Dating Undated Medieval Charters

Dating Undated Medieval Charters

Edited by
Michael Gervers

The Boydell Press

© Editor and Contributors 2000

All Rights Reserved. Except as permitted under current legislation no part of this work may be photocopied, stored in a retrieval system, published, performed in public, adapted, broadcast, transmitted, recorded or reproduced in any form or by any means, without the prior permission of the copyright owner

First published 2000
The Boydell Press, Woodbridge
Reprinted in paperback 2002

In association with
Collegium Budapest
Hungary

ISBN 0 85115 792 0 hardback
ISBN 0 85115 924 9 paperback

The Boydell Press is an imprint of Boydell & Brewer Ltd
PO Box 9, Woodbridge, Suffolk IP12 3DF, UK
and of Boydell & Brewer Inc.
PO Box 41026, Rochester NY 14604-4126, USA
Website: www.boydell.co.uk

A catalogue record for this title is available
From the British Library

Library of Congress Catalog Card Number: 00-026139

This book is printed on acid-free paper

Printed in Hungary by
Séd Nyomda, Szekszárd

TABLE OF CONTENTS

Acknowledgements   vii

Introduction
Michael Gervers (University of Toronto)   1

Part I: Dating by Word-Pattern Matching

The DEEDS Project and the Development of a Computerized Methodology for Dating Undated English Private Charters of the Twelfth and Thirteenth Centuries
Michael Gervers (University of Toronto)   13

An Overview of the Process of Dating Undated Medieval Charters: Latest Results and Future Developments
Rodolfo Fiallos (University of Toronto)   37

Part II: Dating by Formulae and Vocabulary

Dating the Charters of the Smaller Religious Houses in Suffolk in the Twelfth and Thirteenth Centuries
Marjorie Chibnall (Cambridge University)   51

Recherches autour de la datation des actes normands aux Xe–XIIe siècles
Véronique Gazeau (Université de Caen)   61

L'étude du vocabulaire et la datation des actes: l'apport des bases de données informatisées
Benoît-Michel Tock (Université des Sciences Humaines de Strasbourg)   81

The Charters of King Henry II: The Introduction of the Royal *Inspeximus* Revisited
Nicholas Vincent (Christ Church College, Canterbury)   97

Part III: Identifying Forgeries

A New Method for the Dating and Identification of Forgeries? The DEEDS Methodology Applied to a Forged Charter of Count Robert I of Flanders for St. Peter's Abbey, Ghent
Georges Declercq (Vrije Universiteit Brussel)   123

The Identification of a Forgery: Regularities and Irregularities in the
Formulae of the Charters issued by the Székesfehérvár convent of the
Knights of St. John of Jerusalem (1243–1353)
Zsolt Hunyadi (József Attila University, Szeged)   137

The Problems of Dating the Queens' Charters of the Árpádian Age
(Eleventh–Thirteenth Century)
Attila Zsoldos (Institute of History, Hungarian Academy of Sciences)   151

Part IV: Dating by the Association of Names

Social Groups as Recognition Patterns: A Means of Dating Medieval
Charters
Maria Hillebrandt (Westf. Wilhelms-Universität Münster)   163

Beyond DEEDS: A Role for Personal Names?
Trevor Chalmers (Ilford, Essex)   177

Part V: Palaeography and Sigillography

On the Border of Book and Charter Palaeography: The Dating of Some
Hungarian Manuscripts from the Eleventh to the Thirteenth Century
László Veszprémy (Central European University, Budapest)   193

Seals and the Dating of Documents
P. D. A. Harvey (University of Durham)   207

Part VI: Comparative Methodologies

Dendrochronology and History
András Grynaeus (Eötvös Loránd University, Budapest)   213

Dating Problems and Methods in the Middle Ages of Earth History
József Pálfy (Hungarian Natural History Museum, Budapest)   221

The Medieval Charter Collection in the National Archives of Hungary
Iván Borsa (retired; formerly of the National Archives of Hungary)   235

ACKNOWLEDGEMENTS

The contributors to the present volume are especially grateful to the administration and staff of Collegium Budapest/Institute for Advanced Study for hosting the conference upon which it is based, and for having the proceedings printed and published in this form. Particular thanks are due to the Rector, Gábor Klaniczay, to the Secretary, Fred Girod, to the publications manager, Edit Farkas, to Csilla Gyenis for in-house organization and accounting, to Magdolna Balogh for outstanding catering, and to the librarians, Katalin Balkuné Deseő and Hédi Erdős for their constant readiness to assist. The participants would never have been brought together without the advice and assistance of Iván Borsa, Marjorie Chibnall, Paul Harvey, Zsolt Hunyadi, Benoît-Michel Tock, and Nicholas Vincent. Wheel-chair access to the conference was kindly provided by the Hungarian Maltese Order through the thoughtful intervention of Kristóf Kállay. Much support also came from the members of the DEEDS research team at the University of Toronto, especially from Rodolfo Fiallos and Michael Margolin who worked extremely hard to prepare and analyse data and produce charts both for the conference and for these Proceedings, and from Gillian Long who helped with proof reading and editing. Special recognition is due to James Patterson, the copy-editor of Collegium Budapest, for translating Dr Borsa's paper from Hungarian into English, for doing wonders with style and content and seeing that each paper conformed to a single format, and for his skillful preparation of camera-ready copy for the entire volume. We are all much indebted also to Boydell and Brewer for undertaking to publish and distribute the book. Warm thanks are owed in this regard to the director, Richard Barber, and to Caroline Palmer, Helen Barber, and Vanda Andrews. Finally, I should like to acknowledge with gratitude the help and inspiration of István Molnár, who designed the dust-jacket for the volume.

Michael Gervers
Paris, 19 January 2000

For Livia

INTRODUCTION

Michael Gervers

The papers appearing in this volume were first presented at a conference devoted to the subject of charter dating which was hosted by Collegium Budapest/Institute for Advanced Study in March 1999. A major objective of this gathering was the establishment of a critical forum to evaluate the computerised methods for dating undated medieval charters developed by the DEEDS Project at the University of Toronto, and the accuracy and validity of the results produced. To this end, copies of a paper published in 1997 by M. Gervers and R. Fiallos under the title 'The Dating of Medieval English Private Charters of the Twelfth and Thirteenth Centuries'[1] were distributed in advance to participants for comment. Many of the contributions provided welcome additions to, and raised significant queries about, the material discussed in that article. What was proposed there, and is further examined here, is the hypothesis that since language, grammatical forms, syntax, and vocabulary change constantly in response to developments in society at large, word order appearing in any text, and particularly any legal text, should reflect the period in which that text was written. What the DEEDS team has been doing is to establish a corpus consisting of dated English charters from the twelfth and thirteenth centuries (approximately 8 per cent of the total), and to produce a computer program capable of comparing their content and of recognising any word-string occurring more than once among them. The present corpus, made up of 3,353 dated charters, contains 223,158 unique patterns consisting of from two to forty-eight words. Since each pattern carries a date of first and last appearance, identifiable patterns appearing in any document can be used to determine a date for that document. The procedure is elaborated in the paper by Rodolfo Fiallos, who developed this computer program.

There can be no doubt that pattern matching is common to most aspects of enquiry which deal in one way or another with the past. One need only consider the role of such matching in DNA research to see how important it is in the natural sciences.[2] Because researchers in the natural sciences are often faced with enormous quantities of information, it is not surprising that they have gone much further in developing appropriate means of analysis than their counterparts in the humanities and social sciences. It was in recognition of the fact that excellent means of comparing data have long existed outside the historical disciplines, which depend upon the written record, that a palaeontologist and a

---

From *Dating Undated Medieval Charters*. Ed. Michael Gervers. Copyright (by the Editor and Contributors 2000). Published by the Boydell Press (in association with Collegium Budapest), PO Box 9, Woodbridge, Suffolk, IP12 3DF, Great Britain. ISBN 0 85115 792 0.

    1. In *A Distinct Voice: Medieval Studies in Honor of Leonard E. Boyle, O.P.*, ed. Jacqueline Brown and William P. Stoneman, Notre Dame (Indiana), 1997, pp. 455–504.

    2. Lorne T. Kirby, *DNA Fingerprinting: An Introduction, Breakthroughs in Molecular Biology*, vol. 2, New York, 1990.

dendrochronologist were invited to participate in the conference deliberations. While the natural sciences and the human sciences differ to the extent that nature provides a regular and definitive record over time, whereas human activity is invariably irregular and often inconsistent, the student of human history cannot disregard what is incontrovertible for the natural scientist, namely, as József Pálfy points out, that our access to the historical record is dependent upon the preservation of that record and upon our ability to identify what has been preserved. "Collection failure", he writes in terms of gathering the fossil record, "can cause observed ranges – that is, the interval between the first and last appearance of a species – to be shorter than the true life-span of the species." The same is obviously true in the attribution of date ranges to word patterns in the charter record: short of having access to all dated charters ever written, which is an impossibility since so many have been lost, we will never know when a given word or word string first appeared in, and eventually disappeared forever from, documents of this kind. However, with about fifty word patterns available for any given document, it has proven possible to date two-thirds of the charters in the DEEDS corpus to within six to ten years of the stated date of issue – determined either from the dating clause or from other internal evidence – by means of a computer-generated analysis of the date ranges represented by the patterns in that corpus.

Véronique Gazeau, who works with Norman charters of the tenth through twelfth centuries, is quick to remind us that, while charter terminology tended to become formulaic only towards the end of her period of inquiry, several centuries go by in which the scribe's use of the Latin language in drawing up a charter was highly narrative and individualistic. As much can be said of English charters from the time of the Norman Conquest in 1066 until, as Marjorie Chibnall explains, "The presence of numerous medium to small landholders encouraged the growth of a vigorous land market in the twelfth century. Law-suits and title-deeds proliferated; scribes and lawyers flourished. These were conditions likely to hasten the standardisation of legal formulae, so that . . . standard forms of drafting might percolate without too long a delay." Whether produced in the royal chancery or by drafters of private conveyances, few English charters before *c.*1180 bear dates. As a consequence, tests so far run at the DEEDS Project have thrown little light on the more 'literary' style typical of the earlier charter. While it may ultimately prove impossible to attribute to earlier documents the more precise chronology which tests show can be determined for undated charters of the thirteenth century, there is every good reason to suspect that a relative chronology can be established for them. It is important in this context to recognise that the determining factor is not the occurrence of 'set' formulae, but rather of similar words in sequence or of word patterns. Regardless of the total range of vocabulary available to any scribe at any time, and despite the fact that a scribe may never use more than a small part of that vocabulary over an entire career of drawing up legal documents, there will always be a limited number of ways of setting down a particular concept so as to be clearly understood within the society that produced it. The more words used to express a concept, the more concepts occurring in any single charter, and the more repetitions of any such concept in the historical record, the more likely it is that, when taken together, the concepts will reflect a historical period to which a date, or approximate date, can be assigned. In these circumstances, then, methods now employed for word-pattern dating should be able to assist in establishing bench marks which in turn can be used to determine chronological limits for any given document. This approach is only feasible when working with words in sequence for, as Benoît Tock indicates after a thorough investigation of the ARTEM database,[3] single words, once they enter the written record, tend to have such a long lifespan that they cannot be used as chronological determinants. Furthermore, when they do appear in the known record, there is no telling when they were first used in that context. Account must also be taken of the fact that meanings of individual words could, and did, change over time. There is the added difficulty of words appearing in copies before they are known from original documents. Were they inserted by scribes seeking to render a document more meaningful in contemporary terms at the time of recopying, or did they also appear in the original? Benoît Tock cites as an example the word '*fevum*' (fief), which first occurs in that spelling among originals in the ARTEM database in AD 1007, but which is known from later copies of documents which purportedly derive from as early as the ninth century.

The problems inherent in the use of copies as opposed to original documents will forever plague the historian. However, the fact that the great majority of records of this sort have survived as copies precludes any argument in favour of restricting ourselves to the use of originals. What this means, of course, is that medievalists must always proceed with caution when dealing with copies and avoid the temptation of drawing definitive conclusions from what will always be an incomplete and possibly modified record. Georges Declercq reminds us that when describing the extent of change discernible within a copied text we should take care to use the appropriate terminology and to distinguish clearly between what are no more than simple modifications and what are outright forgeries. The difficulty lies in identifying what has been modified or forged. Word-pattern matching can be of considerable assistance in this regard as patterns which turn up outside a core chronological range can easily be singled out and the accuracy of the document or documents in which they appear re-evaluated on an individual basis. Generally speaking, it can be expected that private charters were less prone to modification when they were copied into cartularies, and less likely to have been the object of forgery, than counterparts issuing from papal, royal, episcopal, and baronial scriptoria. As a consequence, and minor modifications notwithstanding, the contents of copies of private charters will continue to serve as sufficiently accurate renditions of the originals to allow them to be used for word-pattern analysis.

Even when dealing with original documents, Véronique Gazeau, understandably cautious when confronted with the enormous diversity of expression appearing in the early, but largely undated, Norman charters available to her, queries

---

3. Atelier de recherches sur les textes médiévaux, Nancy, France.

their usefulness for statistical exploitation and computer assisted examination. She cites the widespread absence of a complete, formal diplomatic text due to a tendency towards brevity and concision in legal documents. As a result, many charters lack proper clauses for the invocation, preamble, or notification. She poses the additional question, when attempting to attribute a date to a document, of what to date: the time when the actual transfer took place, the time when that transfer was recorded in writing or, in the case of copies, the time when the content of an original document was registered in a cartulary? There can be little argument that in the case of dated documents, the date refers to the moment the document was written and not to the time of transfer. Without additional evidence from within the conveyance itself, or from external sources, the actual date of transfer can only be assumed to have occurred at a point reasonably close to when the charter was issued. In response to these concerns, it may be noted that word-pattern matching is compromised by missing diplomatic clauses only to the extent that the length of a document is one determinant of the number of patterns it produces. The likelihood is that the longer the document, the greater the number of patterns bearing date ranges there will be for computational analysis, but it is not unusual for a reasonably accurate date to be calculated from a small number of patterns, especially if their lifetime – the length of the period during which a pattern is current – is short. In fact, an algorithm recently developed by R. Fiallos at DEEDS to select only the unique patterns in a document – that is, patterns which occurred in the document to be dated and in only a single year in the comparison group – produced dating results which were accurate to within ten years of the actual date of issue in 70 per cent of the documents in the corpus. This degree of accuracy was achieved using a corpus consisting predominantly of dated copies and suggests quite firmly that, in terms of private English charters of the twelfth and thirteenth centuries, the differences between an original document and its copy are for the most part insufficient to change significantly a date generated by this algorithm. There is good cause to believe, therefore, that reasons other than scribal modifications at the time of copying lie behind the present inability to date the remaining 30 per cent or so of the documents in the DEEDS corpus to within a decade of their actual dates. As things stand at the moment, an additional 22 per cent – bringing the overall total to 92 per cent of the entire corpus – can be dated to within twenty years of the actual date using the unique patterns, or 'single partner' algorithm.

Allowing for errors of transcription and interpretation made by modern editors of medieval charters, it may well be that a considerable number of the documents falling outside the ten-year accuracy range achieved by the pattern-matching algorithms have to a greater or lesser extent been purposely tampered with, reworked for any number of reasons, or simply forged. There is every reason to suppose that anyone who reworked or forged a charter would have done so for his own advantage, and in order to provide a temporal context for that advantageous moment, it would have been necessary to associate a date with the transaction. In other words, and especially in a territory such as England where the dating of private charters was rare before the beginning of the fourteenth century, it would not be surprising to find that there is a higher proportion of forgeries among charters bearing dates than among those which do not. In areas where, and at times when, the dated charter is an exception, the historian needs therefore, to ask why a given charter should have been dated. The DEEDS corpus consists of charters containing dates, and charters datable to a single twelve-month period based on such specific internal evidence as the name of an official or a known event. Tests to be performed shortly will confirm whether greater accuracy can be achieved in dating documents bearing actual dates or in those to which dates have been assigned. If the former, one may question the reliability of the editor's calculation; if the latter, there is even more reason to suspect the involvement of the forger.

It is in the context of forgeries, whether suspected or not, that word-pattern matching can provide a further major service to the historian. Once an appropriate date range has been established for a word-pattern, the appearance of that pattern outside the range, or in association with chronologically unusual patterns or words, points to an anomaly which will be easily visible to the researcher. Using his own modified version of the DEEDS methodology, Georges Declercq shows how a comparison of the results of word-pattern matching with that of other internal evidence confirm that a charter supposedly issued by the Flemish count Robert I in 1072 for the benefit of St. Peter's Abbey in Ghent was actually fabricated by a monk from that abbey more than a century later. Taking a very similar approach, Zsolt Hunyadi is able to ascertain that a charter dated 1341 and issued by the Knights of St John of Jerusalem in Székesfehérvár (Hungary) in favour of a certain Beke son of Ipoch, was in reality a forgery which was probably produced by Beke's descendants in the last quarter of the fourteenth century. In neither case did the forger attempt to reproduce the handwriting, or the phraseology, concomitant with the date appearing in the charter. Rather, "their only aim was to fabricate a text that would suit contemporary notions of charter drafting". To this end, in both of the cases cited above, the forgers would appear to have been entirely successful in their efforts. The degree to which this kind of forgery was rampant at the highest levels is underlined by Nicholas Vincent in his discussion of the royal *inspeximus*, "the forger's charter par excellence". Dr Vincent, who is preparing a critical edition of the approximately 3,000 known surviving charters attributed to the chancery of King Henry II of England, is fully cognisant of the importance of identifying changes occurring in royal diplomatic as a means of establishing chronological distinctions within this enormous collection of largely undated records. Therein lies another potential application for word-pattern analysis. Although it would prove difficult to assign real dates to documents for which no comparison group of dated material is available, it would certainly be possible to search for all distinct word-patterns and thereafter to order charters according to their appearance in them. It would then be feasible to develop a relative chronology for the entire collection. Since the names appearing in these charters will often be sufficient to date each of them more or less accurately, further precision may be indicated by changes in the diplomatic. All three of these authors concur that machine-generated data which gives rise to suspicions that a document is spurious, or somehow not what it appears to be, must be corroborated by a careful analysis of internal evidence.

There is every reason to suppose that the terminology appearing in the English private charter derives from royal and episcopal precedents. In light of the increasingly widespread growth of the land market in the last decades of the twelfth century, and in the concurrent movement by the royal chancery towards improved record keeping – including the regular introduction of dating to royal documents from the start of the reign of Richard I in 1189 – the availability of the charters of Henry II in machine-readable form will provide an extremely valuable source for comparison.

To this point, the results of all dating experiments performed on the DEEDS corpus of private charters have been derived solely from the evidence provided by matching word-patterns; no distinctions have been made among the individual documents within the collection. In an attempt to make those results even more precise, the next stage of analysis will seek to determine the extent to which differences represented by the present selection of charters may affect the dates attributed by a given algorithm. From now on, therefore, it will be possible to associate a wide range of complementary information to every pattern that can be identified. This information will include: date type (assigned or internal; if internal, by AD, regnal year, feastday, or event); the document type (grant, concord, quitclaim, and so on); whether the source is an original document or a copy, and if a copy, the nature and date of the source; the geographic location(s) with which a conveyance is concerned; the place of issue (if indicated); the general nature of the issuer and recipient (lay or religious); the specific nature of the issuer and recipient (name, title, and occupation for individuals, order in the case of religious houses, or institution); for religious houses, name of the mother house and dates of foundation and dissolution; document length and total number of documents in the source collection. It is expected that, in addition to refining the dates, these attributes considered in conjunction with the occurrence and usage of vocabulary will further lead to the identification of individual scribes, the length of their charter-writing careers, and the place(s) where they worked. A further stage will be the application of XML mark-up language to the long-established diplomatic divisions (protocol, corpus, and eschatocol) and subdivisions of each charter. This procedure will make it possible to analyse each section of a conveyance separately in order to determine, on the one hand, which section(s) are more likely to reflect patterns common to a particular donor or recipient (including institutions), and on the other, in the case of copies or suspected forgeries, whether or not a section is contemporary with the rest of the document, whether it might have been modified at the time of recopying, or whether inconsistencies constituting the various parts of a document point to a total forgery.

A number of the papers in the present volume call for greater exploitation of the more traditional methods used in dating medieval sources, wherever possible with the assistance of computer-generated programmes. Foremost in this regard is the evidence of personal names which, as Maria Hillebrandt describes, received considerable attention at the University of Münster a generation ago when attempts were made to carry out prosopographical studies on the approximately 4,000 surviving charters covering the period 910–1120 from the Abbey of Cluny. Individuals standing behind the approximately 60,000 largely Christian names extracted from these documents could in many cases be identified as one and the same person through their association with similar places and similar name groups. It was then possible to develop patterns of these name groups in dated charters and to use them to date undated ones. Surprisingly, perhaps, the dating of charters at Cluny became increasingly less precise and irregular between the late tenth and the mid-eleventh century, whereupon for a good half-century and more dates disappear altogether. Under these circumstances, the evidence provided by identifiable name-groups would obviously be invaluable in attributing some degree of chronology to this large collection of conveyances. Such is especially true in the case of charters pre-dating the mid-twelfth century in which there was far less conformity in legal phraseology and verbal expression than in later periods. Information garnered from name-groups has great potential, the more so now that packaged computer programs are available to do what individual programmers working with mainframe computers found an enormous challenge – or were quite unable to achieve – twenty years and more ago. Trevor Chalmers proposes just such a solution. Using a readily available Microsoft Access database, he shows convincingly how, by matching identified or unidentified individuals from name-groups in a search set from an unregistered document with their equivalents in a register of dated entries from approximately the same period and topographical region, close temporal parallels can be made. There can be no question that in cases where a sufficient number of personal names are included in a document, or have been retained in a later copy thereof, the chronological evidence to be ascertained from the association of name-groups would be a valuable adjunct to that determined from word-pattern matching.

Paul Harvey points to another still largely unexploited dating factor: the evidence which can be derived from seal impressions. With an estimated 300,000 of these extant in England alone from before 1500, there is obviously much to be said for adding whatever chronological information they can provide to what is becoming increasingly within the historian's reach: a comprehensive database for the medieval charter in which all conceivable aspects of a document or group of documents can be examined in relation to one another. The projected automated union catalogue of British seals which he discusses would include, in addition to a physical description of the seal itself, whatever can be ascertained about the date of the document bearing the seal, as well as "the names of the parties who used – or may have used – the surviving seals, the places they came from, the places the document relates to, and the place where it was sealed, whether there is a sealing clause, and whether the seal explicitly supports or replaces the seal of someone else". With the exception of the physical description, all this information can be determined from the document itself providing, in the case of copies or originals from which the wax impressions have been lost, a vast extension of the field to the study of sigillography without seals.

One approach to dating which at present is entirely dependent upon the survival of originals – and which is represented here by László Veszprémy's study of a series of eleventh- to thirteenth-century Hungarian codices – is the evidence of palaeography. As a discipline, the study of handwriting has made great strides in recent years and when its principles can be applied to written sources more generally through computer-driven programs it will become increasingly possible not only to distinguish one hand from another, but even to develop a repertory of scribes based on surviving examples of their activity. Literary scholars have already proposed methods of identifying authorship, and of distinguishing between joint authors or determining whether or not a text is forged, through machine analysis of vocabulary and, particularly, of style. This approach, known as the CU-SUM technique, was developed, like word-pattern analysis, to be applied to a printed text and can thus be used to identify a writer in the absence of an original handwritten document.[4] What researchers using the CU-SUM methodology need to know from the start, however, is the date or approximate date when the text they are studying was written. DEEDS proposes eventually to incorporate the techniques of author identification into its program of chronological analysis. Once the date of a document has been determined, it should be possible to measure the working lifetime of a particular scribe by the order, sequence, syntax, and style of the word-patterns he employs. This information in turn will serve to confirm the reliability of date-ranges assigned by whatever means to an undated document, and should further assist in the identification of spurious or modified ones. This capacity to determine authorship without recourse to the evidence of handwriting has the potential of extending the palaeographer's scope well beyond the domain of original sources. In cases of original authorship, and with particular reference to an individual scribe's production of charters, he may look forward to the day when he will be able to place texts distinguished by handwriting in the context of what may be a far broader range of works produced by the same 'author', but surviving only in later copies.

A valuable addition to our knowledge of early Hungarian conveyances is Attila Zsoldos' paper on the 200 surviving charters issued by the country's queens from the time Christianity was adopted in the Carpathian Basin in the year 1000 to the end of the thirteenth century. Unlike English royal charters which were not systematically dated until the last decade of the twelfth century, documents emanating from the Hungarian royal chancery almost invariably included some reference to a date, even if it was to a day in the absence of a year. The Hungarian custom, of course, derived directly from the papal tradition which was introduced at the same time as the new religion, while the nearly contemporary English experience was probably determined by the Conqueror's lack of concern for, or unawareness of the historical importance of, temporal markers in the realm of property transfer. When it comes to interpreting and writing history, however, dates are not everything. No matter how vague the chronological record, the 4,000 extant and largely undated charters of Henry II presently being edited by Nicholas Vincent will provide an infinitely richer source for English history between 1154 and 1189 than the 319 predominantly dated royal charters which have survived from the entire twelfth century do for Hungary.

---

4. On the Cu-Sum technique, see p. 29, note 30.

Iván Borsa describes what has survived of medieval charter production in Hungary after centuries of foreign incursion and destruction in the Carpathian Basin. He has also been responsible for initiating a recently completed project to place a calendar of this corpus on a single CD-ROM, available to the public in bookshops for the modest equivalent of 20 US dollars. The CD contains references to well over 315,000 records, of which thirteen cover the period up to and including the tenth century, while there are 228 for the eleventh, 472 for the twelfth, 14,142 for the thirteenth, 74,308 for the fourteenth, 156,223 for the fifteenth, 60,596 for the sixteenth century prior to the Turkish victory over the Hungarians at Mohács in 1526, and 9,865 undated documents (representing only 3 per cent of the total). Included in this collection are 85,007 royal records (27 per cent of the total), of which 1,379 or 1.6 per cent are undated. The calendar is written in Hungarian, which for all intents and purposes limits its use to Hungarian researchers, but as a tool it is a remarkable model towards which scholars from other nations may strive.[5]

We have left to the end the obvious question of why there is such diversity in the tendency to include, or exclude, a date reference in European medieval property conveyances, depending upon where and when they were issued. There can be no doubt that the closer the tie between the issuer and the Roman tradition, the greater the likelihood that a charter would bear a date. While any conclusion must be tentative in the absence of a comprehensive study of dating practices across Europe as a whole from the time of Charlemagne to the fourteenth century, there is growing evidence to suggest that in some of the regions referred to in this volume, namely in Burgundy and in Normandy, the tendency to include dates declined steadily from the late tenth century until the middle of the eleventh century, when they became quite rare. Although situated within the Frankish realm, these territories lay well outside the formal control of the French king. It is above all this detachment from royal administrative supervision which may explain why, when the charters of the French monarchy continued to be dated, those of some, at least, of the more independent outlying provinces did not. To confirm or refute this observation, it will be necessary to review the dating customs apparent in ducal, episcopal, and abbatial records alike from these and other regions, both within France and elsewhere in Europe. Whatever the outcome of such an examination, there is no denying the fact that the English custom of not dating charters at any level of society was introduced by the Normans. The Norman dukes, with only a century and a half of literacy behind them and an administrative system developed when ties with the French Crown were weak, were clearly unconcerned about the formal letter-writing traditions which European monarchs had adopted from the papal chancery. They bothered little with traditional formality, dispensed with all that was not absolutely essential to the message they wished to convey,

---

5. For a concise and useful description of the Hungarian medieval charter archive, see the article by Iván Borsa in this volume. See also Zsolt Hunyadi, '"... scripta manent": Archival and Manuscript Resources in Hungary', in *Annual of Medieval Studies at CEU 1997–98*, ed. Katalin Szende, Budapest: CEU Department of Medieval Studies, 1999, pp. 231–40 (esp. pp. 232–36).

and only occasionally included a date. In a word, they sought brevity and conciseness in their charters and carried that administrative principle with them to England where it became a long-standing tradition in its own right. It was undoubtedly tradition, then, rather than a conscious desire to dispense with the concept of time, that led to the enduring English phenomenon of the undated charter. In Normandy, dating returned to the charter text as royal administrative authority spread in the region, while in England it took the accession of Richard I, whose administrative experience was rather Continental than English, to introduce it to his royal chancery. Attachment to tradition being what it is, however, it still took well over a century for that custom to be adopted by those who drafted charters elsewhere in the realm. The papers which follow propose various means of determining dates for the vast array of undated, or forged, medieval charters preserved in the archives of Europe. The more accurate new methods of dating become, the more useful these documents will be in clarifying the historical record.

PART I
DATING BY WORD-PATTERN MATCHING

THE DEEDS PROJECT AND THE DEVELOPMENT OF A COMPUTERISED METHODOLOGY FOR DATING UNDATED ENGLISH PRIVATE CHARTERS OF THE TWELFTH AND THIRTEENTH CENTURIES

Michael Gervers

> "If we knew the properties of every event which happened and at which time that event happened, then we would know everything."
> Richard Swinburne, 'Mind and Body. A Defense of Substance Dualism', Collegium Budapest, 2 March 1999

It has proved difficult to bring together an international group of scholars from Eastern and Western Europe to discuss means of attributing dates to undated medieval documents, particularly charters, because in the east most documents of this type bear dates and so determining even a relative chronology is neither a question nor a problem. One may well ask why the territories of Western Europe, especially the north-west, and particularly England and Normandy, seem to have fared less well in this regard than the kingdoms and principalities to the east. There are several answers to this question. In the first place, in Hungary, for example, the issuance of charters was far more restricted than in the West, in part because the places of authentication which produced such documents were fewer in number. Initially, these places were cathedral chapters. Since they originated as royal foundations, it is not surprising that scribes were provided to them by the royal chancery. This procedure ensured close ties between the principal chancery of the land and the cathedral chapters and monastic foundations which owed their existence to the king's favour. The royal chancery regularly dated its documents from the commencement of the Christian monarchy in the year 1000, as did the religious institutions which the king brought into being.[1] Secondly, records of this nature predating the fourteenth century are few and far between in most areas of eastern Europe, compared to England which can boast of perhaps as many as a million undated deeds surviving in one form or another for the twelfth and thirteenth centuries alone. By the early fourteenth century – that is, by the end of the

---

From *Dating Undated Medieval Charters*. Ed. Michael Gervers. Copyright (by the Editor and Contributors 2000). Published by the Boydell Press (in association with Collegium Budapest), PO Box 9, Woodbridge, Suffolk, IP12 3DF, Great Britain. ISBN 0 85115 792 0.

Note: The author is grateful to the following for their assistance and advice in the preparation of this paper: Anne Byrne, Rodolfo Fiallos, Gillian Long, Zsolt Hunyadi, Michael Margolin, Daniel J. Power, and Amanda Spencer.

1. György Bónis, 'Les autorités de "foi publique" et les archives des "loci credibiles" en Hongrie', *Archivum* 12 (1962): pp. 87–104; Iván Borsa, 'Zur Beurkundstätigkeit der glaubwürdigen Orte in Ungarn', in *Forschungen über Siebenbürgen und seine Nachbarn. Festschrift für A. T. Szabó und Zs. Jako*, vol. 2, ed. K. Benda, T. Bogyay, and H. Glassl, Munich, 1988, pp. 143–48; Franz Eckhart, 'Die glaubwürdigen Orte Ungarns im Mittelalter', *Mitteilungen des Instituts für Österreichische Geschichtsforschung*, Supplementary vol. 9 (1913/1915): pp. 395–558.

reign of Edward I (1272–1307) – dates are invariably included in English charters too. Thirdly, the private charter, which represents the great bulk of the undated material in the West, is practically unknown in this period in the East.[2] Care must thus be taken not to compare royal, baronial, or episcopal charters on the one hand with private charters on the other. However, it is often a matter of some surprise to our eastern colleagues to learn that for nearly a century and a quarter, from the accession of William the Conqueror in 1066 until that of Richard I in 1189, even the English royal chancery paid little heed to matters of chronology.[3] The situation was similar under the Normans, although when they opted to include dates regularly in their acts in the early thirteenth century, they did so progressively, to the detriment of the witness list which thereafter was largely dispensed with.[4] In practical terms, this exchange of names for dates was as reasonable to those who introduced it as it is regrettable in the eyes of medieval historians who lose track, as a result, of the make-up of the ducal court and of the individuals whose passage in and out of the record serves as one of their primary points of chronological reference. If one of the roles of witnesses was to vouch for the veracity of a document's content, or of the fact that the transaction witnessed had actually taken place, another was to serve as a temporal reminder to subsequent generations of what their predecessors had been privy to, and approximately when. Obviously, the evidence of both dates and witnesses was important, but despite the royal precedent in the late twelfth century it would still be more than a hundred years before the dating clause took its place as a matter of common usage within the diplomatic of the English private charter.[5]

In the absence of dates, editors of charters and charter collections have invariably turned to the evidence of personal names to establish date limits for a given document. If one is fortunate, at least one person may be identified who held office and whose dates of tenure are known; the more such names that appear, the easier it is to narrow down the date of issue of the document in which they occur. The Reverend H. E. Salter was very fortunate in this regard in the course of editing numerous volumes of charters for the Oxford Historical Society. He was able to date nearly 500 charters to the year in which they were issued from the names of the aldermen and sheriffs who appeared in them.[6] Most collections, however,

---

2. László Mezey, 'Anfänge der Privaturkunde in Ungarn und der glaubwürdigen Orte', *Archiv für Diplomatik* 18 (1972): pp. 290–302.

3. Pierre Chaplais, *English Royal Documents: King John–Henry VI*, Oxford, 1971, p. 14; see also the article in the present volume by Véronique Gazeau.

4. Matthieu Arnoux, 'Essor et déclin d'un type diplomatique: les actes passés "coram parrochia" en Normandie (XII–XIII siècles)', *Bibliothèque de l'Ecole des Chartes* 154 (1996): pp. 323–57, esp. pp. 338–40 (hereafter: Arnoux, 'Essor et déclin').

5. Michael Clanchy, *From Memory to Written Record*, 2nd ed., Oxford, 1993, pp. 299–304.

6. Oxford officials appeared in 624 of the charters which Salter edited; 145 of these also bore dates, so enabling him to determine accurate dates for the remaining 479; see the following volumes of the Oxford Historical Society: *Eynsham Cartulary*, vols. 49, 51 (1907–08); *The Oxford Deeds of Balliol College*, vol. 64 (1913); *A Cartulary of the Hospital of St. John the Baptist*, vols. 66, 68, 69 (1914–17); *Oriel College Records* (ed. with C. L. Shadwell), vol. 85 (1926); *Cartulary of Oseney Abbey*, vols. 89, 90, 91, 97, 98, 101 (1929–36).

do not contain anything like such a large proportion of documents bearing the names of individuals who can not only be identified, but who also, in the case of the aldermen at least, only held office for a year. It is far more likely that one or two, certainly rarely more than a few, of the names will be found to have identifiable counterparts elsewhere. And here the trouble begins, for how can we be sure that someone bearing a similar name in an external source is the self-same person that we are dealing with and not simply a namesake? And if it is the same person, how can we know where he or she was in his or her life-span at the time the document in which the name appears was issued? For lack of sufficient contextual evidence inaccurate attributions can easily be made. The trouble then is that once a circa date has been attributed to such a document and the work goes into print, that date tends thereafter to take on a historical value of its own and to be given the benefit of the doubt by subsequent scholars as though it actually belonged to the document in question. In this manner, dates are assigned to undated charters, which in turn are used as evidence in the dating of yet other undated charters. The potential for error in this process is rather greater than we would like it to be and, I fear, greater even than we imagine it to be. In order not to be guilty of throwing the first stone, however, I should like to cite from my own work two examples of erroneous dating which have been brought to light recently by machine analysis of word-patterns.

In 1982, I published the content of what is referred to in the manuscript itself as the '*secunda camera*' of the Cartulary of the Knights of St. John of Jerusalem in England, or Hospitallers.[7] There are 957 entries in this section of the cartulary and all but a few concern the Order's holdings in the county of Essex. To one of these, no. 618, I assigned a date of *c*.1231, and explained the dating as follows:

> Five of the persons appearing in this charter also occur in no. 610 (*c*.1231), with which this must be nearly contemporary. Three more occur *c*.1240 (no. 611). The names of three of the tenants mentioned here appear in a charter of 1275 (no. 669), but the similarity is probably coincidental.

There are many coincidences in the historical record, but this, I now realise, was not one of them. I considered that the association of eight names in common over a ten-year period was a better chronological indicator than the association of three names in a dated charter issued several generations later. It was not, furthermore, the first time I had come across common names designating different people separated by a significant period of time. What brought the matter to the fore was a study of forms of address in charters in which the Knights of St. John were the beneficiaries.[8] The form used in the document (no. 618) to which I had assigned

---

7. Michael Gervers, ed., *The Cartulary of the Knights of St. John of Jerusalem in England, Secunda Camera: Essex*, Records of Social and Economic History, n. s. VI, Oxford University Press for the British Academy, London, 1982 (hereafter: *Hosp. Cart.*, s.c.).

8. Michael Gervers, 'Changing Forms of Hospitaller Address in English Private Charters of the Twelfth and Thirteenth Centuries', forthcoming in *Expanding the Frontiers of Medieval Latin Christianity: The Crusades and the Military Orders*, ed. József Lászlovszky and Zsolt Hunyadi.

the date c.1231 due to the occurrence of such a large number of similar names, was also used in seven other documents in the '*secunda camera*', all of which were invariably dated between the years 1272 and 1280.[9] One of those charters (no. 669) was the one, precisely dated to 1275, in which the names of the three tenants mentioned in the document to which I attributed the date c.1231 (no. 618), also appeared. I am now quite convinced that my original dating based on the common occurrence of eight names between c.1231 and 1240 was off by a good forty years and that the counterparts of names from the 1230s which appear in the 1270s may well have designated the grandchildren of those recorded in the 1230s. Had I nearly twenty years ago had the information available to me now, I would not have hesitated to assign a date of c.1275 to this document, rather than c.1231.

In a second case, I was confronted with a fairly short grant in free alms issued by a certain Richard of Rockhill, whose wife, Matilda, was also mentioned in the document.[10] By good fortune, or so I thought, I found a Richard of Rockhill with his wife Matilda in an external source concerning the same region and precisely dated to 1252.[11] As a consequence, I assigned a date of c.1250 to the document. Some years later, I came across Richard of Rockhill again in a charter addressed to all his men and friends "*Francis et Anglicis*". Students of English history are familiar with this address, usually associating it with a date prior to 1204 because in that year the English renounced their tenure of lands in Normandy.[12] By this time, however, I had found that a Richard of Rockhill was reported to have died in 1222 and that his namesake, identified as his son, had departed in 1277.[13] Three other individuals appearing in the charter, including two clerics, appeared elsewhere c.1220–1230, and so I settled on a date of c.1220 as being appropriate for this second charter, regardless of the reference to "French and English". I dealt with this problem by suggesting that the document may have been a conflation, a conclusion further strengthened by the fact that namesakes occurred both c.1175–1200 and c.1237–1269.

Returning recently to the document mentioning Richard and Matilda, I found that it was addressed to "*deo et beatis pauperibus (hospitalis) Ierusalem*", an address which elsewhere was only current around the third quarter of the twelfth

---

9. The address attributed to c.1231, appearing in Hosp. Cart., s.c. no. 618, is "*Deo et beate Marie et Sancto Iohanni Baptiste et fratribus hospitalis Sancti Iohannis Ierusalem apud Mapeltrestede commorantibus et ibidem deo servientibus*". The same address occurred c.1272–80 in nos. 234, 255, 654, 661, 667, 669, and 670.

10. *Hosp. Cart.*, s.c. no. 371.

11. R. E. C. Kirk, ed., *Feet of Fines for Essex*, vol. 1, Colchester: Essex Archaeological Society, 1899, p. 192, no. 263.

12. Nicholas Vincent, *Peter des Roches: An Alien in English Politics, 1205–38*, Cambridge, 1996, pp. 42–47; Ian Short, 'Tam Angli quam Franci: Self-Definition in Anglo-Norman England', *Anglo-Norman Studies* 18 (1996): pp. 153–75; Arnoux, 'Essor et déclin', as cited in n. 5.

13. Michael Gervers, ed., *The Cartulary of the Knights of St. John of Jerusalem in England, part 2, Prima Camera: Essex*, Records of Social and Economic History, n.s. 23, London: Oxford University Press for the British Academy, 1996 (hereafter: *Hosp. Cart.*, p. c.), p. 60, no. 46 (note); Philip Morant, *The History and Antiquities of the County of Essex*, vol. 1, London, 1763 (reprint: EP Publishing, 1978), p. 99.

century in grants made to the Order of St. John of Jerusalem.[14] That document in turn took me back to the other in which Richard of the same name addressed his men and friends "French and English", and which I had dated *c.*1220 but, had it not been for a majority of the names, I would have dated to before 1204. I have already noted that counterparts of some of the names appeared in the last quarter of the twelfth century. If Richard of Rockhill's name was common to much of the thirteenth century, there seemed to be increasing evidence pointing to the possibility that in these two cases, this was one and the same Richard, or at least that the transactions described belonged to the last quarter of the twelfth century rather than to *c.*1220 or *c.*1250. Had I been guided more by the format of the document and the historical evidence it revealed, than by the common appearance of familiar names, I might have given more credence to the year 1204 as a valid *ante quem* date for all documents addressed to *"Francis et Anglicis"*. The occurrence of this phrase among the 3,353 dated acts, and approximately 1,000 circa-dated Essex documents in the Hospitaller cartulary, which comprise the DEEDS database of English charters, is represented in *Figure 1*.[15] The same form appeared in one other

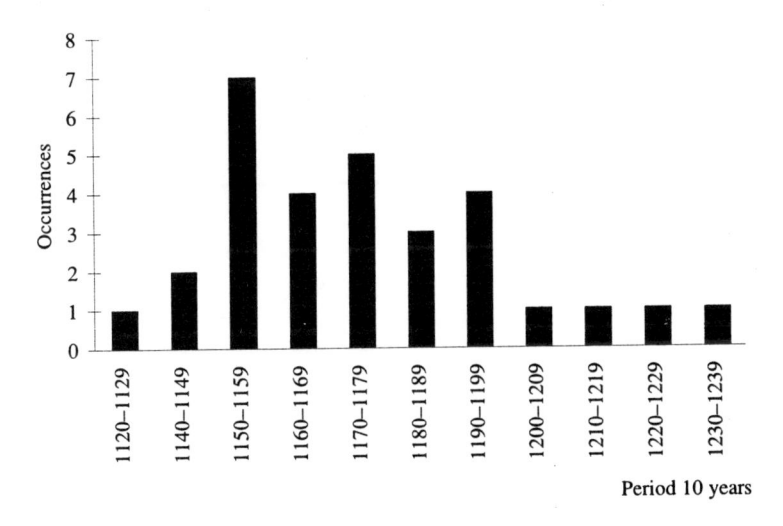

Figure 1 *"francis et anglicis"*

14. *Hosp. Cart.*, s.c. nos. 286 (*c.*1138–53), 298 (*c.*1138–53), 321 (*c.*1155–86), 371 (originally attributed to *c.*1250), 377 (*c.*1175), and 414 (*c.*1160).

15. Bars in this chart representing one document each for the decades 1220–29 and 1230–39 indicate what I now believe to be incorrectly dated charters in *Hosp. Cart.*, p.c., nos. 46 and 79. The bar for a single document in the decade 1210–19 reflects a charter of Geoffrey de Mandeville, Earl of Essex and Gloucester, dated by its editor to the period 1214–16 (Robert B. Patterson, ed., *Earldom of Gloucester Charters. The Charters and Scribes of the Earls and Countesses of Gloucester to AD 1217*, Oxford: Clarendon Press, 1973, no. 93).

document, which I had placed in the second quarter of the thirteenth cen-tury due to the association of names.[16] In this case, the balance was quite even between similar names occurring elsewhere *c.*1245 and those occurring *c.*1185–1198. I opted for the later date, explaining away "French and English" by saying that it "appears to be borrowed from an earlier document". I now think otherwise.

Quite obviously, it was not unusual for similar names to be used by the same families living in or near the same place from one generation to the next. Cases are known of names such as William son of William son of William son of William, or William son of Richard son of William son of Richard, wherein the Christian name succeeds from father to son, or from grandfather to grandson, generation after generation. In the examples I have just cited, the recurrence of names was so widespread that some village rosters at least would appear to have been remarkably similar from one generation to the next for upwards of a hundred years and probably more. It may have been due in part to this situation that, as the population continued to grow in village and town, English administrators towards the end of the thirteenth century and the beginning of the fourteenth found it increasingly attractive not only to date legal documents, and by so doing to provide each one with a precise chronological context, but also to encourage the use of family names. It could well be that those same administrators were running into the difficulty, similar to ours, of not being able to distinguish between generations and, as a consequence, of losing the ability to maintain anything like an accurate historical record at a time when a developing administrative system called for it.

The preceding may seem to be a somewhat pessimistic view of the use of personal names to date the twelfth- and thirteenth-century charters whence they came, and an overly optimistic view of the use of forms of address as an alternative method of reaching the same end. If witness lists could be conflated, which in some cases they very likely were, so also could forms of address be introduced outside what might be considered their proper historical range. I must admit, however, that in view of the cases cited, the evidence provided by changing forms of address and, as we shall see, of word patterns in general, would seem to be a considerably more accurate indicator of chronological change than the association of names in undated sources with their counterparts in dated ones.

Problems arising from the misidentification of different individuals bearing the same name, or of the same individual bearing the same name, not to mention the same individual bearing different names, are compounded in documents whose witness lists were left off at the time when they were copied into a cartulary. Faced sometimes with documents in which no more than two or three names appeared, and those often or not of otherwise unknown social standing, other means were obviously needed to identify chronological change. Palaeography was not an option as the great majority of the sources have survived only in later copies. For the same reason, sigillography was also insufficient, regardless of its importance in those relatively rare cases where originals exist together with their seals.

---

16. *Hosp. Cart.*, p. c., no. 79.

The case previously cited of the address *"Francis et Anglicis"*, in charters which upon careful scrutiny could with few exceptions be attributed to a date before 1204, raised the possibility that other word-patterns within a given document might provide further indication of its date of issue. A concordance of words in context derived from the nearly one thousand charters registered in the *secunda camera* of the Hospitaller cartulary previously cited, served as a point of departure for this enquiry.[17] Over ninety per cent of these charters, it may be noted, were circa-dated, but regardless of the potentially imprecise chronology reflected by the resultant attributions, four stages became quickly apparent. In the first place it was evident that a good number of forms current in the twelfth century were gone by the middle of the next. Such, for example, was the case in grants offered for the salvation "of my friends living and dead" (*amicorum meorum vivorum et mortuorum*) (*Figure 2*), which had a lifespan among the Hospitaller documents of about ninety years, from *c.*1150 to *c.*1240. Secondly, from *c.*1200 and especially after *c.*1225, many new forms began to enter the record and remained in vogue through the third quarter of the century. They were characterised by the highly egocentric vocabulary of what I have referred to elsewhere as the "golden age of subinfeudation" and included expressions to the effect that land was held "of me and my heirs to him and his heirs" (*de me et heredibus meis sibi et heredibus suis*)

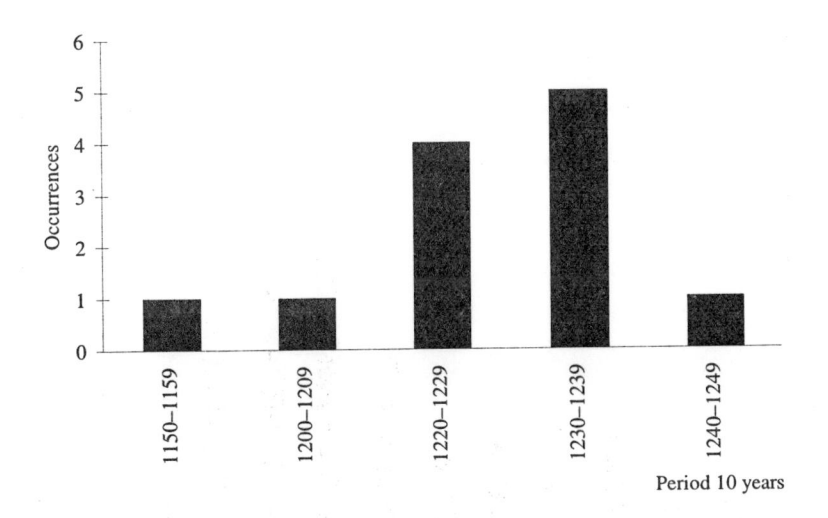

Figure 2 *"amicorum meorum vivorum et mortuorum"*

---

17. Michael Gervers, *A Microfiche Concordance of the Cartulary of the Order of St. John of Jerusalem, secunda camera (British Library, Cotton ms. Nero E VI, fols. 289–467)*, Toronto: Deeds Project (Scarborough Campus, University of Toronto), 1983. Compiled with the technical assistance of L. C. Kordecki.

(*Figure 3*). Third came changes associated with the passage of the Statute of Mortmain in 1279, by which royal license was required to transfer property to religious houses. This statute led to the disappearance of many formulae containing reference to grants made in alms as, for example, in the formula "free and pure and perpetual alms" (*liberam et puram et perpetuam elemosinam*) (*Figure 4*). Lastly were those which resulted from the statute *Quia Emptores*, issued in 1290 to restrict subinfeudation. The latter put an end to much of the language of subinfeudation which had been introduced at the beginning of the second quarter of the century. The context of "I–me–my" would thereafter be confined to the direct action

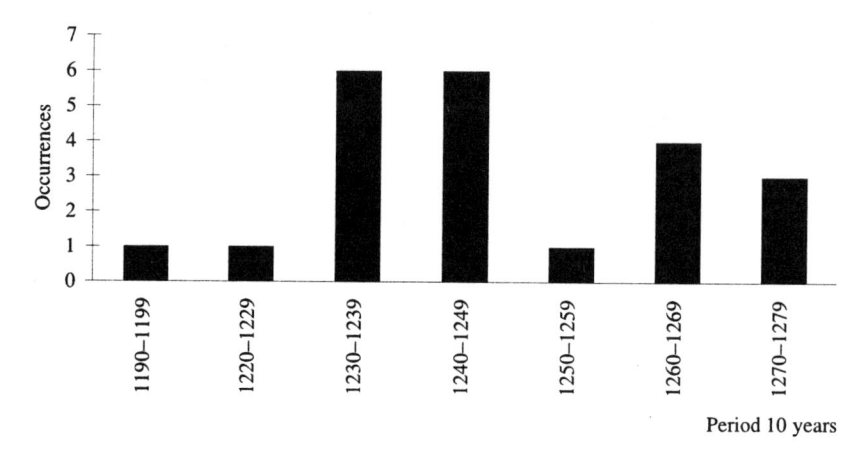

Figure 3 *"de me et heredibus meis sibi et heredibus suis"*

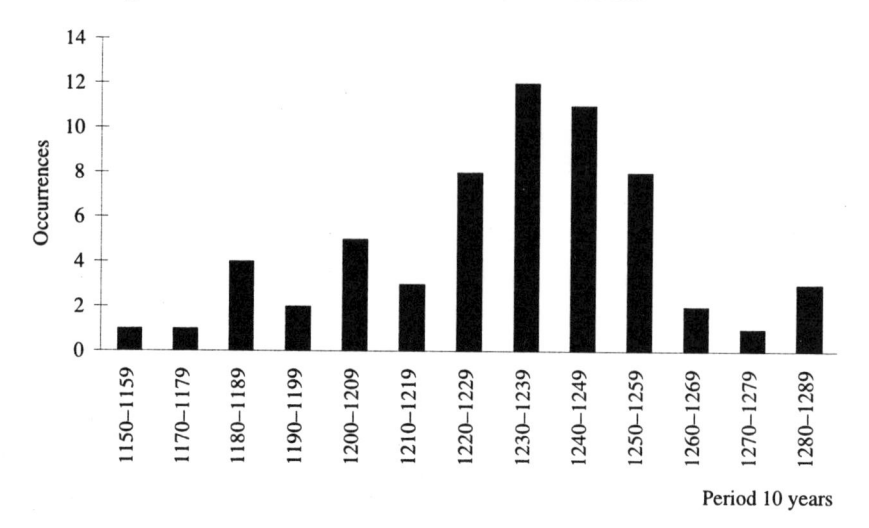

Figure 4 *"liberam et puram et perpetuam elemosinam"*

of conveying, warranting, and sealing, while the concept of tenure would invariably be couched in terms of dependency on the chief lords of the fee (see *Figure 5: de capitalibus dominis feodi*). Simultaneously, mention of scutage, royal service, gersum, gloves, and spice rents disappears from the record (see *Figure 6: scutagium*).

The chronological groupings reflected in the word-patterns from the concordance, and represented by some of the examples previously cited, prompted further consideration of word-pattern matching as a potentially viable means of dating the undated charter. It seemed likely that the four temporal stages mentioned above would not be the only ones which could be distinguished among the tens of

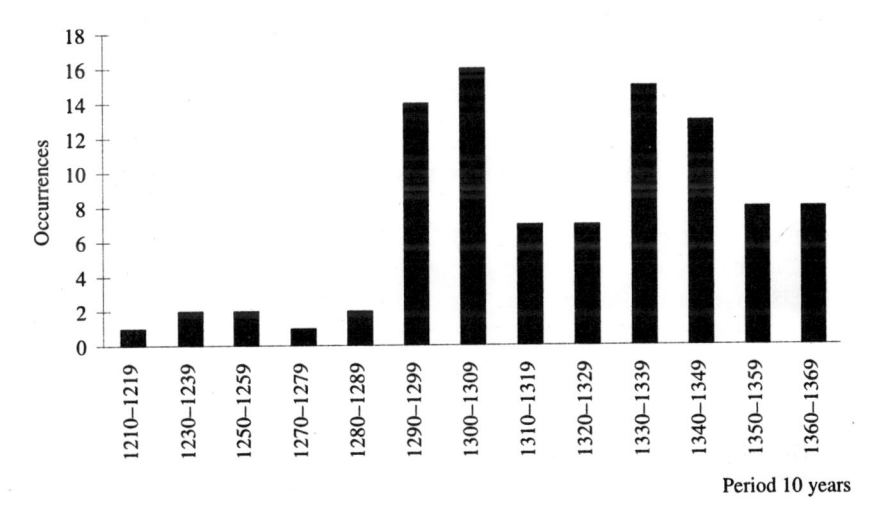

Figure 5 *"de capitalibus dominis feodi"*

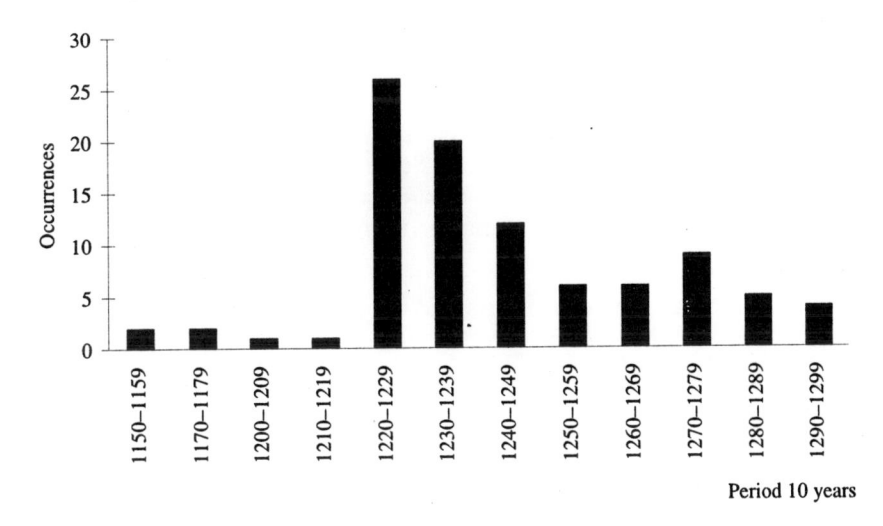

Figure 6 *"scutagium"*

thousands of word-patterns visible in the concordance. In fact, the wide variety of dates associated with the different patterns led me to suspect that rather than being predominantly static, with the occasional change resulting from this or that historical event or from the response to a royal statute, the language of the medieval charter was in constant flux due to any number of heretofore unidentified reasons. Taken as a whole, it seemed reasonable to suppose that if the chronology of change were clear, it should be possible to use the rates of appearance of word-patterns in the record and their disappearance from it to determine a reasonably accurate date for any given document of this sort. Rates of appearance and disappearance have been aptly termed 'origination' and 'extinction rates' by our colleagues in other disciplines; expressions which I shall employ in what follows to add emphasis to the very real degree of change taking place constantly in the wording of charter texts.

As far as the evidence provided by the concordance was concerned, a major problem lay in the fact that only ten per cent at most of the Hospitaller sources from which it was derived bore dates of issue; the rest, having been indirectly dated, contained potentially greater or lesser degrees of chronological error. To overcome this limitation, it was necessary to develop a source collection of dated documents, or documents which could with certainty be dated to within a year of issue. The creation of such a collection has in recent years been the major task of the DEEDS Project at the University of Toronto.[18] After some four years of tedious effort we now have, in machine-readable form, a corpus of 3,353 dated Latin charters from twelfth- and thirteenth-century England. For reasons of time, all of our sources have been selected from published collections. More than 40,000 charters have been searched to this end and we are always on the lookout for the next edition to appear. With few exceptions, the harvest is never very rich, there being seldom more than seven to ten per cent of dated documents in any charter collection.

Although our objective is to retain the highest possible degree of accuracy in our work, there are a number of limitations which we can neither avoid nor overcome. In the first place, we are, as I have mentioned, working entirely with published editions and so are dependent upon the accuracy of the editors who produced them. We do not have the means to check all transcriptions against the original. If editors have unconsciously left out a word or words from the text, then they will be missing from our corpus as well. Some editors take it upon themselves to replace with "etc." what to them are apparently similar word-patterns, but which may in reality incorporate subtle variations bearing temporal boundaries.[19] Others

---

18. Michael Gervers, 'Medieval Charters and the Computer: An Analysis Using Mark IV', *Computers and the Humanities* 12 (1978): pp. 127–36; 'The DEEDS Database of Mediaeval Charters: Design and Coding for the RDBMS ORACLE 5', *History and Computing* 1, no. 3 (1990): pp. 1–12 (co-authored with G. Long and M. McCulloch; 'The Dating of Medieval English Private Charters of the Twelfth and Thirteenth Centuries', *A Distinct Voice: Medieval Studies in Honor of Leonard E. Boyle, O.P.*, ed. Jacqueline Brown and William P. Stoneman, Notre Dame (Indiana), 1997, pp. 455–504; 'Középkori angol oklevelek datálása szóelőfordulások alapján' (Computerised methods for dating undated medieval English charters [in Hungarian]), *Aetas* 2–3 (1997): pp. 189–97.

19. E. O. Blake, ed., *Cartulary of the Priory of St. Denys*, Southampton Records Series, vols. 24 and 25, Southampton: Southampton University Press, 1981.

leave supposedly 'common' forms in abbreviation,[20] while still others limit the reproduction of full Latin texts to charters issued before 1250,[21] or even as early as 1100;[22] the later material being translated or calendared in English regardless of whether it bears a date or not.[23] Then, too, many editions appear as English translations or calendars only.[24] Individual editorial decisions concerning capitalisation, punctuation, and spelling are not a problem, as we disregard the former and have our own standardisation for the latter anyway.

Another potential shortcoming is that relatively few editions are based on original documents. The large majority of texts which have been transcribed are derived from cartulary copies, whose content may represent any number of earlier copyings. This is not to say that such copies are totally unreliable, but rather that they cannot be expected to be exact reproductions of the original. Medieval

---

20. T. B. Dilks, ed., *Bridgwater Borough Archives*, vol. 1: *1200–1377*, Somerset Record Society, vol. 48 (1933):

> In a perfect scheme the complete text of the originals, all words extended, would have been laid before the reader. But exigencies of space have made it necessary to condense. It will be found that oft-recurring forms, such as the enfeoffment clause, the warranty clause, the sealing clause, here have been simply indicated by their initial words, for though the phraseology may vary, the general sense is standardised. Words of frequent occurrence have been shortened. It is hoped that no great inconvenience will be experienced on this account. Important documents and sentences are given verbatim, and translations are added where it has seemed specially desirable. (Introduction, p. xiv)
>
> *Sci. pres. et fut. qd. ego Alicia de Wodefford filia Galfridi de Wodefford dedi concessi quietum clamavi et hac presenti carta mea confirmavi David de Weleton et hered. suis vel assig. totam terram meam quam habui de dono Galfridi de Wodefford patris mei in manerio de Palton cum omn. pert. una cum uno messuagio et curtillagio in villa de Wolleye qd. vocatur La Holdehalle cum omn. pert. suis Hab. et ten. sibi et hered. suis vel assig. Suis . . .* (charter no. 6, undated, p. 6)

21. Mortimer, ed., *Charters of St. Bartholomew's Priory, Sudbury*, Suffolk Charters 15, Woodbridge: Suffolk Records Society/Boydell Press, 1996.

22. E. H. Bates, ed., *Two Cartularies of the Benedictine Abbeys of Muchleney and Athelney in the County of Somerset*, Somerset Record Society, vol. 14 (1889). See in this case the Muchleney cartulary.

23. See n. 21 above.

24. J. H. Bullock, ed., *The Norfolk Portion of the Chartulary of the Priory of St. Pancras of Lewes*, Norfolk Record Society, vol. 12 (1939):

> No attempt, of course, has been made to print the deeds in full . . . Such introductory legal phraseology as *Sciant presentes et futuri*, the commencement of nearly half the documents; *noverint omnes, presentes, universi, etc.; notum sit omnibus*, is left out. Other omissions in the text are indicated by dots, comprising words of common legal form, redundancies and repetitions, such as "the monks who are serving and will go on serving God there", "God and the Church of St. Pancras of Lewes" . . . warranty and sealing clauses have been simply mentioned as such, unless some special wording called for notice. The word "grant" is made to cover the whole phrase *concessi, dedi et hac carta mea confirmavi*. The dots at the end of each charter represent *et multis aliis* or something similar. (Introduction, pp. xviii–xix)

See also: J. K. Kirby, ed., *The Hungerford Cartulary: A Calendar of the Earl of Radnor's Cartulary of the Hungerford Family*, Wiltshire Record Society, vol. 49 for 1993, Trowbridge: Wiltshire Record Society, 1994.

scribes, it may be noted, were not unlike modern editors to the extent that it was not unusual for them to replace common phrases with "etc.", and to leave out what at the time may have been considered extraneous material, such as the witness lists. They may also have applied a degree of standardisation in their preference for the use of letters 'c' or 't', 'i' or 'j', and 'u' or 'v', but I am not aware that a conscious effort was ever made to change formulaic expressions to conform to usage current at the time the copying was carried out. It is fairly safe to say that when formulae turn up in situations which would appear to be chronologically incorrect, there is good reason to believe that the document in question has been consciously tampered with; in other words, that it is either a blatant forgery, or an attempt to reconstruct the presumed content of a lost original. In addition to its potential as an aid in dating, the ability to recognise subsequent modifications to historical texts is a second major contribution which the study of changing word-patterns can make to our verification of the written record.

An example of such modification is another entry in the Hospitaller cartulary of 1442, one which is, in fact, precisely dated to the year 1148.[25] It is a grant to the Hospitallers by a certain Ingram de Merck and his wife, Maza, of six acres of land in a parish called Dunmow. Dunmow is located only two parishes distant from the parish of Chaureth, the site of the Order's first preceptory in Essex, founded in 1151. The charter is addressed to "*deo et beate marie et sancto iohanni baptiste et beatis pauperibus sancti hospitalis ierusalem*", a formula which occurs nine times among the documents from the cartulary which have been published, eight of which can be clearly attributed to the period 1225–1240.[26] Furthermore, while this document is preserved in the Order's mid-fifteenth-century cartulary, it also figures on two cartulary fragments, one of which can be dated to the early thirteenth century and the other to the early fourteenth century. The early thirteenth-century copy contains no dating clause, but has a witness list. The early fourteenth-century copy, which was the source for the example appearing in the cartulary of 1442, includes the dating clause, but has no witness list. There is reason to believe, therefore, that it may have been the scribe associated with the period 1225–1240 – and I do think we are dealing here with an individual scribe – who was responsible for incorporating the address as it now stands into the earlier of the two fragments, and that it could have been the scribe responsible for copying the early fourteenth-century fragment who relinquished the normal incipit (*Notum sit omnibus tam presentibus quam futuris quod ego*) in favour of this dating clause. Certainly, that pattern disappears from charter terminology elsewhere before the end of the thirteenth century (*Figure 7*). The reasons for these emendations are not clear, and while the document in its various forms almost certainly belongs to the twelfth century, the accuracy of the date and the validity of the address may well be questioned.

Despite the potential limitations inherent in copied sources, I am satisfied that, for the most part, the content of the charters which have survived in whatever form

---

25. *Hosp. Cart.*, p.c., no. 161.
26. *Hosp. Cart.*, p.c., no. 156; *Hosp. Cart.*, s.c., nos. 326, 370, 466, 468, 553, 571, 907.

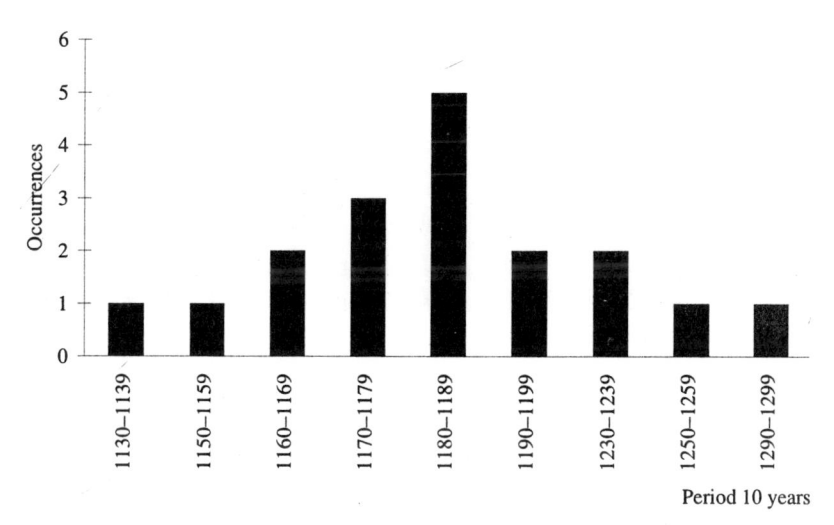

Figure 7 *"notum sit omnibus tam presentibus quam futuris quod ego"*

is generally accurate and that modifications made in subsequent recopyings can be recognised as such. It may well be, therefore, that documents with incorrect dates enter our corpus, but there is a good chance that documents containing later modifications will not pass the scrutiny of word-pattern matching unnoticed. The methodology we have developed is designed to identify the origination and extinction of word-patterns. The relative importance of each pattern in the dating process depends on three principal factors and a series of dependent ones. The principal factors include the word-pattern's chronological range, its currency over the course of that range, and its length in words. The longer and more frequent the pattern over a short chronological range, the more weight it holds as a dating criterion. The success of the method derives not from the assumption, but from the fact that, although the rate of origination of new patterns is not set, new patterns are nevertheless constantly entering the record, while old ones are disappearing from it.

Factors dependent upon the previous three include document type, place concerned, place of issue, issuer, length of document, and total number of documents in the source collection, provided they can be determined. While these aspects have yet to be analysed, there is good reason to suspect that forms may differ according to the type of document in which they appear, the place where the document was issued, and the institution or individual responsible for issuing it.

Our present database of word-patterns, derived from the dated charters in the DEEDS corpus, contains over 223,000 entries. They run from two-word patterns, of which there are 35,000, to forty-eight-word patterns, of which there are 80. We have recently produced bar-charts showing the origination and extinction of the patterns appearing in the database. One of these (*Figure 8*) represents the absolute number of changes and the second (*Figure 9*) the corresponding percentage of

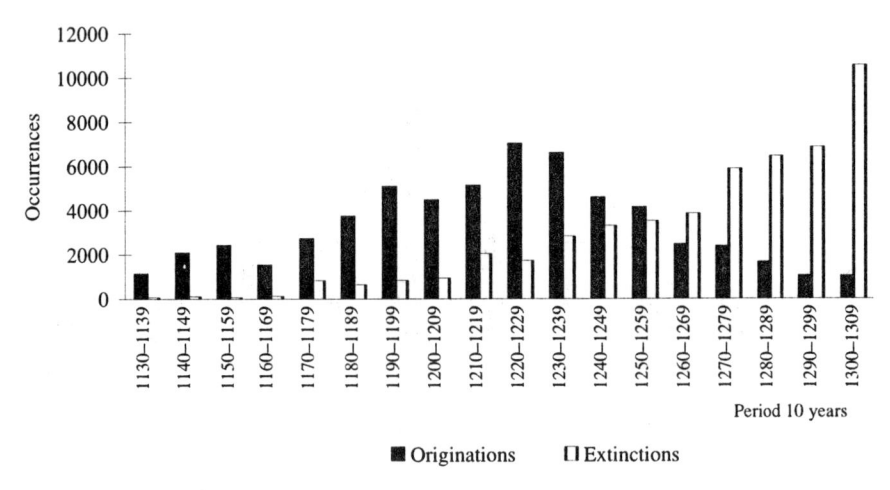

Figure 8 *Number of originations and extinctions of word-patterns, by period*

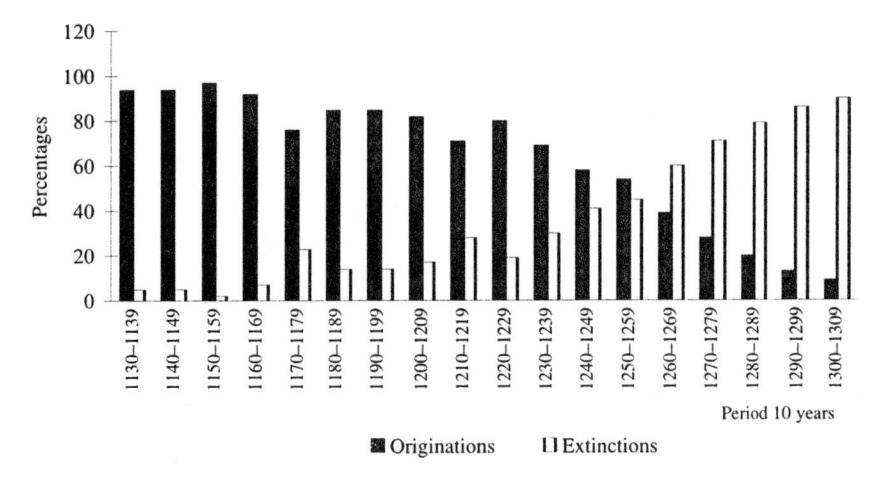

Figure 9 *Percentage of originations and extinctions of word-patterns, by period*

these changes, both being grouped in ten-year periods.[27] A second set (*Figures 10 and 11*), grouped in five-year periods, shows the origination and extinction rates of patterns with a lifetime of ten years or less. They represent nearly 60,000 patterns, over twenty-five per cent of all the patterns in the corpus. We have not yet had the opportunity to interpret these results fully, but some trends are clear,

27. The height of the bar indicating extinctions, and corresponding to the period 1300–1309, is due in part to the fact that the corpus of documents searched for word-patterns ends in that decade. The query, however, was programmed to allow for a degree of continuity of patterns past that decade. The trend by which extinctions increased and originations decreased from *c*.1220 to the end of the century is clearly demonstrated by the percentage of differences visible in the bars for the previous decades.

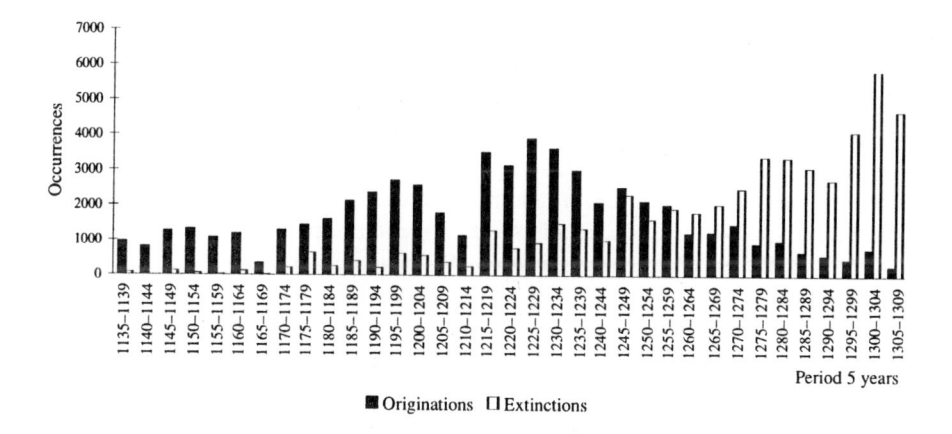

Figure 10 *Number of originations and extinctions of word-patterns with a life-time of 100 years or less, by period*

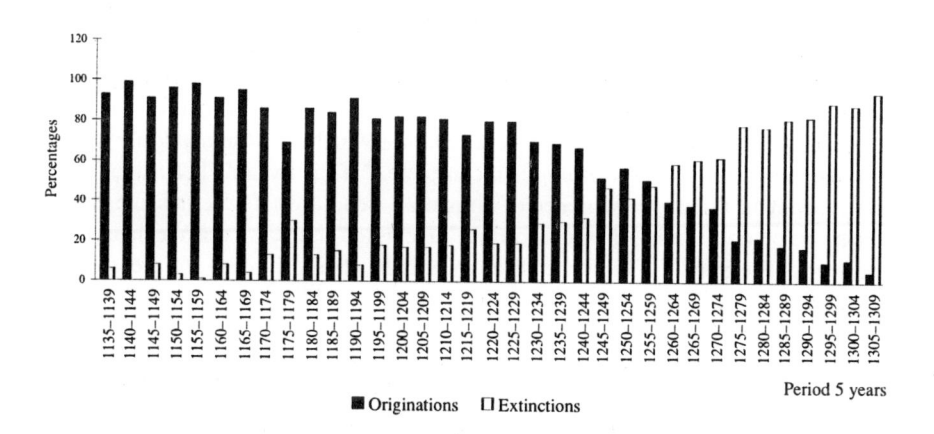

Figure 11 *Percentage of originations and extinctions of word-patterns with a life-time of 100 years or less, by period*

notably that there is a correlation between the portion of new word-patterns manifesting themselves over time and the number of documents present in the corpus for any given period. The fluctuation over time between creation and extinction may be seen in *Figure 11*. These changes may be explained by political, social, and economic developments, not to mention a conscious effort by the judiciary and those who drafted the charters to apply a degree of conformity to this type of record. The process by which this conformity was achieved supports the obvious conclusion that the wording of charters in the twelfth and thirteenth centuries was anything but static.

The number of documents surviving from the twelfth century is small compared to the enormous activity in the land market reflected by the great quantity of documents extant from the first half of the thirteenth century. Furthermore, the relative extinction rate of patterns is negligible until about 1175, and even then it is relatively modest. There is then an increase in the portion of extinctions during the first quarter of the thirteenth century and a visibly steady growth from 1225 to the end of the century. The creation and extinction of patterns reaches a balance in the late 1250s, whereafter extinctions figure noticeably more frequently than creations throughout the remainder of the century. The portion of creations, we know, correlates to the number of new documents available over time. It is interesting that during the course of the thirteenth century the portion of extinctions grows inversely to the number of creations. This phenomenon gives rise to two distinct factors. In the first place we recognise that as far as the dating procedure is concerned, *postquem* limits can be set by creations and *antequem* limits by extinctions. Consequently, it should prove statistically more possible to attribute dates to thirteenth-century documents, where so many patterns are seen to come and go, than to those from the twelfth century, where at present there is relatively little evidence of extinction. Secondly, the decreasing rate of creations and the increasing rate of extinctions during the thirteenth century would suggest that the wording of the English private charter became ever more standardised as the century progressed. One thing to keep in mind regarding an apparently massive extinction at the very end of the thirteenth century, however, is that for all intents and purposes our corpus concludes *c*.1310, past which date the material we have available for computer reckoning is incomplete.[28] This invisible barricade should not, however, affect the evidence of an overall trend towards progressive simplification, or conformity, in the wording of charter sources from the late 1250s onwards. The trend has long been recognised; the charts showing the creation and extinction rates of frequently occurring patterns provide visual proof of the phenomenon.

A final remark regarding the second set of charts concerns the fact that more than twenty-five per cent of the word-patterns in the corpus had a life-time of ten years or less. This phenomenon is particularly significant in two ways. First, the large number of short-lived patterns provides us with reasonably precise *postquem* and *antequem* dates which can be used in attributing dates to undated charters in which similar patterns occur. Secondly, the short lifetimes may well be due to the activity of individual scribes, more about which subject appears below.

To this point, approximately one-hundred published collections have been searched for the dated twelfth- and thirteenth-century charters presently comprising the DEEDS corpus. Initially, an effort was made to select documents coming from what are known as the Home Counties, the assumption being that because of their proximity to London communication would be better and there would be a greater degree of conformity in scribal activity than in places more distant from

---

28. By 1310, most English private charters contain dating clauses.

the capital. This may, in fact, be the case, but we have now gone well beyond these boundaries in our search, taking advantage, for example, of the rich selection of material in W. Farrer and C. T. Clay's edition of *Early Yorkshire Charters*, including ninety-three dated twelfth-century documents.[29] We know that there are important differences in vocabulary between the documents issued in Yorkshire and those from the southern counties, but we have not yet had the opportunity to determine whether these differences are significant enough to alter the chronological scheme into which the rest of the charters fit. What is clear, regardless of a document's source, is that some patterns, sometimes many patterns, turn out to be specific to the institution, or the hand, which produced them. Typical of this tendency is the address formula which, especially in the case of religious houses, regularly differs from one house to the next. Furthermore, forms of address for any one house change over time, making the address alone a useful indicator when attributing a date to a document. In some cases these formulae remained current for considerable periods of time, indicating that they were in one way or another representative of a scribal tradition issuing from a particular chancery. In other cases, particular word-patterns may be associated with a specific house or institution over periods of less than a decade. Examples of this nature, which are numerous, point to the hand of an individual scribe. This is one of the many exciting possible applications of computerised access to charter sources. There is a reasonable chance that word-pattern matching will enable us to identify (i) different scribes, at least by their writing style, if not by name; (ii) the length of time they worked in a particular place; and (iii) their peregrinations in the event they moved from one scriptorium to another. Employing Q-sum technology, a method used increasingly to identify authorship, it should be possible to distinguish between a wide variety of hands working at any given time.[30] Distinctions will, of course, depend not on handwriting, but on stylistic preferences and on the personal rendition of legal formulae.

Is it possible, one may ask, to have a personal rendition of a legal formula? Is not a formula a fixed or set form of words, a stock phrase, a conventionalised statement? Indeed it is, but our sources indicate that many charter formulae came in a great variety of forms, all of which apparently bore the same meaning, but which did not share the same currency, nor the same chronological distribution. For example, turning to a 'typical' Hospitaller formula of address, we find the following (*Figures 12* and *13*):

---

29. W. Farrer, ed., *Early Yorkshire Charters*, 3 vols., Edinburgh: Ballantyne, Hanson and Co., 1914–16; Charles Travis Clay, ed., *Early Yorkshire Charters*, 9 vols., Yorkshire Archaeological Society Record Series, Extra Series, vols. 1–3, 5–9 (1935–65).

30. On Q-sum technology, see Jillian M. Farringdon, *Analysing for Authorship: A Guide to the Cusum Technique* (with contributions by A. Q. Morton, M. G. Farringdon, and M. D. Baker), Cardiff: University of Wales Press, 1996; Paula R. Feldman and Buford Norman, *The Wordworthy Computer: Classroom and Research Applications in Language and Literature*, New York: Random House, c.1987; Andrew Queen Morton, *The Authorship of the Pauline Epistles: A Scientific Solution*, Saskatoon: University of Saskatchewan, 1965; Frederick Mosteller and David Wallace, *Inference and Disputed Authorship: 'The Federalist'*, Reading, MA: Addison-Wesley, 1964.

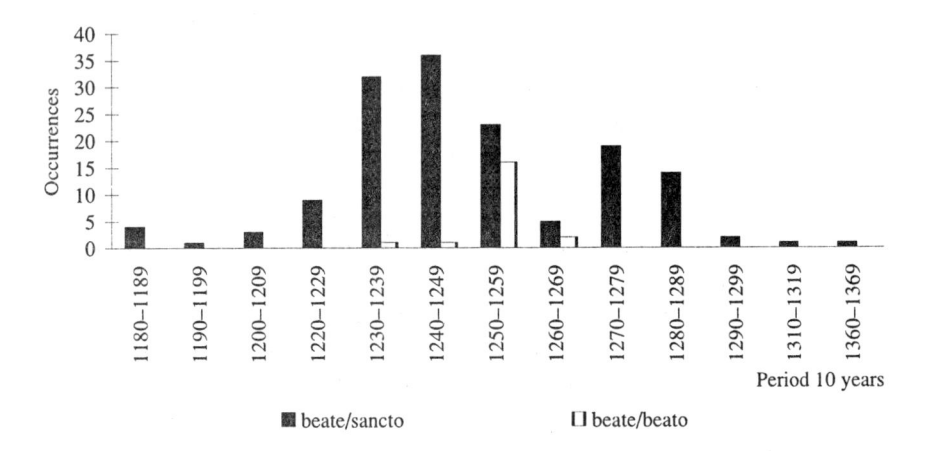

Figure 12 *Chronological distribution of expressions:*
*"deo et **beate** marie et **sancto** iohanni baptiste" (150X c.1180–1370)*
*"deo et **beate** marie et **beato** iohanni baptiste" (20X c.1230–1260)*

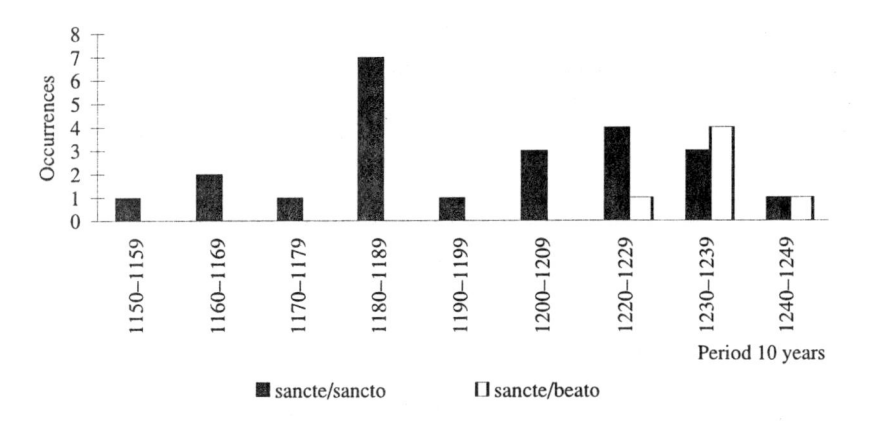

Figure 13 *Chronological distribution of expressions:*
*"deo et **sancte** marie et **sancto** iohanni baptiste" (23X c.1150-1240)*
*"deo et **sancte** marie et **beato** iohanni baptiste" (6X c.1230-1240)*

Each of the foregoing bears the same sense, although the usage of the two adjectives describing Mary and John, *beata/beatus* and *sancta/sanctus*, differs. The first case, addressed to "God and the Blessed Mary and to Saint John the Baptist", is the most common and is current for much of the period covered by the sources. It occurs 150 times in our corpus over the period of 200 years. The second is the same as the first, except that "Saint John" is here rendered "Blessed John". That difference is reflected in the fact that the address occurs only twenty times over the thirty-year period from *c.*1230 to 1260. Like the second, the third example differs from the first only in the descriptive of Mary as "Saint" rather than "Blessed". This form is, in fact, the earliest, occurring twenty-three times between *c.*1150 and c.1240. Finally, there is the fourth form, which differs from the first in two ways: "Blessed Mary" becomes "Saint Mary", and "Saint John" becomes "Blessed John". The address has a very short lifespan, appearing only during the decade 1230–1240, and occurring in surviving documents only six times during that period.

What, one may ask, does this example tell us about the nature of a formula? If it changes, is it the same formula? I would answer that it is not. Clearly, each of the forms has a different chronological range, and from our present viewpoint such chronological distinctions are extremely important. As a dating aid, the first example can hardly be considered useful as it extends over such a long temporal range. The second is considerably more useful because that range is limited to only thirty years. The third is seemingly like the first in its relatively long lifespan, but the end date, c.1240, serves as a useful *antequem* indicator; that is, a document in which it appears can be expected to belong to the period before 1240. The fourth and last example is a particularly interesting case for two reasons. In the first place, it is limited chronologically to a single decade, and secondly, the end of that decade corresponds to the end of the range exhibited by example number three. It is an excellent chronological indicator because of its relatively frequent currency and the short range of its occurrence. I would argue, however, that unlike the other three examples, and certainly the first two, it is not a formula. Rather, its occurrence is more than likely due to the choice and preference of a single scribe. This is not to say that the scribe's activity was restricted to this particular decade, but that he only used this word-pattern at some point during those years. He could well have used any of the other three choices at the same time as this one.

There is another element worthy of recognition in the present discussion: we have seen that both formula three and pattern four have the same end date, c.1240. The point is not coincidental. What determines the final date limit is the reference in the address to "Saint Mary" (*sancte marie*). After that date, the term never occurs in any form in Hospitaller documents, nor as a form of address in any of the other sources searched after 1257.[31] Thereafter, *beate marie* alone appears in this formulaic role. References to *beato iohanni baptiste* follow a similar pattern. They disappear entirely from Hospitaller documents after c.1260, when *sancto iohanni baptiste* becomes the standard form.[32]

It is difficult to determine the motivations which lie behind such changes in charter language. There may be a very specific reason why *sancte marie* gives way definitively to *beate marie* towards the middle of the thirteenth century, after appearing with it concurrently for the previous hundred years or so (*Figure 14*); and, also, why all the other thousands of modifications take place regularly during the period under study. There are obvious cases, as for example the changes precipitated by such royal acts previously mentioned as the statutes of *Mortmain*

---

31. H. E. Salter, ed., *Cartulary of the Hospital of St. John, Oxford 1914–17*, no. 242. The form does, however, continue to appear in the name of churches and festivals dedicated to the Virgin.

32. References to "*beato iohanni baptiste*" do occur later elsewhere, however. See the example, dated 1284/85, in H. E. Salter, *A Cartulary of the Hospital of St. John the Baptist*, vol. 1, Oxford Historical Series, vol. 66 (1914), no. 283, pp. 283–84.

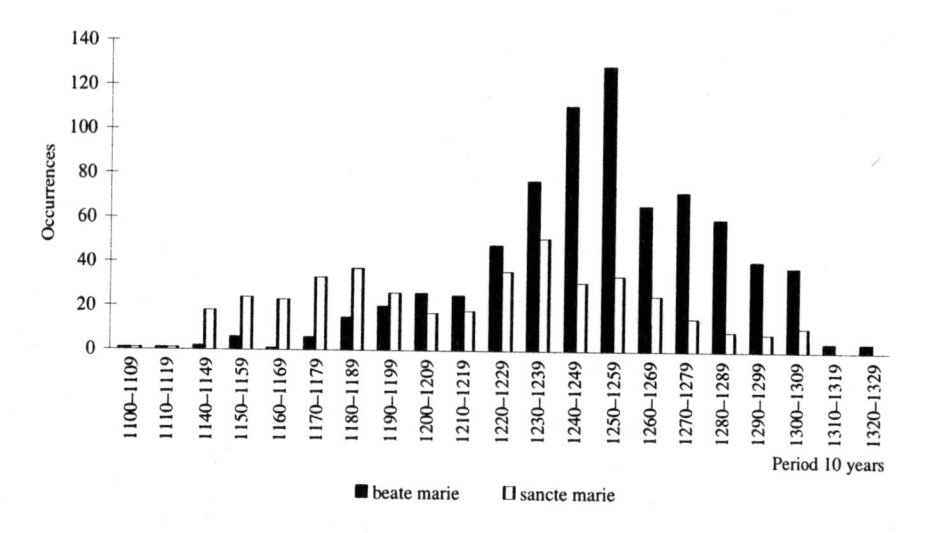

Figure 14 *Chronological distribution of expressions "beate marie" and "sancte marie"*

and *Quia Emptores* in the last quarter of the thirteenth century, but it will likely be next to impossible to determine what lies behind most changes which can be documented as occurring year in and year out during this mysterious age of chronological twilight. Students of English twelfth- and thirteenth-century history are indeed fortunate in having at their disposal, in whatever form, that eight to ten per cent of charters which are dated. That fortune lies, in my opinion, not in the fact that this small portion of the whole provides the historian with a chronological context for individuals whose names can be associated with counterparts appearing in undated documents, but in the multitude of word-patterns which are common to dated and undated charters alike, and to each of which a distinct chronological lifespan and fingerprint can be attributed. It is these patterns which, analysed as a whole and weighted according to currency, duration, and length, provide us with an extremely positive alternative to dating by so-called traditional methods. That alternative, developed by the DEEDS Project at the University of Toronto, is described by Rodolfo Fiallos in his contribution to the present volume.[33]

An enormous effort has been devoted over many years to bringing the DEEDS dating program to the point it has reached today. I myself developed a primitive, manual form of our methodology when attempting, a decade ago, to date a series of charters in the English cartulary of the Knights of the Hospital of St. John of Jerusalem which had been copied without their witness lists. Now that we have at

---

33. See also Rodolfo Fiallos, 'Procedure for Dating Undated Documents Using a Relational Database', in M. Gervers, 'The Dating of Medieval English Private Charters of the Twelfth and Thirteenth Centuries', in *A Distinct Voice: Medieval Studies in Honor of Leonard E. Boyle, O.P.*, ed. Jacqueline Brown and William P. Stoneman, Notre Dame (Indiana), 1997, pp. 480–501.

our disposal, in machine-readable form, a relatively large corpus of dated documents, and an equally large database of word-patterns derived from it, I am able to re-evaluate the chronological accuracy of my previous dating attributions. As we have seen, some of the attributions based on the common occurrence of personal names have turned out to be inaccurate. Those dated by word-pattern matching have fared better, although, as we are all well aware, there is no way in the case of an undated document of ever knowing whether or not an attribution is correct. That is why the DEEDS research team has spent so much time gathering dated documents and testing our methodology against them. However, there is one major question which, as far as I know, no one has ever asked, and that is, why were dates only entered in eight to ten per cent of English twelfth- and thirteenth-century charters? Is there something about the dated charter, other than that it contains a date, which distinguishes it from the over ninety per cent of charters for which a chronological marker was deemed unnecessary? A closer consideration of this question might enable us to understand to what extent contemporaries felt chronological precision to be important, and what they thought chronology to be.

It is our intention to make the dating system developed at DEEDS available to researchers everywhere over the Internet. We have decided to provide remote access to our database and dating program, as well as the ability to browse and search our source collection and word-patterns by means of a Web application. This, in fact, is one of our most pressing current objectives. It must be kept in mind, however, that while historians everywhere may find value in our methodology, our corpus and database will probably only be of use to students of English medieval history. Scholars working in other regions will have to build their own corpus, and to do this effectively a considerable degree of collaboration and co-operation will be required.

I would like initially to call for the co-operation of colleagues working with, and especially editing, English medieval charters belonging to the period 1066 to 1310. Once their manuscripts have been sent to the press, or published, the DEEDS Project would greatly appreciate receiving a machine-readable copy of their transcriptions, with dates and topographic identifications, so we would not have to go through the long task of scanning printed pages and correcting the errors which invariably result from the process. Experience suggests that the larger our corpus of dated documents, the more accurate our dating attributions become. Secondly, I should like to emphasise once again that our methodology has the capacity not only to assist in the dating of undated documents, but also to identify obvious forgeries or later emendations to earlier documents. If the rest of Europe is satisfied with the chronology of its legal documents, all historians can profit from being able to recognise and exclude, or re-evaluate the content of, false or altered ones. If others are prepared to build a corpus of dated documents, or contribute towards the existing DEEDS corpus, we will be only too happy to make our programs available to all who would like to use them.[34]

34. Notices concerning, and publications produced by, the DEEDS Project are posted on its home page on the Internet: http://www.utoronto.ca/deeds/.

Bibliography

Arnoux, Matthieu. 1996. 'Essor et déclin d'un type diplomatique: les actes passés "coram parrochia" en Normandie (XII–XIII siècles).' *Bibliothèque de l'Ecole des Chartes* 154: pp. 323–57.

Bates, E. H., ed. 1889. *Two Cartularies of the Benedictine Abbeys of Muchleney and Athelney in the County of Somerset*. Somerset Record Society. Vol. 14.

Blake, E. O., ed. 1981. *Cartulary of the Priory of St. Denys*. Southampton Records Series, vols. 24 and 25. Southampton: Southampton University Press.

Bónis, György. 1962. 'Les autorités de "foi publique" et les archives des "loci credibiles" en Hongrie.' *Archivum* 12: pp. 87–104.

Borsa, Iván. 1988. 'Zur Beurkundstätigkeit der glaubwürdigen Orte in Ungarn', in *Forschungen über Siebenbürgen und seine Nachbarn. Festschrift für A. T. Szabó und Zs. Jakó*, ed. K. Benda, T. Bogyay, and H. Glassl, pp. 143–48. Vol. 2. München.

Bullock, J. H., ed. 1939. *The Norfolk Portion of the Chartulary of the Priory of St. Pancras of Lewes*. Norfolk Record Society. Vol. 12.

Chaplais, Pierre. 1971. *English Royal Documents: King John–Henry VI*. Oxford.

Clanchy, Michael. 1993. *From Memory to Written Record*, 2nd ed. Oxford: Blackwell.

Clay, Charles Travis, ed. 1935–65. *Early Yorkshire Charters*. 9 vols. Yorkshire Archaeological Society, Record Series, Extra Series, vols. 1–3, 5–9.

Dilks, T. B., ed. 1933. *Bridgwater Borough Archives*. Vol. 1: *1200–1377*. Somerset Record Society. Vol. 48.

Eckhart, Franz. 1913/1915. 'Die glaubwürdigen Orte Ungarns im Mittelalter,' in *Mitteilungen des Instituts für Österreichische Geschichtsforschung*, 395–558. Supplementary vol. 9. N. p.

Farrer, W., ed. 1914–16. *Early Yorkshire Charters*. 3 vols. Edinburgh: Ballantyne, Hanson and Co.

Farringdon, Jillian M. (with contributions by A. Q. Morton, M. G. Farringdon, and M. D. Baker). 1996. *Analysing for Authorship: A Guide to the Cusum Technique*. Cardiff: University of Wales Press.

Feldman, Paula R., and Norman Buford. c.1987. *The Wordworthy Computer: Classroom and Research Applications in Language and Literature*. New York: Random House.

Fiallos, Rodolfo. 1997. 'Procedure for Dating Undated Documents Using a Relational Database', in *A Distinct Voice: Medieval Studies in Honor of Leonard E. Boyle, O.P.*, ed. Jacqueline Brown and William P. Stoneman, pp. 480–501. Notre Dame (Indiana).

Gervers, Michael. 1978. 'Medieval Charters and the Computer: An Analysis Using Mark IV.' *Computers and the Humanities* 12: pp. 127–36.

———. 1983. *A Microfiche Concordance of the Cartulary of the Order of St. John of Jerusalem, secunda camera (British Library, Cotton ms. Nero E VI, fols. 289–467)*. Toronto: Deeds Project (Scarborough Campus, University of Toronto). Compiled with the technical assistance of L. C. Kordecki.

——— (co-authored with G. Long and M. McCulloch). 1990. 'The DEEDS Database of Mediaeval Charters: Design and Coding for the RDBMS ORACLE 5'. *History and Computing* 1, no. 3: pp. 1–12.

———. 1997a. 'The Dating of Medieval English Private Charters of the Twelfth and Thirteenth Centuries', in *A Distinct Voice: Medieval Studies in Honor of Leonard E. Boyle, O.P.*, ed. Jacqueline Brown and William P. Stoneman, pp. 455–504. Notre Dame (Indiana).

———. 1997b. 'Középkori angol oklevelek datálása szóelőfordulások alapján' (Computerised methods for dating undated medieval English charters). *Aetas* 2–3: pp. 189–97.

———. Forthcoming. 'Changing Forms of Hospitaller Address in English Private Charters of the Twelfth and Thirteenth Centuries', in *Expanding the Frontiers of Medieval Latin Christianity: The Crusades and the Military Orders*, ed. József Lászlovszky and Zsolt Hunyadi.

———. ed. 1982. *The Cartulary of the Knights of St. John of Jerusalem in England, Secunda Camera: Essex*. Records of Social and Economic History, n. s. VI. Oxford University Press for the British Academy, London (*Hosp. Cart.*, s.c.).

———. 1996. *The Cartulary of the Knights of St. John of Jerusalem in England, part 2, Prima Camera: Essex*. Records of Social and Economic History, n. s. 23. London: Oxford University Press for the British Academy (*Hosp. Cart.*, p.c.).

Kirby, J. K., ed. 1994. *The Hungerford Cartulary: A Calendar of the Earl of Radnor's Cartulary of the Hungerford Family*. Wiltshire Record Society. Vol. 49 for 1993.

Kirk, R. E. C., ed. 1899. *Feet of Fines for Essex*. Vol. 1. Colchester: Essex Archaeological Society.

Mezey, László. 1972. 'Anfänge der Privaturkunde in Ungarn und der glaubwürdigen Orte.' *Archiv für Diplomatik* 18: pp. 290–302.

Morant, Philip. 1978 (1763). *The History and Antiquities of the County of Essex*. Vol. 1. London: EP Publishing.

Mortimer, Richard, ed. 1996. *Charters of St. Bartholomew's Priory, Sudbury*. Suffolk Charters 15. Woodbridge: Suffolk Records Society/Boydell Press.

Morton, Andrew Queen. 1965. *The Authorship of the Pauline Epistles: A Scientific Solution*. Saskatoon: University of Saskatchewan.

Mosteller, Frederick, and David Wallace. 1964. *Inference and Disputed Authorship: 'The Federalist'*. Reading, MA: Addison-Wesley.

Patterson, Robert B., ed. 1973. *Earldom of Gloucester Charters. The Charters and Scribes of the Earls and Countesses of Gloucester to AD 1217*. Oxford: Clarendon Press.

Salter, Rev. H. E. 1914–17. *A Cartulary of the Hospital of St. John the Baptist*. Oxford Historical Society. Vols. 66, 68, and 69.

———. 1929–36. *Cartulary of Oseney Abbey*. Oxford Historical Society. Vols. 89, 90, 91, 97, 98, and 101.

———. 1907–08. *Eynsham Cartulary*. Oxford Historical Society. Vols. 49 and 51.

——— (ed. with C. L. Shadwell). 1926. *Oriel College Records*. Oxford Historical Society. Vol. 85.

———. 1913. *The Oxford Deeds of Balliol College*. Oxford Historical Society. Vol. 64.

Short, Ian. 1996. 'Tam Angli quam Franci: Self-Definition in Anglo-Norman England.' *Anglo-Norman Studies* XVIII: pp. 153–75.

Vincent, Nicholas. 1996. *Peter des Roches: An Alien in English Politics, 1205–38*. Cambridge.

AN OVERVIEW OF THE PROCESS OF DATING UNDATED MEDIEVAL CHARTERS: LATEST RESULTS AND FUTURE DEVELOPMENTS

Rodolfo Fiallos

Introduction

This paper presents an overview of the process of dating undated medieval charters in development at the DEEDS Project, University of Toronto. The three stages involved in the process are summarised and a chronology of events is used to show milestones in the third developmental stage. The first two developmental stages have been explained in previous publications, so they are described only briefly in this paper. The third and last developmental stage is described in more detail, but what is given here does not pretend to be a complete description. More material will be published later for the purpose of updating the researcher.

References to previous publications and to unpublished material displayed at the DEEDS Project web site (www.utoronto.ca/deeds) are provided in order to allow the making of the appropriate connections. References to "the process of dating undated charters" should be understood to refer to the process of dating undated charters using the method developed at the DEEDS Project.

A Brief Description of the Method of Dating Undated Medieval Charters

The process of creating the system in a relational database was divided into three stages:

Stage 1. Creating a database of dated word patterns.
Stage 2. Comparing the undated charter with the database of dated charters.
Stage 3. Dating the undated charter.

Stage 1. The creation of a database of dated word patterns using a relational database

A collection of dated charters is taken and their wordings are compared to produce a database of word patterns that occur at least twice in the collection. This means that each word pattern has at least two dates associated with it. Word patterns are 'born' the first time they occur in the time-scale and 'die' when they cease to occur. If a word pattern is born and dies in the same year, then its lifetime is one year.

From *Dating Undated Medieval Charters*. Ed. Michael Gervers. Copyright (by the Editor and Contributors 2000). Published by the Boydell Press (in association with Collegium Budapest), PO Box 9, Woodbridge, Suffolk, IP12 3DF, Great Britain. ISBN 0 85115 792 0.

The principle behind this database of dated word patterns is that the more dated charters there are, the more dated word patterns are produced, therefore the more elements of analysis the system has with which to assign a date to the undated charter. The use of a relational database was adopted because of the large amount of information we expected to produce and the flexibility of the SQL (Structured Query Language) language in extracting the information.

A method of producing the database of dated word patterns using a relational database is fully described in an article published by Michael Gervers and Rodolfo Fiallos in 1997.[1] It is still current: researchers can make use of this method or produce their own. At the DEEDS Project, three generations of dated word-pattern databases have been created so far.

The first generation was produced using the 1,167 dated and circa-dated – in fact, only 256 are dated accurately – charters from the Order of the Hospital of St. John of Jerusalem in England.

A second generation of dated word patterns was produced taking the 256 dated charters from the first database and adding dated charters from more than 30 other sources, to make a total of 1,525 charters. This database contained only charters whose dates are known to be accurate within a one-year range. The total number of unique word patterns was 106,676.

The third and current database was produced by adding more dated charters from different sources to the second database to make a total of 3,353 dated charters. It contains almost entirely charters dated within a one-year range. The total number of unique word patterns obtained was 223,158.

Stage 2. The comparison of an undated charter with the database of dated word patterns

A method of comparing an undated charter with a database of dated word patterns using a relational database is also described in Gervers and Fiallos (1996). To compare an undated charter with a database of dated word patterns is a mechanical process. The text of the undated charter is compared word by word with the database of dated word patterns to produce a list of 'matching' word patterns that serve as the foundation for the dating of the charter.

Matching word patterns can be of any length, from two to 48 words. At the DEEDS Project, however, only matching patterns of a minimum of three words were produced to avoid the high volume of two-word matching patterns. It was not until recently that two-word patterns were incorporated in the dating process.

In order to facilitate the testing of different algorithms, the comparison process is carried out independently and in advance of the dating of charters as an intermediate stage. The matching patterns, the product of the comparison stage, are stored in a database that consists of a small repository of matching patterns for

---

1. Michael Gervers and Rodolfo Fiallos, 'The Dating of Medieval English Private Charters of the Twelfth and Thirteenth Centuries', in *A Distinct Voice: Medieval Studies in Honor of Leonard E. Boyle, O.P.*, Notre Dame, Indiana: University of Notre Dame Press, 1997.

every undated charter. When the dating takes place, the comparison process is skipped and the matching patterns are taken from the repository.

To compare a medium-size undated charter with the current database of dated word patterns takes approximately fifteen minutes at the DEEDS Project installations. This represents most of the computing time involved in dating an undated charter.

For the first database, approximately 10 charters were compared. The analysis included word patterns of three or more words. For the second database, 1,484 charters were compared including only patterns with three or more words. For the third database a total of 3,326 charters have been compared and for the first time two-word patterns have been included.

Stage 3. The dating of undated charters

This stage consists of a dating algorithm. The matching word patterns produced by the comparison of an undated charter with the database of dated charters form the basis of this stage, which analyses, evaluates, weighs, filters, and summarises the information related to matching patterns to produce a final date estimate.

The current dating algorithm consists basically of three steps:

1. Assign a weight to every matching word pattern. A description of the weighting mechanism can be found in online documents on the DEEDS web site.[2]
2. Assign the weight from every matching word pattern to the dates in which the matching word patterns occur.
3. Summarise the weighting obtained in step 2 by date and select the most probable date range for the charter based on the best weight/period ratio.

The third stage has evolved from a simple counting of hits to a weighting system that processes matching word patterns according to three variables: (i) length or number of words; (ii) lifetime or years between first and last occurrence; and (iii) currency or average number of years per occurrence.

The following chronology will illustrate the evolution of the dating algorithm and milestones in its development.

---

2. Rodolfo Fiallos, 'An Example of Word-Pattern Dating in which the Patterns in Charter 340207 (dated 1247) are Compared with the 196,632 Patterns in the DEEDS Database', DEEDS Project, December 1997. Rodolfo Fiallos, 'A Description of the Process in which Sample Charter 10662 (dated 1274) is Dated by Comparing its Text with the Text of 1,524 Dated Charters in the DEEDS Database', DEEDS Project, October 1998.

Chronology

1992–93

First talks about the possibility of developing a computerised system to date undated charters by comparing word patterns.

1994

The first database of dated word patterns is created using 1,167 dated and circa-dated charters. Approximately 10 dated charters were dated simulating undated charters using the Tetris algorithm: that is, the counting of hits or number of occurrences of all matching patterns in specific years.

After that, the dating algorithm used a system of points to give weights according to the length of the matching pattern. This algorithm is now called the Points algorithm. Little was accomplished and no consistency was achieved in the results. There was, however, an indication of approximation, as shown in *Figures 1* and *2*.

1996

A second database of word patterns was created using 1,525 dated charters from different sources. It included word patterns with a minimum of three words; two-word patterns were excluded to reduce the amount of information.

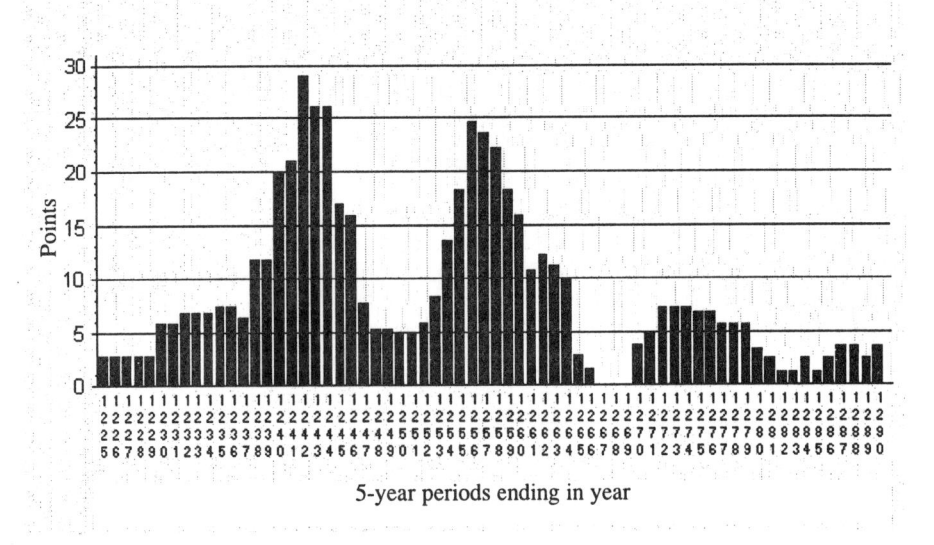

Figure 1 *DEEDS Project: Possible dates for document STP333*

From Gervers and Fiallos (1997). The dating of charter STP333 (dated 1239) in 1994, using the first (1,167-charter) database of dated charters and the Points algorithm, and filtering patterns according to charter type (grant, quitclaim, and so on). The tallest bar represents the best range.

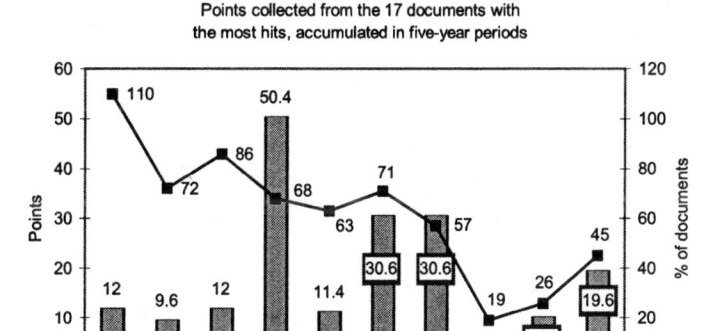

DEEDS PROJECT. Document STP333
Points collected from the 17 documents with
the most hits, accumulated in five-year periods

Figure 2

Document STP333 (dated 1239) is shown here under observation using the first (1,167-charter) database, the Points algorithm, combined with the number of dated charters in the database and filtering in terms of similar charters (dated charters with more matching word patterns).

For the first time, the weighting of matching word patterns in the dating algorithm was based on three variables: length, lifetime, and currency. These three variables generated a number called the MT number (for 'Multiplicador Total' in Spanish, or 'Total Multiplier' in English). The MT number is produced for each matching word pattern and expresses the quality of the word pattern. When dating a charter, matching patterns are filtered according to the MT number, taking into consideration only those with high values.

1997

In order to test undated charters the concept of the Global MT number was introduced. The Global MT number was defined for a given charter as the average MT number of the ten matching patterns with the highest MT numbers.

Selected at random from a pool of 1,525 dated charters, 186 charters were dated. For the first time in the dating algorithm development process, a correlation was discovered between the accuracy obtained and the Global MT number of the charter. The accuracy of the dating depended on the ability of the undated charter to produce matching patterns that were long, had a short lifetime, and had occurred consistently during that lifetime. Charters with these characteristics had a high Global MT number.

Figure 3 shows this group of 186 charters classified in terms of two groups, small and large charters.

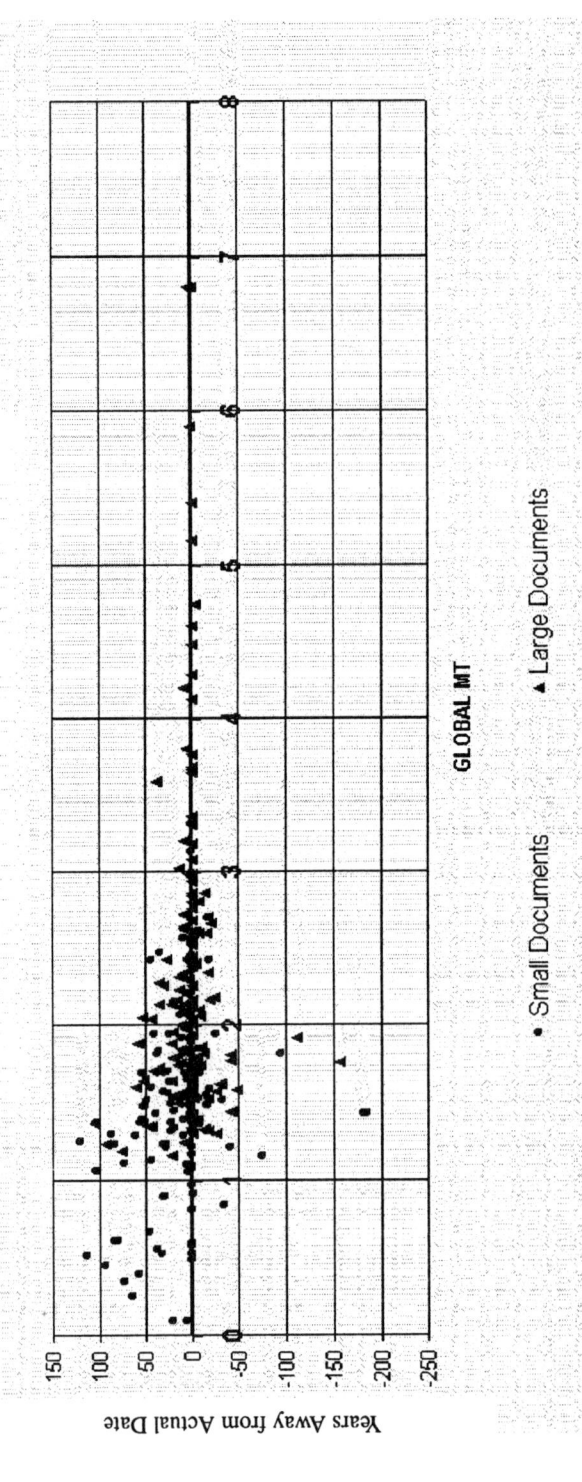

Figure 3 *Distribution of Differences after Dating (Test Groups Small and Large Documents)*

On 18 September 1997, 186 randomly selected, dated charters were dated using the MT number algorithm. For the first time, consistency was achieved. Charters with a high MT number were dated with very little error.

1998

In February 1998, 1,484 dated charters were dated using the MT number algorithm. The results were passed for analysis to the Department of Statistics at the University of Toronto. The idea was to develop an error curve that could indicate the expected error when dating a charter according to its Global MT number.

The error curve in question (*Figure 4*) indicated that the maximum accuracy to be expected according to statistics was plus or minus 8.77 years and the minimum accuracy was plus or minus 24.69 years. However, these results were conservative, as explained in the following extract taken from the report.

> The predicted date was defined as the mid-point of the predicted interval. The discrepancy or delta value was the difference between the actual date and the predicted date.
>
> A plot of the square of delta against the MT number of each document was produced. Each value of delta squared is an estimate of the variance of the predicted year, for a document with a given MT value.
>
> A locally weighted regression line (lowess function) was used to model delta squared as a function of the MT value. For a given MT value, let (MT, y) be the corresponding point on the lowess curve. Then y is the estimated variability of the predicted year, for documents with the given MT value. Then the square root of this value ((sqrt(y)) is the estimated standard error of the predicted value. A 95% confidence interval for the predicted year is ((predicted - 1.96*sqrt(y), (predicted + 1.96*sqrt(y)).
>
> Given a large number of documents with a given MT number, we can say that 95% of the predicted years will lie within the constructed intervals. However, for a given document, we cannot say whether it lies inside or outside the interval.
>
> Since the dispersion in your data is less than would be expected theoretically, the constructed intervals are actually wider than necessary, and hence are conservative. It seems unlikely that you would predict with very little error in almost 1/3 of the documents.
>
> Peter Austin

1999

A third generation of dated word patterns was created based on 3,353 dated charters. This time, however, two-word patterns were included to increase the number of matching patterns produced when dating a charter, so increasing the number of high-quality word patterns. In the current database, there are 34,832 unique two-word patterns out of a total of 223,158 unique word patterns of up to 48 words.

Recently, the comparison process was completed and the first dating of a total of 3,326 charters carried out.

Latest Results

The dating of 3,326 charters with the MT number algorithm was the last stage in the development of the dating algorithm.

On the premise that the more quality word patterns are available, the more accurate the dating of charters will be, two-word patterns were included in the database of dated word patterns.

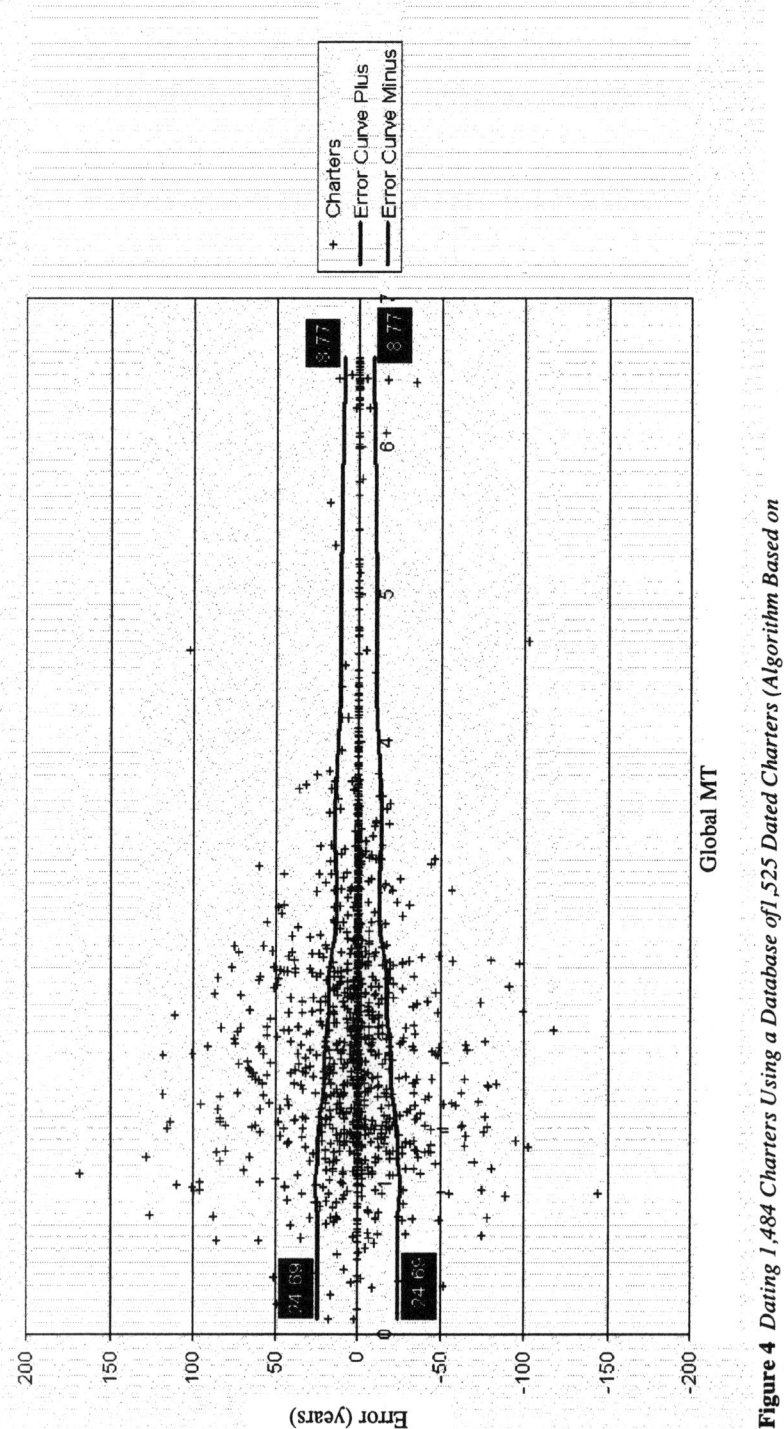

Figure 4 *Dating 1,484 Charters Using a Database of 1,525 Dated Charters (Algorithm Based on Length, Lifetime, and Currency)*

On 6 April 1998 an error curve was developed by the Department of Statistics, University of Toronto. The curve is based on a 95% confidence interval.

Tables *1* and *2* show the results of dating the 3,326 charters from the current database – which includes two-word patterns – compared to the results of dating the 1,485 charters from the previous database (which does not). *Table 2*, however, shows only the charters common to both databases.

Table 1 The results of dating 1,484 charters from the second database (columns 2, 3, and 4) compared with those derived from dating 3,326 charters from the third and current database (columns 4, 5, and 6).

	From the previous 1,525-charter database (using three-word patterns and up)			From the current 3,353-charter database (includes two-word patterns and up)		
Error (years)	Number of charters	%	Accumulated %	Number of charters	%	Accumulated %
0	105	7.1	7.1	195	5.9	5.9
1–5	656	44.2	51.3	1 198	36.0	41.9
6–10	175	11.8	63.1	459	13.8	55.7
11–20	219	14.8	77.8	613	18.4	74.1
21–50	229	15.4	93.3	643	19.3	93.4
51–100	84	5.7	98.9	182	5.5	98.9
101–150	16	1.1	100.0	34	1.0	99.9
Total	1 484	100.0		3 326	99.9	

Table 2 The results of dating 1,455 charters common to the previous and current databases. Using patterns of three words or more (columns 2, 3, and 4) and patterns of two words or more (columns 4, 5, and 6).

	From the previous 1,525-charter database (using three-word patterns and up)			From the current 3,353-charter database (includes two-word patterns and up)		
Error (years)	Number of charters	%	Accumulated %	Number of charters	%	Accumulated %
0	102	7.0	7.0	85	5.8	5.8
1–5	642	44.1	51.1	556	38.2	44.0
6–10	174	12.0	63.1	205	14.1	58.1
11–20	215	14.8	77.9	265	18.2	76.3
21–50	223	15.3	93.2	254	17.5	93.8
51–100	83	5.7	98.9	76	5.2	99.0
101–150	16	1.1	100.0	14	1.0	100.0
Total	1 455	100.0		1 455	100.0	

Apparently, the addition of two-word patterns in the dating of charters had a detrimental effect upon the current dating algorithm. However, the addition of two-word patterns can be converted into a positive step after some adjustments to the algorithm. Some conclusions can be drawn from the latest results and they form the basis for future developments.

Conclusion

Two major changes were made recently to the dating process: the database of dated charters was increased by 120 per cent (from 1,525 to 3,353) and the production of dated word patterns was increased by adding two-word patterns, which amounts to 15 per cent of the total (34,832 of 223,158).

The idea behind these recent changes was to produce more matching patterns to improve accuracy when comparing an undated charter with dated charters. However, this was only partly borne out by the results. Although the amount of matching patterns gives more elements for analysis, the number of matching patterns does not by itself produce better dates. What makes the difference when dating a charter has always been the filtering of matching patterns in order to reach a final selection of the 'best' ones for dating. Hence the need to weight them.

Weighting, however, does not have the same effect in relation to all charters. Some charters can be dated accurately with one weighting system and inaccurately with another. Modifying the weighting formulae for length, lifetime, and currency can change an accurate date for a charter into an inaccurate one. This suggests the absence of one or more variables.

The number of matching patterns also presents a difficulty. How many of those patterns should be considered for dating the undated charter: 25, 50, or 100; 30 per cent or 100 per cent? The current algorithm tries to balance the number of word patterns and their weighting so that it can be applied to all charters and obtain reliable results. This algorithm has proved that selecting and weighting the right matching patterns is an important part of successful dating.

Future Developments

Although far from complete, the present algorithm is a significant step towards achieving our goal. A few options are envisaged for the improvement of the reliability of this method of dating undated charters developed at the DEEDS Project.

Improving the Current Algorithm

Having a larger database of dated word patterns and incorporating the two-word patterns into the process of dating a charter should give more elements for analysis. This has not yet been proved, but there is a strong feeling that this will be the case.

Two problems have been observed in the present algorithm. It gives a great deal of importance to longer word patterns. Its weighting formulae show this by increasing the numeric value (MT number) of the patterns by 20 per cent for each additional word. Although this represents much of the success of the present algorithm, it has a drawback: when the matching patterns are organised in order of importance, long patterns go to the top of the list and short patterns have the almost impossible task of climbing the list to be considered in the dating of the charter. Short patterns therefore tend to get lost in the process.

Another problem is that when an undated charter cannot produce long word patterns, dating occurs based on only two variables, currency and lifetime. The length variable is practically eliminated by the absence of long word patterns because most of the word patterns are similar in length. Dating is then based on short patterns which are abundant with strong currency and short lifetimes, making the selection of the best patterns almost arbitrary.

The solution to these problems might be to develop an alternative method of selecting the first 20-year date range based on the selection of matching patterns, independently of, or in addition to, the three variables in question. One possible method is the selection of matching word patterns that occur only in the undated charter and in one dated charter. These highly selective word patterns point to one year only, so they do not show lifetime or currency. The length is deliberately discarded, or it can be used for weighting. The end result is a collection of single dates. Quartiles are then used to define an initial date range which can be narrowed down to a more precise date using traditional weighting mechanisms. Working with quartiles and single-date word patterns has been done at the DEEDS Project with encouraging results. Work is still in progress.

Including More Variables

A classification of matching word patterns can be carried out in order to identify those that are more similar to the undated charter. The three variables that seem usable are document type, geographic location, and source.

Document type is already available at the DEEDS Project. All 3,353 dated charters are classified according to eight different categories. Weighting can then be increased on those patterns coming from the same type of charter. However, this method is yet to be explored.

Geographic location can be also used to select matching word patterns within a specific region. Geographic location is already available for many of the dated charters of the current database, but the infrastructure for this kind of analysis has to be created.

The use of the charter's source for classifying dated word patterns is already under way at the DEEDS Project. A new classification based on Religious Houses has been defined for use in the dating process in the near future.

Including Date Ranges as Input Parameters

Currently, the dating algorithm selects an initial 20-year period based on the concentration of MT numbers per charter in that period. However, there are cases when the researcher has certain knowledge of the date range in which the undated charter was produced. This external source of information can and must be used to help the dating algorithm to select the initial date range.

Developing an Alternate Dating Method to Cross-Check Dates

Having a second method to date the undated charter can provide an extra source of certainty. Among these, probably the best known is the association of names. Authorship methods can also be used to identify scribes.

The name-association method has been used to date undated charters for a long time. However, it has not been exploited to its full potential. The work presented by Maria Hillebrandt seems to be the most advanced in terms of technical development.

Exploration of writers' habits might also be used to create a list of 'virtual authors', that is, authors created artificially as scribes of the dated charters. These virtual authors would have a working lifetime and a list of charters they might have created would be attributed to them. When an undated charter is to be dated, an analysis of the habits of the scribe will assign the best possible author and therefore a possible date range.

PART II
DATING BY FORMULAE AND VOCABULARY

DATING THE CHARTERS OF THE SMALLER RELIGIOUS HOUSES IN SUFFOLK IN THE TWELFTH AND THIRTEENTH CENTURIES

Marjorie Chibnall

Charters of the twelfth and thirteenth centuries are very different in character from many of the earlier medieval charters discussed by some other contributors to this symposium. Early charters are far more literary; many were drafted by monks or canons, whose language was often idiosyncratic and coloured by Scripture or the Fathers of the Church. Later charters were far more professional; many were written by clerks in royal, episcopal, or baronial chanceries, or at least by men trained in the technicalities of the deeds they were drafting. They were liable to be produced in courts of law as title deeds. Consequently, their language becomes progressively clearer and more concise. Although oral culture remained important and witnesses still had an essential part to play in courts of law, written documents were useful to preserve a record of earlier transactions. Dating them becomes both more possible as the formulae pass into general use, and more important in tracing the slow penetration of literacy in society. The speed of change varied in different regions of Europe.

East Anglia is a region rich in medieval charters. The presence of numerous medium to small landholders encouraged the growth of a vigorous land market in the twelfth century. Law-suits and title-deeds proliferated; scribes and lawyers flourished.[1] These were conditions likely to hasten the standardisation of legal formulae, so that even in smaller properties where the lord, whether individual or institutional, was unlikely to have more than a rudimentary writing office, standard forms of drafting might percolate without too long a delay. In studying the process one must always bear in mind the cautionary comment of C. R. Cheney on English bishops' chanceries: that "at all times in the period (between 1100 and 1250) abnormalities occur, but in the latter part of the period we can at least easily distinguish the normal".[2]

The archives of the religious houses of Suffolk, which are steadily being made available in the Suffolk Charters series of the Suffolk Record Society, contain a wealth of material dealing with the acquisition of both church lands and lay fees.[3] Many of the gifts to religious houses were made up of small holdings of land that had been accumulated from different sources; charters recorded each change of

---

From *Dating Undated Medieval Charters*. Ed. Michael Gervers. Copyright (by the Editor and Contributors 2000). Published by the Boydell Press (in association with Collegium Budapest), PO Box 9, Woodbridge, Suffolk, IP12 3DF, Great Britain. ISBN 0 85115 792 0.

1. See Paul Brand, *The Origins of the English Legal Profession*, Oxford, 1992.
2. C. R. Cheney, *English Bishops' Chanceries 1100–1250*, Manchester, 1950, p. 96.
3. The one drawback in using this series is that from about the middle of the thirteenth century charters are calendared and not transcribed in full.

ownership, and the whole set of charters relating to the transaction might pass into the archives of the final beneficiary. They were the proof, if ownership was challenged, that even if witnesses testified to property being in the hands of a particular owner at an earlier date, his descendants no longer had any valid claim to it. Consequently, these rich archives contain records of lands passing as lay fee from one secular lord to another, as well as of properties – both secular and spiritual – being conveyed to a religious house. Churches and tithes were included in the endowments. So the language of the charters illustrates everything from the details of subinfeudation on lay fees to the changing forms for conveying spiritualities in free alms. The formulae change under the influence of slow standardisation in the king's courts and the changing canon law of the universal Church. Neither ever became rigid and completely stereotyped, and there was always room for some local variation. But standard forms percolated through society. East Anglia was a region susceptible to central influences.

Many of the patrons of new monasteries were men who had thriven in the royal service; men like Ranulf de Glanville, founder of Butley Priory and Leiston Abbey,[4] or Wimond the chaplain, founder of Dodnash Priory,[5] who after making their fortunes as justices and sheriffs were settling down as country gentry with their substantial estates and family monasteries. As men of solid means rather than great wealth they favoured small houses of regular canons, or priories dependent on some great abbey either in England or across the Channel. They were familiar with litigation in the royal courts. The evidence of the *Pedes finium* (Feet of Fines), peculiar to England, is important. From the middle of the twelfth century an increasing amount of private business was being transacted in the royal courts, and the *Rotuli curiae regis*, briefly recording the outcome of cases heard in these courts began to be kept in the 1190s. Although many of the entries relate to serious litigation, a substantial number were the outcome of fictitious lawsuits, in which as soon as the litigants were both before the court they asked for permission to compromise their supposed dispute.[6] A record of the case, in the form of a sealed chirograph, was then given to each of the participants. From 1195 a third copy was written at the foot of the 'final concord' or 'fine', and this was preserved in the treasury.[7] These 'Feet of Fines' were particularly valued by landholders, as a record of the transfer or settlement of landed property. The settlement had to be published; in addition to being recorded it was required to be read out in the court sixteen times.[8] So by written record and oral proclamation the technicalities of land transfer became familiar even to very small land-holders. All this tended towards the standardisation of formulae.

4. Richard Mortimer, ed., *Leiston Abbey Cartulary and Butley Priory Charters*, Suffolk Record Society (hereafter SRS) 1979, pp. 1–2.
5. Christopher Harper-Bill, ed., *Dodnash Priory Charters*, SRS, 1998, pp. 2–3.
6. F. Pollock and F. W. Maitland, *The History of English Law*, 2nd ed., vols. 1–2, Cambridge, 1911, 1.97 and n. 3.
7. M. T. Clanchy, *From Memory to Written Record*, 2nd ed., Oxford, 1993, pp. 87–88.
8. S. R. Scargill-Bird, *A Guide to the Various Classes of Documents Preserved in the Public Record Office*, 3rd ed., London, 1908, pp. 284–85.

There was standardisation also in the changing forms for conveying spiritual property, through the influence of canon law. Once the system of judges delegate was well established, appeals to Rome touched almost all the bishops and many abbots and priors, who were called upon to act as judges delegate. It may seem surprising that such men possessed the necessary expertise. Indeed, by the thirteenth century a number of ecclesiastics were pleading to be exempted from such service, on the grounds of ignorance of the details of the law or pressure of business; but exemption, when granted, was apt to be temporary or conditional.[9] Even though, as has been shown, the degree of standardisation in a bishop's chancery might vary from bishop to bishop, the language of the papal curia was steadily becoming familiar.[10] The diocese of Norwich was sometimes well to the fore in adopting the forms of canon law.[11] There is, therefore, a possibility of finding some regional trends in Suffolk, in spite of the large number of scribes involved in drafting the documents.

Sometimes the scribes identified themselves at the end of the witness lists, as "X the scribe who wrote this charter". The alien priory of Eye, the conventual daughter-house of the Norman abbey of Bernay, which was a house of moderate wealth founded by the family of William Malet, has left records in which three scribes can be clearly identified. William of Eye occurs between about 1180 and 1210; Saerus de Plesseto in the 1240s; and Benedict for about thirty years after 1250.[12] Even if no form of words was specially characteristic of any particular scribe, they tended to conform to the types of formulae in use at the time of writing. The addresses in charters written by William of Eye ring the changes between, "*Notum sit omnibus sancte matris ecclesie fidelibus tam futuris quam presentibus*", or "*omnibus hominibus et amicis et vicinis suis Francis et Anglis*" in the later years of the twelfth century, whereas "*Omnibus hoc scriptum videntibus et audientibus*", or "*Sciant omnes tam futuri quam presentes*" are normal in the charters written by Saerus de Plesseto in the 1240s. Whether or not the scribe used any formulary, the language indicates general changes in terminology. By 1250, when Benedict became active, "*Universis Christi fidelibus ad quos presens scriptum pervenerit*", or "*Sciant presentes et futuri*" are more or less standard in the Eye charters.[13]

The character of the archive varied with the nature of the foundation. Priories which took over the endowment of former secular colleges or minster churches might hold a high proportion of their endowment in parish churches. Such were Blythburgh, a priory of Augustinian canons which replaced a former minster church,[14] or Stoke-by-Clare, where a college of secular canons was replaced by

---

9. See, for example, Mortimer, *Leiston*, no. 91, a charter of Honorius III of March 1225, granting exemption from service to the abbot and prior of Leiston.
10. Cheney, *English Bishops' Chanceries*, pp. 75–76.
11. Brian Kemp, 'Towards Admission and Institution: English Episcopal Formulae for the Appointment of Parochial Incumbents in the Twelfth Century', *Anglo-Norman Studies* 16 (1994): pp. 155–76, at pp. 164–66.
12. Vivien Brown, ed., *Eye Priory Cartulary and Charters*, vols. 1–2, SRS, 1994–96, 2.39.
13. Brown, *Eye*, nos. 120, 155, 158, 160, 161, and passim.
14. Christopher Harper-Bill, ed., *Blythburgh Priory Cartulary*, vols. 1–2, SRS, 1980–81, 1.1-2.

monks of Bec-Hellouin, who took over the churches as the canons died or became monks, and established an alien priory at Stoke nearby.[15] Most of the priories had at least one parish church: even Sibton, the one Cistercian house in Suffolk, acquired the church of St Peter's, Sibton at foundation.[16] Dodnash Priory was granted the church of Thurston by the founder; the parish church already belonged to Battle Abbey and Battle's rights were not to be infringed.[17] Bricett Priory, an alien priory of Augustine canons, was founded in 1114 x 1119 by Ralph son of Brian, who held five knight's fees there of the honour of Peverel, for canons from St Leonard de Noblac in Limoges. Most of its property was given by local lords who held small fractions of a knight's fee; the one church it acquired was Wattisham, and its temporalities accounted for nearly two-thirds of its income in 1291.[18] All the priories held some tithes, though in greatly varying proportions. So although the balance of property between spiritualities and temporalities differed in individual houses, all were exposed to changing formulae for transferring land in free alms and lay fee.

In all the collections some firm dates can be established by comparison with dated Feet of Fines, entries in bishops' registers, and records of changing inheritance on the lands of tenants-in-chief in the royal records. For some, approximate lists of priors, or family trees of donors, can be established. Within these parameters, groups of witnesses and formulae are important instruments for narrowing down possible dates. Where original charters survive, some hints may be gathered from palaeography or seals: the final date or dating range arrived at must often depend on a combination of all these indications. By the reign of Edward I several statutes became influential on formulae, though desirable legislation was sometimes indicated in the wording of charters before the promulgation of any statute, and there were occasional variations for some time afterwards. The 1279 Statute of Mortmain, by forbidding the transfer of lay fee to religious houses unless transfer was licensed, was a response to pressure from lay lords impoverished by the loss of feudal incidents when land was granted away in free alms to religious houses; from the 1250s – and even occasionally earlier – some charters of donation had forbidden the regranting of land to either men of religion or Jews.[19] The statute of *Quia emptores* in 1290, by limiting subinfeudation, caused donors to replace the long lists of dues and services, such as scutage, gloves, or pepper rents owed to lords, by the simple formula "*faciendo inde capitalibus dominis omnia*

---

15. Christopher Harper-Bill and Richard Mortimer, eds., *Stoke-by-Clare Cartulary*, vols. 1–3, SRS, 1982–84, 3.2-3.
16. Philippa Brown, ed., *Sibton Abbey Cartularies and Charters*, vols. 1–4, SRS, 1985–88, 1.136.
17. Christopher Harper-Bill, ed., *Dodnash Priory Charters*, SRS, 1998, pp. 3–4.
18. *Victoria History of the County of Suffolk*, 2.94–95; Christopher Harper-Bill, ed., *English Episcopal Acta 6, Norwich 1070–1214*, British Academy, Oxford, 1990, nos. 20, 45.
19. Sandra Raban, *Mortmain Legislation and the English Church 1279–1500*, Cambridge, 1982, p. 13; P. Brand, 'The Control of Mortmain Alienation in England 1200–1300', in J. H. Baker, ed., *Legal Records and the Historian*, London, 1978, pp. 29–40.

servicia de iure debita et consueta".[20] References to danegeld had disappeared a century earlier. And references to Jews became obsolescent after they were expelled by Edward I in 1290.

Some changes in law were more slowly, and much more erratically, reflected in the language of the charters. The precise nature of tenure in frankalmoign became only slowly defined by the increased activity of the king's courts in the twelfth century. Stenton noted that a charter of the abbot and convent of Welbeck granting a church to Thomas, their clerk, for life, "shows that about the year 1150 the ordinary formulae of enfeoffment were considered appropriate to the grant of a church".[21] From that time language changed, though it would be difficult to chart in precise detail from the language of the Suffolk charters the clearer definition of frankalmoign tenure under the influence of canon law and royal practice. The later twelfth and early thirteenth centuries were a time of great diversity. Among the charters of Sibton, for instance, before c.1200, the formulae vary between "*in puram, liberam et perpetuam elemosinam*", to "*in puram et perpetuam elemosinam*"; but by the early thirteenth century "*in puram, liberam et perpetuam*" had established itself as normal.[22] Dodnash Priory charters show the scribes groping for the best way to describe such grants. A charter of Ada de Tosny not later than 1188 grants land "*in puram et perpetuam elemosinam, liberam ab omni exactione seculari absolutam*"; and a charter of the bishop of Lincoln in September 1188 describes the same grant as "*liberam et quietam ab omni servitio, dominatione et exactione sicut liberam et puram elemosinam*".[23] Other early Dodnash charters vary between "*in liberam et perpetuam elemosinam*" and "*in puram et perpetuam elemosinam*", which gradually became the normal formula. The earliest Bricett charters, before the middle of the twelfth century, give lengthy formulae, such as "*in perpetuam elemosinam . . . liberam et quietam ab omni consuetudine et seculari servitio*" or "*in perpetuam elemosinam . . . ab omni exactione secularis servitii liberam*", before settling down to "*in puram et perpetuam elemosinam*" in the early thirteenth century.[24]

The warranty clauses in charters are of particular interest; to some extent they reflect the gradual changes in the law as it was established in the royal courts.[25] The reflection is somewhat blurred, because of uncertainty among the judges as the law was being developed, and because even when general agreement was

---

20. Michael Gervers, ed., *The Cartulary of the Knights of St John of Jerusalem in England, Part 2, Prima Camera Essex*, British Academy, Oxford, 1996, pp. xxxv–xxxvi.
21. F. M. Stenton, ed. *Documents Illustrative of the Social and Economic History of the Danelaw*, British Academy, Oxford, 1920, p. lxxiv and no. 453.
22. Brown, *Sibton*, nos. 234, 247, 361, 403, 406, 729.
23. Harper-Bill, *Dodnash*, nos. 2, 4.
24. King's College Cambridge (hereafter KCC), Series GBR. I am grateful to the Provost and Fellows of King's College for permission to work in their archives.
25. On warranty in general, see S. F. C. Milson, *The Legal Framework of English Feudalism*, Cambridge, 1976, pp. 42–44, 62–64, 126–32, 183–84; Pollock and Maitland, 1.306–307; 2.662–64.

reached it took some time to penetrate throughout the country. From the early years of Henry III, and particularly in the reign of Edward I, statutes were promulgated which set out general rules to be followed. A statute of 1276 laid down that "a charter of feoffment in which the feoffor uses the words '*dedi et concessi*' and in which no homage is reserved to the feoffor and no clause of warranty is included implies a warranty". Nevertheless, this statute like any other to a great extent confirmed existing practice and was not exhaustive.[26] So the phraseology of warranty clauses can be no more than an indication of date, but it is a useful indication. Warranty might be either implied or explicit. As written records increasingly took over from the memory of witnesses, the courts were deciding how far what was implied in the ceremony of homage bound the grantor even without a charter specifying warranty. Until towards the end of Henry II's reign express warranties were rare in charters. Glanvill did not mention them.[27] They occurred occasionally, often concentrating on the grantor's liability to make escambium if he was unable to warrant the gift. Often warranty was held to be implied when land was granted in return for homage and service – a very common form of grant. That more precision was necessary is shown in a case of 1195, where it was implied that a grant stating '*concessi*' without '*dedi*' did not necessarily imply warranty.[28] Cases of dower caused particular problems, as the heir of the deceased husband of a widow was held to be the warrantor of her dower; and, amongst the complications, it was not at first clear how much 'assigns' were bound no less than heirs. Some charters in which warranty was explicit included both heirs and assigns. The variations in charter phraseology reveal the uncertainties slowly being resolved.

Turning to warranty clauses in the Suffolk charters, we find some approximate indications of date. One of the earliest explicit references to warranty occurs in a charter of Ralph son of Brian, grandson of the founder, towards the end of Henry II's reign.[29] It is a simple warranty to William de Eu and his heirs "*contra omnes homines et feminas imperpetuum*" by the service specified. Characteristically, at that date, there is no mention of assigns. The same formula persisted unchanged in a 1252 charter of Amaury Peche, who had acquired the fee of Ralph son of Brian by marrying the heiress.[30] But many other warranty clauses drafted in the

---

26. S. J. Bailey, 'Warranties of Land in the Thirteenth Century', *Cambridge Law Journal* 8 (1942–45): pp. 274–99, at pp. 281–82.

27. S. J. Bailey, 'Warranties of Land in the Reign of Richard I', *Cambridge Law Journal* 9 (1945–47): pp. 192–209. Glanvill's references to warranty are discussed in G. D. G. Hall, ed., *The Treatise on the Laws and Customs of the Realm of England Commonly Called Glanvill*, London and Edinburgh, 1965, pp. 181–82.

28. Bailey, 'Richard I', p. 206.

29. KCC, GBR 64.

30. KCC, GBR 70. Amaury was the son of Bartholomew Peche, a trusted royal servant and sheriff, who in 1233 had been granted the wardship of the land and marriage of the heirs of Ralph son of Brian (*Close Rolls 1231–1234*, 204). Amaury and his brother Herbert were knighted in 1254 at the same time as Edward the king's son (*Close Rolls 1253–1254*, 271).

first half of the thirteenth century for lords less likely than Amaury and his antecessores to be involved in the royal administration contained much longer, more complicated formulae. One of the early Leiston charters, dated certainly before 1212, included a mention of the *escambium* in case of failure to warrant. A mill was granted to the canons of Leiston with warranty "*contra omnes homines et feminas qui vivere et mori poterunt, et si ita contigerit quod ego et heredes mei warantizare non poterimus, dabimus eis quadraginta marcas sterlingorum*".[31] That women should be explicitly included in the formulae is not surprising, since warranty was involved in many suits for dower. (Women were, however, implicitly included both in "*contra omnes homines*" and "*contra omnes gentes*" which became normal later.) Another group frequently specified from the late twelfth century were the Jews. They were named in formulae which ranged from the minutely detailed (for example, "*warantizabimus et acquietabimus eos de omnibus querelis, de omnibus dampnis, de omnibus expensis et de omnibus placitis contra omnes Cristianos et contra omnes Iudeos quandocumque vexati fuerint vel tracti fuerint in placitum in quacumque curia*"), to the simpler and more common, "*contra omnes homines et omnes feminas et contra omnes cristianos et contra omnes Iudeos in perpetuum*". Mention of them becomes less common after the barons' wars, when feelings had been running strong because debts to the Jews on the security of land had been incurred by many impoverished landowners. After the expulsion of the Jews in 1290 references to them occurred only very occasionally.

Implicit warranty persisted well into the thirteenth century; it was a characteristic of good lordship to warrant the lands of a vassal who had done homage and performed the necessary services for his fee, and such warranty bound also the heirs of the donor. The Bricett charters include many examples of grants in lay fee without mention of warranty. The witnesses of the charter were sometimes the witnesses of the homage: for example, a charter of William le Norreis granted some sixty acres to Hugh, heir of Ralph Ioie, to hold of him and his heirs rendering one pound of pepper annually for the service due. Warranty was not mentioned; but the witnesses included the whole parish of Chippenham who met on Trinity Sunday in the cemetery of the parish church when William received Hugh's homage.[32] A charter could be produced in pleading without explicit mention of homage. Many of the charters include the word '*dedi*', and sometimes a successful action in the king's court confirmed a title. But experience of the kind of difficulties that might arise often led to the reinforcement of gifts by every kind of guarantee.[33] Sometimes the possible complications of dower were avoided by a charter in which a widow abandoned all claims in return for cash down.[34] The

---

31. Mortimer, *Leiston*, no. 63.
32. KCC, GBR 32.
33. KCC, GBR 64, 66, include a series of charters relating to the surrender by Matilda, widow of Laurence of Horshage, of her lands and the establishment of a corrody. One of them is a fine of 1243.
34. For example, KCC, GBR 66.

duplication of guarantees, and the lengthy formulae, are most common in the early and middle years of the thirteenth century. Nevertheless, even after the simple form of warranty *"contra omnes gentes in perpetuum"* was widespread, some more elaborate and detailed warranties persisted, even into the fourteenth century.[35] The maverick can never be completely ruled out.

Because the drafting of English charters was so closely bound up with the development of the common law, many of these criteria would not be helpful in dating continental charters, with the possible exception of twelfth-century Norman charters. Even the gifts of churches, where canon law could influence language, were affected by the issue of frankalmoign tenure, as it was handled in the king's courts. All the evidence derived from formulae needs to be considered in conjunction with older techniques, such as comparing the dates of groups of witnesses. They are, however, an important general indication to add to other techniques. As evidence accumulates and is analysed, through, for example, the building up of material by the DEEDS project of Michael Gervers,[36] it is gradually becoming possible to narrow down charter dates to a much narrower range of dates – even to a decade or less – rather than giving a general indication such as 'probably late twelfth or early thirteenth century' which was once considered adequate.

---

35. For example, Richard Mortimer, ed., *The Charters of St Bartholomew's Priory Sudbury*, SRS, 1996, no. 38.

36. See also the comments of Michael Gervers on dating by formulae, Gervers, *Cartulary*, pp. xxviii–xxxvi.

Bibliography

Manuscripts

Kings College Cambridge, Series GBR.

Printed Sources

Bailey, S. J. 1942–45. 'Warranties of Land in the Thirteenth Century'. *Cambridge Law Journal* 8: pp. 274–99.
———. 1945–47. 'Warranties of Land in the Reign of Richard I'. *Cambridge Law Journal* 9: pp. 192–209.
Brand, Paul. 1978. 'The Control of Mortmain Alienation in England 1200–1300', in *Legal Records and the Historian*, ed. J. H. Baker, pp. 29–40. London.
———. 1992. *The Origins of the English Legal Profession*. Oxford.
Brown, Philippa, ed. 1985–88. *Sibton Abbey Cartularies and Charters*. Vols. 1–4. Suffolk Record Society (hereafter SRS).
Brown, Vivien, ed. 1994–96. *Eye Priory Cartulary and Charters*. Vols. 1–2. SRS.
Cheney, C. R. 1950. *English Bishops' Chanceries 1100–1250*. Manchester.
Clanchy, M. T. 1993. *From Memory to Written Record*. 2nd ed. Oxford.
Close Rolls of the Reign of Henry III. 1902–38. 14 vols. London.
Gervers, Michael, ed. 1996. *The Cartulary of the Knights of St John of Jerusalem in England, Part 2, Prima Camera Essex*. British Academy, Oxford.
Hall, G. D. G., ed. 1965. *The Treatise on the Laws and Customs of the Realm of England Commonly Called Glanvill*. London and Edinburgh.
Harper-Bill, Christopher, ed. 1980–81. *Blythburgh Priory Cartulary*. Vols. 1–2. SRS.
———. 1990. *English Episcopal Acta 6, Norwich 1070–1214*. British Academy, Oxford.
———. 1998. *Dodnash Priory Charters*. SRS.
Harper-Bill, Christopher, and Richard Mortimer, eds. 1982–84. *Stoke-by-Clare Cartulary*. Vols. 1–2. SRS.
Kemp, Brian. 1994. 'Towards Admission and Institution: English Episcopal Formulae for the Appointment of Parochial Incumbents in the Twelfth Century'. *Anglo-Norman Studies* 16: pp. 155–76.
Milsom, S. F. C. 1976. *The Legal Framework of English Feudalism*. Cambridge.
Mortimer, Richard, ed. 1979. *Leiston Abbey Cartulary and Butley Priory Charters*. SRS.
———. 1996. *The Charters of St Bartholomew's Priory Sudbury*. SRS.
Pollock, F., and F. W. Maitland. 1911. *The History of English Law*. Vols. 1–2. 2nd ed. Cambridge.
Raban, Sandra. 1982. *Mortmain Legislation in the English Church 1279–1500*. Cambridge.
Scargill-Bird, S. R. 1908. *A Guide to the Various Classes of Documents Preserved in the Public Record Office*. 3rd ed. London.
Stenton, F. M., ed. 1920. *Documents Illustrative of the Social and Economic History of the Danelaw*. British Academy, Oxford.
The Victoria History of the County of Suffolk.

RECHERCHES AUTOUR DE LA DATATION DES ACTES NORMANDS AUX Xe–XIIe SIÈCLES

Véronique Gazeau

La Normandie est une principauté territoriale constituée en 911 par le roi Charles le Simple pour le Viking Rollon qui depuis la fin du IXe siècle est parfaitement bien inséré dans le jeu des alliances politiques du monde franc. Les actes émanant des *scriptoria* des nombreux établissements monastiques dont la province va progressivement se couvrir ainsi que des diocèses sont fort nombreux. Ils peuvent faire l'objet d'une typologie. Ils se présentent sous la forme de chartes de donation, de chartes contenant le règlement d'un litige, de chartes de confirmation, de pancartes et de notices. Les pancartes qu'on trouve pendant le règne du Conquérant surtout, sont des confirmations juxtaposant des chartes ayant conservé leur forme diplomatique.[1] Les notices sont des textes rédigés en style objectif ou apparemment objectif, non approuvées par une autorité publique quoique certaines le soient après coup.

La grande majorité des actes ne portent pas de date. Qu'ils proviennent des *scriptoria* des abbayes ou moins souvent de la chancellerie ducale, qu'ils enregistrent de simples donations ou qu'ils se proposent à nous comme des actes solennels, ils ne sont pas systématiquement datés.[2] Isolons pour commencer les actes émanés des princes normands. Dans les premiers temps de la principauté lorsque la datation est mentionnée, elle l'est par l'année du règne du roi de France et par elle seule; cette norme est encore en vigueur à la fin du Xe siècle; elle implique la reconnaissance du roi, de sa souveraineté et le respect des usages carolingiens dans la nouvelle principauté.[3] A cet égard force est de constater qu'en ne datant pas systématiquement leurs actes les princes normands vont rompre avec la tradition franque. Les actes conservés des abbayes franques de la partie qui deviendra la Normandie sont pratiquement toujours datés. L'usage de dater par référence au roi de France perdure jusqu'à la fin du règne de Richard II (1026). Avec le principat de Robert le Magnifique, la mention exclusive de l'année du règne du roi de France devient tout à fait exceptionnelle et ne se rencontre que pour des actes non normands.[4] La datation par le millésime prend le relais. Mais elle va devenir et demeurer occasionnelle. Elle peut se placer au début, dans le corps de l'acte ou à

From *Dating Undated Medieval Charters*. Ed. Michael Gervers. Copyright (by the Editor and Contributors 2000). Published by the Boydell Press (in association with Collegium Budapest), PO Box 9, Woodbridge, Suffolk, IP12 3DF, Great Britain. ISBN 0 85115 792 0.

1. Nous suivons la définition donnée par D. Bates, « *Les chartes de confirmation et les pancartes normandes du règne de Guillaume le Conquérant* », Pancartes monastiques des XIe et XIIe siècles, éd. M. Parisse..., Brepols 1998, p. 95.
2. M. Fauroux, *Recueil des actes des ducs de Normandie (911-1066)*, Caen 1961, p. 63.
3. L. Musset, « Sur la datation des actes par le nom du Prince en Normandie (XIe-XIIe siècles) », *Autour du pouvoir ducal normand Xe-XIIe siècles, Cahier des Annales de Normandie*, n°17, 1985, p. 8.
4. Sauf pour l'abbaye de Cerisy, M. Fauroux, *Recueil*, n° 99.

la fin, généralement après ou avant les souscriptions. Elle peut être introduite par *Actum* ou *Acta*. Dorénavant pratiquement tous les documents datés le sont d'après l'année de l'Incarnation. Dans le recueil factice des actes des ducs de Normandie de 911 à 1066 qui comporte 234 actes seulement 40 actes comportent une date, soit 17,09% des actes.[5] On compte 191 actes normands et 26 sont datés, ce qui donne un pourcentage de 13,61%. La récente édition des *Regesta* de Guillaume le Conquérant (1066-1087) compte 52 actes datés par le millésime pour 355 actes ce qui donne un pourcentage inférieur, 14,64%. Il convient de rapporter les 27 actes normands datés à la totalité des actes normands soit 106 actes.[6] Le pourcentage est alors de 25,47%. Le progrès en matière de datation n'est pas confirmé sous le principat d'Henri Ier. On conserve 199 actes. 28 actes comportent une date. Le pourcentage s'élève maintenant à 14,07%. La moitié est datée d'avant 1130 et l'autre moitié d'après cette date, ce qui autorise à considérer qu'à partir des années 1130 et pendant les cinq dernières années du principat la datation est plus fréquente.[7] Plus du tiers des actes datés provient du chartrier du Bec ce qui confirme que les actes continuent d'être rédigés par les destinataires. On sait que les actes d'Henri II ne sont pas datés.[8] Sous Richard Cœur de Lion les actes sont datés en fonction des années du règne.[9] Le millésime est très rarement employé. Jean Sans Terre dont les actes ne sont pas rassemblés n'a pas suivi la pratique de son frère, ses actes n'étant pas toujours datés. Parmi les dignitaires de l'Eglise normande rares sont ceux dont les actes comportent une date. Seuls peut-être les actes de quelques évêques et ceux de l'archevêque de Rouen, Hugues d'Amiens (1130-1164) portent plus fréquemment le millésime mais cette pratique sera négligée par ses successeurs.[10]

La mention d'événements dans le corps des actes, le croisement des personnages cités soit dans l'acte, soit parmi les témoins et/ou les souscriptions fournissent une aide traditionnelle fort utile à celui qui veut dater. C'est ainsi que nous avons relevé 26 actes dans *le Recueil des actes des ducs de Normandie (911–1066)* dont le millésime peut être valablement avancé.[11] On date donc 66 actes ducaux

---

5. M. Fauroux, *Recueil*, n° 2, 3, 9, 12, 13, 14 bis, 15, 18, 34, 35, 36, 61, 64, 90, 92, 99, 101, 114, 115, 122, 124, 125, 126, 127, 130, 131, 132, 133, 136, 142, 143, 150, 156, 157, 158, 229, 230, 231, 232, 233. Nous n'avons pas fait de distinction entre les actes normands et non normands. Un acte dit « normand » est un acte donné pour un établissement situé en Normandie.

6. D. Bates, *Regesta Regum Anglo-Normannorum. The Acta of William I (1066–1087)*, Oxford 1998, n° 26, 27, 30, 58, 60, 64, 144, 145, 175, 179, 179a, 215, 229, 230, 232, 235, 236, 245, 247, 248, 255, 256, 257, 261, 262, 264, 280.

7. H. Chanteux, *Recueil des actes de Henri Ier Beauclerc, duc de Normandie*, thèse manuscrite de l'Ecole des Chartes, 1932, I, pp. 64–66.

8. Ed. L. Delisle et E. Berger, *Recueil des actes de Henri II, roi d'Angleterre et duc de Normandie, concernant les provinces françaises et les affaires de France*, 1909–1927, Introduction, 9.

9. Ed. Cl. Fagnen, *Essai sur quelques actes normands de Richard Cœur de Lion*, thèse dactylographiée de l'Ecole nationale des Chartes, 1977, I, p. xcvi.

10. A titre d'exemple isolé, dans le cartulaire de Montebourg parmi les vingt-sept actes datés figurent six actes des évêques de Coutances (B.N.F., ms. lat. 10087, n° 44, 45, 57, 74, 75, 77). En l'absence d'une édition des actes des évêques normands on se référera à l'article de M. Arnoux, « Essor et déclin d'un type diplomatique: les actes passés *coram parrochia* en Normandie (XIIe–XIIIe siècles) », *B.E.C.*, 154, 1996, p. 330 et en particulier note 30.

11. M. Fauroux, *Recueil* n° 4, 16, 17, 22, 25, 26, 27, 33, 60, 63, 69, 71, 89, 96, 97, 98, 100, 120, 121, 123, 137, 144, 147, 148, 151, 228.

soit 28,20% des actes. Trente-sept actes de Guillaume le Conquérant dont treize normands peuvent aussi faire l'objet d'une datation sans grand risque d'erreur.[12] Ainsi 89 actes de Guillaume le Conquérant sont désormais datés avec un pourcentage en baisse par rapport aux actes d'avant 1066, 25,07%. Si on ajoute aux 27 actes normands datés les 13 que l'on peut dater, cela donne 40 actes à rapporter aux 106 actes normands soit 37,73%. On connaît les travaux de Delisle autour de la formule de suscription dans les diplômes d'Henri II. On trouve « Henricus rex Anglorum » de 1155 jusqu'à 1172–1173 et « Henricus Dei gratia rex Anglorum » depuis 1172–1173 jusqu'à sa mort en 1189.[13] On conjugue l'utilisation de cette clause quand c'est possible avec le lieu d'expédition, et la liste des témoins. C'est jusqu'à maintenant l'unique moyen d'approcher une datation des actes du souverain plantagenêt. La nouvelle édition des actes d'Henri II et de Richard Cœur de Lion qui sera prête en 2003 prévoit l'utilisation de la méthode traditionnelle de la datation par les dignitaires et officiers ecclésiastiques, les grands de l'aristocratie laïque présents dans les actes et par la clause « Dei gratia ».[14]

Il est certain que les Normands n'ont pas éprouvé le besoin de dater leurs actes. Et même si le principat de Richard Cœur de Lion marque un réel progrès, les *scriptoria* d'abbayes ne lui emboîtent pas systématiquement le pas pour les actes qui n'émanent pas du duc-roi.

Tous les actes ducaux conservés sont des originaux ou des copies faites dans les cartulaires. Le cartulaire le plus ancien de la province date de l'extrême fin du XIe siècle, celui de La Trinité-du-Mont de Rouen.[15] Fécamp a préparé très tôt un cartulaire, probablement au XIe siècle, aujourd'hui perdu.[16] Les grandes abbayes de la vallée de la Seine, Fécamp, Saint-Ouen de Rouen, Saint-Wandrille et Jumièges, restaurations ducales des abbayes mérovingiennes, sont documentées grâce à des cartulaires des XIIe, XIIIe, XIVe voire XVe siècles.[17] Les archives municipales d'Avranches conservent la copie du XIIe siècle du cartulaire de l'abbaye du Mont-Saint-Michel dont l'édition est en cours sous les auspices d'une équipe franco-britannique.[18] Les archives départementales d'Evreux conservent

---

12. D. Bates, *Regesta*, n° 46, 59, 139, 146, 158, 163, 166, 214, 231, 238, 243, 244, 246.
13. L. Delisle, *Recueil des actes de Henri II*, Introduction, pp. 12–20.
14. En préparation sous les auspices de Nicholas Vincent (Cantorbéry).
15. Archives départementales de la Seine-Maritime, 27 H 1. Ed. A. Deville, *Cartulaire de la Sainte Trinité-du-Mont de Rouen, Cartulaire de Saint-Bertin*, éd. B. Guérard, Paris 1840, pp. 403–487.
16. D. Bates, « Les pancartes », p. 101.
17. Fécamp: cartulaire du XIIIe siècle (Bibl. mun. Rouen, ms. 1207 (Y 51), cartulaire des XIIIe–XIVe siècles (Archives départementales de la Seine-Maritime, 7 H 9) et cartulaire perdu du XIIe siècle (B.N.F., coll. Moreau, ms 341, f° 1–190).
Saint-Ouen de Rouen: grand cartulaire du XVe siècle (Arch. dép. Seine-Maritime, 14 H 18) et fragment d'un cartulaire du XVe siècle (B.N.F., ms. lat. 12777, pp. 106–125).
Saint-Wandrille: cartulaire des XIIIe–XVIes siècles (Arch. dép. Seine-Maritime, 16 H 14) et cartulaire du XIVe siècle (B.N.F., ms. lat. 17132).
Jumièges: grand cartulaire du XIIIe siècle (Arch. dép. Seine-Maritime, 9 H 4), cartulaire du XVe siècle (Arch. dép. Seine-Maritime, 9 H 4, 9 H 5, 9 H 6).
18. Bibl. mun. Avranches, ms. 210. K. Keats-Rohan et H. Guillotel préparent cette édition.

deux cartulaires de l'abbaye de Saint-Taurin d'Evreux, restaurée également par les ducs, qui ne sont pas édités et qui datent l'un du XIIIe siècle, l'autre du XIVe siècle.[19] Plusieurs abbayes ont perdu la majeure partie de leurs archives; c'est le cas de Cerisy au diocèse de Bayeux, de Conches et de la Croix-Saint-Leufroy au diocèse d'Evreux, du Bec et du Tréport au diocèse de Rouen, de Notre-Dame de Saint-Pierre-sur-Dives au diocèse de Sées, de Bernay, Grestain et Cormeilles au diocèse de Lisieux, de Saint-Sever, Lessay et Saint-Sauveur-le-Vicomte au diocèse de Coutances. Des copies partielles ont parfois été faites à des époques récentes. C'est le cas au diocèse de Bayeux pour Cerisy, au diocèse d'Evreux de Conches, au diocèse de Rouen pour Le Tréport et Le Bec, enfin au diocèse de Coutances de Lessay et de Saint-Sauveur-le-Vicomte.[20] Enfin plusieurs cartulaires des XIIe, XIIIe, XIVe ou XVe siècles sont conservés dans les différents dépôts d'archives départementaux de la Normandie ou à Paris. Il s'agit de Caen, Fontenay, Troarn, Lyre, Saint-Martin de Sées, Saint-Evroult, Préaux et Montebourg.[21] Deux d'entre eux ont fait l'objet d'édition non encore publiées. Il s'agit de Préaux et de Saint-Martin de Sées.[22] La reconstitution du cartulaire de Conches est en cours.[23]

Prenons quatre exemples tirés d'abbayes bénédictines fondées au XIe siècle. Le cartulaire de La Trinité-du-Mont de Rouen terminé en 1097 contient 97 actes. L'abbaye a été fondée en 1030; la fondation a donné lieu à un acte daté par l'année de l'Incarnation, ce qui est la règle quasi systématique dans les actes datés des

---

19. Petit cartulaire du XIIIe siècle (Arch. dép. Eure, H 793) et grand cartulaire du XIVe siècle (Arch. dép. Eure, H 794).

20. Cerisy: copie du XVIIe s. dans le Livre noir (Bibl. mun. Alençon, ms. 114) et traduction française du XIXe s. (B.N.F., ms. n. acq. fr. 21659).

Conches: fragments d'une copie exécutée au XVIIe s. du cartulaire perdu (Arch. dép. Eure, H 262) et fragments d'une copie exécutée au XVIIe s. dans le Livre blanc (B.N.F., ms. lat. 13816, f° 461–476).

Le Tréport: cartulaire du XVIIIe s. (Paris, Bibl. Sainte-Geneviève, ms. 1651).

Le Bec: fragment d'un cartulaire du XIIIe s. (Arch. dép. Eure, H 91); copies faites au XVIIe s. dans un cartulaire du XVe s. (B.N.F., ms. lat. 12884) et au XVIIIe s. (B.N.F., ms. lat. 13905).

Lessay: copie faite au XIXe s. du Livre blanc (B.N.F., ms. lat. 10071, f° 39–93).

Saint-Sauveur-le-Vicomte: copie du Livre noir du XVIIe s. (B.N.F., ms. lat. 17137).

21. Saint-Etienne de Caen: cartulaire des XIIe–XIIIe s. (Arch. dép. Calvados, entrée 1996-135, cote provisoire).

Fontenay: Arch. dép. Calvados, H 5603 à 5737 et musée des Beaux-Arts de Caen, coll. Mancel, ms. 120 (trad. du XVIIIe s. en français).

Troarn: Arch. dép. Calvados, H 7745, 7747, 7750–7753, 7758–7764, 7771–7779 et cartulaire du XIVe s. (B.N.F., ms. lat. 10086).

Lyre: Arch. dép. Eure, H 438–590 et Lenoir (Dom J.-L.), copies du XVIIIe s., dans la collection du marquis de Mathan, vol. 23 et 72.

Sées: Bibl. évêché de Sées, Livre blanc du XIIe s.

Saint-Evroult: cartulaire du XIIIe s. (B.N.F., ms. lat. 11055–110556).

Préaux: cartulaire du XIIIe s. (Arch. dép. Eure, H 711).

Montebourg: cartulaire du XIIIe s. (B.N.F., ms. lat. 10087).

22. D. Rouet, *Le cartulaire de Saint-Pierre de Préaux: étude et édition du manuscrit dans son état de 1227*, thèse de l'Ecole nationale des Chartes, mars 1999 et J.-M. Bouvris pour la préparation de l'édition du cartulaire de Saint-Martin de Sées.

23. On doit ce travail à Madame C. de Haas.

cartulaires normands. L'acte daté le plus récent est de 1091. Sur ces 97 actes on relève 22 actes dont la datation est indiquée à partir de l'année de l'Incarnation, soit un pourcentage de 22,68%.[24] A Montebourg, abbaye fondée par Guillaume le Conquérant en 1066–1087, le cartulaire compte 445 chartes dont seulement 27 comportent une datation, soit un pourcentage de 6,07%.[25] A Lyre, abbaye fondée par Guillaume Fitz Osbern, membre d'une prestigieuse famille de l'entourage de Guillaume le Bâtard vers 1060, on dénombre 8 actes datés pour 107 actes du seul XIIe siècle avec un pourcentage de 7,48%.[26] A Saint-Pierre de Préaux fondé en 1035, le cartulaire rédigé en 1227 se compose de 404 actes. On peut considérer les seuls 317 actes dont on est certain qu'ils ont été passés aux XIe–XIIe siècles; seulement 23 actes sont datés; le pourcentage s'élève à 7,25%.[27] Les pourcentages proches et faibles démontrent l'absence de datation en règle générale. Et surtout il apparaît que chaque *scriptorium* établit ses propres règles. Même les actes de fondation en règle générale ne sont pas datés. Les actes datés émanent des grands de l'aristocratie normande à l'abbaye de Préaux surtout dans la deuxième moitié du XIIe siècle.[28] Cet état de fait correspond à l'abbatiat de Michel, un ancien moine du Bec, abbaye dont on avait déjà souligné la forte propension à dater par le millésime les actes sous le principat d'Henri Ier. Mais ce n'est pas le cas pour Lyre où pas un acte du XIIe siècle émané de la famille fondatrice n'est daté. En revanche dans ce même cartulaire de Lyre sur les 8 actes datés quatre proviennent d'évêques et quatre de petits vassaux de la famille fondatrice.[29] Dans l'ensemble on a l'impression que les membres bienfaiteurs de l'aristocratie laïque agissent par mimétisme. A l'instar des ducs ils ne datent pas leurs actes. La rupture avec la tradition carolingienne est nettement consommée.

De quels moyens empiriques dispose-t-on pour dater ou approcher une date? Le repérage d'événements conjugués ou non à la présence de personnages dans le corps de l'acte ou parmi les souscriptions et les témoins permettent d'améliorer dans d'assez bonnes proportions les scores de datation. Ainsi le professeur L. Musset a montré que 7 personnages interviennent avec une relative fréquence dans la datation des actes normands: le roi de France au début de la période, le pape, le prince normand, l'empereur parfois, l'archevêque de la province, les évêques et les abbés quoique la présence de ces derniers dans les actes soient rares.[30] On y ajoutera les membres de familles prestigieuses dont les dates sont très fréquemment parfaitement connues grâce aux sources narratives. La titulature du prince

---

24. Voir références en note 15.
25. Je dois ces chiffres à Lionel Neuwirth qui prépare sous ma direction à l'Université de Caen un mémoire de maîtrise sur la fondation et le développement de l'abbaye de Montebourg. Cartulaire de Montebourg, B.N.F., ms. lat. 10087, n° 30, 39, 44, 45, 57, 58, 74, 75, 77, 99, 103, 128, 134, 145, 148, 194, 195, 207, 208, 262, 388, 651, 652, 740, 741, 742, 743.
26. Dom Lenoir, t. 23, 472–480 et 490 et Arch. dép. Eure, H 438 et 465.
27. Ces chiffres sont calculés d'après la lecture de la thèse de D. Rouet. Qu'il soit chaleureusement remercié.
28. D. Rouet, *Le cartulaire de Saint-Pierre de Préaux*, 156.
29. Voir références en note 26.
30. « Sur la datation des actes », p. 7.

est d'une grande utilité parfois: ainsi Guillaume est d'abord comte ou duc jusqu'à la conquête de 1066 puis est intitulé *rex* après cette date ce qui fournit une borne chronologique. Plusieurs notices du cartulaire de Préaux portent en exergue le même type d'*incipit*: *Regnante principe Willelmo* ou *Regnante Willelmo Normannorum principe et Anglorum rege.*[31]

Pour le cartulaire de La Trinité-du-Mont de Rouen le nombre d'actes datés passe de 22 à 29 grâce à l'évocation d'un d'événement connu et daté.[32] Le pourcentage d'actes dont la date est donc connue passe de 22,68% à 29,89%. Pour 32 actes on approche une fourchette qui va de 5 à 40 ans. Pour 14 actes la fourchette est inférieure à 12 ans. Seulement 14 actes ne sont datables que grâce aux dates d'un abbatiat. Pour Montebourg 16 actes sur 445 sont datables par ce moyen et il faut se rendre à l'évidence que près de 190 actes semblent a priori impossibles à dater.[33] Mais ce moyen de datation par l'événement doit être manié avec prudence parce qu'il n'est pas impossible que les compilateurs aient introduit au sein des actes des événements, événements datant la donation mais pas la rédaction.

La présence de souscripteurs et de témoins, caractéristique par excellence de la diplomatique normande, est une véritable aubaine pour le chercheur. Même les notices caractérisées par un appareil protocolaire des plus réduits comportent des listes significatives de témoins, qui les valident. Ce sont plus de 400 témoins différents que l'on trouve à Rouen, et plus de mille pour Montebourg. Or les abbayes normandes ont été fondées par des familles qui pour la plupart gravitent dans l'entourage des ducs-rois et qui sont alliées entre elles. On retrouve les mêmes lignages dans plusieurs cartulaires. Une base de données des témoins normands serait un formidable outil de datation des actes. Toutefois il arrive que parfois les listes soient tronquées, le scripteur ayant abrégé sa copie par la formule « *et multi alii* ». C'est le cas à Montebourg mais pas à Préaux. A Montebourg il est tout à fait possible que les listes de témoins soient complètes et que la formule « *et multi alii* » soit devenue purement protocolaire. Quand la comparaison entre la copie et l'original est possible, on constate fréquemment la validité des listes de témoins et de souscripteurs. A Préaux il semble bien que les listes sont complètes. Les listes de témoins du prieuré clunisien de Longueville, connues par des originaux comportent ce genre de clause.[34]

Un autre moyen de datation peut être envisagé dans certains cas. A Montebourg on a repéré la mention de paiement en monnaies différentes. La monnaie angevine apparaît dans les actes dès 1139/1140 mais elle est décrétée « monnaie officielle de l'empire plantagenêt » en 1174.[35] Elle disparaît aussitôt l'annexion de la

---

31. Cartulaire de Préaux, Arch. dép. Eure, H 711, n° 420: « regnante Willelmo Roberti marcionis filio... »; n° 68: « regnante Willelmo Anglorum rege... ».
32. Ed. A. Deville, *Cartulaire de la Sainte Trinité-du-Mont*, n° 6, 7, 8, 57, 63, 64, 69.
33. Cartulaire de Montebourg, B.N.F., ms. lat. 10087, n° 5, 19, 20, 23, 28, 29, 43, 46, 47, 73, 76, 136, 141, 151, 204, 304.
34. Ed. P. Le Cacheux, *Chartes du prieuré de Longueville, de l'ordre de Cluny au diocèse de Rouen, antérieures à 1204*, Rouen et Paris 1934.
35. F. Dumas et J. Pilet-Lemière, « La monnaie » dans M. d'Onofrio (dir), *Les Normands peuple d'Europe, 1030–1200*, catalogue d'exposition, Paris 1994, pp. 60–63.

Normandie réalisée en 1204. Le denier angevin s'efface alors devant le denier tournois, la monnaie du royaume de France. Certes la fourchette est très large mais dans certains cas il est avéré que c'est là le seul moyen de savoir si l'acte a été passé au temps des ducs ou au temps des rois de France. A Montebourg ce sont 190 actes qui restent difficilement datables et le classement des actes dans le cartulaire est loin de fournir une indication en matière de chronologie, les actes étant regroupés par famille de bienfaiteurs.

Une récente étude a montré que des chartes ont été passées « *coram parrochia* » en Basse Normandie, autour de Caen et de Bayeux. Ces actes sont datés des premières décennies du XIIIe siècle.[36] L'apparition de ces actes coïncide avec la disparition des usages anglo-normands dans la diplomatique du duché (absence de millésime, nombreux témoins).

Parmi les raisons qui introduisent un doute sérieux dans la méthode proposée par le projet DEEDS, on évoquera les caractéristiques des actes de certains cartulaires. D'une manière très générale l'absence d'originaux et l'obligatoire recours à des copies rendent le processus de datation quelque peu aléatoire. A Montebourg il est certain qu'au moins un acte et très vraisemblablement davantage a perdu sa date au moment de la transcription dans le cartulaire.[37] La seconde partie du cartulaire de Préaux se présente comme une série d'actes qui sont davantage des notices que des chartes, savoir des résumés assez souvent abrégés; certaines notices font l'objet de deux voire trois rédactions différentes. Leur rédaction a été effectuée par plusieurs moines à différentes époques. Certains actes se présentent comme de véritables récits susceptibles d'être complétés. Enfin dans certaines notices l'indication de la date par un événement ou un règne indique plutôt la translation et pas la rédaction de l'acte.[38] Des considérations identiques valent pour les notices de La Trinité-du-Mont.[39] Des observations proches peuvent être portées à ce dossier à propos des pancartes et grandes chartes de confirmation de Guillaume le Conquérant si fréquentes dans les cartulaires normands. Elles se présentent comme de très longs actes rassemblant des dispositions nombreuses, arrêtées à des époques diverses et dues à plusieurs auteurs. Elles font l'objet de remaniements et d'adjonctions. En outre, les scribes cherchent à obtenir le plus grand nombre de souscriptions possibles. Cohabitent ensemble dans un même acte des *signa* inconciliables. Il faut commencer par considérer les expéditions successives de ces actes avant toute utilisation. Il faut bien distinguer ce qui doit être attribué à l'époque de la donation et ce qui doit être attribué à l'époque de la fabrication de la pancarte ou de la confirmation. Ces actes sont de véritables histoires de l'abbaye et des étapes successives de la formation de son patrimoine. Mais le souci d'harmoniser les éléments chronologiques des pancartes et confirmations n'a jamais animé l'esprit des rédacteurs. La date de ces actes est donc celle de la

---

36. M. Arnoux, « Essor et déclin », pp. 323–357.
37. B.N.F., ms. lat. 10087, n° 138.
38. Ces considérations proviennent de la thèse de D. Rouet, *Le cartulaire de Saint-Pierre de Préaux*, p. 140 et suiv.
39. Une grande partie des actes du cartulaire sont des notices.

confirmation faite par le duc-roi mais il faut avoir à l'esprit la séparation entre les donations successives et la confirmation qui intervient à l'occasion d'un événement majeur.[40] En règle générale les actes sont susceptibles de transformations entre le moment de la rédaction et celui de leur insertion dans le cartulaire.

Une autre objection réside dans la suppression de plusieurs caractères internes dans les actes normands. Sous le principat d'Henri Ier la tendance est à l'extrême concision des actes. Les *scriptoria* monastiques n'agissent pas différemment. C'est le cas pendant toute la période à La Trinité-du-Mont de Rouen, à Lyre, à Préaux et à Montebourg. Bien des actes ne comportent ni invocation, ni préambule. Parfois encore la notification a disparu, ce qui est fréquent dans le cas des simples notices.[41] Le manque d'homogénéité des caractères internes des actes normands des XIe–XIIe siècles semble interdire toute exploitation statistique et donc informatique. Ne serait-ce pas le signe que les actes ne sont pas tant une suite de formules stéréotypées qu'un exercice de narration, qui laisse au rédacteur une assez grande souplesse.

A Lyre nous avons considéré 15 actes qui sont tous des chartes sans date, tous émanés d'un comte de Leicester, Robert II (1118–1168) ou son fils Robert III (1168–1190); grâce essentiellement à la présence dans les chartes des épouses des comtes et dans une moindre mesure à celle d'autres personnages on peut distinguer les actes de l'un des actes de l'autre. Ils sont les héritiers de la famille fondatrice et à ce titre ont grandement doté l'abbaye de Lyre. Notre enquête a porté sur les adresses.[42] En effet invocations et préambules ont disparu. Quant au protocole final il est si peu homogène que son utilisation est difficile. On comptabilise 13 adresses différentes dans lesquelles on retrouve les mêmes termes agencés différemment, *omnibus, baronis, hominibus, filiis sancte Ecclesie, presentibus, futuris*. On a l'impression que ces termes ont été choisis par le rédacteur, comme s'il avait puisé dans un formulaire ou un glossaire au gré de sa volonté. Certes une certaine normalisation se met en place avec la disparition des préambules et des invocations mais le rédacteur semble conserver une certaine liberté.

A La Trinité-du-Mont de Rouen, un tableau a été constitué, englobant les rares invocations et préambules, et surtout les notifications, les adresses et les termes du dispositif. Les résultats des tris effectués se sont avérés très minces. Deux actes (68 et 93) présentent les mêmes notification, adresse et dispositif. L'un est daté très vaguement de l'abbatiat d'un abbé. Peut-on émettre l'hypothèse qu'il en est de même du second acte? Le second résultat associe « *dedit* » et « *notum sit* » (55 et 77). L'acte 55 est daté de 1068. On aura remarqué la grande diversité des adresses. La fréquence de « *notum sit* » s'explique par le grand nombre de notices dans le cartulaire rouennais réduites souvent au strict minimum quant aux formes diplomatiques.

A Préaux la difficulté réside dans la composition même du cartulaire qui comporte d'une part des chartes, d'autre part une grande quantité de notices dont il a

---

40. Voir à ce sujet les travaux de L. Musset, *Les actes de Guillaume le Conquérant et de la reine Mathilde pour les abbayes caennaises*, Caen 1967, 25–41 et ceux de D. Bates, *Regesta*, pp. 22–30.
41. Voir en annexe le tableau consacré aux actes de La Trinité-du-Mont de Rouen.
42. Voir en annexe les adresses des actes des comtes de Leicester en faveur de Lyre.

été démontré qu'elles ont dans leur ensemble subi des modifications, suppressions, adjonctions de toutes sortes à tel point qu'elles n'ont presque plus rien à voir avec les textes originaux. En outre Dominique Rouet, qui vient d'achever l'édition non encore publiée du cartulaire de Préaux considère qu'il a existé un recueil primitif, sorte de cartulaire chronique, dont la trace est visible dans le cartulaire conservé du XIIIe siècle. Que s'agit-il de dater?

Dans le cartulaire de Montebourg nous avons commencé à relever les formules de corroboration pour aboutir au même constat que celui que nous avions dressé pour les adresses de Lyre.[43] Le rédacteur des actes dispose d'une infinie possibilité. On a peine à croire que chaque formule correspond à une date ou une période bien précise. En outre à Montebourg on connaît la date de 43 des 445 actes. Rappelons qu'ici il s'agit de dater environ 190 actes qu'on ne peut dater avec les moyens traditionnels. La plupart des actes datés émanent des autorités ecclésiastiques, papes et évêques, des membres de la famille cofondatrice et de trois comtes proches de l'entourage ducal. Quatre autres actes viennent de petites familles vassales des cofondateurs et sont datés des années 1196 pour deux d'entre eux, 1201 et 1202.[44] Or d'une part on ne peut pas mettre en parallèle les actes épiscopaux plus souvent datés avec la grande masse des actes provenant de la petite aristocratie et qui précisément ne sont pas datés. Les caractères internes de ces deux catégories d'actes affichent trop de dissemblances. D'autre part un acte est daté de 1160 et se présente comme une confirmation de biens et n'a rien à voir avec la multitude des petits actes de donation qu'on cherche à dater.[45] Enfin l'échantillon utilisable d'actes datés, les quatre des années 1196, 1201 et 1202, n'offre pas un éventail chronologique assez large.

Nous ne contestons pas l'utilisation de l'outil informatique pour la datation des actes en général et notre enquête nous aura permis de lire et relire les actes avec un œil nouveau. Mais les rédacteurs d'actes et à leur tour les copistes qui constituent les cartulaires font preuve d'une inventivité telle qu'il nous faut nous résoudre à une grande humilité. En Normandie il faut attendre le XIIIe siècle pour qu'apparaisse une standardisation des formules encore que dans les premières décennies du siècle la diplomatique normande et la diplomatique française ont cohabité. Les sondages effectués par exemple dans la documentation de l'abbaye cistercienne de Barbery située dans le diocèse de Bayeux et fondée dans les années 1180 montre d'une part que les actes sont dans leur grande majorité datés à partir de 1206, d'autre part que les formules diplomatiques sont standardisées dès le début du XIIIe siècle, enfin que les listes de témoins disparaissent. Environ 25% des actes seulement ne sont pas datés et il devrait être possible d'améliorer le pourcentage grâce à DEEDS.[46] L'abbaye cistercienne de Bonport au diocèse

---

43. Voir en annexe l'échantillon incomplet des formules de corroboration pour l'abbaye de Montebourg.
44. B.N.F., ms. lat. 10087, n° 195, 196, 262, 388.
45. B.N.F., ms. lat. 10087, n° 148.
46. Nous suivons ici les travaux en cours de R. Da Cruz qui prépare un mémoire de maîtrise à l'Université de Caen sous ma direction, consacré à l'abbaye de Barbery.

d'Evreux, fut fondée par Richard Cœur de Lion en 1190. 42,42% des actes sont datés durant la période normande.[47] Par la suite seulement deux actes postérieurement à 1204 ne porteront pas de date. Parmi les actes non datés figurent des actes émanés de grands de l'aristocratie même si l'on est enclin à penser que l'habitude de dater de Richard Cœur de Lion a dû influencer le scribe. A moins que les Cisterciens aient attaché davantage d'importance à la question de la datation que les Bénédictins. Les actes rouennais quelle que soit leur provenance semblent aussi, passés les débuts du XIIIe siècle obéir à des règles plus uniformes qui contrastent avec le manque d'homogénéité de la période précédente. En règle générale, passé 1204, la proportion d'actes datés s'accroît dans des proportions considérables. Mais les changements sont parfois longs à se mettre en place et l'on observe des poches de résistance qu'il faudrait pouvoir inventorier, l'archevêque de Rouen, Gautier de Coutances, la famille de Beaumont-Meulan.[48]

La documentation normande est immense; elle compte plus d'une centaine de cartulaires qui ne sont pas nombreux à avoir fait l'objet de publication. Plusieurs milliers d'actes sont à la disposition des chercheurs. La plupart des établissements bénédictins restaurés et fondés aux Xe–XIe siècles ne sont connus que par des copies d'actes collationnées dans des cartulaires dont on a vu qu'ils pouvaient avoir subi des transformations. Que date-t-on? La donation, l'inscription des témoins sur l'acte ou l'insertion dans le cartulaire? De nombreux cartulaires contiennent de vraies chartes, mais aussi des notices difficilement exploitables. Tout de même une ample liberté préside à la rédaction des actes et il faut redire que la chance des historiens de la Normandie des Xe–XIIe siècles tient à la multiplicité des témoins qui doivent impérativement être placés dans une base de données. L'utilisation des formules diplomatiques pour une datation relative n'est certainement pas à négliger même si nos propres essais ne sont pas concluants. L'érudition normande accuse un réel retard, trop peu de cartulaires ayant fait l'objet d'une édition.

De très nombreuses questions restent en suspens. Ainsi par exemple on doit se demander si un scribe qui place dans le corps de l'acte un événement datant pour l'historien, a bien l'intention de dater et dans l'affirmative pourquoi il ne date pas par le millésime. Ensuite on a vu des *scriptoria* dater davantage et nous voulons parler ici du Bec au début du XIIe siècle. Est-ce à lier à l'existence d'une école monastique particulièrement active? Les actes rouennais de La Trinité-du-Mont présentent un nombre beaucoup plus élevé d'actes datés que les abbayes de Lyre, Montebourg et Préaux. Cet établissement jouit d'un triple avantage; il est urbain et proche des centres de décision royale et archiépiscopale et profite d'une certaine modernité. Mais les actes des archevêques de Rouen, dont l'édition reste à faire, sont datés de façon très irrégulière. Les actes de l'archevêque de Rouen, Hugues d'Amiens (1130–1164), semblent porter davantage le millésime que ceux de ses prédécesseurs et successeurs. Les influences réciproques entre l'Angleterre et la Normandie avant et après la Conquête méritent à elles seules une étude.[49]

---

47. J. Andrieux, *Cartulaire de l'abbaye royale de Notre-Dame de Bonport (1190–1467), de l'ordre de Cîteaux, au diocèse d'Evreux*, Evreux 1862.
48. M. Arnoux, « Essor et déclin », p. 339 et note 60 et J. Andrieux, *Bonport*, n° x et xii (vers 1190).
49. Le point de départ de cette étude, réside dans les travaux de D. Bates, *Regesta*, Introduction.

Bibliographie

Andrieux, A. 1862. *Cartulaire de l'abbaye royale de Notre-Dame de Bonport (1190–1467), de l'ordre de Cîteaux, au diocèse d'Evreux.* Evreux.
Arnoux, M. 1996. 'Essor et déclin d'un type diplomatique: les actes passés *coram parrochia* en Normandie (XIIe–XIIIe siècles).' *B. E. C.* 154: p. 330.
Bates, D. 1998. 'Les chartes de confirmation et les pancartes normandes du règne de Guillaume le Conquérant', in *Pancartes monastiques des XIe et XIIe siècles*, éd. M. Parisse et al. Brepols.
———. 1998. *Regesta Regum Anglo-Normannorum. The Acta of William I (1066–1087).* Oxford.
Chanteux, H. 1932. *Recueil des actes de Henri Ier Beauclerc, duc de Normandie.* Thèse manuscrite de l'Ecole des Chartes. 3 vol.
Delisle, L., and Berger, E. 1909–27. *Recueil des actes de Henri II, roi d'Angleterre et duc de Normandie, concernant les provinces françaises et les affaires de France.* Introduction.
Deville, A. 1840. *Cartulaire de la Sainte Trinité-du-Mont de Rouen, Cartulaire de Saint-Bertin*, ed. B. Guérard, pp. 403–87. Paris.
Dumas, F., and J. Pilet-Lemière. 1994. 'La monnaie', in M. d'Onofrio (dir.), *Les Normands peuple d'Europe, 1030–1200*, pp. 60–63. Catalogue d'exposition. Paris.
Fagnen, Cl. 1977. *Essai sur quelques actes normands de Richard Cœur de Lion.* Thèse dactylographiée de l'Ecole nationale des Chartes. 8 vol.
Fauroux, M. 1961. *Recueil des actes des ducs de Normandie (911–1066).* Caen.
Le Cacheux, P. 1934. *Chartes du prieuré de Longueville, de l'ordre de Cluny au diocèse de Rouen, antérieures à 1204.* Rouen et Paris.
Lenoir (Dom J.-L.). Copies du XVIIIe s., dans la collection du marquis de Mathan, 76 cahiers in 4°.
Musset, L. 1985. 'Sur la datation des actes par le nom du Prince en Normandie (XIe–XIIe siècles)', in *Autour du pouvoir ducal normand Xe–XIIe siècles, Cahier des Annales de Normandie*, no. 17. Caen.
———. 1967. *Les actes de Guillaume le Conquérant et de la reine Mathilde pour les abbayes caennaises*, pp. 25–41. Caen.
Rouet, D. 1999. *Le cartulaire de Saint-Pierre de Préaux: étude et édition du manuscrit dans son état de 1227.*

Echantillon incomplet de formules de corroboration dans
le cartulaire de Montebourg (actes de bienfaiteurs laïcs)

Ut hoc firmum permaneat in presentis scriptis et sigilli mei testimonio confirmo (222).

Ut autem haec donatio rata sit et inconcussa et firmiter in perpetuum teneatur sancte Crucis + munio et impressione sigilli mei confirmo (224).

Et ut haec donatio sit rata signo sancti Crucis presentem cartam imprimo + sigilli mei auctoritate communio (256).

Et ut ratum et inconcussum permaneret sigilli mei confirmavi (260).

Et haec donatio rata et firma sit in perpetuum signo sancte Cru+cis confirmo (274).

Et hoc in perpetuum firmiter teneatur presens scriptum signo sancte Crucis + confirmo et sigilli mei impressione corroboro (276).

Et hoc ratum et stabile permaneat in futurum presenti scripto et sigilli mei munimine roboravi (279).

Ego R. signum sancte Crucis propria manu imprimens hanc donationem confirmo (390).

Et ut haec donatio sit rata et inconcussa signo Crucis confirmo et anuli mei auctoritate sigillo (427).

Et ut hoc ratum et stabile permaneat in futurum presentem cartam sigilli mei auctoritate roborare curavi (467).

Et ut haec donatio firma et rata signo sancte Crucis confirmo (484).

Et ut hoc ratum et stabile perseveret presentem cartam sigilli mei munimine confirmavi (552).

Et ut haec donatio firma sit in perpetuum et stabilis presentis scripti pagina et sigilli mei munimine roboravi (594).

Exemples de notices du cartulaire de La Trinité-du-Mont de Rouen (XIe siècle)

N° 56

Quidam nobilium, nomine Hugo, cognomento Taleboth, dedit Sanctae Trinitati decimam de Sanreith. Cujus donationi Walo de la Roca, ad quem praedictae terrae possessio devenit postea, libenter annuit. Post hos successor illorum Osbernus de Ansevilla, accepta societate monasterii, predictorum virorum donationem et ipse annuendo confirmavit.
Signum Hugonis Talebot. Signum Walonis de la Roca. Signum Osberni de Ansevilla. Signum Osberni de Hotot. Testes: Gulbertus de Ou; Osbernus de Alberti Villa; Heddo de Canaan; Rodulfus, filius Hermeri; Rodulfus de Pauliaco; Osbernus, filius Goiffredi de Ou; Gozelinus de Alladio.

N° 57

Ea tempestate qua Guillelmus, dux Normannorum egregius, cum classico apparatu ingentique exercitu, Anglorum terram expetiit, quidam miles, nomine Osmundus de Bodes, cum aliis illuc profectus, et langore correptus atque ad extrema perductus, pro animae suae remedio, dedit Sanctae Trinitati omnem decimam terrae suae in alodio, quam domini sui Rodolfi de Warenna tenebat beneficio. Unde eidem domino suo Rodulfo, ut hoc annueret, XXX solidos dedimus: quod et fecit ante altare Sanctae Trinitatis.
Signum Rodulfi de Warenna; Signum ejusdem Osmundi; Signum Rodulfi heredis Osmundi. Testes: Alveredus de la Bruere; Goiffredus del Busc; Ricardus de Drincurt; Ilbertus de Longo Campo; Bernardus, cocus; Robertus, pistor.

N° 58

Anno ab incarnatione Domini MLXIII., quidam vir de Sancti Petri Ponte, nomine Germundus, cum uxore sua Bersenta, Romam, orationis causa pergens, eo quod steriles erant, hereditatem suam monachis Sanctae Trinitatis, pro commissa fraternitate, post obitum suum jure perpetuo tradiderunt: scilicet domum suam cum ustensilibus, annonam et foenum, et hortum, quattuor acres terrae, quos de Waleranno de Dalbuet et Azore de Rolvilla pro XII solidis annorum quattuor termino in vadimonium habebant, pro animae suae remedio obtulerunt, et in eadem villa unum acrem et dimidium de beneficio Durandi forestarii, annuente eodem Durando, perpetualiter largiti sunt, coram his testibus:
Signum Durandi, forestarii; Signum ipsius Germundi; Signum uxoris ejus Bersendis; Signum Rogerii, fratris Durandi; Signum Rozelini; Signum Rainoldi; Signum Bernardi, coci; Signum Huelini, fratris ejus.

N° 72

Donatio Wigerii de Torduit et uxoris ejus Osmodis, de omni terra quam de illis tenebat Ebroinus de Portmort in Warcliva.
Signum Wigerii. Signum Osmodis, uxoris ejus. Testes: Rogerius, filius Odelardi; Durandus, nepos ejusdem Wigerii; Ricardus, senescal.

Cartulaire de Lyre: étude de l'adresse et du salut dans les 15 actes des comtes de Leicester, principaux bienfaiteurs de l'abbaye au XIIe siècle (Dom Lenoir, t. 23).

Robert II (1118–1168)

Acte 12 (1118–1155/1158): omnibus baronibus et ministris et hominibus suis Normannie salutem (p. 460).

Acte 13 (1120–1168): omnibus filiis sancte Ecclesie et E. de B. et omnibus baillivis et ministris et hominibus suis de Normannia salutem (p. 460).

Acte 17 (1120–1168): cunctis baronibus suis atque hominibus tam citra mare quam ultra constitutis presentibus et futuris salutem (p. 461).

Acte 19 (1118–1168): E. de B. et omnibus baronibus et hominibus suis et fidelibus de Normannia salutem (p. 462).

Acte 26 (1120–1168): E. de B. et omnibus baronibus et hominibus suis totius Normannie salutem (p. 464–465).

Acte 27 (1118–1168): omnibus hominibus suis francis et anglis salutem (p. 465).

Robert III (1168–1190)

Acte 4 (1168–1190): sancte matris Ecclesie filiis salutem (p. 453).

Acte 5 (1168–1190): omnibus hominibus francis et anglis presentibus salutem et pacem (p. 457–458).

Acte 6 (1168–1190) et acte 22 (1164–1168): omnibus sancte matris Ecclesie fidelibus et omnibus hominibus suis de Normannia salutem (p. 458).

Acte 8 (1168–1190): omnibus hominibus suis et amicis tam presentibus quam futuris salutem (p. 458).

Acte 9 (1164–1168): omnibus hominibus suis Normannie salutem (p. 459).

Acte 10 (1168–1190): omnibus ad quos presens scriptum pervenerit... salutem (p. 459).

Acte 18 (1168–1190): omnibus hominibus suis tam presentibus quam futuris salutem (p. 462).

L'acte 11 est difficile à attribuer à l'un ou l'autre comte (l'adresse est la même que celle de l'acte 18): omnibus hominibus suis tam presentibus quam futuris salutem (p. 459–460).

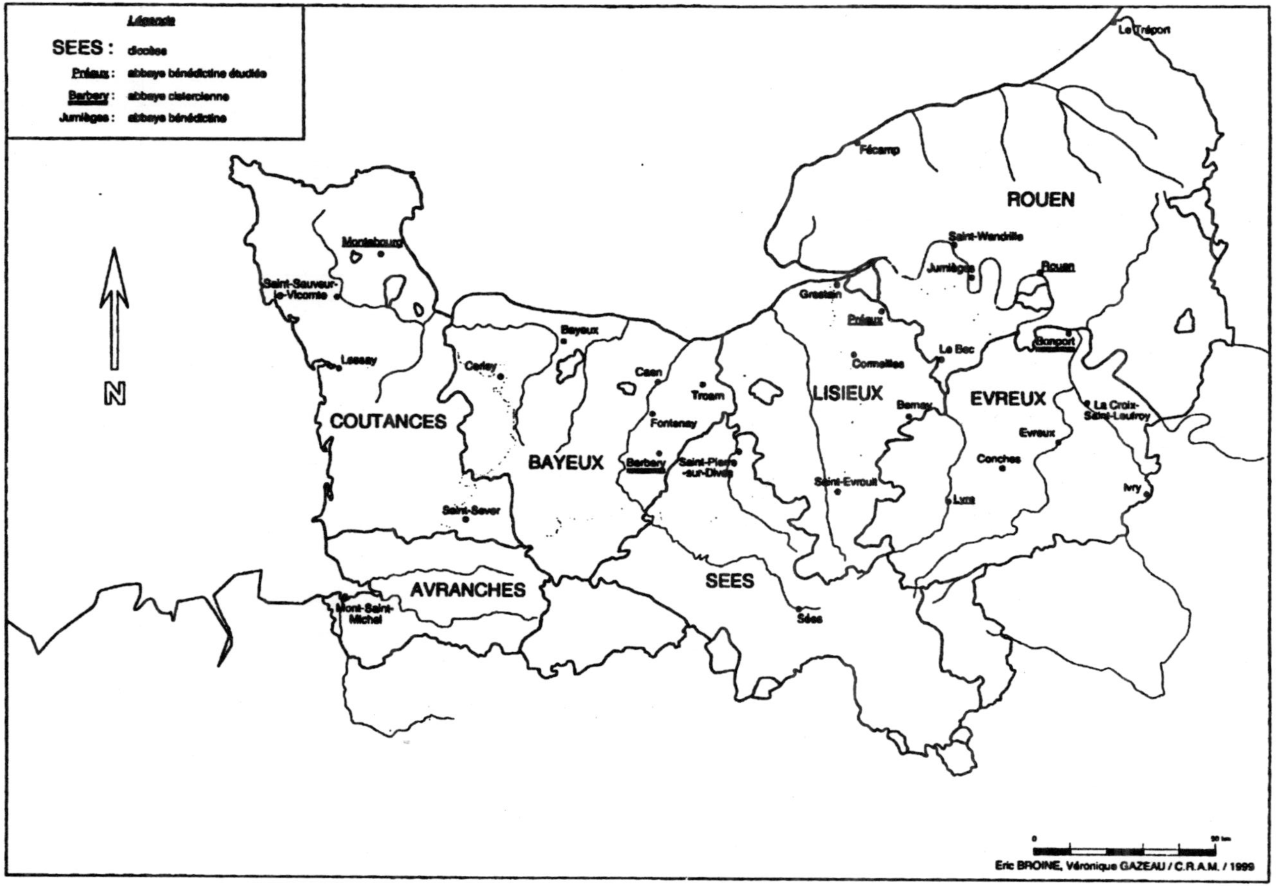
Légende
SEES : diocèse
Préaux : abbaye bénédictine étudiée
Barbery : abbaye cistercienne
Jumièges : abbaye bénédictine
N
ROUEN
EVREUX
LISIEUX
BAYEUX
COUTANCES
AVRANCHES
SEES
Le Tréport
Fécamp
Saint-Wandrille
Jumièges
Rouen
Grestain
Préaux
Le Bec
Bonport
Cormeilles
Bernay
La Croix-Saint-Leufroy
Evreux
Conches
Ivry
Lyre
Saint-Evroult
Troarn
Caen
Fontenay
Barbery
Saint-Pierre-sur-Dives
Bayeux
Cerisy
Montebourg
Saint-Sauveur-le-Vicomte
Lessay
Saint-Sever
Mont-Saint-Michel
Sées
0
50 km
Eric BROINE, Véronique GAZEAU / C.R.A.M. / 1999

Formules diplomatiques dans le cartulaire de La Trinité-du-Mont de Rouen

N° Deville	N° Fx ou Bates	Date indiquée	Date présumée	Invocation	Préambule	Notification	Adresse	Dispositif
1	F 61	1030		INSIT	si fidelium nostrorum petitionibus	notum esse	omnibus christianae religionis fidelibus presentibus scilicet ac futuris	concedimus
2	F 104		1035–1047			pateat		
3	F 81		1030–1035				Christi fidelibus	tradiderunt
4	F 118		1040–1051			pateat	cuncti fideles tam presentes quam futuri	dedit
5	F 82		1030–1035			noverint		dedit
6	F 96		c. 1040					dederunt
7	F 123		1051 ?					dedit, donavit et tradidit
8	F 60		c. 1030	in Dei nomine		notum sit	omnibus christianae fidei cultoribus presentibus scilicet et futuris	
9	F 83		1030–1035					largitus est
10	F 221		1060–1066					tradiderunt
11								vendidit
12								
13								tradidit
14								dederunt
15								largitus est
16	B 234		1066–1077				Christi fidelibus	
17								
18								donatio
19			1051–1077					emit
20			1051–1077					emit
21			1051–1077					emit
22								dedit
23	F 201		1051–1066					concesserat

N° Deville	N° Fx ou Bates	Date indiquée	Date présumée	Invocation	Préambule	Notification	Adresse	Dispositif
24	F 84		1030–1035					concedo
25		1059						tradiderunt et dederunt
26			1051–1077					tradidit
27	F 135		1037–1055		préambule	notum fecimus	cunctis tam presentibus quam et nostris minoribus	emimus
28	F 206		1055–1066					vendidit
29	F 143	1059						vendiderunt
30			post 1059					dedit et tradidit
31			1051–1077					vendidit
32		1060						dedit et tradidit
33								vendidit
34		1062						vendidit
35		1074				notum sit filiis	omnibus sanctae Ecclesiae vendiderant	
36								tradidit
37	F 130	1053				liceat	omnibus sanctae Dei ecclesiae fidelibus	vendidit
38	F 138		1050–1056					dederunt
39	F 233	1066				pateat	cunctis Christi fidelibus	perdonavit
40			1051–1077			agnoscant famulantes	omnes Jeshu Christo vendidit	
41			1051–1077					vendidit
42								emimus
43	F 200		1051–1066					vendidit
44			1051–1077					tradidit
45			1051–1077					
46	F 202		1051–1066			manifestum sit	omnibus sanctae Dei ecclesiae filiis	donaverunt
47	B 233		1068–1071			pateat	fidelibus Christi	redemimus

N° Deville	N° Fx ou Bates	Date indiquée	Date présumée	Invocation	Préambule	Notification	Adresse	Dispositif
48								dedit
49	F 119		1040-1050		celestis regni promereri			dedi
50				in Dei nomine		notum sit	omnibus Christi et sanctae Ecclesiae fidelibus	donavit et tradidit
51	F 101	1043						misit super altare donationem
52								tradidit
53								invadiavit
54		1047						vendidit
55		1068				notum sit		dedit
56			1066					dedit
57								tradiderunt
58		1063						emimus
59		1059						vendidit
60			1051-1077					dedit
61								tradidit
62								condonavit
63	B 231		marc-dec 1067					dedit
64			1066					
65			1055-1066				omnibus in Christum credentibus	largiti sunt
66								dedit
67	B 232	1069	1077-1120					dedit
68						notum sit	omnibus	concessit
69		1063	1049					dedit
70								vendidit
71								tradidit
72								donatio
73								donatio

N° Deville	N° Fx ou Bates	Date indiquée	Date présumée	Invocation	Préambule	Notification	Adresse	Dispositif
74								tradidit
75		1068						invadiaverat
76			1030–1051			notum sit	omnibus Christum colentibus	emit
77						notum sit	omnibus fidelibus	dedit
78		1044						donavit
79						notum sit	cunctis fidelibus	do
80								dedit
81			1051–1077			notum sit	omnibus Christi fidelibus	dederunt
82	B 235	1080				notum sit	cunctis fidelibus	dederunt
83		1091	1051–1077					tradiderunt
84								dono
85								do
86						pateat	cunctis fidelibus Christi	invadiaverat
87								dedit
88								dono
89	B 236	1080				notum sit	omnibus catholicae Ecclesiae filiis	damus
90		1084						dedit
91								reddidit
92		1084				notum sit	omnibus	concessi
93						pateat		dedit
94							cunctis fidelibus Christi	dederunt
95								dederunt
96						notum sit	omnibus	reddit
97								

L'ÉTUDE DU VOCABULAIRE ET LA DATATION DES ACTES: L'APPORT DES BASES DE DONNÉES INFORMATISÉES

Benoît-Michel Tock

L'étude du vocabulaire est depuis longtemps utilisée de manière empirique pour dater un acte non daté et, d'ailleurs aussi, pour critiquer l'authenticité d'un acte (ce qui souvent revient à en contester la date d'élaboration). La constitution, récente, de bases de données informatisées de textes diplomatiques permet de renouveler l'approche, en sécurisant la recherche, mais entraîne la nécessité de définir des règles de travail.[1] On songe évidemment à la publication récente du *Thesaurus Diplomaticus*, qui comprend environ 6000 actes antérieurs à 1200 relatifs aux territoires correspondant à l'actuelle Belgique.[2] Mais j'utiliserai surtout la base de données en cours de développement à l'Atelier de recherches sur les textes médiévaux de Nancy, relative aux chartes originales antérieures à 1121 conservées en France et riche de près de 4800 actes.[3] La base de l'Artem constitue donc un ensemble appréciable d'actes. Malgré l'importance du chiffre, ces actes ne représentent sans doute qu'un pourcentage assez faible de l'ensemble des actes conservés pour cette période, sans même parler de ceux qui ont été perdus. Mais la valeur de cette base repose sur trois atouts: le nombre des actes; leur diversité;[4] le fait que seuls les originaux soient repris, ce qui permet d'éviter à coup sûr les erreurs ou les modifications dues aux copistes.

1. Qu'apportent les bases de données aux études de vocabulaire?

L'étude du vocabulaire d'un corpus de textes peut passer soit par la lecture attentive des textes en question, soit par l'utilisation d'un fichier manuel établi le plus souvent par les éditeurs de ces textes sous la forme d'*index verborum*, soit enfin par l'utilisation de bases de données informatisées. C'est évidemment à ces

---

From *Dating Undated Medieval Charters*. Ed. Michael Gervers. Copyright (by the Editor and Contributors 2000). Published by the Boydell Press (in association with Collegium Budapest), PO Box 9, Woodbridge, Suffolk, IP12 3DF, Great Britain. ISBN 0 85115 792 0.

1. Voir déjà Michel Parisse, 'A propos du traitement automatique des chartes: chronologie du vocabulaire et repérage des actes suspects', *La lexicographie du latin médiéval et ses rapports avec les recherches actuelles sur la civilisation du Moyen Age*, Paris 1981, pp. 241-249. Benoît-Michel Tock, 'Les mutations du vocabulaire latin des chartes au XIe siècle', *Bibliothèque de l'Ecole des Chartes* 155 (1997): pp. 119-148.
2. *Thesaurus Diplomaticus*, Turnhout 1998 (un CD-Rom).
3. ARTEM, membre de l'UPRESA 7002 'Moyen Age', Université de Nancy 2/C.N.R.S. Voir Michel Parisse, 'Inventaire des actes originaux du Haut Moyen Age conservés en France: un premier bilan', *Académie des Inscriptions et Belles-Lettres. Comptes-rendus des séances* (1984), pp. 352-369. Les nombreux actes que nous utilisons ici sont cités d'après leur numéro dans cette base de données (p. ex. Artem 3602). Un inventaire de ces actes sera publié prochainement. Le travail n'étant pas encore fini, on a utilisé pour cette étude une version provisoire, riche de 4798 actes.
4. L'Artem travaille sur la France actuelle, ce qui signifie qu'y sont représentés aussi bien le royaume de France que ceux de Germanie, de Bourgogne, de Provence, voire d'Aquitaine.

dernières qu'on donnera la préférence actuellement. L'avantage de pouvoir consulter d'un coup d'oeil plusieurs milliers d'actes, plusieurs millions de mots, n'échappe à personne. Toutefois, les autres avantages, mais aussi les inconvénients de ces bases de données n'apparaissent pas toujours clairement.

Commençons par les avantages. Les bases de données ne permettent pas seulement de consulter beaucoup de mots, elles permettent également la consultation de n'importe quel mot, alors que les index sont forcément toujours sélectifs:[5] et comme les critères de la sélection des mots ne sont pas précisés, il n'est guère facile, quand un mot est absent, de savoir si c'est parce qu'il n'est pas employé dans les textes édités ou parce que l'éditeur n'y a pas prêté attention.

Les bases de données peuvent aussi améliorer les informations qu'elles trouvent dans les éditions. C'est vrai pour des problèmes de datation, d'authenticité, mais aussi et plus simplement d'établissement du texte. Ainsi, le *Thesaurus diplomaticus* a collationné des milliers d'actes, tandis que l'Artem a réédité directement à partir des originaux tous les actes traités. Par rapport à des éditions parfois anciennes et / ou fautives, c'est un atout important.

Les bases de données ne sont cependant pas exemptes de reproches. Tout d'abord, et même si c'est un peu trivial, elles peuvent ajouter des fautes aux éditions qu'elles utilisent. En général aussi elles omettent tout ou partie, ou elles simplifient à tout le moins, les identifications et les commentaires diplomatiques ou historiques qui accompagnent l'édition d'un texte.

D'autre part, la plupart traitent directement le vocabulaire, sans passer par une lemmatisation. Or la diversité des graphies médiévales est, on le sait, très grande. A titre d'exemple, et sauf erreur ou oubli, le lemme *abbatia* apparaît, dans la base de l'Artem, sous les graphies *abacia, abadia, abathia, abatia, abbacia, abbadia, abbathia, abbatia, abbazia* et *habatia*, ceci sans compter les formes déclinées (*abatias, abbaciam...*) et les formes dérivées (*abatiola, abbaciola, abbatiola*). En sens inverse, certains mots peuvent en cacher d'autres. Quand on cherche les bourgeois, on rencontre aussi l'évêque de Burgos, *Burgensis episcopus*. Quand on cherche les villes, et donc le mot *oppidum*, on rencontre une dame *Opida*. Tout le travail d'harmonisation lexicale, de lemmatisation en fait, accompli par l'indexeur d'un texte est ici négligé, et doit donc être accompli par l'utilisateur de la base de données.

Enfin, la constitution d'une base de données, qui est un travail lent et progressif, ne permet généralement pas de procéder à une critique d'authenticité attentive des actes qu'on y reprend. Concrètement, on se contente de mentionner les informations disponibles, sans plus. Un acte qui n'est pas déclaré comme faux peut avoir échappé à cette infamie simplement parce qu'il n'a jamais fait l'objet d'une critique attentive. Il en va de même pour les problèmes de datation: un acte non daté est daté de façon plus ou moins approximative, mais sans enquête particulière.

---

5. Il faut toutefois noter que, grâce à l'aide de l'informatique, les *index verborum* sont maintenant beaucoup plus détaillés qu'avant. Voir p. ex. le *Recueil des actes de Louis VI, roi de France (1108–1137)*, éd. Jean Dufour, t. 4, Paris 1994, p. 123.

2. Le vocabulaire et la datation des actes: problèmes généraux

Pour que le vocabulaire puisse être d'une quelconque utilité pour la datation des actes non datés, il faut qu'il ait évolué, soit par l'apparition de mots nouveaux, soit par la disparition de mots anciens et périmés, soit enfin par la modification du sens des mots.

L'apparition de mots nouveaux dans le lexique médio-latin est bien connue. C'est, par exemple, *feodum, vassus, ligius, bireta*...[6] Il importe cependant de noter que ces mots nouveaux sont relatifs à une réalité sociale, juridique, économique, politique, institutionnelle ou simplement matérielle qui est en général à peu près aussi nouvelle qu'eux. Pour reprendre un exemple célèbre, l'hommage lige apparaît vers la moitié du XIe siècle à Vendôme:[7] un acte utilisant le lemme *ligius* ne peut donc être antérieur à cette date. De même, la brouette n'est inventée que dans la seconde moitié du XIIe siècle, et ne peut donc être mentionnée avant.[8] Mais cette constatation ne permet pas de faire beaucoup avancer les choses: on n'a pas attendu l'invention de l'ordinateur et des bases de données pour se méfier des actes parlant d'hommage lige ou de brouette au IXe siècle.

On a accordé beaucoup moins d'intérêt à la disparition de mots, ce qui permettrait de nourrir certaines espérances. Hélas, c'est un phénomène rare. Une étude menée il y a quelques années n'avait pu, pour le vocabulaire des chartes "belges" du XIe s., mettre en relief que trois disparitions définitives:[9] *coenobita* et *ingenuilis*, qui renvoient à une réalité institutionnelle,[10] et *inexquisitus*, qui de toute façon est un terme très rare.[11] On ne peut donc certes pas écarter cette méthode, mais il ne faut pas s'en exagérer l'importance.

C'est donc surtout les changements dans l'utilisation des mots qui retiendront notre attention. Ces changements peuvent porter sur le sens, mais aussi sur le contexte d'utilisation des mots.

---

6. On ne tient évidemment pas compte ici, parce que cela n'a pas d'intérêt pour la datation des actes, de tout le vocabulaire ecclésiastique, mis au point en général dans l'Antiquité tardive ou au début du Moyen Age, et qui passe tant par la création de nouveaux mots (souvent importés du grec) que par le détournement de mots existants. On retrouvera une période de création de mots intellectuels dans le monde universitaire au XIIIe s., mais ce lexique ne se retrouvera guère dans les chartes; de surcroît, cela dépasse la période traitée ici.

7. Voir Dominique Barthélemy, *La société dans le comté de Vendôme de l'an mil au XIVe siècle*, Paris, 1993, pp. 617–18, qui insiste avec raison sur le fait que l'institution a précédé sa dénomination. Voir aussi, p. ex., *Novum glossarium mediae latinitatis ab anno DCCC usque ad annum MCC*, t. 1, Copenhague 1957, pp. 134–35.

8. M. J. T. Lewis, 'The Origins of the Wheelbarrow' *Technology and Culture* 35 (1994): pp. 453–475. De fait, elle n'est pas mentionnée dans la base de l'Artem, ni même dans celle du *Thesaurus Diplomaticus*, sauf peut-être comme sobriquet (*Boroete*, en 1198).

9. B.-M. Tock, *Les mutations du vocabulaire latin* (n.1), p. 124.

10. Le terme est de toute façon rare: onze attestations à l'époque patristique et soixante-cinq au Moyen Age (y compris au XIIe s. chez Bernard de Clairvaux ou Philippe de Harvengt), contre respectivement 1608 et 6009 pour *monachus*, d'après le *Cetedoc Index of Latin Forms*, Turnhout 1999 (un CD-Rom).

11. Le même *Cetedoc Index of Latin Forms* n'en relève que trois mentions à l'époque patristique et trois à l'époque médiévale.

Mais avant d'en parler, il est nécessaire de rappeler les conditions de travail des rédacteurs d'actes médiévaux. Les rédacteurs de chartes ne vivaient pas que dans un monde de chartes. C'étaient en général des clercs, vivant soit dans un monastère, soit dans une église cathédrale ou collégiale, soit enfin auprès d'une chapelle royale ou princière, mais en tout cas toujours dans un contexte latin et religieux. Ils chantaient journellement des psaumes, entendaient la messe, la Bible, les Pères latins de l'Eglise. Ils ne consacraient à l'écriture ou la rédaction de chartes qu'une partie de leur travail, simplement parce qu'ils n'avaient pas assez de matière pour y travailler à temps plein.[12]

La conséquence que nous devons en tirer, c'est que leur connaissance du latin était nettement plus importante que ce qu'ils en montrent dans les chartes.[13] C'est-à-dire qu'ils disposaient d'un potentiel lexical latin nettement plus important que ce qu'ils utilisaient concrètement dans les actes. Et de ce potentiel ils tiraient parfois quelques mots, pas forcément parce qu'ils étaient à la mode, mais parce qu'ils avaient envie de les utiliser. Prenons l'exemple du lemme *machinatio*. Il se trouve dans six actes: un diplôme d'Otton Ier le 10 mars 956 pour Saint-Maximin de Trèves, un diplôme suspect d'Henri Ier pour Guillaume, chevalier de Corbeil, une charte douteuse aussi de 1070 d'Adalbéron III, évêque de Metz, pour Saint-Arnoul de Metz, une notice de la donation d'un chevalier Otbert en faveur de l'abbaye de Marmoutier vers 1096, une notice de la fin du XIe siècle de la donation de Guillaume Correle pour l'abbaye de Nouaillé, une charte donnée en 1105 par l'évêque d'Amiens Godefroid pour l'abbaye de Saint-Fuscien.[14] Il est difficile de vouloir établir un lien entre ces actes: il n'y a pas eu influence d'un rédacteur sur un autre, il n'y a pas eu milieu intellectuel commun, école identique, il y a eu

---

12. Sur l'hésitation à utiliser le mot de "chancellerie" au XIIe s. voir par exemple Peter Rück, *Die Urkunden der Bischöfe von Basel bis 1213*, Bâle 1966, pp. 191–193. Anton Gössi, *Das Urkundenwesen der Bischöfe von Basel im 13. Jhdt (1216–1274)*, Bâle 1974, p. 163, voit les choses différemment pour le XIIIe s. Mais pour soixante ans il n'a que 190 chartes, soit à peine plus de trois par an! Sur d'autres activités des agents des chancelleries épiscopales, voir Marie Bláhová, 'Bischöfliche Beamte als Geschichtsschreiber im Ostmitteleuropa des frühen und hohen Mittelalters', *Die Diplomatik der Bischofsurkunde vor 1250 [Actes colloque Innsbruck, 1993]*, éd. Christoph Haidacher et Werner Köfler, Innsbruck 1995, pp. 187–195. Dans le cadre monastique, voir le beau cas présenté par Michel Parisse, 'Un scribe champenois du XIIe siècle et l'évolution de son écriture' *Archiv für Diplomatik* 29 (1983): pp. 229–241: il s'agit d'un moine cistercien de Trois-Fontaines qui, entre 1169 et 1188 écrit 41 actes (plus encore un en 1191 et un en 1196), tous sauf un pour sa propre abbaye. Même quarante actes en vingt ans, cela laisse du temps au moine pour vaquer aux obligations régulières et à d'autres travaux.

13. "Deeds by their nature made limited demands on vocabulary": Richard Sharpe, 'Vocabulary, Word formation and Lexicography', F. A. C. Mantello et A. G. Rigg, *Medieval Latin. An Introduction and Bibliographical Guide*, Washington, 1996, pp. 93–105, à la p. 94.

14. On trouvera ces actes respectivement dans *Conradi I., Heinrici I. et Ottonis I. diplomata*, t. 1, Hanovre 1879–1884 (*MGH. Diplomata regum et imperatorum Germaniae*), n° 179, pp. 260–262 (Artem 1836); Jacques Boussard, 'Actes royaux et pontificaux de Saint-Maur-des-Fossés', *Journal des savants* (1972): pp. 81–113, aux pp. 107–109 (Artem 2082); Arch. dép. Moselle, H 24 (Artem 335); Charles Métais, *Marmoutier. Cartulaire Blésois*, Blois 1889–1891, n° 69, pp. 80–81 (Artem 2179); P. de Monsabert, *Chartes de l'abbaye de Nouaillé de 678 à 1200*, Poitiers 1936 (Archives historiques du Poitou, 49), n° 179, pp. 284–285 (Artem 1381); Joseph Estienne, 'Chartes de s. Geoffroi évêque d'Amiens (1105–1112)', *Bibliothèque de l'Ecole des Chartes* 90 (1929): pp. 37–50, n° 1, pp. 44–46 (Artem n° 932).

utilisation indépendante, par six rédacteurs différents, d'un mot par ailleurs largement utilisé dans les textes de base de la culture monastique.[15]

Dans d'autres cas cependant, il est difficile de ne pas mettre en relation deux occurrences d'un même mot. Ainsi, *taciturnitas* n'apparaît que deux fois dans le corpus de l'Artem. Ces deux occurrences sont parisiennes et datent du début du XIIe s., et constituent donc sans doute l'indice d'une origine identique: au moins une même école, sans doute un même rédacteur.[16] Mais ces actes sont datés: le rapprochement est donc aisé et sûr. S'ils ne l'avaient pas été, aurions-nous pu, sur la seule base de cet usage identique de *taciturnitas* et de leur origine géographique commune, associer ces deux documents?[17] Assurément non. D'ailleurs, le *Thesaurus Diplomaticus* indique une utilisation du même mot, dans une bulle de Grégoire VII pour l'évêque de Liège datée du 23 mars 1073, donc sans rapport avec les deux actes précédents.[18]

L'apparition de mots nouveaux ne permet donc pas d'obtenir des résultats probants, sauf en ce qui concerne le vocabulaire institutionnel.[19]

Comment voir ces modifications dans l'usage des mots? Il faut distinguer les changements dans le sens et les changements dans le contexte d'utilisation.

Il n'est pas toujours facile de suivre, de dater, ces changements de sens, tant est grande la part d'interprétation qui figure dans notre compréhension des textes médiévaux. Pour prendre un exemple célèbre, à partir de quand *miles* signifie-t-il chevalier? Malgré la difficulté de la tâche, il ne faut pas perdre cette possibilité de vue. De nouveau, le vocabulaire institutionnel permet des démarches plus aisées. Ainsi, c'est vers l'an mil que le mot *altare*, particulièrement dans le Centre et le Nord de la France – et c'est l'occasion de rappeler qu'évidemment, le cas échéant, les disparités locales doivent être prises en compte – commence à désigner, par

---

15. La *Cetedoc Library of Christian Latin Texts*, version 3, Turnhout, 1997 (un CD-Rom), le montre utilisé une fois dans la Bible, douze fois chez Augustin, vingt-et-un fois chez Grégoire le Grand, deux fois chez Bède. Le *Cetedoc Index of Latin Forms* (n. 10) cite 132 attestations à l'époque patristique et 136 au Moyen Age.

16. Les contextes sont cependant différents. Charte de Galon, évêque de Paris, pour l'abbaye Saint-Maur-des-Fossés, en 1107, éd. R. de Lasteyrie, *Cartulaire général de Paris*, t. 1, Paris 1887, n° 143, pp. 161–163: critique de la *taciturnitas* de prélats qui se taisent devant les méfaits commis par des méchants. Charte de Ste-Geneviève de Paris pour le chapitre cathédral, en 1116, éd. Benjamin Guérard, *Cartulaire de l'église Notre-Dame de Paris*, t. 1, Paris 1850, p. 449, définissant dans le préambule l'*oblivio* comme la *taciturnitatis mater*. Il y a bien un troisième emploi, une charte de Baudouin évêque de Noyon pour l'abbaye Saint-Eloi de Noyon en 1063 (Artem 248), mais cette charte est suspecte: Olivier Guyotjeannin, 'Noyonnais et Vermandois aux Xe et XIe siècles: la déclaration du trésorier Guy et les premières confirmations royales et pontificales des biens du chapitre cathédral de Noyon', *Bibliothèque de l'Ecole des Chartes* 139 (1981): pp. 143–189, à la p. 160, n. 4.

17. S'il est absent de la Bible, ce mot se trouve dix-huit fois chez Augustin, cinq fois chez Bède, neuf fois chez Grégoire le Grand (*Cetedoc Library of Christian Latin Texts*). Et au total 274 fois à l'époque patristique et 206 fois à l'époque.

18. Ed. Erich Caspar, *Das Register Gregors VII.*, 2 vol., Berlin 1920–1923, n° II-61, t. 1, pp. 215–216.

19. Cette remarque est d'ailleurs vraie aussi, évidemment, pour les problèmes d'apparition ou de disparition des mots. Dans l'étude citée plus haut (B.-M. Tock, *Les mutations du vocabulaire* (n. 1), p. 123), on peut voir que le verbe *laudare* n'apparaît qu'une fois dans les actes 'belges' antérieurs à l'an mil, pour seize fois au XIe siècle. Faut-il mettre en doute la datation ou l'authenticité de cet acte? Evidemment non: n'importe quel clerc médiéval connaît le verbe *laudare*, et est susceptible de l'utiliser.

opposition à l'*ecclesia*, les éléments les plus proprement ecclésiastiques d'une église paroissiale: nomination du prêtre, revenus du culte, partie de la dîme affectée à l'entretien du prêtre...[20] Dès lors, si une mention de donation *super altare facta* ne permet pas de dater l'acte, une donation de l'*altare cum oblationibus* permet au moins d'avancer un *terminus a quo*.

Le contexte dans lequel un mot est utilisé peut, lui aussi, être révélateur, et cela parfois de façon surprenante. Qui penserait qu'un mot outil comme *proinde* peut avoir un quelconque intérêt? Il est d'ailleurs présent dans 175 chartes originales antérieures à 1121 conservées en France, ce qui est un beau chiffre. Pourtant, quand on classe ces occurrences par ordre chronologique, il faut attendre la 44e, vers 846, pour trouver un acte qui ne soit pas royal ou impérial.[21] Et sur les 44 occurrences suivantes (jusque 918), seules 9 ne sont pas des diplômes royaux ou impériaux. On retrouve la même chose, plus fort encore, dans l'actuelle Belgique: la première attestation non royale date de 1039.[22] Ce n'est pas tout. *Proinde* n'est pendant longtemps utilisé qu'en tête de phrase, pour marquer justement l'intervention royale, après le long récit de l'action juridique que le roi confirme. Sous Louis le Pieux, ce mot peut aussi être placé, et il l'est de plus en plus, après le préambule. Et sous Charles le Chauve, il arrive qu'il figure au milieu d'une phrase, sans plus de rapport donc avec l'intervention royale. C'est-à-dire qu'il y a un lent processus d'abandon, par la chancellerie royale elle-même, du caractère royal de ce mot. D'où sa reprise, soit par des pouvoirs qui essayent de se grandir, soit par d'autres qui ignorent ce caractère royal.[23]

Un peu de la même manière, la *magnificentia* ne peut être que royale ou divine jusqu'à ce qu'en juin 941 ou 942 le comte de Poitiers Guillaume s'arroge cette qualité, rapidement suivi par d'autres actes.[24]

---

20. Voir Benoît-Michel Tock, 'Altare dans les chartes françaises antérieures à 1121', dans *Roma, Magistra Mundi. Itineraria culturae medievalis. Mélanges offerts au Père L. E. Boyle à l'occasion de son 75e anniversaire*, éd. J. Hamesse, Louvain-la-Neuve 1998, t. 2, pp. 901–926.

21. En l'occurrence, une charte de l'archevêque de Sens Wanilo (Artem 1780). Sur cette charte, voir Maurice Prou, 'Le transfert de l'abbaye de Saint-Remy de Sens à Vareilles', *Bulletin de la société archéologique de Sens* 28 (1913): pp. 254–321. En revanche, le mot figure dans plusieurs *formulae andecavenses*, éd. Karl. Zeumer, *Formulae Merowingici et Karolini aevi*, Hanovre 1886, § 31, 33, 44 (en ne cherchant que les débuts de phrases). De même, dans les *formulae Marculfi*, il est dans deux formules d'acte royal (I, 9 et 37), mais aussi dans une formule d'acte privé (II, 7). Il n'y a rien à ce sujet dans Rudolf Falkowski, 'Studien zur Sprache der Merowingerdiplome', *Archiv für Diplomatik* 17 (1971): pp. 1–125.

22. Nicolas Huyghebaert, 'Hugo Tornacensis ecclesiae cancellarius. Examen critique de la charte de fondation de l'abbaye de Phalempin (1039)', *Bulletin de la commission royale d'histoire* 128 (1962): pp. 183–273. Il y a une exception, mais c'est une lettre transmise par une *Vita*, celle de s. Amand [Bruno Krusch et Walter Levison, *Passiones Vitaeque sanctorum aevi merovingici*, Hanovre-Leipzig 1910 (*MGH. Scriptores rerum merovingicarum*, 5), pp. 483–485].

23. Dans le premier cas figure l'acte de l'archevêque Wanilo, cité ci-dessus, et le concile de Pîtres de 861, éd. Wilfried Hartmann, *Die Konzilien der karolingischen Teilreiche, 860–874*, Hanovre 1998, n° 6, pp. 53–56. Dans le deuxième, la donation d'Emmon pour l'abbaye de Nouaillé en août 857, éd. P. de Monsabert, *Les chartes de l'abbaye de Nouaillé* (n. 14), n° 17, pp. 31–33.

24. Acte de Guillaume pour Saint-Hilaire de Poitiers, en janvier 941 ou 942, éd. Rédet, *Documents pour servir à l'histoire de l'église de Saint-Hilaire de Poitiers*, 2 vol., Poitiers 1848–1852, au t. 1, n° 18, pp. 22–23 (Artem 1109). Acte de Regimbold pour Saint-Arnoul de Metz (*voir la page suivante*)

On aura constaté qu'aucun des exemples avancés ne concernait un vocabulaire plus abstrait, plus spirituel. C'est qu'en fait, ce vocabulaire, évidemment plus rare dans les actes, même ceux, très expressifs, du XIe siècle, que le vocabulaire institutionnel, économique, juridique... connaît une grande stabilité du IXe au XIIe siècle.[25] Même si on prend des mots liés, par exemple, à la réforme grégorienne, on s'aperçoit que celle-ci a repris des mots existants plus qu'elle n'en a inventé. Ainsi, le mot *libertas*. On sait quelle importance ce mot a revêtue pour la réforme. Et on le trouve de fait davantage au XIe siècle qu'avant.[26] Mais il est tout de même présent, dès 830, dans des diplômes, des bulles, des actes privés, même s'il y désigne moins souvent la liberté ecclésiastique, ou si celle-ci est alors davantage concédée par le roi que par le pape.

Un autre concept important de la réforme grégorienne est celui de *vita apostolica*. Mais c'est là un concept qu'on ne rencontre presque pas dans les chartes:[27] la *vita* n'est pas *apostolica*, elle est *eterna*, elle est *canonica*. Et la *vita canonica*, elle, ne se trouve de fait qu'au temps grégorien.[28] Mais on revient là dans un vocabulaire plus institutionnel.

3. Le vocabulaire et la datation des actes: application

Il a paru intéressant de compléter cet exposé théorique par l'étude de deux cas particuliers. Tout d'abord une donation d'un certain *Jarimbertus* au chapitre cathédral de Langres, datable de 901-933.[29] Ce *Jarimbertus* est diacre, *levita indignus* dit-il. L'adjectif *indignus* se rencontre à travers toute la période, comme le terme *levita*. Mais ce dernier connaît une période faste au Xe et dans la première moitié du XIe s.[30]

(*suite de la page précédente*) éd. *Histoire générale de Metz*, t. 3, Metz 1775, preuves, pp. 71-73 (Artem 212). Acte de Nouaillé pour Thetaldus le 21 juin 961 ou 964, éd. P. de Monsabert, *Les chartes de l'abbaye de Nouaillé* (n. 14), n° 64, pp. 107-109 (Artem 1127).

25. Richard Sharpe, *Vocabulary* (n. 13), dit justement p. 94 qu'au cours des IXe-XIe siècles rares furent les créations de mots. L'utilisation même des mots anciens ne doit pas être jugée trop vite. C'est à tort, par exemple, que Joseph Avril, "La fonction épiscopale dans le vocabulaire des chartes (Xe-XIIIe siècles) *Horizons marins, itinéraires spirituels (Ve-XVIIIe siècles)*, t. 1: *Mentalités et sociétés*, éd. Henri Dubois et al., Paris 1987, pp. 125-133, à la p. 130, pense que c'est au cours de la seconde moitié du XIIe siècle que les évêques parlent de leur *administratio*: on en a des exemples dès le XIe, le premier dans une charte de l'évêque de Cambrai Liébert pour l'abbaye Saint-Aubert de Cambrai, en 1057 (Le Glay, *Glossaire topographique de l'ancien Cambrésis*, Cambrai 1849, p. 8; Artem 376).

26. Sur 204 actes concernés, on en compte vingt-quatre jusque 1000, 180 après, soit respectivement 11,27 et 88,72 %, alors qu'on compte 25,19 et 74,80 % des actes avant et après l'an mil.

27. Une exception dans une charte douteuse de l'évêque de Metz Adalbéron Ier pour St-Arnoul de Metz, datée de 944, éd. *Gallia Christiana*, t. 13, 2e éd., Paris 1874, col. 387-389 (Artem 304).

28. Charte d'Isarn, évêque de Toulouse, pour le chapitre cathédral de cette ville, datable d'environ 1073 (Devic et Vaissette, *Histoire du Languedoc*, t. 5, Toulouse 1875, pp. 626-631).

29. La date est proposée par P. Gautier, *Catalogue des actes des évêques de Langres du VIIe siècle à 1136*, th. Ec. Chartes, t. 3, pr., n° 3, pp. 126-127 (Artem 170).

30. Il est attesté dans 190 actes sur 4798, soit 3,9 %, mais dans trente-deux actes sur 259 entre 901 et 950, soixante-deux actes sur 447 entre 951 et 1000 et cinquante-trois actes sur 653 entre 1001 et 1050, soit respectivement 12,3, 13,8 et 8,1%.

Il y a dans ce texte deux éléments rares. L'expression *Christum colentibus* n'apparaît que deux autres fois, mais ses attestations sont dispersés en 916 et 1092.[31] Le mot *onoma* apparaît quatre fois au total depuis cette charte jusque 1024 ou 1026;[32] il est d'ailleurs inconnu dans les chartes "belges".[33]

A l'inverse, des mots comme *obitus, clarissimi, facinus, implorare, indominicatum, mancipia, anniversarius, perversus, carta* sont extrêmement fréquents bien avant et bien après la période considérée. Enfin, il y a dans ce texte deux *hapax*, deux mots qu'on ne trouve pas ailleurs dans la base de l'Artem: le verbe *superare*, le substantif *abscessus*. *Superare* ne se trouve que sept fois dans les chartes "belges" antérieures à 1200, mais sa première attestation est tardive: 1088.[34] Cependant, l'intensité de l'utilisation du mot dans d'autres sources interdit de tirer quelque avantage que ce soit de cette constatation.[35] Même s'il est plus rarement utilisé dans les autres sources, le mot *abscessus* n'est pas inconnu: on le trouve notamment dans deux actes "belges".[36] C'est tout simplement une manière plus littéraire de désigner l'*obitus*.

Que tirer comme conclusion de tout cela? Que notre acte doit dater de la période au cours de laquelle les rédacteurs de chartes se sont sentis les plus libres de forger un nouveau vocabulaire, ou de se constituer un lexique à partir de sources très diverses. En clair, les Xe et XIe siècles.[37] Cela reste évidemment très vague: nous

---

31. Diplôme de Charles le Simple du 7 juin 916 pour Attigny (*Recueil des actes de Charles III le Simple, roi de France*, éd. Philippe Lauer, t. 1, Paris 1940, n° 86, pp. 192–196; Artem 2048) et charte de Gérard II évêque de Cambrai pour Anchin en 1092 (Arch. dép. Nord, 1 H 34/380 (Artem 420). Elle est attestée dans les chartes "belges" à partir de 1016 (charte d'Helecinus, prévôt du chapitre de Saint-Omer, éd. B.-M. Tock, *Les mutations* (n. 1), pp. 147–148).

32. Charte d'Eudes, abbé de Saint-Mihiel, pour Etienne et Gui en 972 (André Lesort, *Chronique et chartes de l'abbaye de Saint-Mihiel*, Paris 1909–1912, n° 30, pp. 130–132; Artem 108): *onomata autem qui hec viderunt monachi*. Charte d'Arnoul, archevêque de Tours, pour l'abbaye St-Julien de Tours, le 26 octobre 1024 (L.-J. Denis, *Chartes de Saint-Julien de Tours (1002–1227)*, Le Mans 1912, n° 10, pp. 15–17; Artem 1566): *miles ... Vualterius onomate dictus*. Charte de Richard II, duc de Normandie, pour l'abbaye Saint-Ouen de Rouen, datable de 1015–1026 (Marie Fauroux, *Recueil des actes des ducs de Normandie (911–1066)*, Caen 1961, n° 42, pp. 146–148; Artem 2679): *Inenarrabili onomate summae Trinitatis...*

33. Quelques autres cas évoqués par le *Novum glossarium latinitatis medii aevi ab anno DCCC usque ad annum MCC*, t. 2, col. 496, qui connaît la plupart des attestations citées ici. Le mot se trouve trente-six fois dans le *Cetedoc Library of Christian Latin Texts*, dont vingt-et-une fois dans des textes médiévaux (toujours grammaticaux) et quinze fois dans des textes patristiques (souvent grammaticaux, mais aussi Augustin et Jérôme): aucune de ces occurrences ne désigne un nom propre.

34. Charte de Reine, fille du comte Conon, pour l'abbaye de Marcigny, éd. Jean Richard, *Le cartulaire de Marcigny-sur-Loire (1045–1144). Essai de reconstitution d'un manuscrit perdu*, Dijon 1957, n° 30bis, pp. 26–28.

35. Le terme se trouve 4140 fois dans la *Cetedoc Library of Christian Latin Texts*.

36. Charte de Bernard, abbé d'Echternach, du 8 octobre 789, éd. Camille Wampach, *Geschichte der Grundherrschaft Echternach im Frühmittelalter*, t. 1–2, Luxembourg 1930, n° 98, pp. 164–166. Lettre du chapitre cathédral de Liège à son homologue d'Utrecht, datable de 1102–1112, éd. Fz. S. Muller et A. C. Bouman, *Oorkondenboek van het sticht Utrecht tot 1301*, t. 1, Utrecht – La Haye 1920, n° 265, pp. 243–247.

37. Olivier Guyotjeannin, 'Penuria scriptorum. Le mythe de l'anarchie documentaire dans le France du Nord (Xe – première moitié du XIe siècle)', *Bibliothèque de l'Ecole des Chartes* 155 (1997): pp. 11–44. Dans le même volume, voir aussi Michel Zimmermann, 'Langue et lexicographie: l'apport des actes catalans', pp. 185–205.

aboutissons donc à un constat d'échec. Et c'est en fait sur des critères paléographiques que l'on peut attribuer l'acte, sans certitude d'ailleurs, au début du Xe siècle.

Le deuxième acte que l'on va étudier de près est une donation, au profit du chapitre cathédral de Clermont (aujourd'hui Clermont-Ferrand, en Auvergne), due à un certain Etienne de *Randoano*, et dans un premier temps datée, très largement, de 901–1000.[38] Plusieurs mots ont fait l'objet d'une recherche. Ainsi *capellanos*, qui est doublement suspect. Car *capellanus*, s'il est utilisé dès le VIIIe s., désigne d'abord et pendant longtemps les seuls chapelains royaux ou impériaux, qui ne sont pas en cause ici.[39] On trouve bien deux mentions hors cadre royal dans les années 960, mais dans deux actes douteux.[40] Ce n'est qu'au début du XIe siècle qu'il y a des mentions sûres, mais elles s'appliquent à un chapelain princier ou épiscopal.[41] Il faut attendre 1041 pour trouver mention de plusieurs chapelains, en l'occurrence ceux de l'archevêque de Besançon Hugues de Salins,[42] et 1035–1045 pour trouver des *capellani* attachés à un lieu de culte, comme c'est le cas dans notre acte clermontois.[43]

Un autre problème vient de l'utilisation, à plusieurs reprises, du mot *fevum*, "fief". L'histoire de ce mot a déjà fait couler beaucoup d'encre, et on ne peut reprendre le problème entièrement ici. Evitant un peu lâchement le débat sur le sens du mot et son évolution, mais qui ne nous concerne pas, on rappellera simplement qu'il est généralement admis que ce mot, bien que d'un usage oral sans doute beaucoup plus ancien, n'apparaît dans les textes, quelques rares exceptions mises à part, que dans la seconde moitié du Xe siècle.[44] Or la base de données de

---

38. Arch. dép. du Puy-de-Dôme, 3 G armoire 18 sac A n° 7 (Artem 3695).

39. Mais ce terme nous permet d'insister sur la complémentarité des bases de données et sur les différences entre les types de textes: le *Cetedoc Index of Latin Forms*, à partir de sources essentiellement théologiques et spirituelles, ne renseigne ce mot qu'à partir du IXe siècle (Rathier de Vérone).

40. Actes de Roricon, évêque de Laon, pour l'abbaye Saint-Vincent de Laon, daté du 1er octobre 961, éd. René Poupardin, "Cartulaire de Saint-Vincent de Laon. Analyses et pièces inédites" *Mémoires de la société de l'histoire de Paris* 29 (1902): pp. 173–267, au n° 6, pp. 22–23 (Artem 741) et d'une certaine *Gostrudis* pour le chapitre cathédral de Langres le 18 janvier 969 (Arch. dép. Haute-Marne, 2 G 1166/18; Artem 162).

41. Acte de Raoul, comte de Bayeux, pour l'abbaye Saint-Ouen de Rouen, du 15 septembre 1011, arch. dép. Seine-Maritime, 14 H 917 A (voir Marie Fauroux, 'Deux autographes de Dudon de Saint-Quentin (1011, 1015)', *Bibliothèque de l'Ecole des Chartes* 111 (1953): pp. 229–234 (Artem 2665): le chapelain en question est le célèbre Dudon de Saint-Quentin. Notice d'un accord entre Francon, évêque de Paris (1020–1030), et Eudes II, comte de Champagne (996–1037), éd. Benjamin Guérard, *Cartulaire de l'église Notre-Dame de Paris*, t. 1, Paris 1850, p. 325 (Artem 2070). Acte de Thibaud comte de Blois pour l'abbaye de Toussaints-en-l'Ile de Châlons, le 13 décembre 1075 (Artem 82).

42. Dans une charte pour l'abbaye de Murbach du 6 novembre 1041: voir Bernard de Vrégille, *Hugues de Salins, archevêque de Besançon, 1031–1066*, 3 vol., Lille, s. d., au t. 3, n° 17, pp. 49*–53* (Artem 547).

43. Acte d'un comte Isembard pour l'abbaye de Montier-en-Der, arch. dép. Haute-Marne, 7 H 25 (Artem 189).

44. K. J. Hollyman, *Le développement du vocabulaire féodal en France pendant le haut moyen âge*, Paris 1957. Elisabeth Magnou-Nortier, 'Note sur le sens du mot fevum en Septimanie et dans la marche d'Espagne à la fin du Xe et au début du XIe siècle', *Annales du Midi* 76 (1964): pp. 141–152. Jean-Pierre Poly, 'Vocabulaire "féodo-vassalique" et aires de culture durant le Haut Moyen Age', *La lexicographie du latin médiéval et ses rapports avec les recherches actuelles sur la civilisation du*

(voir la page suivante)

l'Artem, qui se limite, rappelons-le, aux actes originaux, est formelle: on ne trouve qu'une seule attestation antérieure à 1000, et cela sous la forme *feuz*.[45] La forme *fevum*, attestée dans 211 actes, l'est pour la première fois le 7 novembre 1007 dans un acte du comte de Palhars pour l'abbaye de La Grasse.[46] Ce qui signifie que presque toutes les attestations des IXe et Xe siècles déjà relevées pour la France se trouvent dans des copies. La netteté du phénomène oblige donc à se demander si l'utilisation de ce mot dans des actes des IXe-Xe siècles n'est pas due plus à des copistes postérieurs. Dans l'état actuel des choses, ce n'est cependant là qu'une hypothèse.

On pourrait dire la même chose de la *sextariata*, la sétariée de terre, pour laquelle on ne trouve aucune attestation du Xe siècle dans le corpus des chartes originales.[47] Mais ici, il faut reconnaître que le mot est de toute façon rare: notre conclusion n'est donc peut-être pas catégorique, d'autant qu'ici aussi on trouve par ailleurs d'autres attestations anciennes.[48] On profitera de cet exemple pour revenir sur la diversité des graphies, déjà évoquée ci-dessus, puisque notre acte d'Etienne de Randoano, à lui seul, reprend quatre graphies différentes du mot: *sectoriada*, *sesteriadda*, *sisteirada*, *sisteriadda*, ce qui décourage toute envie de chercher à dater un acte d'après la graphie des mots. *Civada*, un mot méridional désignant l'orge ou l'avoine, n'apparaît qu'à partir d'un acte du 13 avril 1017, si l'on excepte deux actes difficilement datables et attribués, peut-être un peu rapidement, au Xe siècle.[49]

Et puis, il y a un argument qui peut paraître plus étonnant. Il est question de chapelains qui chantent. Si évidemment le chant liturgique existe au Xe siècle, et depuis longtemps, il n'est guère mentionné dans les chartes: on en trouve une attestation en 862, et la suivante date de 991.[50] C'est surtout à partir du deuxième tiers du XIe que les mentions se multiplient, jusqu'à ce qu'à la fin du siècle un

---

(*suite de la page précédante*)
Moyen Age, Paris 1981, pp. 167–190. François-Louis Ganshof, *Qu'est-ce que la féodalité?*, 5e éd., Paris 1982, pp. 168–177. Susan Reynolds, *Fiefs and Vassals. The Medieval Evidence Reinterpreted*, Oxford 1994, pp. 160–163.

45. Echange entre Blidegarius et Auricius, dans la région de Nîmes, le 9 juin 956, avec la phrase *et ad Bernardum cuius erat feuz* (éd. Alexandre Teulet, *Layettes du Trésor des Chartes*, t. 1, Paris 1863, n° 12, pp. 14–15; Artem 2761). On a cherché aux formes *fedium*, *feodum*, *fevum*, *feovum*, *feu*, *feuz*, *feveium*, *pheodum*, *pheu*.

46. Ed. Elisabeth Magnou-Nortier et Anne-Marie Magnou, *Recueil des chartes de l'abbaye de La Grasse*, t. 1, Paris 1996, n° 91, pp. 140–141.

47. La plus ancienne attestation se trouve dans une charte, clermontoise elle aussi, datable de 1017–1021, éd. Emmanuel et Henry Chardon du Ranquet, *L'église Notre-Dame du Port de Clermont-Ferrand*, Clermont-Ferrand 1932, pp. 18–19.

48. Voir Charles Du Cange, *Glossarium mediae et infimae latinitatis*, éd. L. Favre, t. 7, Niort 1886, p. 463, *s. v. sextarata*. Jan F. Niermeyer, *Mediae latinitatis lexicon minus*, Leyde, 1986, p. 968, *s. v. sextariata*.

49. Acte de 1017: donation d'Elie au chapitre de Clermont (arch. dép. Puy-de-Dôme, 3 G arm. 18 sac A n° 13; Artem 3700. Les deux autres actes sont une donation de Durand Raimond pour l'abbaye de Moissac (Arch. dép. Tarn-et-Garonne, G 570; Artem 4579) et une concession de biens du chapitre de Clermont à Robert de Mercoriolo (arch. dép. Puy-de-Dôme, 3 G arm. 18 sac A n° 10; Artem 4738).

50. On ne tient pas compte ici des mentions de *cantor* isolé.

prêtre desservant une église paroissiale puisse être appelé le *presbiter cantaturus*.[51]

Si les arguments de la *civada* et de la *sextariata* ne paraissent pas déterminants, à cause du faible nombre d'occurrences concernées, il n'en va pas de même de *capellanus*, de *cantare*, voire même de *fevum*, qui permettent de replacer la date de notre acte au plus tôt au début du deuxième tiers du XIe siècle.

4. Conclusion

Le bilan que l'on peut tirer de cette étude est évidemment mitigé. Disons en peu de mots que c'est essentiellement d'un vocabulaire plutôt concret, attaché à des réalités institutionnelles, juridiques, économiques ou sociales que l'on peut attendre une aide pour dater un document; encore cette datation restera-t-elle approximative. Toutefois, l'historien doit se méfier, et rester attentif: il peut avoir des surprises, comme on l'a vu plus haut, par exemple avec *cantare*. En revanche l'étude du vocabulaire grâce aux bases de données permet de mieux connaître l'évolution des réalités ainsi attestées.

Peut-on espérer qu'en transposant à l'étude des mots la méthode développée par le professeur Gervers pour les formules, c'est-à-dire en évaluant la période de plus grande fréquence de chacun des mots d'un acte, on puisse aboutir à une estimation plus ou moins fiable? Je ne le pense pas, parce que là où l'étude des formules permet d'englober toutes les expressions parvenues jusqu'à nos jours, l'étude des mots compris dans des textes diplomatiques ne permettra jamais que d'atteindre le vocabulaire utilisé par, et non le vocabulaire connu des rédacteurs médiévaux.

---

51. Diplôme de Charles le Chauve du 19 septembre 862 pour l'abbaye de Saint-Denis (éd. *Recueil des actes de Charles le Chauve*, éd. Georges Tessier, t. 2, Paris 1952, n° 247, pp. 56–57; Artem 3019); acte d'Eudes, *levita, scole cantorum magister* pour l'évêque du Puy le 19 juillet 991 (Bibl. nat. de France, n. a. l. 2184/63; Artem 2580); acte de Gigo pour l'abbaye de Psalmodi, premier tiers du XIe siècle (Arch. dép. Gard, H 116; Artem 994); acte de Mainard, évêque de Troyes, pour l'abbaye de Montier-en-Der en 1035 (Arch. dép. Haute-Marne, 7 H 25; Artem 167); acte douteux de Thierry, évêque de Verdun, pour la Ste-Madeleine de Verdun, 1047 (Jean-Pol Evrard, *Les actes des évêques de Verdun des origines à 1107*, Nancy 1977, n° 54, p. 109–111; Artem 111); acte d'Elie pour le chapitre cathédral de Clermont datable de 1031–1052 (Arch. dép. Puy-de-Dôme, 3 G arm. 9 sac J n° 2; Artem 3686).

5. Annexe: documents étudiés

5.1 Premier tiers du Xe siècle

Jarimbertus *donne différents biens au chapitre cathédral de Langres.*

A. Original sur parchemin, Chaumont, Arch. dép. Haute-Marne, 2 G 662.

Indiqué: Artem 170.

/01/ (*Chismon*) In nomine domini Jhesu Christi. Ego igitur Jarinbertus, levita indignus, materque mea /02/ Gottelendis, notum volumus fore omnibus Christi colentibus, nostris propriis parentibus propensius, /03/ qualiter concedimus, post obitum nostrum[a], vobis clarissimis fratribus ecclesie Lingonensium filiis, tam vobis quam et /04/ successoribus vestris, pro nostris facinoribus; et ut post abscessum nostrum domini misericordiam devotius /05/ et acceptabilius libeat vel placeat implorare, res quas jure possidere videmur, videlicet: /06/ in pago Lingonico et in loco quem Catennacum dicunt, mansum indominicatum aliaque mansa /07/ bene constructa VIIII, assa vero VII, cum omnibus illorum aspicienbus[b] mancipia quoque /08/ inibi degentia quorum hec sunt onomata Arnaldum, Amalricum, Eldierium cum uxore /09/ sua et infantibus III, Ariaudum, Lanbertum cum libero I. Denique pratum indominicatum /10/ et alia necnon et sylvam et quicquid ad supradicta mansa legaliter aspicere cernitur /11/ cum omnibus pretaxatis mancipiis et supradictis rebus quas jure ereditario videmur possidere /12/ in futurum vobis tradimus et conferimus possidendas ea dumtaxat conditione ut dies obitus /13/ nostri et Arnaldi ex quo omnia remanserunt anniversarius nobis exinde preparetur et a vobis vestrisque suc-/14/-cessoribus memoria nostri decentius atque congruentius celebretur. Si quis vero, quod ac-/15/-cidere non credimus, si nos ipsi aut ullus heredum nostrorum vel quislibet futurus perversus /16/ mutare vel minuere seu inpedire cessionem nostram tenptaverit, non valeat superare /17/ quod requerit sed jure convictus et judito legali superatus, auri libras V persolvat, /18/ posteaque presens largitio in perpetuum firma et stabilis permaneat stipulatione subnixa. /19/ Ego Jarinbertus, levita indignus, hanc chartam facere libenter rogavi /20/ et firmavi. /21/ Signum Gotthelendis.

a) *post obitum en interligne, de la même écriture.*
b) *sic A.*

5.2 XIe siècle

Etienne de Randoano *donne aux chapellains de l'église Notre-Dame de Clermont divers manses, champs, jardins, prés, terres, vignes, et des redevances en vin et avoine.*

A. Original sur parchemin, Clermont-Ferrand, Arch. dép. Puy-de-Dôme, 3 G armoire 18, sac A, n° 7.

Indiqué. M. Cohendy, *Inventaire de toutes les chartes antérieures au XIIIe siècle qui se trouvent dans les différents fonds d'archives du dépôt de la Préfecture du Puy-de-Dôme*, Clermont-Ferrand 1855, 14–15. – Artem 3695.

/01/ Breve memoratorio Stephano de Randoano. /02/ In primis pro redemptione anime meae, dimit-/03/-to ad sacrificium quarta parte de uno manso /04/ qui fuit Sanctae Mariae, campos et vineas et pratos /05/ cum agro et curto et orto totum et ab integrum /06/ in villa Jusaraddo, ad illos presbiteros capellanos /07/ que ad altare Sanctæ Mariae sedis cantent. /08/ Et dimito Sancta Maria in communia ad sepultura /09/ uno manso in Jusaraddo Fabrenco et in ipsa villa /10/ uno furno cum apendaria et olca et in ipsa villa /11/ fevo Arnulfo uno campo de sesteriaddas III et /12/ cortilio et orto, et ipsa villa Jusarad /13/ alio maso qui fuit Johan Montiso cum to-/14/-to capmasio et in tale conventu hubi mors /15/ me advenerit, in calecumque loco ut Sanctae Marie /16/ in communia remaneat. Et dimito alio manso Sancta /17/ Maria a Pontelio totum et ab integrum et I apenda-/18/-ria a la Font Adreiag, ad Otazag pratos del /19/ fevo Guido sectoriadas V et alia terra sisteriaddas IIII /20/ quem Johannes habet, et dimitto fevo Aimenrico cum filio suo clero /21/ cum XIIcim sesteriaddas de terra. /22/ Et dimitto ad meo formimento fevo Bernardo /23/ de Iciago, in Cuciago solidos IIII de gardas et de /24/ terra sisteriaddas III in Jusaraddo, et vinea I, et in Aizio /25/ Ademaro simodio de vino et emina de civadda, /26/ in Sedoc et in ipso loco sisteriada I de terra /27/ et in Ischenio dimedio maso, que Puncte eo teniat /28/ totum et ab integrum et in Cornol dimedio maso to-/29/-tum et ab integrum, et in Cabannas una apendaria /30/ ab quantum respicit, et in Latfolio dinerios VI, /31/ et in Cornol maso I totum excepto illa terra que donavit /32/ Sancti Petri et Sancti Juliani et hoc sunt X sisteriadas. /33/ Propter visitationem ad lignum domini dono de terra sisteiradas IIII /34/ in Jusarad, in Otazag sisteriadas IIII de terra Arbertenea, /35/ et dimito fevo Asterio de solicias apendarias V decoren /36/ in ipso conventum fevo Giraldo Adrebaldo totum et ab integrum. /37/ Sed donacio facta firma omnique tempore permaneat et si homo est /38/ qui ullam calomniam movere voluerit, ira Dei omnipotentis super illos /39/ incurrat. S. Petrono. S. Aimoino. S. Bertranno. S. Johan. /40/ S. Neviono.

Bibliographie

Avril, Joseph. 1987. 'La fonction épiscopale dans le vocabulaire des chartes (Xe–XIIIe siècles)', in *Horizons marins, itinéraires spirituels (Ve–XVIIIe siècles)*, t. 1: *Mentalités et sociétés*, ed. Henri Dubois et al., pp. 125–133. Paris.
Barthélemy, Dominique. 1993. *La société dans le comté de Vendôme de l'an mil au XIVe siècle*. Paris.
Bláhová, Marie. 1995. 'Bischöfliche Beamte als Geschichtsschreiber im Ostmitteleuropa des frühen und hohen Mittelalters', in *Die Diplomatik der Bischofsurkunde vor 1250 [Actes colloque Innsbruck, 1993]*, ed. Christoph Haidacher and Werner Köfler, pp. 187–95. Innsbruck.
Boussard, Jacques. 1972. 'Actes royaux et pontificaux de Saint-Maur-des-Fossés.' *Journal des savants*: pp. 81–113.
Caspar, Erich. 1920–23. *Das Register Gregors VII*. 2 vols. Berlin.
Cetedoc Index of Latin Forms. 1999. Turnhout. (CD-Rom.)
Cetedoc Library of Christian Latin Texts. 1997. Version 3. Turnhout. (CD-Rom.)
Chardon du Ranquet, Emmanuel, and Henry Chardon du Ranquet. 1932. *L'église Notre-Dame du Port de Clermont-Ferrand*. Clermont-Ferrand.
Cohendy, M. 1855. *Inventaire de toutes les chartes antérieures au XIIIe siècle qui se trouvent dans les différents fonds d'archives du dépôt de la Préfecture du Puy-de-Dôme*. Clermont-Ferrand.
Conradi I., Heinrici I. et Ottonis I. Diplomata. 1879–84. Vol. 1. Hanover. (*MGH. Diplomata regum et imperatorum Germaniae.*)
Denis, L.-J. 1912. *Chartes de Saint-Julien de Tours (1002–1227)*. Le Mans.
Devic et Vaissette. 1875. *Histoire du Languedoc*. Vol. 5. Toulouse.
Du Cange, Charles. 1886. *Glossarium mediae et infimae latinitatis*, ed. L. Favre. Vol. 7. Niort.
Estienne, Joseph. 1929. 'Chartes de saint Geoffroi évêque d'Amiens (1105–12).' *Bibliothèque de l'Ecole des Chartes* 90: pp. 37–50.
Evrard, Jean-Pol. 1977. *Les actes des évêques de Verdun des origines à 1107*. Nancy.
Falkowski, Rudolf. 1971. 'Studien zur Sprache der Merowingerdiplome.' *Archiv für Diplomatik* 17: pp. 1–125.
Fauroux, Marie. 1953. 'Deux autographes de Dudon de Saint-Quentin (1011, 1015).' *Bibliothèque de l'Ecole des Chartes* 111: pp. 229–34.
———. 1963. *Recueil des actes des ducs de Normandie (911–1066)*. Caen.
Gallia Christiana. 1874. Vol. 1. 2nd ed. Paris.
Ganshof, François-Louis. 1982. *Qu'est-ce que la féodalité?* 5th ed. Paris.
Gautier, P. n. d. *Catalogue des actes des évêques de Langres du VIIe siècle à 1136*. th. Ec. Chartes.
Gössi, Anton. 1974. *Das Urkundenwesen der Bischöfe von Basel im 13. Jhdt (1216–1274)*. Bâle.
Guérard, Benjamin. 1850. *Cartulaire de l'église Notre-Dame de Paris*. Vol. 1. Paris.
Guyotjeannin, Olivier. 1981. 'Noyonnais et Vermandois aux Xe et XIe siècles: la déclaration du trésorier Guy et les premières confirmations royales et pontificales des biens du chapitre cathédral de Noyon.' *Bibliothèque de l'Ecole des Chartes* 139: pp. 143–89.
———. 1997. 'Penuria scriptorum. Le mythe de l'anarchie documentaire dans le France du Nord (Xe – première moitié du XIe siècle).' *Bibliothèque de l'Ecole des Chartes* 155: pp. 11–44.
Hartmann, Wilfried. 1998. *Die Konzilien der karolingischen Teilreiche, 860–874*. Hanover.
Histoire générale de Metz. 1775. Vol. 3. Metz.

Hollyman, K. J. 1957. *Le développement du vocabulaire féodal en France pendant le haut moyen âge*, pp. 168–77. Paris.
Huyghebaert, Nicolas. 1962. 'Hugo Tornecensis ecclesiae cancellarius. Examen critique de la charte de fondation de l'abbaye de Phalempin (1039).' *Bulletin de la commission royale d'histoire* 128: pp. 183–273.
Krusch, Bruno, and Walter Levison. 1910. *Passiones Vitaeque sanctorum aevi merovingici*. Hanover–Leipzig. (*MGH. Scriptores rerum merovingicarum*, 5.)
Lasteyrie, R. de. 1887. *Cartulaire général de Paris*. Vol. 1. Paris.
Le Glay. 1849. *Glossaire topographique de l'ancien Cambrésis*. Cambrai.
Lesort, André. 1909–12. *Chronique et chartes de l'abbaye de Saint-Mihiel*. Paris.
Lewis, M. J. T. 1994. 'The Origins of the Wheelbarrow.' *Technology and Culture* 35: pp. 453–75.
Magnou-Nortier, Elisabeth. 1964. 'Note sur le sens du mot fevum en Septimanie et dans la marche d'Espagne à la fin du Xe et au début du XIe siècle.' *Annales du Midi* 76: pp. 141–52.
Magnou-Nortier, Elisabeth, and Anne-Marie Magnou. 1996. *Recueil des chartes de l'abbaye de La Grasse*. Vol. 1. Paris.
Métais, Charles. 1889–91. *Marmoutier. Cartulaire Blésois*. Blois.
Monsabert, P. de. 1936. *Chartes de l'abbaye de Nouaillé de 678 à 1200*. Poitiers (Archives historiques du Poitou, 49).
Muller, Fz. S., and A. C. Bouman. 1920. *Oorkondenboek van het sticht Utrecht tot 1301*. Vol. 1. Utrecht–La Haye.
Niermeyer, Jan F. 1986. *Mediae latinitatis lexicon minus*. Leyde.
Novum glossarium mediae latinitatis ab anno DCCC usque ad annum MCC. 1957. Vol. 1. Copenhagen.
Parisse, Michel. 1981. 'A propos du traitement automatique des chartes: chronologie du vocabulaire et repérage des actes suspects', in *La lexicographie du latin médiéval et ses rapports avec les recherches actuelles sur la civilisation du Moyen Age*, pp. 241–49. Paris.
———. 1984. 'Inventaire des actes originaux du Haut Moyen Age conservés en France: un premier bilan.' *Académie des Inscriptions et Belles-Lettres. Comptes-rendus des séances*: pp. 352–69.
———. 1983. 'Un scribe champenois du XIIe siècle et l'évolution de son écriture.' *Archiv für Diplomatik* 29: pp. 229–41.
Poly, Jean-Pierre. 1981. 'Vocabulaire "féodo-vassalique" et aires de culture durant le Haut Moyen Age', in *La lexicographie du latin médiéval et ses rapports avec les recherches actuelles sur la civilisation du Moyen Age*, pp. 167–90. Paris.
Poupardin, René. 1902. 'Cartulaire de Saint-Vincent de Laon. Analyses et pièces inédites.' *Mémoires de la société de l'histoire de Paris* 29: pp. 173–267.
Prou, Maurice. 1913. 'Le transfert de l'abbaye de Saint-Remy de Sens à Vareilles.' *Bulletin de la société archéologique de Sens* 28: pp. 254–321.
Recueil des actes de Charles le Chauve, ed. Georges Tessier. 1952. Vol. 2. Paris.
Recueil des actes de Charles III le Simple, roi de France, ed. Philippe Lauer. 1940. Vol. 1. Paris.
Recueil des actes de Louis VI, roi de France (1108–1137), ed. Jean Dufour. 1994. Vol. 4. Paris.
Rédet. 1848–52. *Documents pour servir à l'histoire de l'église de Saint-Hilaire de Poitiers*. 2 vols. Poitiers.
Reynolds, Susan. 1994. *Fiefs and Vassals. The Medieval Evidence Reinterpreted*. Oxford.

Richard, Jean. 1957. *Le cartulaire de Marcigny-sur-Loire (1045–1144). Essai de reconstitution d'un manuscrit perdu.* Dijon.

Rück, Peter. 1966. *Die Urkunden der Bischöfe von Basel bis 1213.* Bâle.

Sharpe, Richard. 1996. 'Vocabulary, Word formation and Lexicography', in *Medieval Latin. An Introduction and Bibliographical Guide*, ed. F. A. C. Mantello and A. G. Rigg, pp. 93–105. Washington.

Teulet, Alexandre. 1863. *Layettes du Trésor des Chartes.* Paris.

Thesaurus Diplomaticus. 1998. Turnhout (CD-Rom.)

Tock, Benoît-Michel. 1998. 'Altare dans les chartes françaises antérieures à 1121', in *Roma, Magistra Mundi. Itineraria culturae medievalis. Mélanges offerts au Père L. E. Boyle à l'occasion de son 75e anniversaire*, ed. J. Hamesse, vol. 2, pp. 901–26. Louvain-la-Neuve.

———. 1997. 'Les mutations du vocabulaire latin des chartes au XIe siècle.' *Bibliothèque de l'Ecole des Chartes* 155: pp. 119–48.

Vrégille, Bernard de. n. d. *Hugues de Salins, archevêque de Besançon, 1031–1066.* 3 vols. Lille.

Wampach, Camille. 1930. *Geschichte der Grundherrschaft Echternach im Frühmittelalter.* Vols. 1–2. Luxembourg.

Zeumer, Karl. 1886. *Formulae Merowingici et Karolini aevi.* Hanover.

Zimmermann, Michel. 1997. 'Langue et lexicographie: l'apport des actes catalans.' *Bibliothèque de l'Ecole des Chartes* 155: pp. 185–205.

THE CHARTERS OF KING HENRY II: THE INTRODUCTION OF THE ROYAL *INSPEXIMUS* REVISITED

Nicholas Vincent

It is hardly surprising that in his search for datable linguistic formulae in undated English charters, Michael Gervers, like Sir Frank Stenton before him, has drawn attention to the all-pervasive influence of the royal chancery.[1] This is not to say that every innovation in the wording of charters was first devised by the king or his officials. Nonetheless, since the terminology of private charters marched a step behind, but always in dogged attendance upon the terminology and processes of the law, and since, by the late twelfth century, it was royal law that dominated most forms of property transaction, it was the king and his courts who did most both to inspire and to police the evolution of new forms in the phrasing of private charters. To this extent, an understanding of the forms and phraseology of the King's own charters is fundamental to any search for the evolution of forms and phrases outside the royal chancery. In the present paper, I hope to show, with reference to the charters of King Henry II (1154–89), how the study of one particular turn of phrase, later to develop into the instrument known as the royal *inspeximus*, might assist us in understanding quite how perilous it may be to rely upon phraseology as a criterion for dating. My discussion here will be founded very firmly upon the work of two previous scholars: the Frenchman Léopold Delisle and the Englishman Vivian Galbraith. Between them, Delisle and Galbraith set a standard for the precise study of the language of twelfth-century charters that has seldom been bettered. There is still much to be learned about the linguistic developments of Henry II's chancery. Nonetheless, as an indication of the lines for future enquiry, and as an introduction to the perils and pitfalls of editing royal charters, I hope that the present enquiry may be of some use, even to those whose work lies far distant from twelfth-century England or the Plantagenet court.

As always with the charters of Henry II, our starting point must be the massive enterprise of Léopold Delisle. From his days as an aspiring *chartiste* in the 1840s, through to the year of his death in 1910, in advanced old age, Delisle sought to assemble a complete collection of those of King Henry II's charters that concerned the King's dominion in France. The results of this enquiry began to appear only shortly before Delisle's death, but by 1910 he had published half-a-dozen articles on the subject and the first introductory volume of what he intended to be

---

From *Dating Undated Medieval Charters*. Ed. Michael Gervers. Copyright (by the Editor and Contributors 2000). Published by the Boydell Press (in association with Collegium Budapest), PO Box 9, Woodbridge, Suffolk, IP12 3DF, Great Britain. ISBN 0 85115 792 0.

1. M. Gervers, 'The Dating of Medieval English Private Charters of the Twelfth and Thirteenth Centuries', in *A Distinct Voice: Medieval Studies in Honor of Leonard E. Boyle, O.P.*, ed. J. Brown and W. P. Stoneman, Notre Dame, pp. 455–56, citing Stenton.

a complete edition of texts, together with an *Atlas* of photographic facsimiles of originals.[2] The edition itself was completed posthumously, in a further three volumes edited by Delisle's pupil, Elie Berger.[3] In all, Delisle and Berger published more than 800 texts of Henry II. Their edition, and in particular Delisle's *Introduction*, remains fundamental to our understanding of the Plantagenet chancery. For the purposes of the present discussion, the most dramatic and rightly famous of Delisle's discoveries concerned the use of the formula *Dei gratia* in the King's title, *Henricus Dei gratia rex Anglorum*.[4] Previously regarded as a haphazard element of chancery phrasing, the *Dei gratia* formula was shown by Delisle to have been introduced at a fairly specific point, midway in the King's reign, at some time in 1172 or 1173. Until Delisle's enquiry many charters of Henry II had proved impossible to date save within the very broadest of perimeters. Delisle's discovery changed all this, suggesting that the presence or absence of *Dei gratia* could be used to determine whether a charter dated from the first or the second half of Henry's reign, from 1154 to 1173, or from 1172 to 1189.

Delisle's claims did not go unchallenged, especially since, to begin with, taken aback by the brilliance of his own discovery, he himself was tempted to exaggerate its infallibility. John Horace Round, whose attitude to the Ecole des Chartes and to all things French had soured considerably as a result of his own researches in the Norman archives, poured scorn upon Delisle's new theory.[5] With his customary mixture of precision and brutality, Round pointed to a number of flaws in Delisle's initial report, and in particular, questioned whether charters that survived only in cartulary or later copies, as opposed to originals, could be dated according to their inclusion or omission of *Dei gratia*. All too frequently, as Round showed in example after cruel example, a later copyist might introduce the *Dei gratia* formula, imposing the most recent practices of the English royal chancery upon documents which in their original state clearly belonged to the years before 1172–73. The criticism here was a serious one, and Delisle was forced to take account of it in the more detailed treatment of *Dei gratia* which he contributed to his *Introduction* of 1909.[6] Nonetheless, and despite various later challenges and qualifications, in particular with respect to cartulary copies and to originals produced

---

2. L. Delisle, *Recueil des Actes de Henri II roi d'Angleterre et duc de Normandie concernant les provinces françaises et les affaires de France: Introduction* (henceforth Delisle, *Introduction*) and *Atlas* of facsimiles (Paris, 1909) (henceforth Delisle, *Atlas*). Articles in the *Bibliothèque de l'Ecoles des Chartes* 67 (1906): pp. 361–401; 68 (1907): pp. 272–314, 525–36; 69 (1908): pp. 541–80, 738–40.

3. *Recueil des Actes de Henri II*, ed. L. Delisle and E. Berger, 3 vols, Paris, 1916–27 (henceforth Delisle and Berger, *Recueil*).

4. See Delisle, 'Mémoire sur la chronologie des chartes de Henri II', *Bibliothèque de l'Ecole des Chartes* 67 (1906): pp. 361–401.

5. J. H. Round, 'The Chronology of Henry II's Charters', *Archaeological Journal* 64 (1907), pp. 63–79. For Round's experiences in France, see the extremely amusing study by Edmund King, 'John Horace Round and the "Calendar of Documents Preserved in France"', in *Proceedings of the Battle Conference on Anglo-Norman Studies* 4 (1982): pp. 93–103, esp. p. 103, where in writing to Maxwell-Lyte, Round expresses the hope that his remarks on *Dei gratia* might leave Delisle "a crumpled heap".

6. Delisle, *Introduction*, pp. 12–38, and for Delisle's immediate reply, see *Bibliothèque de l'Ecole des Chartes* 68 (1907): pp. 515–36.

by beneficiaries outside the royal chancery, the rule that Delisle devised remains a classic, arguably *the* classic, example of the use of linguistic formulae in the dating of otherwise poorly dated medieval charters.[7]

The chief flaw in Delisle's edition lay not with diplomatic, of which he was master *sans-pareil*, but in his failure to extend his search for the charters of Henry II much beyond the archives of northern France. Delisle did assemble lists of original charters of the King in the British Museum and the Public Record Office, and, by correspondence with H. E. Salter at Oxford, and Canon Foster at Lincoln, came to appreciate at least something of the riches that still awaited discovery in the English archives.[8] However, just as Round's work on the *Calendar of Documents Preserved in France* appears to have bred in Round a raging francophobia, in the same way, Delisle's experiences in England, and in particular his fight to secure the return of French manuscripts looted by the thief and bibliophile Libri, and thence sold to the utterly insufferable Lord Ashburnham, may have blunted the Frenchman's enthusiasm for the *entente-cordiale*.[9] As a result, Delisle and Berger, in publishing their 800 texts for French beneficiaries or issued in France, merely scratched the surface of the vast mountain of Henry II's charters that awaited discovery in England.[10]

With this English material a start had been made, half a century earlier, by the Rev. R. W. Eyton, who in his *Court, Household and Itinerary of King Henry II* had attempted to reconstruct the King's movements by reference to the chronicles, the Exchequer records, and to the place of issue with which Henry II's charters end: *Testibus X apud Z*.[11] "Facts, simple facts", declared Eyton, "These are the primary and most essential elements of pure history", a sentiment with which some but by no means all latter-day medievalists might agree.[12] Eyton's *Itinerary* was

---

7. See in particular R. L. Poole, 'The Dates of Henry II's Charters', *English Historical Review* 22 (1908): pp. 79–83; J. de Font-Réaulx, review of the first volume of Delisle and Berger's *Recueil*, in *Le Moyen Age* (1915–16): p. 417, and the especially valuable study by H. Prentout, 'De l'origine de la formule 'Dei Gratia' dans les chartes de Henri II', *Mémoires de l'Académie Nationale des Sciences, Arts et Belles-Lettres de Caen* (1918–20): pp. 341–93, republished in pamphlet form (Caen, 1920). Pierre Chaplais, *English Royal Documents, King John–Henry VI, 1199–1461*, Oxford, 1971, p. 13, seeks to date the change to 1172. This, however, does not conclusively settle the matter.

8. These English charters form the subject of the articles by Delisle in the *Bibliothèque de l'Ecole des Chartes* 68 (1907): pp. 272–314; 69 (1908): pp. 541–80, 738–40, assembled at least in part as a counterblast to Round's attack upon Delisle's theory on *Dei gratia*.

9. The story of Delisle and the Libri thefts is best told by A. N. L. Munby, 'The Earl and the Thief', and 'The Triumph of Delisle', as printed in Munby, *Essays and Papers*, ed. N. Barker, London, 1978, pp. 175–205.

10. Perhaps most remarkable was Delisle's failure to consult the so-called Norman Rolls in the Public Record Office at London (henceforth PRO), class C64, which are a treasure-trove of early Norman charters, but which Delisle knew only imperfectly and at second hand, from the transcripts in Paris and elsewhere by Bréquigny, Lenoir, and others. The limitations of Delisle's work in England did not prevent at least one reviewer, Charles Bémont (who should really have known better), from criticising the *Recueil* for its publication of too many English texts: *Bibliothèque de l'Ecole des Chartes* 77 (1916): pp. 341–42. The date of this review helps to explain Bémont's particular concern for the glory and honour of France.

11. R. W. Eyton, *Court, Household and Itinerary of King Henry II*, London, 1878.

12. Eyton, *Itinerary*, p. iii.

widely used by Delisle and Berger: on occasion with unfortunate results. As had been remarked, again by the ubiquitous Round, Eyton's attempt "to assign to each charter its probable date [could prove] a very dangerous and misleading practice",[13] tempting those who came after him to assume that a charter issued, say, at Canterbury, must be assigned to one of the King's dozen or so recorded visits to that city, despite the fact that for weeks, indeed for months on end, the King's movements were entirely unrecorded in chronicles or Pipe Rolls, and that, as a result, there were many hundreds of days when the court could have been resident at Canterbury or at any other of the locations where charters were issued. Eyton's dating of charters was itself heavily dependent upon conjectures, many of which have wilted in the light of later discoveries, most notably Delisle's exposure of the date at which *Dei gratia* became common form. Furthermore, although Eyton did his best from the cartularies and editions published by 1878, to assemble all references to the King's charters, he knew of only a small fraction of the total that has since come to light, and only a fraction of Eyton's fraction, being directly relevant to France, was used by Delisle and Berger.

As a result, and despite the remarkable labours of Eyton, Delisle, and Berger, historians of the Plantagenet court continued to seek a more comprehensive edition of Henry II's charters: an edition that would span both sides of the Channel, and assemble materials from both the French and the English archives. Within a decade of Delisle's death, Vivian Galbraith had clearly begun to toy with the idea of such an edition, in the process making several important discoveries. As we shall see, it was Galbraith who first investigated the introduction of the *inspeximus* form to Henry's chancery. In addition, Galbraith drew attention to the work of one particular chancery scribe, Stephen of Fougères, whose activities could be clearly traced from the peculiarity of his script, allowing for the dating by palaeographical criteria of numerous original charters of Henry II.[14] Galbraith's lead here was taken up by T. A. M. Bishop, who began by collecting further examples of the work of Stephen of Fougères, in the process demonstrating that the phrase *omnibus hominibus* in the address to royal charters served as something of a linguistic signature, allowing many charters containing this formula to be assigned to the period before Stephen's promotion as bishop of Rennes in 1168.[15] From this, Bishop went on to examine the work of other chancery scribes, tracing as many as possible of the surviving originals issued in the names of kings Henry I, Stephen, and Henry II. Having meticulously listed these documents and supplied photographic facsimiles in his *Scriptores Regis* of 1961, Bishop sought both to reveal the inner workings of the chancery and to provide dating criteria for original charters based upon the career-dates of their scribes, and in some cases upon linguistic 'signatures' similar to that revealed in the work of Stephen of

---

13. Round, 'Chronology', p. 63.
14. V. H. Galbraith, 'Seven Charters of Henry II at Lincoln Cathedral', *The Antiquaries Journal* 12 (1932): pp. 269–78.
15. T. A. M. Bishop, 'A Chancery Scribe: Stephen of Fougères', *Cambridge Historical Journal* 10 (1950): pp. 106–107.

Fougères.[16] As with Eyton's *Itinerary*, this proved a useful but on occasion a hazardous enterprise, depending as it does upon identifications of scripts and their authors that in many cases remain speculative or unproved. Many dozens of originals, it transpired, could not be assigned to the work of any particular royal scribe, suggesting both that many of these 'originals' are forgeries, and that the beneficiaries of individual charters, rather than the king's writing office, continued to produce a large number of the documents to which the royal seal was applied, at least during the earlier part of Henry II's reign.[17] Moreover, like Galbraith before him, Bishop balked at the prospect of a complete edition of Henry II's charters, French and English, originals as well as cartulary or later copies.

Working at much the same time as Bishop, Professor van Caenegem in 1959 produced a groundbreaking edition of one particular type of royal document, the writ, traced from its origins through to the reign of Henry II.[18] However, it was not until the 1970s that a scheme for a definitive edition of all of Henry II's charters was seriously entertained. Its proposer, J. C. – now Professor Sir James – Holt, obtained funding for a research assistant from the British Academy, and over the next twenty-five years built up an impressive archive in the History Faculty at Cambridge, assembling photographs and xeroxes of all known manuscript copies of Henry II's charters, which could then be filed and assigned a particular reference number, organised by beneficiary in alphabetical order, charter by charter.[19] By 1994, Holt and his researchers, most notably Richard Mortimer, had assembled files on nearly 2,000 texts of Henry II, collected chiefly from the British Library and the Public Record Office in London, but including all of the items published by Delisle and Berger from France. In addition, and in order that the work might be carried beyond the reign of Henry II, they extended their search to include the chanceries of King Richard I, Queen Eleanor, and of John prior to his accession as King, thereby laying the basis for what was conceived of as an edition of all surviving Plantagenet royal charters from 1154 to 1199. From 1199, as all English and at least some continental historians are aware, the English royal chancery began to make enrolments of its outgoing charters and letters, through the various series of Cartae Antiquae, Charter, Patent, Close and other Rolls, still

---

16. T. A. M. Bishop, *Scriptores Regis*, Oxford, 1961, in part superseded by *Regesta Regum Anglo-Normannorum 1066–1154*, ed. H. W. C. Davis, H. A. Cronne, R. H. C. Davis, and others, 4 vols, Oxford, 1913–69, vol. 4.

17. On this see the remarks of Richard Mortimer, 'The Charters of Henry II: What Are the Criteria for Authenticity?', *Anglo-Norman Studies* 12 (1990): pp. 119–34. For a valuable comparison with the chancery of the French King Philip Augustus, see J. Dufour, 'Peut-on parler d'une organisation de la chancellerie de Philippe Auguste?', *Archiv für Diplomatik* 41 (1995): pp. 249–61, suggesting that a large number of the documents issued in the name of the King of France, as late as the 1220s, continued to be written outside the embryonic royal chancery.

18. R. C. van Caenegem, *Royal Writs in England from the Conquest to Glanvill*, Selden Society 77 (1959).

19. For the history of this project, see J. C. Holt, 'The Acta of Henry II and Richard I of England 1154–1199: The Archive and its Historical Implications', in *Fotografische Sammlungen mittelalterlicher Urkunden in Europa*, ed. P. Rück, Sigmaringen, 1989, pp. 137–40; 'The Writs of Henry II', *Proceedings of the British Academy* 89 (1995): pp. 47–64.

preserved in the Public Record Office in London and by now published, at least as far as the sixteenth century, either *in extenso* or in calendar form.[20] In 1986, Holt and Mortimer produced a provisional *Handlist* of original charters of Henry II and Richard I surviving in archives in the United Kingdom.[21] Beyond this, the existence of their archive in Cambridge encouraged the writing of further articles, including a particularly valuable study of forgery in the charters of Henry II, published by Richard Mortimer in 1990.[22]

I myself first became involved with the project in 1994, working initially in France as Professor Holt's research assistant funded by the Leverhulme Trust, and since 1996 as his successor as Director. Professor Holt now serves as the project's Chairman and chief mentor, supervising the funds contributed by the British Academy and by Trinity College Cambridge and providing sage counsel to the project's endeavours. From France, and after a comprehensive search of the English archives, involving visits in person to more than 300 libraries and archives, I and my own research assistants, first Michael Staunton and more recently Kate Dailinger, have managed since 1994 to assemble references to a further 1,000 charters of Henry II, bringing the total close to 3,000, and including nearly 100 charters for beneficiaries in France that were unknown to Delisle and Berger.[23] In 1997, I began the process of putting all of this material onto computer, and thereafter have proceeded, letter by letter, through the collection as a whole, editing all the texts that are on file, and supplying historical apparatus, identifying placenames and the dates of individual documents. All 3,000 texts of Henry II are now machine-readable, and the final editorial process has reached letter 'L', covering the first half of the collection. The edition itself is under contract for publication in four volumes of more than a million words, to appear from the Oxford University Press in 2003.

---

20. The classic account of these enrolments remains that by H. G. Richardson, in his introduction to *The Memoranda Roll for the Michaelmas Term of the First Year of the Reign of King John (1199–1200)*, Pipe Roll Society n.s. xxi (1943), p. xxi ff., and for listings of the various editions and calendars, see *Texts and Calendars: An Analytical Guide to Serial Publications*, ed. E. L. C. Mullins, Royal Historical Society Guides and Handbooks vii (1958), especially lists 1–5, 30.

21. *Acta of Henry II and Richard I: Handlist of Documents Surviving in the Original in Repositories in the United Kingdom*, ed. J. C. Holt and R. Mortimer, List and Index Society Special Series xxi (1986).

22. See, in particular, J. C. Holt, 'The Assizes of Henry II: The Texts', in *The Study of Medieval Records: Essays in Honour of Kathleen Major*, ed. D. A. Bullough and R. L. Storey, Oxford, 1971, pp. 85–106; T. K. Keefe, 'Place–Date Distribution of Royal Charters and the Historical Geography of Patronage Strategies at the Court of King Henry II Plantagenet', *The Haskins Society Journal* 2 (1990): pp. 179–88; Holt, 'The Writs of Henry II'; Mortimer, 'Criteria for Authenticity'.

23. For the additions from France, see *Acta of Henry II and Richard I Part Two: A Supplementary Handlist of Documents Surviving in the Original in Repositories in the United Kingdom, France, Ireland, Belgium and the USA*, ed. N. Vincent, List and Index Society Special Series xxvii (1996); N. Vincent, 'Les Actes de Henri II Plantagenet concernant la Normandie inconnues à Léopold Delisle', *Cahiers Léopold Delisle* (forthcoming). Taken together, the two Handlists of 1986 and 1996 cite 54 original charters of Henry II entirely unknown to Bishop. A further 20 originals have come to light since 1996, bringing the total of additional originals unknown to Bishop to 65, and the grand total of Henry II originals to c.520. For some remarks on the implications of this, see Vincent, *Handlist* (1996), pp. 25–26.

We have thus progressed far beyond the point reached by Eyton, Delisle, or Berger, and with the aid of modern technology, at last have access to all, or nearly all, of Henry II's 3,000 surviving charters, searchable at the touch of a computer keyboard in a way unimaginable in the days of Delisle, Galbraith, or Bishop. What, however, can be learned from such a search? Here it is that we return to the chief matter of this enquiry: the question of the *inspeximus*.

In a brief but seminal article published in 1937, V. H. Galbraith advanced a number of theories about the introduction of the *inspeximus* form to English royal charters.[24] In accordance with the standard authorities on continental diplomatic – Bresslau and Giry – Galbraith proposed that the *inspeximus* (or *vidimus* as it is known in France), originated with the practice of episcopal chanceries, in response to the growth of papal jurisdiction.[25] From around the year 1100, continental bishops in receipt of papal mandates would occasionally rehearse the text of such mandates, with the application of the bishop's seal and the insertion of brief introductory and corroborative clauses, in order to broadcast such letters to the diocese at large. From this, it was but a relatively simple step towards the rehearsal in similar terms of other, non-papal, letters, including earlier episcopal or private charters, should a bishop seek to renew the privileges of a monastery or other religious corporation. Beginning in this way as an episcopal innovation, inspired by the new authority of the post-Gregorian popes, the form slowly took root in English episcopal chanceries, and at much the same time in the chancery of the English Kings. In the episcopal chanceries of England, the verb *inspeximus* makes its first recorded appearance in such a context in the 1120s, and it was not until the 1170s that the English bishops began to issue full recitals of earlier awards.[26] As for the royal chancery, well into the reign of King Stephen

---

24. V. H. Galbraith, 'A New Charter of Henry II to Battle Abbey', *English Historical Review* 52 (1937): pp. 67–73.

25. H. Bresslau, *Handbuch der Urkundenlehre für Deutschland und Italien*, 2nd ed., 2 vols, Leipzig and Berlin, 1912–31, I, p. 301ff; A. Giry, *Manuel de Diplomatique*, 2 vols, Paris, 1925, I, pp. 16–22. It is hardly necessary here to emphasise the distinction between the *inspeximus* form and the *pancarte*, more analogous to a cartulary copy: *Pancartes monastiques des XIe et XIIe siècles*, ed. M. Parisse, P. Pégeot, and B.-M. Tock, Brepols, 1998.

26. For detailed discussion of the episcopal *inspeximus*, see C. R. Cheney, *English Bishops' Chanceries 1100–1250*, Manchester, 1950, pp. 90–96. However, many of the earliest examples adduced by Cheney come from the archives of Rochester and Gloucester, where there is evidence of such widespread forgery that any use of the *inspeximus* must be treated with grave suspicion. In a more recent analysis, *English Episcopal Acta II: Canterbury 1162–1190*, ed. C. R. Cheney and B. E. A. Jones, Oxford, 1986, pp. lxvi-viii, Cheney accepted a date after *c*.1170 for the adoption of the full-blown *inspeximus* form, tracing the earliest genuine examples to the diocese of Worcester. The form, he suggests, remained rare, even amongst episcopal chanceries, until *c*.1200. For what may be the earliest use of the verb *inspeximus* in the episcopal confirmation of earlier episcopal and royal charters (by bishop Everard of Norwich, 1121/22), and for what may be the earliest full-blown *inspeximus* charter reciting an earlier award word for word (by bishop Roger of Worcester, 1164 X 1179), see *English Episcopal Acta VI: Norwich 1070–1214*, ed. C. Harper-Bill, Oxford, 1990, no. 45; M. G. Cheney, *Roger Bishop of Worcester 1164–1179*, Oxford, 1980, pp. 112, 306, no.75; *The Cartulary of Worcester Cathedral Priory*, ed. R. R. Darlington, Pipe Roll Society n.s. xxxviii (1968), p. 34 no. 55. In the decade to 1180, the full recital of earlier awards appears for the first time in the dioceses of Bath, London, and York. At Canterbury, it first appears 1181 X 1184 (*cont. on next page*)

(1135–54), although it was customary for the King to renew the privileges of his ancestors, or on occasion to confirm gifts recorded in private charters, such confirmations tended merely to paraphrase the earlier award to be confirmed, sometimes by direct copying from an earlier charter down to precise details of field-names and word order, sometimes in more general terms by stating simply that the new King confirmed all the gifts of his ancestors or of private individuals, whatever they might be, without entering into specific detail: *sicut carte donatorum* (or *antecessorum meorum*) *testantur*.[27] From Stephen's reign, however, and in tandem with the development of similar formulae by the English bishops, the King or his chancery officials might from time to time dictate a clause to the effect that the King himself had seen with his own eyes the charters which he hereby confirmed.[28] It is just such phrases that occur in a handful of the early charters of Henry II.

Galbraith knew of at least two examples of this formula, both of them the work of the chancery scribe Stephen of Fougères: a charter to Eynsham Abbey, issued between December 1159 and May 1162, confirming an earlier award by King Henry I, *quam vidi oculis meis*; and a charter to Lincoln cathedral, 1163 X October 1164, confirming an earlier charter of King William I, *quam vidi*.[29] To these we can now add a writ for Burton Abbey, 1155 X 1158, confirming a charter of Henry I, *quam oculis mei(s) vidi*;[30] a charter to Bury St Edmunds, c.May 1157, confirming a charter granted by Edward the Confessor, *quam vidi*,[31] and a charter confirming the foundation of the leper house at La Flèche, 1156 X 1159, renewing charters of the King's father, Geoffrey Plantagenet, and of Geoffrey de Claris his steward, *quas oculis meis vidi*.[32] Only the last of these, with its address to *omnibus hominibus et amicis et fidelibus*, can tentatively be assigned to the work of Stephen of Fougères. The Burton writ is supported by a further letter of Queen Eleanor of Aquitaine, issued before 1167, referring to Henry II's confirmation as the *cartam domini mei que testatur quod ipse oculis suis vidit cartam H(enrici) regis aui sui*.[33] In this way, the new clause remained something of a

---

(*cont. from previous page*) (*English Episcopal Acta* II, p. lxvii); at Hereford 1174 X 1186 (*English Episcopal Acta VII: Hereford 1079–1234*, ed. J. Barrow, Oxford, 1993, p. xcv); at Lincoln 1192/93 (*English Episcopal Acta IV: Lincoln 1186–1206*, ed. D. M. Smith, Oxford, 1986, pp. xxxix–xl, no. 188a); and at Winchester not until 1206 X 1218 (*English Episcopal Acta IX: Winchester 1205–1238*, ed. N. Vincent, Oxford, 1994, pp. lxx–lxxi, no. 1).

27. For examples, see Delisle, *Introduction*, pp. 185–93.

28. See the charter of King Stephen to Peterborough, 1140 X 1154, printed in *Regesta* III, no. 660: *carta . . . quam oculis meis vidi et hoc eis testor*, as noted by Galbraith, 'New Charter', p. 70. For episcopal examples, see *English Episcopal Acta II*, p. lxvi.

29. Galbraith, 'Seven Charters', pp. 271–73, nos. 1, 7. Here, and in what follows, the dates given for individual documents are based upon standard criteria, most notably the King's itinerary and the witness lists, all of which will be fully explained in my edition of Henry II.

30. London, British Library (henceforth BL) ms. Loans 30 (Burton cartulary) fo.13r, as calendared by G. Wrottesley, 'The Burton Chartulary', *William Salt Archaeological Society Collections for a History of Staffordshire* V, part 1 (1884), p. 12.

31. Best preserved in PRO E368/84 (Memoranda Roll 7 Edward II) m. 92, with an inferior text printed by D. C. Douglas, *Feudal Documents from the Abbey of Bury St Edmunds*, British Academy Records of the Social and Economic History of England and Wales VIII (1932), p. 105, no. 101.

32. Delisle and Berger, *Recueil*, no. 106.

33. BL ms. Loans 30 (Burton Cartulary) fo.6r, whence 'Burton Chartulary', p. 12.

rarity, used only sparingly during the first decade of the reign, and not at all thereafter.

Even before 1154, a charter supposedly issued by Henry II as Duke of Normandy, witnessed by Richard de Bohun as chancellor – which would place it in the period September X December 1151 – claims to confirm earlier charters awarded by the ancestors of Jordan Taisson and Duke Henry himself to the monks of Fontenay, referring specifically to the *charta fundatoris* . . . *que incipit Quisquis Deo*, and the *charta confirmationis quam predicti abbas et monachi habent a Willelmo tunc duce Normannie* . . . *que incipit In Nomine Sancte et Indiuidue Trinitatis, que charte crucibus sunt signate secundum antiquam consuetudinem*, stating that these charters had been recognised by Jordan before the Duke and his barons at Rouen, and confirmed by Duke Henry 'word for word' (*de verbo ad verbum*).[34] The editors of Henry's ducal charters accepted this award as genuine, presumably on the basis of its, admittedly plausible, witness list. However, the terminology of the charter, with its address to *omnibus tam presentibus quam futuris*, and its distinctly episcopal-sounding corroboration *quod ut statum (?ratum) sit et stabile in perpetuum presenti scripto et sigilli mei munimine confirmaui*, combined with the charter's reference to the earlier privileges by their *incipits* – reminiscent of much later practice – all argue strongly against authenticity. Almost certainly, the Fontenay charter is a forgery.

Standing slightly apart from the development of the *inspeximus* charter, we should note that already by the 1160s it was accepted that the King might add his authority and confirmation to non-royal charters simply by the application of the royal seal. In this way, Pierre Chaplais has identified a copy of the canons of the Council of Lillebonne of 1080 as an exemplification submitted to King Henry II for sealing, probably in February 1162, with a final clause inserted in the hand of one of Henry II's known chancery scribes, noting merely that the Council's rulings had been devised by the bishops and the King.[35] Such a use of the royal seal, to authenticate an instrument not in the King's name, can be found again in May/June 1169, when the King's seal was appended to a cyrograph drawn up in the names of the abbess of Fontevraud and the abbot of Bourgueil, and at some time between 1177 and 1179 when the King, together with the archbishop of Canterbury, sealed a cyrograph drawn up between the Canterbury monks and Reginald of Cornhill.[36]

---

34. Delisle and Berger, *Recueil*, no. 42*; *Regesta* III, no. 325, from much later copies at Caen and Rouen, also printed in *Gallia Christiana*, 16 vols, Paris 1715–1865, XI, instr. col. 82.

35. P. Chaplais, 'Henry II's Reissue of the Canons of the Council of Lillebonne of Whitsun 1080 (?25 February 1162)', *Journal of the Society of Archivists* IV (1973): pp. 627–32, reprinted in Chaplais, *Essays in Medieval Diplomacy and Administration*, London, 1981, ch. 19, noting the final clause *Hec omnia suprascripta que ad iura ecclesiastica spectare dinoscuntur, episcoporum tantum, cetera omnia regis erunt*, in the hand of Bishop's scribe XXXV.

36. Delisle and Berger, *Recueil*, no. 283, with original exemplars now Angers, Archives départementales de Maine-et-Loire 173H2, no. 27; Poitiers, Archives départementales de la Vienne Carton 12 dossier 1 no. 1, only the first of these being noticed by Delisle and Berger. For the Canterbury cyrograph, see W. Urry, *Canterbury under the Angevin Kings*, London, 1967, pp. 409–10, nos. 29–30, from Canterbury Cathedral Library Chartae Antiquae C846, C849, the royal seals now missing. The Canterbury settlement was thereafter confirmed in a full royal charter, paraphrasing the original cyrograph: Urry, *Canterbury*, pp. 410–11, nos. 31–32.

For the next development affecting the *inspeximus* proper, Galbraith referred to a well-known story in the *Battle Chronicle*, a narrative source composed at Battle Abbey in Sussex: attributed by its most recent editor to the last decade of Henry II's reign, but perhaps more correctly dated to the 1190s, given its reference at one point to the "time of King Henry", as if the King were already dead when the chronicler was writing.[37] The general consensus on the Chronicle is that, although making use of eleventh- and early-twelfth-century charters that are undoubtedly forged, the chronicler himself provides a reliable account of the process by which these forged charters were employed after 1154 by the Battle monks, eventually obtaining confirmation from King Henry II. Here, as part of an extended account of the election of abbot Odo of Battle in 1175, the chronicler reports Odo's attempt to have his earlier charters of liberty and exemption confirmed by the King. The abbot, who had been blessed by the archbishop of Canterbury at Malling on 28 September 1175,[38] travelled thereafter to the royal court carrying with him a charter of King William I, Battle's founder, "which had decayed with age". The King was unwilling to confirm this charter without judgement of his court, but was won round after a speech in council from his justiciar, Richard de Lucy, brother of the previous abbot of Battle, Walter de Lucy (d.1171). Calling for Master Walter of Coutances, who the chronicler describes as chancellor, but who in fact at this time was discharging a subsidiary office in chancery:

> The King ordered that a new charter be made in the royal name and sealed with his own seal, following the form of the old charter, and specifying that in the new charter it be stated that he had confirmed it for the love of God and at the petition of abbot Odo, wishing the name and merit of the abbot to be recorded. Now, whereas in the charters and muniments given by various persons at different times concerning the same matter, it is the custom that the later documents mention the earlier ones, so that the latter seem to require the evidence of the former, for example in such words as *sicut carta illa, vel illius N., testatur*, the King would put in no such phrase, but himself dictated another phrase, never before employed (*antea inusitatam*), bearing witness in his own person concerning what he had seen in these words: *quoniam inspexi cartam Willelmi proaui mei, in qua prescripte libertates et quietancie et libere consuetudines ab eo prefate ecclesie concesse continebantur.*

---

37. *The Chronicle of Battle Abbey*, ed. E. Searle, Oxford, 1980, and see the detailed review by Martin Brett in *Medium Aevum* l (1981): pp. 319–22. In her introduction (p. 9), the editor suggests that the chronicler himself died between 1184 and 1189. However the chronicle (pp. 228–29), in recounting litigation over the church of Mildenhall, suggests that after the late 1150s the canons of Leeds Priory withdrew their claim against Battle 'for the time of King Henry [d.1189] and abbot Walter [d.1171]' (*ad tempus quieuerunt a lite, domino scilicet rege Henrico et abbate Waltero superstitibus*). Litigation over Mildenhall was revived in the time of Pope Celestine III (1191–98), and continued, with interventions by the monks of Bury St Edmunds, until at least 1206: *English Episcopal Acta VI*, no. 332n. The chronicler's remarks here can leave little doubt that he was aware of the dispute's revival after 1191.

38. *Chronicle of Battle*, pp. 300–307.

The chronicler then goes on to report the King's explanation for this new formula, inserted so that the new charter might stand independently of its archetype, removing the necessity for both the earlier charter of William I and its confirmation by Henry II to be produced in evidence. The King is furthermore said to have ordered that the new charter be written out and sealed with the royal seal in three separate exemplars, so that the monks would always have a copy at hand, even if one or two of the exemplars were in use elsewhere, presumably so that the charter might be produced simultaneously before different sessions of the King's courts, meeting in eyre in other counties or in other places where the monks claimed lands or liberties.[39]

As Galbraith pointed out, the chronicler's account here is of fundamental significance to our understanding of the evolution of the instrument later to be known as the royal *inspeximus*, suggesting that the term *inspexi* was first introduced to the charters of Henry II in 1175 or shortly thereafter, for very practical reasons. Some previous writers who had known of the Battle chronicler's remarks had dismissed them as mere fiction.[40] Such a dismissal had come to seem all the more justified once it became clear to modern historians that, from at least the mid-twelfth century onwards, the monks of Battle were engaged in widespread forgery, attempting to invent for themselves an exemption from the local diocesan authority of the bishops of Chichester on the basis of spurious charters of King William I. The charter confirmed by Henry II in 1175 may well have been just such a forgery, supposedly issued by King William before 1089, but in fact composed some seventy years later.[41] It was Galbraith's achievement not only to refocus attention upon the chronicler's account of the new clause introduced in 1175, but to bring to light one of the three authentic exemplars which, as the chronicler claims, the King ordered to be written and sealed in favour of the Battle monks. This document, now British Library Additional Charter 70981, unlike so many other twelfth-century charters from Battle, is of undisputed authenticity, written in the hand of a chancery scribe identified by Bishop as scribe XL, active from at least 1163 until 1187, dated at Winchester, and witnessed by Geoffrey bishop of Ely and eight other courtiers. Since, in accordance with the chronicler's remarks, this surviving charter refers to abbot Odo, and since it is witnessed by Richard de Lucy, who retired from court in April 1179 and died that August, it can be dated without doubt to the period between September 1175 and April 1179, probably to

---

39. *Chronicle of Battle*, pp. 308–313, the translation above being adapted from that by Searle.

40. Thus Sir Thomas Hardy, in *Rotuli Chartarum*, London, 1837, p. v, dismissing the earlier notice afforded the chronicler's remarks by Lord Coke and Sir Francis Palgrave. Delisle (*Introduction*, pp. 184–85) was less sceptical.

41. The principal authority here is Eleanor Searle, 'Battle Abbey and Exemption: The Forged Charters', *English Historical Review* 83 (1968): pp. 449–80. Credit for the first proper exposure of these forgeries belongs to Sir Frank Stenton, in a series of notes appended to David Knowles' study of the Battle charters in *The Downside Review*, n.s. xxxi (1932): pp. 431–32. Searle (*Battle Chronicle*, 312n.) relates Henry II's charter of *c.*1175 to the forged charter of William I, now BL ms. Cotton Charter xvi.28, as printed by Searle, 'Forged Charters', pp. 462–63, 477, no. 8, and in *Regesta Regum Anglo-Normannorum: The Acta of William I 1066–1087*, ed. D. Bates, Oxford, 1998, pp. 147–50, no. 19.

early in that period, shortly after abbot Odo's consecration. Its identity with the charter described in the chronicle is supported by its contemporary endorsement *triplex*, suggesting that it was indeed produced in triplicate as the chronicler claims. Most significantly of all, its corroborative clause is more or less identical to that described by the chronicler: *quia inspexi cartam regis Willelmi proaui mei in qua prescripte libertates et quietancie et libere consuetudines ab eo prefate ecclesie concesse continebantur*.[42] Nor does the proof end here. Unknown to Galbraith, a duplicate exemplar of the same original survives in the East Sussex Record Office at Lewes, in more or less identical terms, save for the omission of the last two witnesses, and written in yet another recognisable chancery hand, identified by Bishop as that of scribe XLV, whose career spanned the service of both Henry II and Richard I, from c.1175–1189.[43]

From his discovery of the first of these original charters, Galbraith drew a number of conclusions. To begin with, he suggested that the appearance of the *inspexi* clause in the Battle charter, although genuine, was unique and that it was never again employed during Henry's reign. When King Richard came, in 1198, to devise an instrument by which he could recite and renew charters issued earlier in his reign word for word, as a means of making large sums of money for the renewal under his second great seal of charters issued under an earlier seal temporarily lost on Crusade, he adopted a formula which made no use of *inspexi* or *inspeximus*, but instead spoke of the "renewal" (*innovatio*) of previous awards.[44] The *inspeximus* form did not gain general currency in the royal chancery until 1227, when King Henry III, once again from financial motives, began to issue large numbers of *inspeximus* charters, renewing the charters of his ancestors in return for payments from the beneficiaries who wished them confirmed, and thereby setting a trend that was to survive for several centuries to come. In 1227, however, Henry III and his officials took their lead not from the embryonic *inspeximus* clause invented by Henry II, but quite independently, in emulation of a model provided by the English bishops.[45] Finally, by proving the authenticity of

---

42. BL ms. Additional Charter 70981, as printed by Galbraith, 'New Charter', p. 73. For the scribe, see Bishop, *Scriptores Regis*, p. 52, no. 328 and plate xxxiv(a). The charter had earlier been printed in the *Proceedings of the Society of Antiquaries*, 2nd series iii (1867), pp. 408–11; see also B. Scofield, 'The Lane Bequest', *British Museum Quarterly* 11 (1937): pp. 73–76.

43. Lewes, East Sussex Record Office ms. BAT7, noticed by Holt and Mortimer, *Handlist*, p. 30, no. 10, and for the scribe see Bishop, *Scriptores Regis*, p. 37, no. 26 and plate xxxvii(b). Later, cartulary and chancery copies, for the most part from the BL version of the original, are to be found as PRO C66/431 (Patent Roll 10 Henry VI part 1) m.21; PRO C52/7 (Cartae Antiquae Roll G) no. 5; PRO C56/12 (Confirmation Roll 2 Henry VII part 3) m.1 no. 5; San Marino, Huntington Library ms. BA29 (Battle Cartulary) fos.36v–37r; London, Lincoln's Inn Library ms. Hale 87 (Battle Cartulary) fo.17v; BL ms. Cotton Vitellius D ix (Cartulary of St Nicholas' Exeter) fos.25v–26r; Oxford, Bodleian Library ms. Tanner 342 fo.170r, noticed from the lost cartulary of Brecon Priory. Brecon and St Nicholas' Exeter were both dependencies of Battle Abbey.

44. For the renovation formula, see Delisle, *Introduction*, p. 192; *The Itinerary of King Richard I*, ed. L. Landon, Pipe Roll Society n.s. xiii (1935), pp. 173–82.

45. Galbraith, 'New Charter', pp. 70–71, 73: 'There can be little doubt that, when in 1227 the royal chancery adopted the charter of *inspeximus* and *confirmamus*, the *formulae* were directly borrowed from the ecclesiastical chanceries. For there is no trace in royal charters, if we except the unique Battle confirmation, of any such intermediate form as that illustrated above . . . nor did the chancery clerks revert, as we might have expected, to the *formulae* of Richard I's innovations.'

the Battle chronicler's story of the *inspeximus* clause, Galbraith appeared to lend verisimilitude to others of the chronicler's remarks, not only on the events of 1175, but in respect to the chronicle's account of other charters and confirmations supposedly issued by King Henry II.

By uncovering the surviving original of Henry II's *inspeximus* charter, Galbraith rendered a major service to the history of diplomatic. However, in most of the conclusions that he drew from this discovery, he may well have been in error. Let us begin with the supposed uniqueness of the Battle charter with its use of the clause *inspexi*. With the help of our 3,000 machine-readable texts, we do not need to look very far to find almost exactly the same formula as that of the Battle charter employed in a charter of Henry II in favour of bishop John of Chichester, confirming the bishop's rights of free warren as inspected in the charters of the King's predecessors: *sicut carta regis Willelmi et carte regis Henrici aui mei quas ego inspexi et carte mee testantur*.[46] This Chichester charter, unknown to Galbraith, was issued at Portsea in Hampshire, and must date after the consecration of John of Greenford as bishop, in October 1174, and before his death c.April 1180. Although it survives only in copies, the earliest of them from the thirteenth century, there is no reason to doubt its basic authenticity. Since the King was in France from October 1174 until May 1175, and since the charter is witnessed by Geoffrey count of Brittany, who made no recorded visit to England after Easter 1179, we can probably narrow its dating perimeters to the period between May 1175 and April 1179, or to very much the same period in which the *inspeximus* for Battle was issued. Now, this is most remarkable. To find two charters of Henry II employing the new formula is in itself no more than intriguing, until we bear in mind that the beneficiaries of our two charters, the monks of Battle and the bishops of Chichester, were the very bitterest of rivals. The chief motive behind the writing of the *Battle Chronicle* lay in its attempt to account for and to describe, in terms entirely favourable to Battle, a dispute between monks and bishops that was to last from the 1150s until at least the 1230s, and which involved an attempt by the monks to prove their exemption from the episcopai authority of Chichester on the basis of forged charters which they claimed to have received from King William I. To find both Battle and Chichester in receipt of *inspeximus* charters in the period 1175–79 is surely no mere coincidence. Rather, it suggests that as part of their longstanding rivalry one or other of the parties reacted to the award of the first *inspeximus* charter by demanding a similar charter for itself. The formula of the Chichester charter is less fully developed than the formula used at Battle, suggesting that it may even have been the Chichester charter that was the first to be issued. During the period in question, the King definitely visited Portsmouth, close by Portsea, in May 1175, and again in July and August 1177, travelling to or from France. In theory, the Chichester charter issued at Portsea could date from some six months before the earliest possible date for the *inspeximus* charter granted to Battle.[47] To accept that the Chichester charter was

---

46. Best preserved in PRO C53/125 (Charter Roll 12 Edward III) m.22, in an *inspeximus* of 1338, whence *Calendar of Charter Rolls 1327–41*, p. 440, no. 5.

47. For the King's movements, see Eyton, *Itinerary*, pp. 190, 216–18, bearing in mind the limitations of our knowledge of the King's movements already remarked upon.

the first to be issued, we would have to discount the claim of the Battle chronicler that, in granting his charter for Battle, the King was improvising something "previously unattempted" (*antea inusitatam*).

Beyond the Battle and Chichester texts, and discounting very obvious forgeries, I have found only three further uses of the verb *inspexi* in Henry II's charters, all of them known to, but dismissed as spurious by Galbraith.[48] Two occur in charters for the monks of Fécamp in Normandy, surviving as purported originals at Rouen and in the Musée de la Bénédictine at Fécamp. Both of these Fécamp originals are problematic. Neither is written by a scribe attached to the royal chancery. One of them is prepared for sealing in a way that would be most peculiar for a chancery production.[49] The other is perished at the foot, so that it is impossible to prove that it was even prepared for sealing.[50] Both might be genuine acts of the King, written by the beneficiary's scribe and merely submitted to the King for the application of the great seal. This would seem to be the interpretation placed upon them by Berger, and more reluctantly by Delisle.[51] However, there are other aspects to these charters that suggest forgery. In particular, although from their identical witness lists and place of issue, at Westminster, they can both be assigned to the period before the death of Warin fitz Gerald, and hence before the King's crossing to Normandy in August 1158, they both adopt the *Dei gratia* clause. As such they join a small group of original charters of Henry II supposedly issued before 1172 with the *Dei gratia* clause. Leaving aside two charters which Bishop identified as "chancery renovations" renewing earlier grants of Henry II under the forms current after 1172–73, and which present particular problems of their own,[52] this group comprises three charters for Fécamp, three charters from the archive of the Fitz Hardings at Berkeley, and a further charter for Battle, all of them, for one reason or another, deeply suspect.[53] The language

---

48. Galbraith, 'Seven Charters', p. 272, n. 3. For other, undoubted forgeries, see Delisle, *Introduction*, pp. 182–84, whence Delisle and Berger, *Recueil*, nos. 137, 467, 714. To these can be added a purported *inspeximus* charter of Henry II to Combermere Abbey reciting in full the text of a charter of Robert de Baskerville, with impossible date, written throughout in the first person plural, first fully recorded in 1400 but perhaps already forged by 1253; *Calendar of Charter Rolls 1341–1417*, pp. 395–96, and cf. *Calendar of Charter Rolls 1226–57*, pp. 427–28. Equally spurious is the purported *inspeximus* of Henry II to Kingswood Abbey in Gloucestershire, again reciting in full a charter of King Henry I, with mixed first person singular and plural, and improbable liberties: London, Lincoln's Inn Library ms. Hale 30 pp. 701–702, reciting the charter of Henry I printed as *Regesta* II, no. 1496.

49. Rouen, Archives départementales 7H12 pièce non coté, as printed in facsimile in *Les Archives de Normandie et de la Seine-Inférieure*, ed. P. Chevreux and J.-J. Vernier, Rouen, 1911, plate 17; Delisle and Berger, *Recueil*, no. 58; Bishop, *Scriptores Regis*, p. 69, no. 672; Vincent, *Handlist*, p. 69, no. 54, sealed *sur double queue* on a parchment tag through a single slit, seal impression missing. Chancery practice tended to favour three slits for the tag.

50. Fécamp, Musée de la Bénédictine, charte no.18 (formerly no.16), printed, with facsimile by Delisle and Berger, *Recueil*, no. 57 and Delisle, *Atlas*, plate 5; Bishop, *Scriptores Regis*, p. 47, no.221; Vincent, *Handlist*, pp. 67–68, no. 52.

51. Delisle, *Introduction*, pp. 18, 286; Delisle and Berger, *Recueil*, nos. 57–58.

52. Bishop, *Scriptores Regis*, 19n., pp. 34–35. Of the originals there cited, only Bishop nos. 288 and 724, for Bordesley and Mont-St-Michel, both in identifiable chancery hands, fit the category of pre-1172 awards recopied as originals under the *Dei gratia* formula after 1172

53. Holt and Mortimer, *Handlist*, pp. 74–77, nos. 107–108, 111; Vincent, *Handlist*, p. 42, no. 9, pp. 67–69, nos. 52–54.

of the Fécamp charters is itself most peculiar. The first of the two charters claims to confirm to Henry abbot of Fécamp all the lands in England and Normandy granted by Duke Richard of Normandy and King William I, free from all subjection, *absque omni subiectione et dominatione baronum vel principum et omnium aliorum et absque omni inquietatione cuiuslibet iudiciarie potestatis vel inminutione dignitatis sicuti res ad fiscum dominicum pertinentes*, forbidding pleas save before the King or his chief justiciar *quia diligenter inspexi cartas Ricardi ducis Normannorum et Willelmi regis Anglorum*.[54] The second confirms abbot Henry in possession of all the lands in England granted by King William I, namely Steyning and Bury in Sussex, together with the liberties contained in the first charter, described in near identical terms, forbidding pleas save before the King or his capital justice *quia inspexi diligenter cartas regis Willelmi et aliorum predecessorum meorum*.[55] The clauses on exemption here are borrowed from a privilege of questionable authenticity but undoubtedly of the eleventh century, supposedly issued to Fécamp by Duke Richard II of Normandy in 1025.[56]

More damaging to the case of the two Fécamp originals is the fact that the second of them, concerning Steyning, is modelled upon and perhaps written in the same hand as a forged charter of King William I, whose forgery Pierre Chaplais has dated nearer to the end than the middle of the twelfth century, and which, Chaplais speculates, was forged so that Fécamp's Norman liberties might be extended across the Channel to the abbey's lands in England.[57] The likelihood that the Steyning original of Henry II is a forgery is increased by our knowledge that the monks of Fécamp undoubtedly possessed one other forgery of Henry II relating to their lands at Steyning, now known only from an early thirteenth-century copy in the *Cartae Antiquae Rolls*. The witnesses to this charter are anomalous, including both Warin fitz Gerald, who died before 1161, and Gilbert Foliot bishop of London, consecrated only in 1163; its terminology, and especially its corroborative clauses, are clearly not the work of the royal chancery, and like several others of the Fécamp charters of Henry II, supposedly issued in the 1150s, it carries the tell-tale *Dei gratia* clause that we would expect only after 1172.[58] If

54. Delisle and Berger, *Recueil*, no. 57.
55. Delisle and Berger, *Recueil*, no. 58.
56. *Recueil des Actes des Ducs de Normandie de 911 à 1066*, ed. M. Fauroux, Caen, 1961, p. 130, no. 34; also in C. H. Haskins, *Norman Institutions*, New York, 1918, appendix B pp. 250–51, where the eleventh-century clause reads *Hec omnia . . . concedo . . . ut habeant, teneant et possideant absque ulla inquietudine cuiuslibet secularis vel iudiciarie potestatis sicuti res ad fiscum dominicum pertinentes*. The Fécamp exemptions have been intensively analysed by J.-F. Lemarignier, *Etude sur les privilèges d'exemption et de juridiction ecclésiastique des abbayes Normandes depuis les origines jusqu'en 1140*, Paris, 1937, esp. pp. 50–63, 192–204, 220–27, 247–54; and cf. D. C. Douglas, 'The First Ducal Charter for Fécamp, in *L'Abbaye Bénédictine de Fécamp: ouvrage sciéntifique du XIIIe centenaire*, Fécamp, 1959, I, pp. 45–56, who suggests that the abbey's exemption may have been more ancient than the date of 1006 proposed by Lemarignier, but that the supposed charter of 1025 was actually drawn up, at the earliest, after 1031.
57. P. Chaplais, 'Une charte originale de Guillaume le Conquérant pour l'abbaye de Fécamp; la donation de Steyning et de Bury (1085)', in *L'Abbaye Bénédictine de Fécamp*, I, pp. 93–104, with detailed commentary at p. 100, reprinted with additional material in Chaplais, *Essays in Medieval Diplomacy*, ch.16, whence the commentary in Bates, *Regesta*, pp. 469–71, no. 141.
58. PRO C52/18 (Cartae Antiquae Roll S) m.2 no. 6, whence *Cartae Antiquae Rolls*, ed. L. Landon and J. Conway Davies, 2 vols, Pipe Roll Society n.s. xvii, xxxiii (1939–60), II, no. 546.

this charter and the original relating to Steyning both fail the test of authenticity, then we must also condemn two other closely related charters: the more general privilege extending Fécamp's Norman liberties to England, employing the clause *inspexi* considered above;[59] and another charter, which survives as an original at Rouen, with the same witness list and place–date as the charters of *inspeximus* but without use of the *inspeximus* clause.[60] With this last charter, from Rouen, we may at last obtain some insight into the true nature of the Fécamp forgeries, since the Rouen original is written in a hand, clearly not a chancery hand, found elsewhere in a pair of duplicate originals of a charter granted by Henry II, before August 1158, to the men of London. Like the Fécamp charters, the London city charter is dated at Westminster, suggesting to T. A. M. Bishop that the scribe who wrote it may have been employed in the Westminster Abbey scriptorium.[61] Westminster Abbey, it hardly needs emphasising, was a prolific source of forgery throughout the 1150s and 1160s.[62] On this basis, we might conclude that the original charter of Henry II for Fécamp now at Rouen was written at Westminster by a scribe who combined work for the royal chancery with freelance forgery, and that this Westminster production in turn provided the model for the two originals containing the *inspeximus* clause preserved at Rouen and in the Musée de la Bénédictine, themselves both forgeries, probably of the late twelfth century. By thus disposing of three of the supposed originals issued in King Henry's name before 1172 under the *Dei gratia* clause, we further call into question the authenticity of all other originals employing *Dei gratia* before 1172, comprising the three charters from the Berkeley archive and a further original for Battle, all of which I would condemn on historical as well as palaeographical grounds.[63]

59. Delisle and Berger, *Recueil*, no. 57, also preserved in the same enrolment as the forged charter on Steyning: PRO C52/18 no.2, whence *Cartae Antiquae Rolls*, II, no. 542.

60. Rouen, Archives départementales de la Seine-Maritime 7H12 pièce non coté, printed with facsimile in Chevreux and Vernier, *Archives*, plate 16; Delisle and Berger, *Recueil*, no. 56 and Delisle, *Atlas*, plate 4; Bishop, *Scriptores Regis*, p. 69, no. 671; Vincent, *Handlist*, p. 68, no. 53. Written in a distinctive, possibly monastic book hand.

61. London, Guildhall Library ms. City Charters nos. 2–2a; Bishop, *Scriptores Regis*, p. 55, nos. 394–95, and cf. p. 10 ("the hand is probably that of a casually employed local scribe"), p. 34, n. 3 ("probably written by a Westminster scribe"). The award to London itself is accepted as an authentic act of Henry II by C. W. Hollister, 'London's First Charter of Liberties: Is It Genuine?', in Hollister, *Monarchy, Magnates and Institutions in the Anglo-Norman World*, London, 1986, pp. 206–207. However, if genuine, its final clause, allowing for the confirmation of *omnes alias libertates et liberas consuetudines quas habuerunt tempore regis H(enrici) aui mei quando meliores vel liberiores habuerunt*, does not sit well with Hollister's suggestion that Henry II deliberately failed to renew the Londoners' privilege to elect their own mayor and to pay a reduced farm to the King, as allowed by their supposed charter of Henry I.

62. P. Chaplais, 'The Original Charters of Herbert and Gervase abbots of Westminster (1121–1157)', in *A Medieval Miscellany for Doris Mary Stenton*, ed. P. M. Barnes and C. F. Slade, Pipe Roll Society n.s. xxxvi (1962), pp. 89–110, reprinted with additions in Chaplais, *Essays in Medieval Diplomacy*, ch.18, and cf. C. N. L. Brooke, 'Approaches to Medieval Forgery', in Brooke, *Medieval Church and Society*, London, 1971, pp. 106–108.

63. The Berkeley charters form the subject of a spirited rearguard action by R. B. Patterson, 'Robert Fitz Harding of Bristol', *Haskins Society Journal* 1 (1989): pp. 112–13, and 'The Ducal and Royal 'Acta' of Henry Fitz Empress in Berkeley Castle', *Transactions of the Bristol and Gloucestershire Archaeological Society* 109 (1991): pp. 117–37, where Patterson supplies facsimiles (*cont. on next page*)

For the moment, having disposed of the Fécamp charters, we are left with only one other charter of Henry II, besides the Chichester and Battle *inspeximuses* of 1175–79, in which the verb *inspexi* makes an appearance. The charter in question, settling a dispute over knight's fees at Dogmersfield and Dinder in favour of bishop Reginald of Bath, is dated at Geddington, and can be assigned by its witnesses to the opening weeks of 1177. In two separate places it refers to a charter of King Henry I *quam ego coram baronibus meis vidi et inspexi*.[64] Galbraith, who knew of it only from an inferior chancery copy, suspected that it was forged.[65] Certainly it is peculiar in its terminology, and in particular employs a phrase, *cum placitum esset in curia mea*, otherwise unique in the entire corpus of Henry II's charters. However, its extremely long list of twenty-nine witnesses contains no obvious anomalies; it is referred to in detail in a papal confirmation of April 1179;[66] its text was fully recited, within a decade, in an apparently genuine *inspeximus* charter of Archbishop Richard of Canterbury to be dated 1181 X 1184,[67] and it ends with the clause *per manum Walteri Constant' archid(iaconi) Oxenef' tunc sigillar(ii)*, similar to a clause found elsewhere in a royal charter of August 1177 X April 1178, lending circumstantial support to the authenticity of the Bath *inspeximus*, and suggesting a direct connection to the earlier *inspeximus* for Battle, which the King is said to have ordered from the hands of the same Master Walter of Coutances.[68] If we accept the Bath charter as authentic, then we may add it to the Chichester charter as yet a third genuine example of the royal *inspeximus* form which Galbraith believed was unique to Battle.

We thus have two or possibly three genuine examples of the use of the clause *inspexi*, rather than the unique example posited by Galbraith. Equally significant, and again contrary to Galbraith's conclusions, there is evidence that this, or a very similar clause, continued in use, in the royal chancery and in the subsidiary

---

(*cont. from previous page*) to argue that the charters are genuine, the work of a contemporary Bristol scribe submitted for sealing by the King. My own reasons for doubting their authenticity, partly set out in N. Vincent, 'Nine New Charters of Henry Plantagenet Duke of Normandy (1150–1154)', *Historical Research* (forthcoming 2000), must await a proper airing elsewhere.

64. Best preserved in PRO E159/97 (Memoranda Roll 17 Edward II) m.185d; E159/94 (ibid.) m.37. Printed from a corrupt copy in *Calendar of Charter Rolls 1300–26*, pp. 471–72. To be dated after the consecration of Bishop Reginald of Bath, and hence after the restoration of Hugh earl of Chester, deprived of his earldom from 1174 until the Northampton council of January 1177 at which another of the witnesses, Wido dean of Waltham, resigned from office.

65. Galbraith, 'Seven Charters', p. 272, n. 3.

66. *Papsturkunden in England II*, ed. W. Holtzmann, Berlin, 1935, p. 386, no. 189.

67. *English Episcopal Acta II*, no. 51, where the charter of Henry II is misdated to February 1176 on the basis of Eyton, *Itinerary*, p. 200. Cheney (*English Episcopal Acta II*, p. lxvii) identifies this as the first genuine example of the use of the *inspeximus* form at Canterbury.

68. For the charter of 1177–78 in favour of Chartres Cathedral, *data per manum magistri Walteri de Constantiis apud Turon*, see Paris, Bibliothèque Nationale ms. nouv.acq. Latin 2231 no.2, printed with facsimile by Delisle and Berger, *Recueil*, no. 563, and Delisle, *Atlas*, plate 21; Bishop, *Scriptores Regis*, p. 68, no. 654, with discussion and somewhat reluctant acceptance of its authenticity at p. 10; Vincent, *Handlist*, p. 57, no. 35. For Master Walter, in 1177 described as *sigillarius regis*, being commanded to issue a royal writ, see P. Grosjean, 'Vies et miracles de S. Petroc', *Analecta Bollandiana* 74 (1956): p. 181.

chanceries of the King's immediate family, until at least the early years of King John. Here we need to take account of two charters of King Richard I, the first of them issued at Canterbury on 26 November 1189, reciting in full eight earlier royal charters to the bishops of Bath: a privilege of King William Rufus, four of Henry I, and a further three of Henry II, including the charter of 1177 over Dogmersfield and Dinder considered above.[69] Richard's charter, it is true, does not make use of the verb form *inspexi* or *inspeximus*, but instead speaks of the earlier charters as those *quas de verbo ad verbum fecimus annotari ... sicut in prescriptis cartarum rescriptis continetur*: a formula that is nonetheless entirely distinct from the formula of renovation that was to govern royal charters reissued under the King's second seal after May 1198, and which at the very least suggests that by 1189 the King's chancery had accepted the basic principle that the charters of the King's ancestors might not merely be paraphrased as part of a general confirmation, but recited word for word as part of an instrument in many respects analogous to the *inspeximus* charter as developed after 1227.

A second charter of King Richard, supposedly issued at Jaffa on 26 August 1192, is equally remarkable.[70] Written in a hand that is clearly not English, it recites in full an award made by Snelman of Ospringe in Kent in the crusader army at Acre, confirming a tenement held from Gervase of Ospringe to Snelman's nephew John, witnessed by various courtiers, including Roger of Préaux, Stephen of Thurnham, and Stephen de Marçay, the King's seneschal, as well as by a group of lesser men.[71] Snelman's original charter survives elsewhere in the same archive, written in the same professional hand as the King's confirmation.[72] The confirmation, perhaps assenting to a deathbed grant by one of the King's fellow crusaders, once again avoids any use of the *inspeximus* formula, but instead speaks of the King's confirmation and assent to Snelman's charter *sicut carta ipsius testatur sub his verbis*, ending *Nos igitur hanc donationem et concessionem iuxta prescriptum tenorem factam approbantes et prorsus habentes, eam ut indissolubilis et in perpetuum firma permaneat, presenti scripto et sigilli nostri appensione sancimus*. That this is a distinctly ecclesiastical turn of phrase is

---

69. The charter is most easily approached in the version printed as *Calendar of Charter Rolls 1300–26*, pp. 470–73, with further cartulary copies in BL ms. Egerton 3316 (Bath cartulary) fos.82r–84r; Wells Cathedral Library ms. Liber Albus I fos.15v–17r.

70. Cambridge, St John's College muniments D8/121, described with full witness lists in Vincent, *Handlist*, pp. 168–69, no. 220.

71. For Stephen de Marçay, *alias* Stephen of Tours, seneschal of Anjou under King Henry II, founder of the Maison-Dieu at Angers, disgraced in 1189 but thereafter ransomed by Richard, released in time to witness a royal charter at Luçon in May 1190, see Delisle, *Introduction*, pp. 459–63; E. M. Hallam, 'Henry II, Richard I and the Order of Grandmont', *Journal of Medieval History* 1 (1975): pp. 171–72, 175–76; *Itinerary of Richard I*, ed. Landon, p. 32, no. 286. The use of the title 'seneschal' in the charter issued at Jaffa is peculiar but not a certain proof of forgery. Gervase of Ospringe is recorded independently in the Exchequer account for 1190, paying an amercement of 54 shillings in Kent: *The Great Roll of the Pipe for the First Year of the Reign of King Richard the First*, ed. J. Hunter, London, 1844, p. 234.

72. Cambridge, St John's College muniments D8/200, sealed *sur double queue*, parchment tag, seal impression missing.

substantiated by the dating clause, *per manum Philippi tunc regis sigillarii*, supplying the date according to the year of the incarnation and the Roman calendar, rather than the customary royal formula of day, month, and regnal year. I suspect that what we have here is not a forgery but a diplomatic oddity, produced by a foreign, possibly Italian scribe, more accustomed to ecclesiastical than royal practice.[73] The list of crusader witnesses it provides is of considerable interest, as is its reference to the King's seal, temporarily lost in a shipwreck off Cyprus in April 1191, but recovered thereafter. Once again, it suggests that as early as 1192, albeit in exceptional circumstances, the King was experimenting with the full recital, not merely of earlier royal charters, but of the charters of such obscure private individuals as Snelman of Ospringe.

Elsewhere, from much the same period, we have clear evidence that a prototype of the *inspeximus* clause was in use in the chanceries both of Queen Eleanor, and of the brother of Richard I, John count of Mortain, the future King John. Thus in a charter to Hugh bishop of Coventry, 1189 X 1198, Count John speaks of charters of his father and brother, Henry II and Richard I, which *propriis oculis inspexi et inspecta approbaui*.[74] A confirmation by John to the monks of Canterbury Cathedral opens with a reference to an earlier charter of Richard I, witnessed by John himself, *Sciatis me vidisse cartam domini et fratris mei regis Ricardi . . . et quod ego in eadem carta testis sum*,[75] whilst a confirmation to Fécamp, apparently unrelated to the earlier, suspect charters of Henry II considered above, once again employs the verb *inspexi*: *Sciatis quod inspexi cartas comitis Richardi et aliorum dominorum de Normannia*.[76] A similar use of *inspexi* may well have been made in John's charter to Tewkesbury Abbey, today known only from an abstract in the Tewkesbury cartulary.[77] Most remarkably of all, a charter issued by John to Geoffrey de Marsh and dated at Nottingham on 29 August 1193 appears to anticipate by more than thirty years much the same formula that was to be officially

---

73. For comparison, see H. E. Mayer, 'Die Kanzlei Richards I. von England auf dem Dritten Kreuzzug', *Mitteilungen des Instituts für Osterreichische Geschichtsforschung* 85 (1977): pp. 22–35; J. Sayers, 'English Charters from the Third Crusade', in *Tradition and Change: Essays in Honour of Marjorie Chibnall*, ed. D. Greenway, C. Holdsworth, and J. Sayers, Cambridge, 1985, pp. 195–213, esp. 196–201, dealing with other royal charters issued on Crusade by the hand of Master Philip of Poitiers, the King's clerk.

74. Lichfield Cathedral Library ms. Magnum Registrum Album fo.115r, whence W. Dugdale and R. Dodsworth, *Monasticon Anglicanum*, ed. J. Caley, H. Ellis, and B. Bandinel, 6 vols, London, 1846, VI, p. 1248.

75. Canterbury Cathedral Library mss. Register A fos.82v–83r, 148v (158v); Register E fo.21v; Register I fo.76v.

76. Rouen, Archives départementales Seine-Maritime 7H20 pièce non coté, in a copy of 1721 taken from a lost original, also in Rouen, Bibliothèque Municipale ms. 1210 (Fécamp cartulary) no. 24; Paris, Bibliothèque Nationale ms. nouv.acq. Latin 2412, p. 24.

77. BL ms. Cotton Cleopatra A vii (Tewkesbury cartulary) fo.75v, printed in Dugdale and Dodsworth, *Monasticon*, II, p. 69, no. 20: *Confirmatio I(ohannis) comitis Moritonie qua dicitur quod inspectis cartis antecessorum suorum R. filii Haimonis et Roberti filii regis H(enrici) primi et Willielmi filii eius comitis Glouc', vidit et intellexit quod R. filius H. dederat et concesserat ecclesie sancte Marie de Theok' et monachis decimas omnium reddituum suorum de Cairdif et de toto dominico suo in Wallia*.

adopted by the chancery of Henry III after 1227: *Sciatis me cartam venerabilis patris I(ohannis) Dublinensis archiepiscopi inspexisse in hec verba*, followed by a full recital of the archbishop's charter, and closing *Ego autem hanc eius donationem ratam habens et firmam eam presenti scripto confirmo et sigilli mei appositione communio*.[78] Being almost too good to be true, this last formula must arouse the suspicion that it has been reworked or forged in imitation of the thirteenth-century royal *inspeximus: Inspeximus cartam X in hec verba . . . Nos igitur hanc concessionem . . . confirmamus*.[79] Nonetheless, even after becoming King in 1199, although many of the experimental devices used by John as count seem to have disappeared from his chancery practice, there is at least one instrument entered on the official chancery rolls that deserves to be regarded as in some respects analogous to the later *inspeximus*: a charter issued in April 1200, granting Henry de Bohun the third penny of the county of Hereford, in return for Bohun's agreement that, should King John have a legitimate heir, there could be no further claim to the lands and liberties contained in a charter of Henry II, first issued in 1155, which is recited in full in King John's award: *cartam H(enrici) regis patris nostri quam ipse habuiit in hac forma*. This charter had been deposited in Winchester Cathedral Priory, to be "broken and destroyed" should King John have legitimate issue: *frangenda et destruenda si heredem de uxore nobis deponsata habuimus*.[80] Since the charter of Henry II was recited here in order that it might be annulled, rather than inspected and confirmed, John's charter deserves to be regarded as perhaps the first example of what would later be described as the royal exemplification, distinct from but clearly related to the charter of *inspeximus*. An exemplification merely recites the terms of an earlier award, without claiming to confirm them: an *inspeximus*, by contrast, not only recites but confirms. As yet another prototype for the *inspeximus* form, we should note a charter of Queen Eleanor, John's mother, issued in July 1199, confirming the privileges of Duke William of Aquitaine and Richard I to the abbey of Ste-Croix at Bordeaux, including the phrase *inspeximus priuilegia quibus pater noster et predictus filius noster rex Ricardus*, confirming, although not reciting these earlier charters, which *presentis scripti testimonio et sigilli nostri authoritate confirmamus*.[81]

---

78. Dublin, National Library of Ireland ms. 2530 (Red Book of Ormond) fos.31v–32r, whence the copy in Lambeth Palace Library ms. 608 fo.10r. Printed in *The Red Book of Ormond*, ed. N.B. White, Irish Manuscripts Commission, Dublin, 1932, pp. 86–87, no. 31, and cf. J. T. Gilbert, *National Mss of Ireland: Account of Facsimiles*, Dublin, 1884, p. 101.

79. For various examples of this formula from the reign of Henry III, see *Rotuli Chartarum*, p. vi ff.

80. *Rotuli Chartarum*, p. 53, from PRO C53/1 (Charter Roll 1 John), and cf. p. 61b for Bohun's reciprocal charter on this agreement, once again reciting the earlier award by Henry II.

81. Bordeaux, Archives départementales de la Gironde H640 (Cartulary of St-Croix) fos.4r–5v, printed in *Cartulaire de l'abbaye de S.-Croix de Bordeaux*, Archives Historiques du département de la Gironde xxvii (1892), pp. 7–8, no. 5, with further copies in Paris, Bibliothèque Nationale mss. Latin 12666 fos.89r–90r, 166v–167v; Latin 17116, p. 379; Latin 13817 fo.44r; Dupuy 841 fo.150r–v, and cf. *Calendar of Patent Rolls 1232–47*, p. 393.

In light of all this, it is clear that Galbraith's conclusions on the date and circumstances in which the *inspeximus* clause came into being are in need of revision. Galbraith was correct to suppose that the *inspeximus* clause proper did not become a regular feature of chancery practice until Henry III's coming of age in 1226–27. However, long before that, the royal chancery had experimented with several very similar instruments. Beginning with the two or three surviving uses of the *inspexi* clause by Henry II in the mid 1170s, and continuing thereafter under King Richard I and his mother and brother with the occasional use of the verb *inspexi* or *inspeximus*, by 1199 we already find the royal chancery and its satellites making a full recital of earlier charters and privileges, including those not only of kings, but of bishops and of relatively minor private individuals. In England, the royal *inspeximus* developed in tandem with, or even in advance of the episcopal *inspeximus*, which itself emerged several decades later than some scholars have supposed. Since the *inspeximus* was the forger's charter *par excellence* – used to lend spurious authenticity to what purported to be much earlier awards – forgeries abound amongst the earliest examples of the form. In the chancery of the kings of France, for example, where the full-blown *inspeximus* developed after *c*.1210, some twenty or thirty years later than in England, both of the earliest examples of the form have been rejected by Michel Nortier as thirteenth-century forgeries or as deeply suspect.[82] We have seen already that various of the charters employing the verb *inspexi*, supposedly issued by Henry II, are probably forged. At Rochester, as late as the 1260s, the monks were concocting what purported to be *inspeximuses*, and even *inspeximuses* of *inspeximuses*, supposedly issued by the twelfth-century archbishops of Canterbury, as a means of authenticating Rochester's remarkable collection of twelfth-century forgeries.[83] In these circumstances, every *inspeximus* charter purporting to date from before 1200 needs to be very closely examined. After examination, only a few such charters – including those of Henry II and Richard I for Battle, Chichester, Bath, and possibly Ospringe examined here – can be accepted as genuine, the rest being subject to a greater or lesser suspicion of forgery. Even the genuine examples, such as the Battle *inspeximus* first studied by Galbraith, now put in context alongside the charter of a similar date for Chichester, suggest that the Battle chronicler's account of the emergence of the *inspeximus* is less than entirely accurate. To quite what extent the chronicler can be believed in other respects is a story that I intend to tell elsewhere.[84] Meanwhile, I hope to have shown that even so common a linguistic formula as the *inspeximus* clause requires careful handling, and the

---

82. M. Nortier, 'Les actes faussement attribués à la chancellerie de Philippe Auguste', *Comptes Rendus des séances de l'Académie des Inscriptions et Belles-Lettres* (1981): pp. 661, 668, rejecting entirely the supposed *inspeximus* of 1180, and casting considerable doubt upon what would thereafter be the earliest full recital of an earlier royal charter, supposedly issued in 1209.

83. M. Brett, 'Forgery at Rochester', *Fälschungen im Mittelalter*, Monumenta Germaniae Historica Schriften 33, no. iv (1988), pp. 397–412.

84. N. Vincent, 'King Henry II and the Monks of Battle: The Battle Chronicle Unmasked', in *Belief and Culture*, Oxford, forthcoming.

application of all manner of tests – palaeographical, diplomatic, and historical – before it can itself be used as a benchmark for the dating of otherwise undated twelfth-century charters. The flowering of the royal *inspeximus* in the 1220s was one whose roots and tendrils stretched back through the reigns of Henry III's father and uncle to first germination in the reign of King Henry II. To trace its origins we must proceed with caution and, as Michael Gervers himself has warned, without any crude assumption that computers alone will tell us all that we need to know.

Bibliography

Bates, D., ed. 1998. *Regesta Regum Anglo-Normannorum: the Acta of William I 1066–1087*. Oxford.

Bishop, T. A. M. 1950. 'A Chancery Scribe: Stephen of Fougères'. *Cambridge Historical Journal* 10: pp. 106–107.

———. 1961. *Scriptores Regis*. Oxford.

Caenegem, R. C. van. 1959. *Royal Writs in England from the Conquest to Glanvill*. Selden Society lxxvii.

Bresslau, H. 1912–13. *Handbuch der Urkundenlehre für Deutschland und Italien*. 2nd ed. 2 vols. Leipzig and Berlin.

Brett, M. 1988. 'Forgery at Rochester'. *Fälschungen im Mittelalter*, Monumenta Germaniae Historica Schriften 33, no. iv: pp. 397–412.

Chaplais, P. 1959. 'Une charte originale de Guillaume le Conquérant pour l'abbaye de Fécamp; la donation de Steyning et de Bury (1085)', in *L'Abbaye Bénédictine de Fécamp*. Fécamp.

———. 1962. 'The Original Charters of Herbert and Gervase abbots of Westminster (1121–1157)', in *A Medieval Miscellany for Doris Mary Stenton*, ed. P. M. Barnes and C. F. Slade. Pipe Roll Society n.s. xxxvi.

———. 1971. *English Royal Documents, King John – Henry VI, 1199–1461*. Oxford.

———. 1973. 'Henry II's Reissue of the Canons of the Council of Lillebonne of Whitsun 1080 (?25 February 1162)'. *Journal of the Society of Archivists* 4: pp. 627–32.

———. 1981. *Essays in Medieval Diplomacy and Administration*. London.

Cheney, C. R. 1950. *English Bishops' Chanceries 1100–1250*. Manchester.

Cheney, C. R., D. Smith, et al., eds. 1980–. *English Episcopal Acta*. 17 vols. Oxford.

Cheney, M. G. 1980. *Roger Bishop of Worcester 1164–1179*. Oxford.

Chevreux, P., and J.-J. Vernier. 1911. *Les Archives de Normandie et de la Seine-Inférieure*. Rouen.

Davis, H. W. C., H. A. Cronne, and R. H. C. Davis, eds. 1913–69. *Regesta Regum Anglo-Normannorum 1066–1154*. Oxford.

Delisle, L. 1906. 'Mémoire sur la chronologie des chartes de Henri II'. *Bibliothèque de l'École des Chartes* 67: pp. 361–401.

———. 1909. *Recueil des Actes de Henri II roi d'Angleterre et duc de Normandie concernant les provinces françaises et les affaires de France*. Introduction (and *Atlas* of facsimiles). Paris.

Delisle, L., and E. Berger, eds. 1916–27. *Recueil des Actes de Henri II*. 3 vols. Paris.

Douglas, D. C. 1959. 'The First Ducal Charter for Fécamp', in *L'Abbaye Bénédictine de Fécamp: ouvrage sciéntifique du XIIIe centenaire*. Fécamp.

Dufour, J. 1995. 'Peut-on parler d'une organisation de la chancellerie de Philippe Auguste?'. *Archiv für Diplomatik* 41: pp. 249–61.

Eyton, R. W. 1878. *Court, Household and Itinerary of King Henry II*. London.
Fauroux, M., ed. 1961. *Recueil des Actes des Ducs de Normandie de 911 à 1066*. Caen.
Galbraith, V. H. 1932. 'Seven Charters of Henry II at Lincoln Cathedral'. *The Antiquaries Journal* 12: pp. 269–78.
———. 1937. 'A New Charter of Henry II to Battle Abbey'. *English Historical Review* 52: pp. 67–73.
Gervers, M. 1997. 'The Dating of Medieval English Private Charters of the Twelfth and Thirteenth Centuries', in *A Distinct Voice: Medieval Studies in Honor of Leonard E. Boyle, O.P.*, ed. J. Brown and W.P. Stoneman. Notre Dame.
Giry, A. 1925. *Manuel de Diplomatique*. 2 vols. Paris.
Hardy, T. D., ed. 1837. *Rotuli Chartarum*. London.
Haskins, C. H. 1918. *Norman Institutions*. New York.
Hollister, C. W. 1986. *Monarchy, Magnates and Institutions in the Anglo-Norman World*. London.
Holt, J. C. 1971. 'The Assizes of Henry II: The Texts', in *The Study of Medieval Records: Essays in Honour of Kathleen Major*, ed. D. A. Bullough and R. L. Storey, pp. 85–106. Oxford.
———. 1989. 'The Acta of Henry II and Richard I of England 1154–1199: The Archive and Its Historical Implications', in *Fotografische Sammlungen mittelalterlicher Urkunden in Europa*, ed. P. Rück, pp. 137–40. Sigmaringen.
———. 1995. 'The Writs of Henry II'. *Proceedings of the British Academy* 89: pp. 47–64.
Holt, J. C. and R. Mortimer, eds. 1986. *Acta of Henry II and Richard I: Handlist of Documents Surviving in the Original in Repositories in the United Kingdom*. List and Index Society Special Series xxi.
Holtzmann, W. 1930–52. *Papsturkunden in England*. 3 vols. Göttingen and Berlin.
Keefe, T. K. 1990. 'Place-Date Distribution of Royal Charters and the Historical Geography of Patronage Strategies at the Court of King Henry II Plantagenet'. *The Haskins Society Journal* 2: 179–88.
Landon, L. 1935. *The Itinerary of King Richard I*, Pipe Roll Society n.s. xiii.
Landon, L. and J. Conway-Davies. 1939–60. *Cartae Antiquae Rolls*. 2 vols. Pipe Roll Society n.s. xvii, xxxiii.
Lemarignier, J.-F. 1937. *Etude sur les privilèges d'exemption et de juridiction ecclésiastique des abbayes Normandes depuis les origines jusqu'en 1140*. Paris.
Mayer, H. E. 1977. 'Die Kanzlei Richards I. von England auf dem Dritten Kreuzzug'. *Mitteilungen des Instituts für Osterreichische Geschichtsforschung* 85: pp. 22–35.
Mortimer, R. 1990. 'The Charters of Henry II: What Are the Criteria for Authenticity?'. *Anglo-Norman Studies* 12: pp. 119–34.
Nortier, M. 1981. 'Les actes faussement attribués à la chancellerie de Philippe Auguste'. *Comptes Rendus des séances de l'Académie des Inscriptions et Belles-Lettres*.
Parisse, M., P. Pégeot, and B.-M. Tock, eds. 1998. *Pancartes monastiques des XIe et XIIe siècles*. Brepols.
Patterson, R. B. 1989. 'Robert Fitz Harding of Bristol'. *Haskins Society Journal* 1: pp. 112–13.
———. 1991. 'The Ducal and Royal "Acta" of Henry Fitz Empress in Berkeley Castle'. *Transactions of the Bristol and Gloucestershire Archaeological Society* 109: pp. 117–37.
Poole, R. L. 1908. 'The Dates of Henry II's Charters'. *English Historical Review* 22: pp. 79–83.
Prentout, H. 1918–20. 'De l'origine de la formule 'Dei Gratia' dans les chartes de Henri II'. *Mémoires de l'Académie Nationale des Sciences, Arts et Belles-Lettres de Caen*: pp. 341–93.

Richardson, H. G., ed. 1943. *The Memoranda Roll for the Michaelmas Term of the First Year of the Reign of King John (1199–1200)*. Pipe Roll Society n.s. xxi.

Round, J. H. 1907. 'The Chronology of Henry II's Charters'. *Archaeological Journal* 64: pp. 63–79.

Sayers, J. 1985. 'English Charters from the Third Crusade', in *Tradition and Change: Essays in Honour of Marjorie Chibnall*, ed. D. Greenway, C. Holdsworth, and J. Sayers, pp. 195–213. Cambridge.

Searle, E. 1968. 'Battle Abbey and Exemption: The Forged Charters'. *English Historical Review* 83: pp. 449–80.

Searle, E., ed. 1980. *The Chronicle of Battle Abbey*. Oxford.

Vincent, N. 1996. *Acta of Henry II and Richard I Part Two: A Supplementary Handlist of Documents Surviving in the Original in Repositories in the United Kingdom, France, Ireland, Belgium and the USA*. List and Index Society special series xxvii.

———. Forthcoming 2000. 'Nine New Charters of Henry Plantagenet Duke of Normandy (1150–1154)'. *Historical Research*.

———. Forthcoming 2001. 'King Henry II and the Monks of Battle: The Battle Chronicle Unmasked', in *Belief and Culture*. Oxford.

———. Forthcoming. 'Les Actes de Henri II Plantagenet concernant la Normandie inconnues à Léopold Delisle'. *Cahiers Léopold Delisle*.

PART III
IDENTIFYING FORGERIES

A NEW METHOD FOR THE DATING AND IDENTIFICATION OF FORGERIES? THE DEEDS METHODOLOGY APPLIED TO A FORGED CHARTER OF COUNT ROBERT I OF FLANDERS FOR ST PETER'S ABBEY, GHENT

Georges Declercq

During the Middle Ages, and particularly in the eleventh and twelfth centuries, charters were forged or reworked in large quantities. The evaluation of this enormous amount of falsified charter evidence is not unproblematic. This is mainly due to the fact that the extent to which medieval documents were tampered with could vary greatly. Some falsifications are based on a genuine document of which the content has been wholly or partially altered, while other forgeries have no authentic basis at all and are completely fabricated. Still another possibility is that only a few words or a single sentence have been changed or interpolated in a broadly trustworthy charter, or that a later copyist has emended the text of an earlier charter in order to adjust it to the conditions of his own time. Furthermore, one has to distinguish between formal or material forgeries, on the diplomatic level, and intellectual forgeries, on the juridical level.[1] In view of this complexity scholars often remain undecided, preferring to use rather vague qualifications as 'doubtful', 'suspicious', or 'dubious', instead of more clear-cut notions such as 'forged', 'interpolated', or 'reworked'.

A problem closely linked to the identification of forgeries is the dating of their fabrication, for it is generally external and/or internal anachronisms that permit the detection of documents which are not what they appear to be, and which, as a consequence, do not belong to the purported date. In the case of originals – or rather apparent or so-called pseudo-originals – the evidence of the handwriting allows the determination of a more or less approximate date. If only copies have been preserved, everything depends on internal criteria, for example, the use of an anachronistic title or the mention of a dignitary not yet in function in the witness list, but these at best result only in the determination of a *terminus post quem*. On the other hand, an explicit mention or the confirmation of a forgery in a later charter may render a *terminus ante quem*. Occasionally it may even be possible to link

---

From *Dating Undated Medieval Charters*. Ed. Michael Gervers. Copyright (by the Editor and Contributors 2000). Published by the Boydell Press (in association with Collegium Budapest), PO Box 9, Woodbridge, Suffolk, IP12 3DF, Great Britain. ISBN 0 85115 792 0.

1. Giles Constable, 'Forgery and Plagiarism in the Middle Ages', *Archiv für Diplomatik* 29 (1983): pp. 1–41, esp. pp. 10–11. See also Christopher Brooke, 'Approaches to Medieval Forgery', in *Medieval Church and Society. Selected Essays*, London, 1971, pp. 100–120, and Michael T. Clanchy, *From Memory to Written Record: England 1066–1307*, 2nd ed., Oxford–Cambridge, Mass., 1993, pp. 318–27. A general discussion of the phenomenon can be found in Raoul C. Van Caenegem (with the collaboration of François-Louis Ganshof), *Guide to the Sources of Medieval History*, Amsterdam–New York–Oxford, 1978, pp. 70–73, and in Olivier Guyotjeannin, Jacques Pycke, and Benoît-Michel Tock, *Diplomatique médiévale*, Turnhout, 1993, pp. 367–78.

a falsification with a specific dispute or with particular circumstances, so making possible the establishment of a quite accurate date. In most instances, however, this is not the case. Sometimes one has no other choice but to accept the approximate date of compilation of a cartulary as the only reliable *terminus ante quem*. As a result, many forgeries can be ascribed only to a date range extending over several decades, or, if the apparent original is preserved, to such inaccurate indications of time as 'early', 'middle', or 'late' in a given century.

The assignation of such vague dates, or of broad spaces of time, to forged or reworked charters considerably diminishes their value as historical sources, which to a large extent depends upon the ability to determine the circumstances in which they were fabricated and the intentions, motivations, and justifications of the people who forged them.[2] A method allowing a more accurate dating of falsifications would therefore be very helpful. The computer-assisted DEEDS methodology developed at the University of Toronto by Professor Michael Gervers to identify chronological changes in charter terminology and word order appears to open new prospects in this connection.[3] The method relies upon the fact that the vocabulary and formulae of medieval charters changed constantly and regularly over time, "so much so in fact that when looked at as a whole and compared with other similar documents (of known date), the make-up of a given charter (without date) can provide an accurate indication of its own date".[4] In other words, it may be assumed that the date of an undated charter can be determined with some accuracy by means of a comparison of its text with a database of word patterns obtained from dated documents, because – as Professor Gervers stresses – "each word and string of words in context has its unique chronological pattern or fingerprint". Although this methodology was designed primarily to provide a possible date for undated private charters, it is obvious that the same procedure can also be applied to the detection and dating of forgeries and other documents of which the language, form, and syntax cannot be reconciled with their purported date. The idea of using the vocabulary of a charter to verify its authenticity is not new of course, but up to now only words out of context, usually technical terms – for example, the anachronistic use of a word such as *feodum* – were singled out for analysis.[5]

---

2. On the value of forgeries as historical sources in their own right, see Constable, 'Forgery and Plagiarism', p. 2: "Forgeries and plagiarism follow rather than create fashion and can without paradox be considered among the most authentic products of their time." The distinction between intent, motivation, and justification is stressed by Elisabeth A. R. Brown, 'Falsitas pia sive reprehensibilis. Medieval Forgers and Their Intentions', in *Fälschungen im Mittelalter. Internationaler Kongress der Monumenta Germaniae Historica: München, 16.–19. September 1986*, vol. I, Hanover, 1988, p. 103.
3. DEEDS is an acronym for 'Documents of Essex England Data Set'. On the methodology, see the contributions of Michael Gervers and Rodolfo Fiallos in this volume.
4. Michael Gervers, 'The Dating of Medieval English Private Charters of the Twelfth and Thirteenth Centuries', in *A Distinct Voice. Medieval Studies in Honor of Leonard E. Boyle OP*, ed. Jacqueline Brown and William P. Stoneman, Notre Dame, 1997.
5. See, for example, Léon Voet, 'Etude sur deux bulles de Benoît VIII pour Saint-Vaast d'Arras', *Bulletin de la Commission Royale d'Histoire* 109 (1944): pp. 206–208 (anachronistic use of the word *bercaria*), and Albert Derolez, 'De valse oorkonde van graaf Arnulf I van Vlaanderen voor het Sint-Donatiaanskapittel te Brugge (961, juli 31)', *Bulletin de la Commission Royale* (*cont. on next page*)

The DEEDS methodology, on the contrary, allows for a more systematic and contextual approach to the whole text of a given document, including its formulaic parts. As the results of initial tests carried out by Professor Gervers and his collaborator Rodolfo Fiallos, using dated documents as a means of control, have proved to be very encouraging, it seemed interesting to test the potential of the methodology with regard to the identification and dating of forgeries.

For this test, we selected a charter from the archives of St Peter's Abbey in Ghent, Flanders, one of the great centres of charter falsification in Western Europe during the Middle Ages. Of the some 400 charters preserved for this monastery up to 1200, 40 or so are forgeries – that is, completely fabricated or heavily falsified – 63 are later 'renovations', while 15 other documents have been subjected to minor alterations, such as a limited interpolation or the attachment of a forged seal.[6] The selected document is a charter dated 1072 by which the Flemish count Robert I, surnamed 'the Frisian', apparently confirmed, in very general terms, the possessions granted to the abbey by his predecessors.[7] In the edition of the charters of the counts of Flanders from 1071 to 1128, published in 1938 by Fernand Vercauteren, this document is still regarded as without suspicion.[8] In 1950, however, Maurits Gysseling and Anton Koch pointed out that the handwriting of the so-called original, of which only the lower part has been preserved, in fact dates from the middle or the second half of the twelfth century.[9] A palaeographical detail allows us to specify somewhat, as the ligature of the letters 'd' and 'e', formed by the addition of the small head of an 'e' in the upper swing of the round 'd', occurs in the archives of the Ghent abbey only from the 1160s onwards.[10] A seventeenth-century drawing representing the now lost seal even offers an

---

(*cont. from previous page*) *d'Histoire* 140 (1974): p. 456 (anachronistic use of the words *feodum* and *prebendatus*). The possibilities offered in this respect by the creation of databases of medieval charters are highlighted by Michel Parisse, 'A propos du traitement automatique des chartes: chronologie du vocabulaire et repérage des actes suspects', *La lexicographie du latin médiéval et ses rapports avec les recherches actuelles sur la civilisation du Moyen Age*, Paris, 1981, pp. 241–49, and Benoît-Michel Tock, 'Les mutations du vocabulaire latin des chartes au XIe siècle', *Bibliothèque de l'Ecole des Chartes* 155 (1997): pp. 119–48, esp. pp. 142–46.

6. Georges Declercq, 'Centres de faussaires et falsification de chartes en Flandre au Moyen Age', in *Falsos y falsificaciones de documentos diplomaticos en la edad media*, Zaragoza, 1991, p. 66.

7. For the text of this charter, see Appendix.

8. Fernand Vercauteren, *Actes des comtes de Flandre (1071–1128)*, Brussels, 1938, pp. 4–5 (no. 2); however, see also pp. civ–cv of the introduction, where Vercauteren has to concede that the now lost seal, which is known only by way of a seventeenth-century engraving (see infra), appears to have been a later forgery, but this, in his opinion, does not affect the authenticity of the charter as such ("il faut vraisemblablement conclure que ce sceau est un faux appendu au plus tôt à la fin du XIIe ou au XIIIe siècle à l'acte comtal. L'authenticité de ce dernier est cependant à l'abri de tout soupçon").

9. Maurits Gysseling and Anton C. F. Koch, *Diplomata Belgica ante annum millesimum centesimum scripta*, vol. I, Brussels, 1950, p. 215 (no. 120).

10. The first original charter in which this ligature is used dates from 1163 (Ghent, Rijksarchief, Sint-Pieters, charters, no. 282). Many examples can be found in the additions from the 1160s in the *Liber Traditionum* of the abbey (Ghent, Rijksarchief, Sint-Pieters, II, no. 2bis, fol. 3r–v, 103r–106v, 107v–108r). On this ligature, see, in general, also Bernard Bischoff, *Latin Palaeography. Antiquity and the Middle Ages*, Cambridge, 1990, p. 122.

absolute *terminus post quem*.[11] On this seal, of the equestrian type, the counts' shield bears a representation of a 'lion rampant', although this coat of arms was first introduced, notably on the seal of the count, in 1163 by the young count Philip of Alsace.[12] The external criteria thus clearly point to the fact that this single sheet of parchment is a pseudo-original fabricated during the last third of the twelfth century. The content of the charter, on the other hand, at first sight does not arouse any suspicion whatsoever. There are no apparent anachronisms, and the names of the witnesses are known from other documents for St Peter's Abbey dating from the reign of count Robert the Frisian (1071–1093).[13] The application of the DEEDS methodology, however, demonstrates that the vocabulary cannot be reconciled with the purported date either.

Using the guidelines of this method, we compared the text in question with a word concordance of all charters for St Peter's up to 1200, provided to us some years ago by the CETEDOC ('Centre de traitement électronique des documents', UCL, Louvain-la-Neuve).[14] Not all documents occurring in the CETEDOC database were useful in this respect. The undated charters had to be discarded of course, as were the numerous forgeries and 'renovations'. We also left out the royal diplomas, the papal privileges and letters, and the *'notitiae'* or abridged copies in the *Liber Traditionum* of the abbey.[15] What remains is a fairly homogeneous collection of some 160 authentic and precisely dated charters, most of which were probably drafted by the Ghent monks themselves.[16] During the comparison,

---

11. Oliverus Vredius, *Sigilla comitum Flandriae et inscriptiones diplomatum ab iis editorum*, Bruges, 1639, p. 6 (with the following description: "anno 1072 diploma edidit sigillo munitum in quo scutum est, leonis typo impressum; diplomati sic inscripsit: Robertus Dei gratia comes Flandrie"); the drawing is reproduced in René Laurent, *Les sceaux des princes territoriaux belges du Xe siècle à 1482*, vol. II, Brussels, 1993, plate 5 (no. 4).

12. Laurent, *Les sceaux*, I/1, p. 150, note 61. On the introduction of this new type of seal in 1163, see Thérèse de Hemptinne and Adriaan Verhulst, *De oorkonden der graven van Vlaanderen (Juli 1128–September 1191)*. II. Uitgave [edition]. Band I: *Regering van Diederik van de Elzas (Juli 1128–17 Januari 1168)*, Brussels, 1988, pp. lxxxix–xci (with plate XII), and Laurent, *Les sceaux*, I/1, p. 142.

13. See, in particular, Arnold Fayen, *Liber Traditionum Sancti Petri Gandensis*, Ghent, 1906, pp. 120 and 122–23 (nos. 129–31).

14. The charters of St Peter's in this word concordance form part of a much larger database of some 5,000 charters originally created at the CETEDOC in connection with the 'Dictionnaire du latin médiéval' and now included in the *Thesaurus Diplomaticus* (CD-Rom, Turnhout: Brepols, 1997). On this project, see Georges Declercq, Philippe de Monty, Katrien Naessens, and Guy Trifin, 'L'informatisation de la "Table chronologique" d'A. Wauters. Méthodologie du nouveau répertoire des documents diplomatiques belges antérieurs à 1200', *Bulletin de la Commission Royale d'Histoire* 153 (1987): pp. 223–302.

15. Charters which originally were not intended for St Peter's Abbey, but entered its archives at a later date, were also left aside. On the other hand, we did take into account some twenty, mostly unedited charters that are absent from the database.

16. As the CETEDOC database is to a large extent based on the defective edition of Auguste Van Lokeren, *Chartes et documents de l'abbaye de Saint Pierre au Mont Blandin à Gand*, vol. I, Ghent, 1868, it was necessary to make rectifications to the text and especially to the date of some charters. This is, for example, the case with Van Lokeren, *Chartes et documents*, nos. 183 (1109 instead of 1110), 185 (1191 instead of 1112), 186 (1193 instead of 1114), and 243 (1151 instead of 1150). Slight textual corrections had to be introduced in Van Lokeren, *Chartes et documents (cont. on next page)*

which we performed manually, it quickly became clear that the language and the formulae of the charter attributed to count Robert the Frisian in fact belong to the twelfth century. Some of the formulae that bear witness to this are quite common. So, for example, the trinitarian invocation *In nomine patris et filii et spiritus sancti* that is first concluded by the word *amen* in 1142;[17] or the dating formula *Actum anno Domini* which occurs for the first time in 1157.[18] Other interesting word patterns are less formulaic. In the tenth and eleventh centuries, St Peter's Abbey was generally qualified as a *monasterium* or a *coenobium*, in combination with the original name of the institution, that is, *Blandinium* (or the genitive form *Blandiniensis*).[19] From the middle of the twelfth century onwards, however, the traditional name of the abbey was more and more replaced by the denomination *ecclesia Sancti Petri Gandensis*, which we also read in this document dated 1072.[20] In total we eventually selected twenty-two 'matching' word patterns of a minimum of three words, existing in both the charter of Robert I and the word

---

(*cont. from previous page*) nos. 185 (*appensione et testium* instead of *appensione testium*), 243 (*patris et filii* instead of *patris filii*), 311 (*dominice* instead of *domini*), 317 (*quam presentibus in perpetuum* instead of *quam presentibus*), 356 (*dominice* instead of *domini*), and 361 (*patris et filii* instead of *patris filii*, and *sigilli mei appensione* instead of *sigilli nostri appensione*). These rectifications are founded either on the original (Ghent, Rijksarchief, Sint-Pieters, charters) or on copies in the oldest cartulary, the so-called *Liber Antiquus* from the middle of the thirteenth century (Ghent, Rijksarchief, Bisdom, B 2955).

17. Van Lokeren, *Chartes et documents*, no. 231. The charters from before this date that begin with the same formula are either forgeries (for example, Van Lokeren, *Chartes et documents*, no. 132, dated 1056, but according to Gysseling and Koch (*Diplomata Belgica*, vol. I, p. 408) forged in the middle of the twelfth century), or later renovations (for example, Van Lokeren, *Chartes et documents*, nos. 144-145, both dated 1070, and Van Lokeren, *Chartes et documents*, no. 155, dated 1074; the handwriting of the first two charters points to a renewal in the thirteenth century, that of the third dates from the end of the twelfth or the beginning of the thirteenth century). Without 'amen', the trinitarian invocation is used in genuine, renewed, and forged charters from the second quarter of the eleventh century onwards (see Gysseling and Koch, *Diplomata Belgica*, vol. I, nos. 58, 68, 77, 88, 89, 90, 95, 103, 104, and 108).

18. Van Lokeren, *Chartes et documents*, no. 254. All charters prior to 1157 that have the same formula are later renovations; see, for example, Van Lokeren, *Chartes et documents*, nos. 155 (dated 1074, renewed in the late twelfth or early thirteenth century), 166 (dated 1099, renewed in the thirteenth century), 172-74 (dated 1101, renewed respectively in the last quarter of the twelfth century, the second half of the twelfth century and the first quarter of the thirteenth century), and 195 (dated 1119, renewed in the first quarter of the thirteenth century).

19. See, for example, Gysseling and Koch, *Diplomata Belgica*, vol. I, nos. 56 (a° 955: *ad monasterium loci Blandiniensis*), 64 (a° 975: *ad monasterium famoso nomine Blandinium nuncupatum*), 92 (a° 1038: *monasterium Sancti Petri, quod vocatur Blandinium in Gandavo*), 96 (a° 1047: *coenobio Sancti Petri apostolorum principis, quod situm est in monte Blandinio in territorio Gandensi*), 116 (a° 1070: *abbas Gandensis seu Blandiniensis coenobii*), and 124 (a° 1088: *in coenobio Gandensi seu Blandiniensi and in coenobio Blandinium nuncupato*).

20. See the word pattern *ecclesiam Sancti Petri Gandensis* in Van Lokeren, *Chartes et documents*, nos. 244-45 (a° 1150), 304 (a° 1166), 307 (a° 1167), and 330 (a° 1177); *ecclesie Sancti Petri Gandensis* in Van Lokeren, *Chartes et documents*, nos. 266 (a° 1161), 312 (a° 1168), 349 (a° 1184), 352 (a° 1186), 356 (a° 1187), and 357 (a° 1189); *ecclesia Sancti Petri Gandensis* in Van Lokeren, *Chartes et documents*, no. 374 (a° 1196). Without *ecclesia*, the pattern *Sancti Petri Gandensis* occurs already from the 1120s onwards; see, for example, Van Lokeren, *Chartes et documents*, nos. 197 (a° 1120), 207 (a° 1129), and 213 (a° 1133).

concordance, which were considered useful and appropriate to date the fabrication of this text. They occur in seventy-four different charters between 1109 and 1200.[21] The selection of the best word patterns for dating is, according to Professor Gervers, one of the critical points of the method, because "the historian's treatment of the records in the resultant file may amplify, or decrease, the accuracy of the date selected".[22] The decisions involved in this selection process are arbitrary and may for that reason influence the eventual outcome. We tried to limit such arbitrary decisions to a minimum, in order to be able to use as many word patterns as possible. We therefore discarded only two-word patterns, as well as word patterns with a lifetime longer than seventy-five years. On the other hand, we did not take account of the lack of currency of some word patterns, although this factor plays an important part in the DEEDS methodology, particularly in its more refined version.

At the outset, the method rested exclusively upon the length of the matching word patterns. They were grouped numerically (by frequency of occurrence) and chronologically (by occurrence over time) according to the number of words they contained. Each word pattern received a numerical value as a weighting factor in order to emphasise its length. The longer the pattern, the higher the number it collected. Once these factors had been distributed over the different years in which the matching word patterns occur, they were totalled for each year and finally accumulated in periods of twenty, ten, or five years. The date range with the highest total was considered to indicate the most likely date of issue for the undated document under consideration.[23]

In its perfected form the method has become more sophisticated. For each word pattern three variables, based respectively on length (number of words), lifetime (difference in years between the first and the last occurrence), and currency (average number of years – 'lifetime' – and occurrences) are taken into consideration. They are valued by numerical modifiers in such a way as to emphasise long patterns, with short lifetime and short currency. Taken together, these three variables result in a so-called 'MT number' (or 'total multiplier'), and only those word patterns with the highest numbers are considered valid and useful for the dating process, because the basic assumption is that "there will be a high concentration of word patterns with high value near to the real date of the charter". Next, the MT numbers are totalled and accumulated on a chronological basis, and finally used to calculate the ratio in respect of the total number of dated charters in the database

---

21. A list of the selected word patterns, with the indication of their lifetime and occurrences, can be found in the table on p. 135. Word patterns embedded in longer word patterns were, in accordance with the guidelines of the method (Gervers, 'Dating', pp. 478 and 491–93), removed. The word pattern *patris et filii et spiritus sancti amen*, for example, occurs, in fact, thirty-two times in our database; but twenty-four of these occurrences are embedded in the larger pattern *in nomine patris et filii et spiritus sancti amen*. Consequently, only the eight charters where that is not the case were taken into consideration for the shorter pattern.

22. Gervers, 'Dating', p. 479.

23. Gervers, 'Dating', pp. 476–79 and 494–99.

for the same period. The period in which the ratio is the highest is considered to represent the most probable date for the undated charter.[24]

In our case, this sophisticated method appears to be less applicable. This is mainly due to the fact that the charter in question does not produce enough high-value word patterns. Some of the word patterns we selected have too long a lifetime to be of much use according to the calculation formula used, while other patterns, with irregular currency, have to be eliminated altogether according to the same formula.[25] I also have the impression that this formula developed – arbitrarily – to calculate the MT number tends to overemphasise the word patterns which occur only once. As a result of all this, the charter of Robert the Frisian has only a global MT number – that is, the average of the ten best MT numbers – of 1.3, which means that the date produced on this basis will be less accurate and thus rather speculative. That is the case indeed, as the ratio between the accumulated MT numbers and the total number of charters in twenty-year periods is highest in the range 1132–1151, a date that is impossible in view of conclusions already drawn from the external criteria. Moreover, the result obtained in this way is anything but clear-cut, as periods as far apart as 1138–1157, 1142–1161, and 1176–1195 produce an identical ratio that almost equals that of the range 1132–1151. The result is even more inconclusive if we narrow the date range to a ten-year period, for in that case the periods 1133–1142 and 1179–1188 both share the highest ratio.

We therefore decided on a different approach, combining the original methodology, in which the selected word patterns are valued only in reference to their length, with a crucial part of its perfected version. According to the weighting method used to emphasise the value of longer patterns, a three-word pattern receives a value of 1, while an increment of 20 per cent is added for each longer word string thereafter. Thus, four-word patterns receive a value of 1.2, five-word patterns a value of 1.4, and so on.[26] Accumulated in twenty-year periods, the weighting factors in our example reach their highest total between 1180 and 1199. It would be too premature a conclusion, however, to think that this is the most likely range for the fabrication of the charter in question, because the range 1180 to 1199 is also the period in which the total number of charters in the CETEDOC database is the highest. To avoid any misinterpretation it seems necessary to verify whether or not the values accumulated by the selected word patterns in any given period are proportional to the total amount of documents in the same

---

24. More information about this perfected version of the method, and particularly the formula used for generating the MT number, can be found in a short paper by Rodolfo Fiallos entitled 'A Description of the Process in which Sample Charter 10662 (actually dated 1274) was Dated by Comparing its Text with the Text of 1524 Charters in the DEEDS Database', accessible on the website of the DEEDS-project (http://www.utoronto.ca/deeds).

25. The MT number for each of the selected word patterns is indicated in the chart on p. 135 as 'Value 2'.

26. Gervers, 'Dating', p. 479. The weighting factor for each of the selected word patterns is indicated in the chart on p. 135 as 'Value 1'.

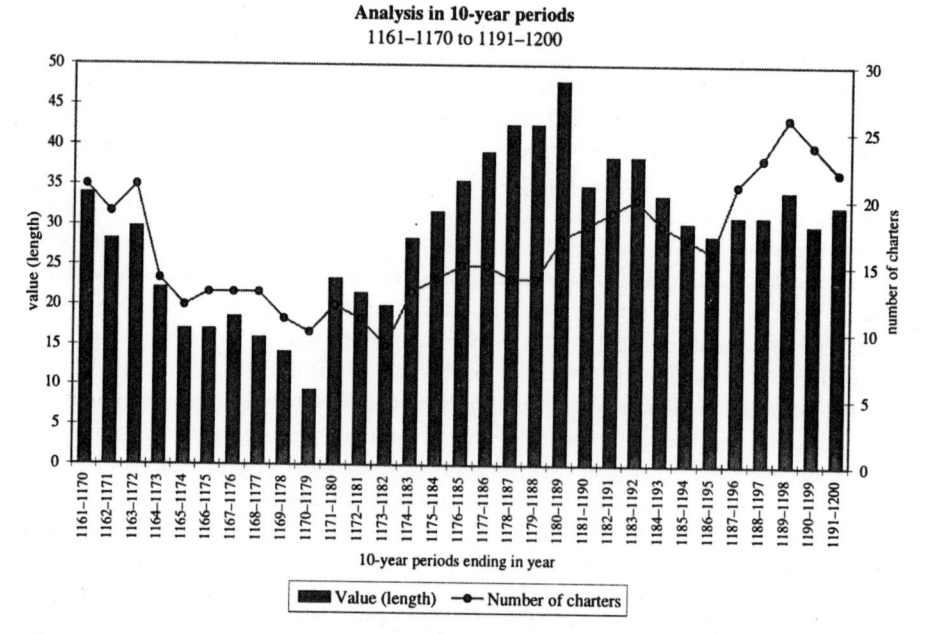

Analysis in 10-year periods
1161–1170 to 1191–1200

Figure 1 *The accumulation of dated charters (line) and weighting factors (columns) in 10-year periods ending in the years 1170 to 1200. The weighting factors, based on the length of the word-patterns, are at their highest in the range 1180–1189, while the number of charters reaches its highest total in the period 1189–1198.*

period. For that reason the selection of a possible date should rather be based on the ratio between the weighting factors and the number of charters, as in the refined version of the DEEDS methodology. If we apply this calculation to our data, we observe that the ratio reaches its highest peak in the range 1169 to 1188. As this is not an impossible date, we tried to narrow the date range to a ten-year period. This time there was more agreement between the range indicated by the accumulated values and that indicated by the ratio. The weighting factors are at their highest value in the years 1180–1189 (*Figure 1*), while the best ranges with regard to the ratio are 1178 to 1187 and 1179 to 1188, which both have exactly the same value (*Figure 2*). The fact that the adjoining ranges 1180 to 1189, and 1177 to 1186 have the second and the third highest ratio respectively, seems to support the result of the dating process.[27] We did not try to narrow the date range further because of the unequal distribution of the documents in the word concordance (for the twelfth century, 115 dated charters distributed over sixty different years).

In conclusion, the timespan 1178–1188 appears, according to this methodology, to be the most likely range for the composition of the charter concerned. The

---

27. It should also be noted that no proportion is shown between the weighting factors and the amount of charters, which reaches its highest total in the period 1189–1198.

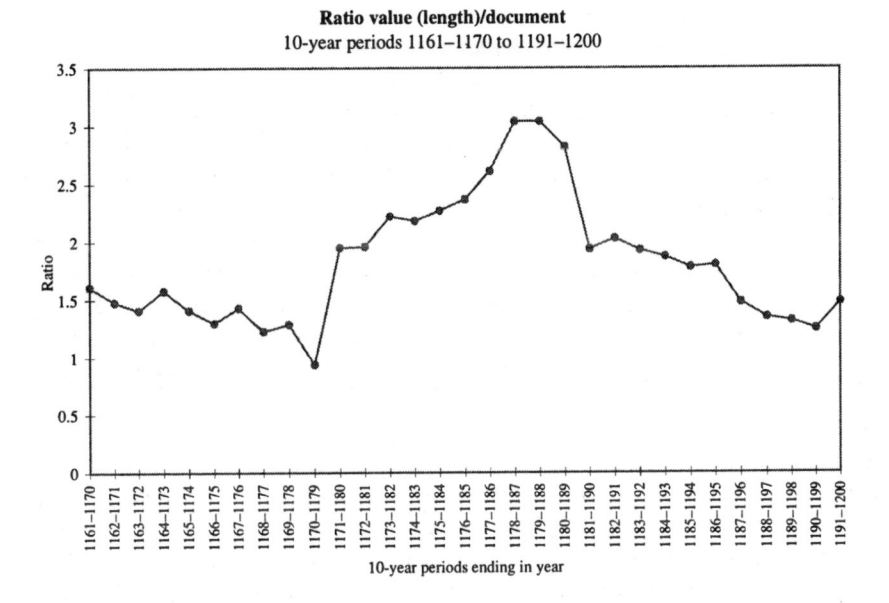

Ratio value (length)/document
10-year periods 1161–1170 to 1191–1200

Figure 2 *The ratio between the weighting factors based on the length of the word-patterns and the number of charters is the highest in the ranges 1178–1187 and 1179–1188, which both have exactly the same value.*

accuracy and reliability of this possible date remain, however, open to some speculation. The reasons for this are twofold. First, several of the word patterns we used have a rather long lifetime or a high currency, and, as the tests carried out by Professor Gervers and his team have shown, this may have a negative impact on the accuracy of the date produced. Partly because of this, we were even forced to apply the method in a creative manner in order to obtain a conclusive result. Secondly, one should bear in mind that medieval diplomatics, and particularly the way charters were drafted, do not obey scientific laws, and that therefore a computer-assisted methodology can, at best, only produce a possible date, which has to be corroborated by other evidence. For that reason, it also seems better not to narrow the date range to a period of less than ten years.

In our case, the speculative nature of the result obtained should not be exaggerated, for the external criteria, as we have seen, clearly point to a fabrication of this forgery in the last third of the twelfth century. Thus, the potential chronological error of the selected date can at most be twelve years or so. Moreover, internal evidence confirms the possibility that the forgery was indeed composed between 1178 and 1188, or in any case somewhere around 1180 or 1190:

1. the proem or '*arenga*' of the forged charter contains a biblical quotation (Ps. 3,9; 3,3; 143,10: *Quoniam Domini est salus et non est vera salus nisi in eo qui dat salutem regibus*), part of which was used in only one other

charter for St Peter's before 1200, namely in a charter issued by abbot Gerard in 1190 (*salus in eo qui vera est salus*);[28]

2. the adverb *proinde*, which links the '*arenga*' with the text proper, occurs only twice in the same position in non-royal and non-papal documents for St Peter's before 1200, namely, in a charter of bishop Everard of Tournai dated 1180 and in a charter of count Philip of Flanders and Vermandois dated 1189;[29]

3. the word pattern *sigilli nostri appensione et testium* occurs as part of the '*corroboratio*' in a charter of Richildis, lady of Oudenaarde, dated 1191, and in another one issued by William, lord of Dendermonde, and his wife Mathildis in 1193;[30] with a slight variation (*mei* instead of *nostri*), this formula can also be found in charters drafted in the name of count Philip of Flanders and Vermandois in 1189 and of count Baldwin IX of Flanders and Hainaut in 1198.[31]

A final indication that this forgery was effectively fabricated around 1180/90 is that all useable charters in the database between 1179 and 1189 contain at least one matching word pattern.[32] The background against which the falsification should be placed is not clear, but it should be noticed that the possible date 1178 to 1188 almost coincides with the abbacy of Gerard (1177–90) at St Peter's, although this may be a coincidence. During his abbacy there were several problems with the officials of the count, which may perhaps have occasioned the drafting of this false charter attributed to count Robert the Frisian.[33]

However that may be, this test has, in my opinion, clearly demonstrated the potential of the DEEDS methodology for the dating of forgeries, particularly with regard to the identification of forged or falsified documents. The application of this method has established beyond all doubt that the charter dated 1072 is not only a material forgery, but also an intellectual and juridical one. All the matching patterns with a lifetime shorter than seventy-five years that we came upon in the word concordance, from the first occurrence of a common string in 1109 to the last one in 1200, all date from the twelfth century. This encouraging result does not mean, however, that the method will be as easily applicable to all forgeries or reworked documents. Everything depends on the way the forger proceeded. Many forgers – among them the monk of St Peter's who fabricated the charter of Robert

---

28. Van Lokeren, *Chartes et documents*, no. 364.
29. Van Lokeren, *Chartes et documents*, nos. 334 and 361. The possible use of the adverb 'proinde' for dating purposes is indicated by Benoît-Michel Tock in his paper in this volume.
30. Van Lokeren, *Chartes et documents*, nos. 185 (incorrectly dated 1112) and 186 (incorrectly dated 1114).
31. Van Lokeren, *Chartes et documents*, nos. 361 and 380. These two charters were, like the vast majority of the twelfth-century charters of the Flemish counts for the St Peter's Abbey (35 out of a total of 39), drafted by the monks themselves.
32. Van Lokeren, *Chartes et documents*, nos. 331, 332, 333, 334, 342, 343, 344, 347, 349, 350, 351, 352, 356, 357, 359, and 361; Ghent, Rijksarchief, Bisdom, B 2955, fol. 136r–v (a° 1189) and 148v–149r (a° 1187).
33. See Van Lokeren, *Chartes et documents*, nos. 351 (a° 1185) and 352 (a° 1186). On abbot Gerard, see *Monasticon Belge*, tome VII: *Province de Flandre Orientale*, 1, Liège, 1988, pp. 112–13.

the Frisian – did their best "to produce a record in a form which was acceptable, particularly in courts of law, at the time it was made".[34] In other words, they did not try to imitate ancient handwriting or to follow the language and formulae of ancient charters; their only aim was to fabricate a text that would suit contemporary notions of charter drafting.[35] Other forgers, however, went to great lengths to alter or rework the content of much older genuine charters, the formulae of which they left untouched. Sometimes they added only a short passage or a few significant words to an authentic document. In such cases the method will probably be less applicable and the result will be, at the very least, confusing. This reservation with respect to some types of forgery does not of course alter the fact that the DEEDS methodology developed by Professor Gervers has great potential and will be very helpful in the identification and, to a certain extent, also in the dating of forgeries.

---

34. Clanchy, *Memory*, p. 318.

35. The only effort the forger of this charter made in this respect was to use three documents from the abbey's *Liber Traditionum* to compose the witness list; see Fayen, *Liber*, pp. 120 and 122–23 (nos. 129–31). The first part of the list is clearly based on Fayen, *Liber*, no. 130 (a° 1073), the central part on no. 131, and the end on no. 129 (these two undated texts can be assigned to the last quarter of the eleventh century).

Appendix

A° 1072. Confirmation by Robert I, count of Flanders, of the possessions granted by his predecessors to St Peter's Abbey in Ghent (forgery).
A. Apparent original (damaged; the upper part is missing): Ghent, Rijksarchief, charters, no. 150.
B. Copy from the middle of the thirteenth century in the *Liber Antiquus* of St Peter's: Ghent, Rijksarchief, Bisdom, B 2955, fol. 68v–69r.
Printed: Auguste Van Lokeren, *Chartes et documents de l'abbaye de Saint Pierre au Mont Blandin à Gand*, I, Ghent, 1868, no. 150, p. 101. – Fernand Vercauteren, *Actes des comtes de Flandre 1071–1128*, Brussels, 1938, no. 2, pp. 4–5.

[**In nomine patris et filii et spiritus sancti, amen. Robertus, Dei gratia comes Flandrie, tam futuris quam presentibus in perpetuum**. Quoniam Domini est salus et non est vera salus nisi in eo qui dat salutem regibus, toto cordis affectu et corporis gestu, si salvari volumus, eius servituti insudare debemus, quippe cum ei servire, regnare sit. Sed quia terrenis negotiis occupati, vix aliquando possumus reminisci salvatoris nostri, magnopere nobis studendum est, ut faciamus nobis amicos, qui recipiant nos in eterna tabernacula, cum defecerimus. Proinde petitioni dilecti nobis abbatis Folcardi et fratrum in **ecclesia Sancti Petri Gandensis** Deo servientium, et pro nobis iugiter orantium, assensum prebentes, ne aliquorum] infestatione [in futuro molestentur et per hoc a Dei] servitio [et nostri memoria retardentur, presentis scripti testimonio omnia] **a predecessoribus nostris** in immobilibus [et mobilibus, in] villis, terris, silvis, redditibus [et decimis predicte ecclesie tradita contradimus, et sicut a] regibus, predecessorum meorum peticionem, prelibate ecclesie confirmata sunt et nos prona(a) animi devocione confirmamus ut omnia **integre, quiete et** pacifice possideant et teneant. **Ut autem hoc** omnibus notum sit et **ratum et inconvulsum permaneat, presentem paginam sigilli nostri appensione et testium** corroboratione signari precipimus. **Actum anno Domini** M°LXXII, regnante rege Francorum Philippo. S. Roberti marchisi. S. Folkardi castellani Gandensis. S. Lamberti filii eius. S. Alardi fratris eius. S. Balduini. S. Eustachii. S. Hugonis. S. Arnulfi filii eius. S. Ascrici de Afsna. S. Reineri fratris eius. S. Erpolfi de Suinarde. S. Ascrici de Munte. S. Roberti de Diekelvena. S. Razonis de Melna. S. Iohannis de Morceka. S. Ecberti de Rosebeka. S. Iohannis de Puttem. S. Arnulfi de Hardoia. S. Sefridi de March. S. Eustachii de Sancto Audomaro. S. Walteri de Nivela.

(a) Van Lokeren and Vercauteren both read 'propria'.

Note: The text in square brackets represents the part missing in the apparent original. The word-patterns used in the dating process are indicated in bold.

Lifetime and Occurrences of the Selected Word-Patterns

Word-pattern	Length	First occurrence	Last	Lifetime	Occurrences	Value 1 (length)	Value 2 (MT)
In nomine patris et filii et spiritus sancti amen N. Dei gratia	12	1156	1180	25	3	2.8	1.28
N. Dei gratia comes Flandriae tam futuris quam presentibus in perpetuum	11	1133	1133	1	1	2.6	2.6
In nomine patris et filii et spiritus sancti amen	9	1142	1199	58	24	2.2	0.96
patris et filii et spiritus sancti amen	7	1109	1183	75	8	1.8	0.05
tam futuris quam presentibus in perpetuum	6	1129	1196	68	23	1.6	0.38
ratum et inconvulsum permaneat presentem paginam	6	1161	1161	1	1	1.6	1.6
sigilli nostri appensione et testium	5	1191	1193	3	2	1.4	1.4
N. Dei gratia comes Flandriae	5	1120	1187	68	7	1.4	0.09
tam futuris quam presentibus	4	1126	1200	75	18	1.2	0.11
ecclesia Sancti Petri Gandensis	4	1196	1196	1	1	1.2	1.2
presentem paginam sigilli nostri	4	1148	1189	42	2	1.2	0
permaneat presentem paginam sigilli	4	1200	1200	1	1	1.2	1.2
permaneat presentem paginam	3	1120	1133	14	2	1	0.63
ratum et inconvulsum	3	1157	1157	1	1	1	1
actum anno Domini	3	1157	1198	42	7	1	0.57
ut autem hoc	3	1120	1167	48	4	1	0
ecclesia Sancti Petri	3	1126	1180	55	7	1	0.26
sigilli nostri appensione	3	1190	1190	1	1	1	1
presentem paginam sigilli	3	1200	1200	1	1	1	1
appensione et testium	3	1189	1198	10	2	1	0.87
a predecessoribus nostris	3	1156	1156	1	1	1	1
integre quiete et	3	1150	1150	1	2	1	1

Bibliography

Bischoff, Bernard. 1990. *Latin Palaeography. Antiquity and the Middle Ages.* Cambridge.
Brooke, Christopher. 1971. 'Approaches to Medieval Forgery', in *Medieval Church and Society. Selected Essays*, pp. 100–20. London.
Brown, Elisabeth A. R. 1988. 'Falsitas pia sive reprehensibilis. Medieval Forgers and Their Intentions', in *Fälschungen im Mittelalter. Internationaler Kongress der Monumenta Germaniae Historica: München, 16.-19. September 1986*, pp. 101–19. Vol. I. Hanover.
Clanchy, Michael T. 1993. *From Memory to Written Record: England 1066–1307.* 2nd ed. Oxford–Cambridge Mass.
Constable, Giles. 1983. 'Forgery and Plagiarism in the Middle Ages.' *Archiv für Diplomatik* 29: pp. 1–41.
Declercq, Georges. 1991. 'Centres de faussaires et falsification de chartes en Flandre au Moyen Age,' in *Falsos y falsificaciones de documentos diplomaticos en la edad media*, pp. 65–74. Zaragoza.
Declercq, Georges, Philippe de Monty, Katrien Naessens, and Guy Trifin. 1987. 'L'informatisation de la "Table chronologique" d'A. Wauters. Méthodologie du nouveau répertoire des documents diplomatiques belges antérieurs à 1200.' *Bulletin de la Commission Royale d'Histoire* 153: pp. 223–302.
Derolez, Albert. 1974. 'De valse oorkonde van graaf Arnulf I van Vlaanderen voor het Sint-Donatiaanskapittel te Brugge (961, juli 31).' *Bulletin de la Commission Royale d'Histoire* 140: pp. 431–99.
Fayen, Arnold. 1906. *Liber Traditionum Sancti Petri Gandensis.* Ghent.
Gervers, Michael. 1997. 'The Dating of Medieval English Private Charters of the Twelfth and Thirteenth Centuries', in *A Distinct Voice. Medieval Studies in Honor of Leonard E. Boyle OP*, ed. Jacqueline Brown and William P. Stoneman, pp. 455–504. Notre Dame.
Guyotjeannin, Olivier, Jacques Pycke, and Benoît-Michel Tock. 1993. *Diplomatique médiévale.* Turnhout.
Gysseling, Maurits, and Anton C.F. Koch. 1950. *Diplomata Belgica ante annum millesimum centesimum scripta.* Vol. I. Brussels.
Hemptinne, Thérèse de, and Adriaan Verhulst. 1988. *De oorkonden der graven van Vlaanderen (Juli 1128–September 1191).* II. Uitgave [edition]. Band I: *Regering van Diederik van de Elzas (Juli 1128–17 Januari 1168).* Brussels.
Laurent, René. 1993. *Les sceaux des princes territoriaux belges du Xe siècle à 1482.* Brussels.
Monasticon Belge. Tome VII: *Province de Flandre Orientale.* Vol. 1. Liège, 1988.
Parisse, Michel. 1981. 'A propos du traitement automatique des chartes: chronologie du vocabulaire et repérage des actes suspects', in *La lexicographie du latin médiéval et ses rapports avec les recherches actuelles sur la civilisation du Moyen Age*, pp. 241–49. Paris
Tock, Benoît-Michel. 1997. 'Les mutations du vocabulaire latin des chartes au XIe siècle.' *Bibliothèque de l'Ecole des Chartes* 155: pp. 119–48.
Van Caenegem, Raoul C. (with the collaboration of François-Louis Ganshof). 1978. *Guide to the Sources of Medieval History.* Amsterdam–New York–Oxford.
Van Lokeren, Auguste. 1868. *Chartes et documents de l'abbaye de Saint Pierre au Mont Blandin à Gand.* Vol. I. Ghent.
Vercauteren, Fernand. 1938. *Actes des comtes de Flandre (1071–1128).* Brussels.
Voet, Léon. 1944. 'Etude sur deux bulles de Benoît VIII pour Saint-Vaast d'Arras.' *Bulletin de la Commission Royale d'Histoire* 109: pp. 187–242.
Vredius, Oliverus. 1639. *Sigilla comitum Flandriae et inscriptiones diplomatum ab iis editorum.* Bruges.

THE IDENTIFICATION OF A FORGERY: REGULARITIES AND IRREGULARITIES IN THE FORMULAE OF THE CHARTERS ISSUED BY THE SZÉKESFEHÉRVÁR CONVENT OF THE KNIGHTS OF ST JOHN OF JERUSALEM (1243–1353)

Zsolt Hunyadi

As an important part of my ongoing doctoral project ('A History of the Order of the Knights of St John in Hungary, c.1150–1400'), I have investigated a good number of written records issued by the Székesfehérvár Convent as a place of authentication (*locus credibilis*) in the Árpád and Angevin Age up to the mid-fourteenth century. Accordingly, I have carried out a close investigation of the charters, especially their formulaic sets, issued between 1243 and 1353.[1] During my survey, a suspicious anomaly appeared, that is, a charter, dated to 1341,[2] which differed somewhat from the usage of the conventual *scriptorium*. In order to interpret this interesting record, it is necessary to enumerate the formulaic sets applied by the scribes of the convent.

The places of authentication (*loca credibilia*), as peculiarly Hungarian institutions, issued charters to testify private legal transactions under their authentic seal upon the request of the parties involved.[3] During Béla III's reign (1173–96) the participation of the beneficiary party (*destinatarius*) in the issuance of charters came to an end, and the king made the royal chancellery available for the issue of all required charters. According to several Hungarian scholars, Béla III was

---

From *Dating Undated Medieval Charters*. Ed. Michael Gervers. Copyright (by the Editor and Contributors 2000). Published by the Boydell Press (in association with Collegium Budapest), PO Box 9, Woodbridge, Suffolk, IP12 3DF, Great Britain. ISBN 0 85115 792 0.

1. Zsolt Hunyadi, 'The Knights of St. John and Hungarian Private Legal Literacy up to the Mid-Fourteenth Century', in *The Man of Many Devices, Who Wandered Full Many Ways. Festschrift in Honor of János M. Bak*, ed. Marcell Sebők and Balázs Nagy, Budapest, 1999, pp. 507–19. See also Zsolt Hunyadi, 'A székesfehérvári johannita konvent hiteleshelyi tevékenysége az Árpád-korban' [The Székesfehérvár convent of the Order of St. John of Jerusalem in Hungary as a place of authentication in the Árpád Age], in *Capitulum I. Tanulmányok a középkori magyar egyház történetéből*, ed. László Koszta, Szeged, 1998, pp. 35–67.

2. 28 May 1341. National Archives of Hungary, Collectio Antemohacsiana DF 266 373 (henceforth DL # and DF #)

3. See György Bónis, 'A közhitelűség szervei Magyarországon és a magyar hitaleshelyi levéltárak' [The offices of authentication in Hungary and the archives of the Hungarian places of authentication], *Levéltári Szemle* 14 (1964), p. 125; see also György Bónis, 'Les autorités de "foi publique" et les archives des "loci credibiles" en Hongrie', *Archivum* 12 (1962), pp. 97–104; Imre Szentpétery, *Magyar oklevéltan* [Hungarian diplomatic], Budapest, 1930, pp. 118–20; János M. Bak, György Bónis, and James Ross Sweeney, eds., *The Laws of the Medieval Kingdom of Hungary. 1000–1301 Decreta Regni Mediaevalis Hungarie 1000 to 1526*, Bakersfield, 1989 (henceforth: *DRMH*) ser. I/2 p. 257; Ferenc Eckhart, *Magyar alkotmány és jogtörténet* [History of Hungarian law and constitution], Budapest, 1946, pp. 176–83. The best concise work on this topic is Franz Eckhart, 'Die glaubwürdigen Orte Ungarns im Mittelalter', *MIÖG*, Ergbd. 9 (1913/1915), pp. 395–558.

influenced by foreign models, either Byzantine or western European.[4] Another school of thought emphasises that the emergence of the places of authentication should be understood as an organic evolution, and as such it might be deduced from the 'institution' of the bailiffs (*pristaldus*),[5] along with the role played by major chapter houses in administering ordeals.[6] The importance of the bailiffs was indirectly reduced by a decree of Pope Alexander III, which stated that after the death of the witnesses of transactions the unsealed documents lost their validity. Yet the early charters issued by a number of cathedral and collegiate chapters were unsealed. In such cases the basis of their authenticity was nothing other than the trustworthiness of the ecclesiastical institutions.[7]

The major collegiate and cathedral chapters began to issue charters as early as the end of the twelfth century: Veszprém in 1181, Székesfehérvár in 1184, Buda in 1211, and Arad in 1221. Soon thereafter, the convents of Pannonhalma (Benedictine), Jászó (Premonstratensian), Esztergom (Knights of St. Stephen), and Székesfehérvár (Knights of St. John) became important places for private legal literacy. In subsequent centuries, besides chapter houses,[8] the convents of the Benedictines,[9] the Premonstratensians,[10] the Knights of St. John,[11] and the Order of St. Stephen acted as places of authentication. There is no sign of similar activity in the case of either the Cistercian or the mendicant orders.[12]

The activities of the places of authentication can be divided into 'internal' and 'external' acts. The activity was internal when the chapters and convents: (i) issued letters of record (*litterae fassionales*) concerning the private legal transactions

4. László Mezey, 'A pécsi egyetemalapítás előzményei (A deákság és a hiteleshely kezdeteihez)' [The precedents of the foundation of the university in Pécs], in *Jubileumi Tanulmányok*, ed. Andor Csizmadia, Pécs: JPTE, 1967, pp. 66–68. See also László Mezey, 'Anfänge der Privaturkunde in Ungarn und der glaubwürdigen Orte', *Archiv für Diplomatik* 18 (1972): pp. 290–302; László Mezey, 'A hiteleshely a közhitelűség fejlődésében és III. Béla szerepe' [Place of authentication in the development of public authenticity and the role of Béla III], in *Középkori kútfőink kritikus kérdései*, ed. János Horváth and György Székely, Budapest, 1974, pp. 315–32.

5. Cf. *DRMH*, ser. I/1, p. 141, I/2, p. 249.

6. Cf. *DRMH*, ser. I/1, p. 148. László Solymosi, 'A székesfehérvári káptalan hiteleshelyi működésének főbb sajátosságai az Árpád-korban' [The major characteristics of the activity of the Székesfehérvár chapter as a place of authentication], in *A székesfehérvári Boldogasszony bazilika történeti jelentősége*, ed. Gábor Farkas, Székesfehérvár, 1996, pp. 181–82.

7. Ferenc Eckhart, 'Hiteles helyeink eredete és jelentősége' [The origin and importance of the Hungarian places of authentication], *Századok* 47 (1913): p. 650. See also I. Borsa, 'Zur Beurkundstätigkeit der glaubwürdigen Orte in Ungarn', in *Forschungen über Siebenbürgen und seine Nachbarn. Festschrift für Attila T. Szabó und Zsigmond Jakó*, vol. 2, ed. Kálmán Benda, Tamás Bogyay, and H. Glassl, Munich, 1988, pp. 143–47.

8. According to Ferenc Eckhart (Hiteles helyeink, 182) fifteen cathedral and nine collegiate chapters acted as place of authentication before 1526. In contrast, Zoltán Miklósy recognised twenty-eight chapter houses: see Zoltán Miklósy, 'Hiteles hely és iskola a középkorban' [Places of authentication and schools in the Middle Ages], *Levéltári Közlemények* 18–19 (1940–41): p. 171.

9. Thirteen convents, cf. Bónis, 'A közhitelűség szervei', p. 132.

10. Six convents, cf. Bónis, 'A közhitelűség szervei', p. 132.

11. There were eight convents up to 1353; cf. Bónis, 'A közhitelűség szervei', p. 132; Eckhart, Hiteles helyeink', p. 182.

12. László Solymosi, 'Észrevételek a Ciszterci Rend magyarországi repertóriumáról' [Notes on the repertoire of the Cistercian Order in Hungary], *Levéltári Közlemények* 55 (1984): pp. 242, 248–50.

of the parties involved (for example, conveyance of property rights); (ii) wrote reports (*litterae relationales*) upon out-of-court legal actions, or upon phases of a trial accomplished under the mandate of the king or that of the major dignitaries of the country. In addition, these institutions (iii) issued certified transcriptions (*litterae transcriptionales*) of charters (i–ii). On the basis of the formal characteristics of these documents, three types of charters can be distinguished: privileges (*litterae privilegiales*), letters patent (*litterae patentes*), and letters close (*litterae clausae*). This division, according to several scholars in the field, is mirrored in the formulae of the records, that is, in their set phraseology.[13] What follows is a brief survey of these phrases.[14]

As the charters issued by the Székesfehérvár Convent do not contain an *invocatio*, the first element of the formulaic set to be investigated is the *intitulatio*. This formula can be found in each charter (66 *in extenso* surviving) of the conventual *scriptorium*, in the first position in the privileges and in the second position in the letters of relation (*relatio*) which were answers to – for example, royal – mandates. The intitulatio denominated the exact title of the charter issuer, thus providing a basis for its identification.

The first few occurrences indicate the unsettled use of this phrase. In light of the sequence of the formulae, the first *intitulatio* (1243) seems quite irregular (*Nos conventus fratrum domus hospitalis de Alba et magister Ambrosius Budensis canonicus generalis procurator eiusdem domus vicem magistri provincialis gerens*),[15] and the following two identical formulae did not become the practice of the Convent either: *Capitulum domus hospitalis Iherosolomitani de Alba* (1256, 1259).[16] The *Capitulum* expression, which is identical with the circumscription of the conventual seal, presumably reflected an activity similar to that of the cathedral and collegiate chapter houses. Nevertheless, later – between 1264 and *c.*1338 – a relatively constant use can be observed. In the case of privileges, the *intitulatio* was *Conventus domus hospitalis Iherosolomitani de Alba*, while the letters patent and close were introduced with *Nos conventus domus hospitalis de Alba*. The first sign of transition appeared as early as 1292 and continued in the course of the first third of the fourteenth century, in which the cruciferorum expression completed the title more frequently.[17] Eventually, by the end of the period under investigation, the *intitulatio* of the privileges was *Conventus (cruciferorum) domus hospitalis ecclesie beati regis Stephani*. Those of the letters patent and close was the same, completed with the *Nos* beginning. However, the letters of relation have almost the same *intitulatio* only with a different *Nos* beginning. By the mid-fourteenth century, the patron saint of the Székesfehérvár house was added to the formula. The distinctive use of *Nos* – differentiating between the privileges and the letters close and patent – corresponds to the practice of the places of authentication.

13. Originated by Imre Szentpétery (Szentpétery, Magyar oklevéltan, passim).
14. See the overall structure of the charters in the Appendix of this study.
15. 1243 (DL 99 844).
16. 13 June 1256 (DL 83 128), 1259 (DF 262 482).
17. For instance, in the charters of 1292, 1322, 1323, and 1333.

The frequency of the *inscriptio* and addressee formulae is lower than that of the previous one, since the *inscriptio* formed part of the privileges only, while addressee can be found exclusively in the letters of relation being issued in folded and sealed form. The first formula is rather a stereotype, since it does not point to the person whom the charter concerns. The most frequent expression – 'developed' by the beginning of the 1270s – is *Omnibus Christi fidelibus (tam presentibus quam futuris) presentes litteras inspecturis*. The use of this pattern was not of course exclusive. In the rest of the letters close and patent the *intitulatio* was directly followed by the *promulgatio*.

In contrast to the general denomination of the *inscriptio*, the addressee formula named the receiver precisely, as the later *missilis* or present-day letters, and then came the *intitulatio*. The letters of relation usually addressed the king in this way: *Excellentissimo domino* or *Serenissimo principi ipsorum N. dei gratia inclito regi Hungarie*,[18] while the palatines were 'honoured' with *Discreto et honesto viro N. palatino* or *Viro magnifico*.

The *salutatio* formula, similarly to the *inscriptio*, formed part of the privileges and letters of relation only. However, it differed slightly, since the composition of the *salutatio* was more permanent. Up to 1334 it mostly reads s*alutem in domino sempiternam*, and afterwards *salutem in omnium salvatore*. Regarding the practice of the places of authentication, it can be noted that the general use of this formula was not completely uniform. While, for example, the Pozsega Chapter[19] and the Szekszárd Convent[20] omitted the *salutatio* from the letters patent only, the same formula in the case of the Vasvár Chapter was rare even in the privileges.[21] Nevertheless, there was a universal feature concerning the structure of the protocollum part of the charters, namely, that the *intitulatio, inscriptio* and *salutatio* formulae were formulated within one sentence.

In accordance with Hungarian practice, the rarest element of the Székesfehérvár charters – found exclusively among the privileges – is the *arenga*. Usually, independent of the content of a document, this formula emphasised the importance of literacy, likewise the solemnity of the affair in question. The texts of the six *arengae* found in the documents are somewhat different from one another, but basically they belong to the *memoria–oblivio* type, and so are to be counted in the group of *arengae* widespread in Hungary and Europe.[22] The papal bulls

---

18. 31 January 1346 (DL 51 366), 31 January 1346 (DL 51 367), and 23 June 1347 (DL 76 844).
19. László Koszta, 'A pozsegai káptalan hiteleshelyi tevékenysége 1353-ig' [The activity of the Pozsega Chapter as a place of authentication up to 1353], *Századok* 132 (1998): p. 16.
20. Ferenc Szakály, 'A szekszárdi konvent hiteleshelyi és oklevéladó működése 1526-ig' [The activities of the convent of Szekszárd as a place of authentication up to 1526], *Tanulmányok Tolna megye történetéből* 1 (1968): p. 27.
21. Péter Kóta, 'A vasvári káptalan korai oklevelei' [The early charters of the Vasvár Chapter], *Levéltári Szemle* 37 (1987): p. 19.
22. On Hungarian practice, see Kóta, 'A vasvári káptalan', p. 20. On European patterns, see Heinrich Fichtenau, *Arenga. Spätantike und Mittelalter im Spiegel von Urkundenformeln*, Graz–Köln, 1957, pp. 129–35; Gabriella Trostovszky, 'Az esztergomi káptalan XIII–XIV századi oklevelei az országos levéltár diplomatikai levéltárában' [The 13th- and 14th-century charters of the Esztergom chapter in the National Archives of Hungary], *Levéltári Közlemények* 60 (1989): p. 66. *(cont. on next page)*

and the German – mainly royal – charters emphasised the significance of literacy using very similar 'arguments' from the second half of the twelfth century.

Inasmuch as the manner in which the charters were sealed can determine the type of a given document, the *promulgatio* is the internal characteristic of privileges, and letters close and patent. Similar to other places of authentication, this element of the charters had been established relatively slowly. Between 1240 and 1270 the *scriptorium* of the Convent hardly issued two identical *promulgationes*. This was not exceptional in the period in question; for instance, each charter of the Pozsega Chapter contained different forms up to 1279.[23] The *promulgatio* of the charters containing *arenga* was usually introduced with the *proinde* expression. On the other hand, the *promulgatio* cannot be found in the letters of relation, thus the transcription of a certain letter of mandate was followed by the addressee.[24]

In practical terms, the *narratio, dispositio* formula was the most important element of a document from the point of view of the parties involved. It contained the description of the affair in question, its precedents, and the disposition of judges (for example, *probi viri*) involved in the procedure. On the basis of the amount of data available for my investigation, it is difficult to produce a typology, as had occasionally been feasible in respect of other places of authentication.[25] However, it is possible to point out particular elements of the *dispositio* section which became formulaic expressions.

In the case of declarations before the place of authentication, the expression of the appearance of the parties, and later the announcement itself, was set: '*constitutus . . . et viva voce et relatum (extitit).*' In those charters which reported conveyances (gifts, pledges, sales, or purchases) the verbs of transfer were repeated: *donatio, assignatio, inpignoratitio,* and *ad possidendam, habendam et tenendam.* Likewise, the manner of possession was indicated with the words '*perpetuo, irrevocabiliter, pacifice et quiete*', and so on. When describing the boundaries of an estate, the phrases were also fixed. The *pertinentia* formula, concerning the (usually moveable) belongings of an estate, or the transfer of immovable goods, appeared as early as 1264 and was expressed in the following form: *cum omnibus suis iobagionibus de Woytha et aliis ad ipsum pertinentibus fructus et utilitates possessionis sue.*[26] Legal formulae were used to describe protestations and prohibitions. The letters of relation, including the result of an inquest, necessarily contained the indication of the inquiry (*ad inquerendo*) and the official report or statement (*veritas*).

(cont. from previous page) See also Ágnes Kurcz, 'Az antikvitás hatásának nyomai XIII. századi oklevelekben' [Traces of the influence of antiquity in thirteenth-century charters], *Antik Tanulmányok* 8 (1961): passim; Ágnes Kurz, 'Arenga und narratio in der ungarischer Urkunden des XIII. Jahrhunderts', *MIÖG* 70 (1962): passim.

23. Koszta, 'A pozsegai káptalan', p. 17.

24. Bernát L. Kumorovitz, 'A leleszi konvent oklevéladó működése' [Charter issuance of the Lelesz Convent], *Turul* 42 (1928): p. 16.

25. For example, Trostovszky, 'Az esztergomi káptalan', pp. 67–74.

26. 24 June 1325 (DL 2304); see also 15 September 1325 (DL 99 941), 1 August 1327 (DL 90 933), 30 September 1334 (DL 2854).

The additional clauses (*clausulae*) of the dispositio secured the obligations (*obligatio*) undertaken by the parties, namely, the warranty which they provided for their opponents before the court. Probably, due to the proximity of the Székesfehérvár Collegiate Chapter – one of the very first places of authentication – this formula was already part of the earliest surviving charter of the Convent issued in 1243. Although the formula was variable, its most frequent occurrences were: *obligo* (or *obligando*) *tenebuntur defendere* (or *liberare*, or *expedire*) *propriis laboribus et expensis*. This frame was, of course, completed with the names of the parties to the given affair.

The parties who did not keep the conditions of an agreement were threatened with amercement. The *sanctio* formula frequently occurred in the charters of the Convent, especially in the cases of pledge of landed property. If the repayment of the given loan was not carried out in time, the owner had to pay double the amount of money lent.[27] Those who desisted from a contract were subject to the same conditions.

An indispensable element of the privileges was the *corroboratio* formula which reported the charter's issuance, its confirmation, the warning of the future litigants,[28] and very often the manner in which the charter was sealed. From time to time, the receiver of the charter also appeared in the *corroboratio*. With two exceptions, the Székesfehérvár Convent used *corroboratio* in the privileges only. However, general Hungarian practice was not so strict.

The *corroboratio* of the very first charter (1243) is somewhat unusual, but the circumstances of its sealing provide clarification of this extraordinary solution (*quia proprium sigillum nostrum erat in maritima propter metum tartarorum . . . litteras . . . concessimus . . . fratris Juliani custodis, fratris Luce preceptoris domus nostre et predicti magistri Ambrosii sigillis communitas*). Regarding the practice evolved in the conventual *scriptorium*, temporal changes and shifts can be observed. Thus, during the first three decades the following form was in use: *In cuius rei memoriam/testimonium . . . sigilli nostri munimine roboratas*. Afterwards, it was replaced by *In cuius rei dedimus . . . litteras sigillo nostro communitas*. From the end of the thirteenth century the most frequent composition was the *In cuius rei memoriam (firmitatem or stabilitatem) . . . (pendentis) sigilli nostri (authentici) munimine roboratas (et consignatas)*.[29] An unusual case is the letter patent of 1276 which was supplied with a pendant seal, but there is no *corroboratio* in the document. In another case, there is a chirograph to be found in the corpus whose *corroboratio* does not indicate the procedure by which it was made.

On the other hand, the introduction of the term '*authenticum sigillum*' in the Székesfehérvár Convent in 1292 corresponded to the practice of other places of authentication. The use of the *authenticum* adjective was inconsistent in Hungary up to the middle of the fourteenth century. This terminology referred to the use of

---

27. For example, in 1277 (DL 968).
28. 1243 (DL 99 844), 13 June 1256 (DL 83 128), 1 August 1327 (DL 90 933), 2 March 1343 (DF 229 977), and so on.
29. 22 August 1338 (DL 3172).

the larger conventual seal, as opposed to the memorial one. The legal difference between the validity of the seals was established in the course of a relatively long process. Nevertheless, it can be supposed that up to the mid-fourteenth century, in spite of the absence of this adjective, the privileges were indeed sealed with the *authenticum sigillum*.

The dates of the charters (*datum*) exactly coincide with Hungarian practice, although differences appeared in the use of the *datum* formula. The first surviving charter – in its known form – was issued without the day's date. Nevertheless, from the second record up to 1295, the privileges were issued with the Roman indication of time, that is, a day was expressed by its proximity to the significant days of the Roman months (*Kalendae, Nonae, Idus*). The dating formula was introduced with the word *datum* (or *data*), referring to the date of the charter issue, while in two cases the scribe recorded the date of the event with the actum expression.[30]

After 1295, the letters patent and close, as well as the privileges, were dated by using both the 'mobile' and 'fixed' Christian feasts (for example, *Datum in octavis Pasche* or *Datum feria tertia ante festum ascensionis domini*).[31] Some exceptions are to be found among the privileges when they contain Roman dating.[32] Additionally, by the middle of the fourteenth century, the *mensis* (month) expression appeared in the charters of the Convent. In those cases when the documents report temporal judicial decisions, the indication of the year could be omitted.[33] Occasionally, the year or the given Christian feast cannot be found at the end of the document; one can read a reference to the date only in the *narratio* (for example, *Anno ut supradicto*).[34]

Similar to several other formulae we have mentioned, the *series dignitatum* (list of dignitaries) can be found only in privileges. In the practice of the Székesfehérvár Convent, the local dignitaries and not the witnesses (*testes*) of the issue or of the transaction were always listed. The name of the provincial master occurred only in the first – somewhat irregular – charter, but the names and titles of the preceptor and the general procurator of the Székesfehérvár house can be found in the *corroboratio*. Besides the fact that the preceptor was almost always among the '*dramatis personae*' in the list of dignitaries, the amalgamated offices of the priors and *custodes*, up to the last decade of the Árpád Age (–1301), were often indicated at the end of the charters. In the Angevin period, chiefly the name of the preceptor – often coupled with the office of the *custos* – appeared in this part of the charter. By the middle of the fourteenth century, the provincial superior, the Prior of Vrana, was added to this list: *Religiosis viris et honestis fratre Baudino Cornuti per Hungariam et Sclavoniam priore et prelato nostro*.[35] This

---

30. 1243 (DL 99 844), 1261 (DL 515, DF 283 246).
31. 29 April 1326 (DF 249 085) and 11 April 1333 (DF 283 213).
32. 7 July 1328 (DL 977), 10 October 1347 (DL 30 646), and 6 May 1353 (DL 3261).
33. Around 20 August 1268–1269 (DL 25 035) and *c.*14 July 1280 (DL 25 766).
34. 1289 (DF 266 353), 1299 (DL 104 898), 1332 (DL 91 256), 1343 (DL 51 223), and so on.
35. 6 May 1353 (DL 3261).

may indicate the shift of emphasis to the houses in the Trans-Drava region (present-day Croatia).

Having acquainted ourselves with the formulaic set of the records issued by the Székesfehérvár Convent, we should return to the 'suspicious anomaly' already mentioned, that is, a charter dated to 1341.[36] Since original charters have survived both from the previous and the subsequent periods, it is possible – and advisable – to begin with a paleographical examination. Compared to some thirty privileges issued between 1353 and 1400, the script of the charter in question may be accepted as a singular variant hand. Nevertheless, this document could not have been written earlier than the last third or quarter of the fourteenth century. Partly the handwriting itself, partly the type and use of abbreviations point to a later hand. Such an argument, of course, is not sufficient, thus it is necessary to compare the 'set phraseology' of this particular charter with the formulaic sets used by the Convent both prior and subsequent to the given year. Therefore, I have extended my investigation up to 1400.[37]

Starting with the *protocollum* part, the *intitulatio* formula of the charter strikes an odd note, stating that it was issued by the *Conventus cruciferorum ordinis Sancti Johannis Jerosolomitani domus hospitalis ecclesie beati regis Stephani de Alba*. Although the (royal) mandates sometimes mentioned the name of John the Baptist, the Convent itself did not use this expression in its privileges before 1358,[38] and it became regular from 1364/1368 onwards.[39] The rest of the protocollum differs slightly from the most frequent forms, but it has no great significance.

The *narratio* of the *contextus* section reports that James and Dominic, sons of Chumur[40] from Hothvon village (Sárhatvan, Fejér County)[41] had sold some of his possessions and a part of the patronage of a church (St. Stephen) to Beke, son of Ipoch from the village of Boch (Bacs, Fejér County).[42] Moreover, it is also stated that the same James and Dominic had already pledged the property and patronage to the aforementioned Beke, which was recorded in another charter of the Székesfehérvár Convent. And now – due to their urgent necessity – James and Dominic had decided on the sale of their property consisting of three parts to Beke for forty marks of Buda denarius, *perpetuo et irrevocabiliter*, and what is more, the vendors had already received the mentioned sum.

The *narratio* is followed by the common clauses, but the end of the *contextus*, the *corroboratio* formula, contains something unexpected: *litteras nostras privilegiales pendentis et autentici sigilli nostri maioris munimine roboratas duximus*

---

36. 28 May 1341 (DF 266 373).
37. The investigation concerned 140 '*in extenso*' extant charters issued by the convent.
38. 1 November 1358 (DL 99 580).
39. 21 December 1364 (DL 20), 27 April 1368 (DL 100 421, DL 10 348), 25 January 1373 (DL 71 311), and 29 March 1373 (DL 71 232).
40. Uncertain reading.
41. Cf. György Györffy, *Az Árpád-kori Magyarország történeti földrajza* [Historical topography of Hungary in the Árpád Age], Budapest, 1987, vol. 2, pp. 387–88.
42. Györffy, *Az Árpád-kori Magyarország*, p. 347.

concedendas. Although by this time the indication of the authenticity of the seals was reasonably fixed (*sigillum authenticum, sigillum memoriale*), the scribes of the Convent never emphasised the size of the seal. According to my present knowledge, the *maius* adjective appeared in the formula as late as 1368, and became regular from 1389/1394 onwards.[43]

The eschatocollum of the charter seems to be the most suspicious part. While the dating formula is ordinary, the *series dignitatum* contains several 'mistakes'. It reads as follows: *Religiosis viris dominis fratribus Petro Cornuti priore Aurane prelato nostro, Donato preceptore, Andrea lectore, Johanne custode, ceterisque fratribus predicti ecclesie existentibus et jugiter famulantibus regi sempiterno.* The first problem is the appearance of the Prior of Vrana. Peter Cornuti was indeed the superior of the Order in this period, but the conventual *scriptorium* identified the provincial dignitaries only after 1353. On the other hand, according to the charter, Donat was only the preceptor and a certain John was the *custos*. There is a contradiction here, since between 1332 and 1343 Donat was not only the preceptor but the *custos* of the house, that is, both before and after 1341.[44] In addition, the presence of the lector in the formula is even more peculiar. The leader of the conventual *scriptorium*, unlike the cathedral and collegiate chapter houses, was the *custos* or the prior. Thus, the appearance of the lector might be connected to the establishment of the conventual school. Consequently, the presence of the lector with his office – as well as his name in the *series dignitatum* – is supposed to be permanent. In the practice of the Székesfehérvár Convent this permanence was characteristic only of the last decades of the fourteenth century.[45] The very last divergence is the '*intitulatio*' of the brethren who served the king in perpetuity: *jugiter famulantibus regi sempiterno*. In spite of the fact that the Knights of St. John in Székesfehérvár or elsewhere in Hungary were indeed among the *fidelissimi* adherents of the realm, this expression was a regular part of the charter of the Convent only between 1373 and 1396, as well as later in the fifteenth century.[46] This type of expression was not rare in the practice of other places of authentication. Similar closing forms can be found in the practice of the Bács[47]

43. 27 April 1368 (DL 100 421, DL 10 348), 3 June 1389 (DL 30 646), 26 June 1394 (DL 7949), 4 January 1395 (DL 72 247), 11 January 1395 (DL 71 225), 21 February 1395 (DL 72 248), 8 May 1396 (DL 8156, DL 8157, DL 8402), 12 December 1397 (DL 42 661), 20 June 1398 (DL 69 300), and 6 October 1400 (DL 8850).

44. 30 September 1334 (DL 2854) and 2 March 1343 (DF 229 977).

45. 27 April 1368 (DL 100 421, DL 10 348), 27 May 1385 (DL 45 459), 3 June 1389 (DL 30 646), 27 May 1390 (DL 90 933, DL 86 989, DL 88 128), and so on. See also Ede Reiszig, *A jeruzsálemi Szent János lovagrend Magyarországon* [The Order of the Knights of St. John of Jerusalem in Hungary], Budapest, 1928, vol. 2, pp. 135–37.

46. 25 January 1373 (DL 71 311), 29 March 1373 (DL 71 232), 5 November 1374 (DL 71 223), 14 April 1379 (DL 7550), 17 April 1380 (DL 42 150), 27 May 1385 (DL 45 459), 3 June 1389 (DL 30 646), 27 May 1390 (DL 90 933, DL 86 989, DL 88 128), 3 July 1390 (DL 71 224), 13 November 1392 (DL 7811), 17 January 1393 (DL 49 304, DL 49 307), 26 June 1394 (DL 7949), 4 January 1395 (DL 72 247), 11 January 1395 (DL 71 225), 21 February 1395 (DL 72 248), and 8 May 1396 (DL 8156, DL 8157, DL 8402).

47. Márton Parlagi, *A bácsi káptalan hiteleshelyi tevékenysége az Árpád-korban* [The Bács Cathedral Chapter as a place of authentication in the Árpád Age] Szeged, 1999 (unpublished MA thesis), p. 25.

and Pécs Cathedral and the Buda Collegiate Chapters, as well as that of the Benedictine monastery in Pécsvárad.[48] The scribes of the *scriptorium* of the Pécs Chapter closed their charters with the form [*iugiter*] *Deo devote famulantibus et existentibus* from 1312 and its final variant from 1343 onwards.[49]

All these facts taken together prove – I believe – that the charter dated to 1341 is a forgery. As for the conveyance, it is obvious that it could have been in Beke's interest to fake such a charter, since he was the last named beneficiary. Nevertheless, based on the details presented, it can be stated that the forgery was prepared some time between 1373 and 1396. Thus, Beke's descendants are most probably to blame. On the other hand, it is very likely that the forger was not a member of the conventual *scriptorium*. In that case, he could have checked a strictly contemporary charter of the Convent in order to identify the appropriate formulaic set, the current dignitaries of the house, and so forth. Accordingly, the forger was not circumspect enough. Or is there such a thing as a perfect forgery? As long as there is no satisfactory answer to such questions, statistical methods should be taken into consideration, such as the method elaborated for dating charters by the DEEDS Project in Toronto. Through the profound analysis of word-patterns one can determine slight chronological changes.[50] With the help of this method, even those who have never dealt with the practice of the Székesfehérvár Convent could reveal that almost 600 years ago someone deviated from the set patterns of the conventual *scriptorium*.

---

48. For example, '*ceterisque fratribus una nobiscum Deo famulantibus iugiter et devote*' February 1267 (DF 244 448); '*ceterisque fratribus nobiscum Deo iugiter famulantibus et devote*' September 1296 (DL 86 881); '*ceterisque fratribus una nobiscum Deo iugiter famulantibus et devote*' April 1298 (DL 86 888); '*ceterisque fratribus una nobiscum iugiter Deo famulantibus et devote*' 14 July 1355 (DF 265 857), 29 June 1358 (DL 77 232).

49. László Koszta. *A pécsi székeskáptalan hiteleshelyi tevékenysége (1214–1353)* [The Pécs Cathedral Chapter as a place of authentication (1214–1353)], Pécs, 1998, pp. 76, 158.

50. See Michael Gervers et al., 'The DEEDS Database of Medieval Charters: Design and Coding for RDBMS Oracle 5', *History and Computing* 2 (1990): pp. 1–11. Michael Gervers, 'Középkori angol oklevelek datálása szóelőfordulások alapján' [Dating of medieval English charters by word-pattern matching], *Aetas* 2–3 (1997): pp. 189–97.

Bibliography

Bak, János M., György Bónis, and James Ross Sweeney, eds. 1989. *The Laws of the Medieval Kingdom of Hungary. 1000–1301 Decreta Regni Mediaevalis Hungarie 1000 to 1526*. Bakersfield: Charles Schlacks Jr.

Bónis, György. 1962. 'Les auctorités de "foi publique" et les archives des "loci credibiles" en Hongrie'. *Archivum* 12: pp. 97–104.

———. 1964. 'A közhitelűség szervei Magyarországon és a magyar hiteleshelyi levéltárak' [The offices of authentication in Hungary and the archives of the Hungarian places of authentication]. *Levéltári Szemle* 14: pp. 118–42.

Borsa, Iván. 1988. 'Zur Beurkundstätigkeit der glaubwürdigen Orte in Ungarn', in *Forschungen über Siebenbürgen und seine Nachbarn. Festschrift für Attila T. Szabó und Zsigmond Jakó*, vol. 2., ed. Kálmán Benda, Tamás Bogyay, and H. Glassl, pp. 143–47. München.

Eckhart, Ferenc. 1913. 'Hiteles helyeink eredete és jelentősége' [The origin and importance of the Hungarian places of authentication]. *Századok* 47: pp. 640–55.

———. 1946. *Magyar alkotmány és jogtörténet* [History of Hungarian law and constitution]. Budapest: Franklin.

Eckhart, Franz [Ferenc]. 1913/1915. 'Die glaubwürdigen Orte Ungarns im Mittelalter.' *MIÖG Ergbd.* 9: pp. 395–558.

Fichtenau, Heinrich. 1957. *Arenga. Spätantike und Mittelalter im Spiegel von Urkundenformeln*. Graz–Köln: Verlag Hermann Böhlaus Nachf.

Gervers, Michael. 1997. 'Középkori angol oklevelek datálása szóelőfordulások alapján.' [Dating of medieval English charters by word-pattern matching]. *Aetas*, nos. 2–3: pp. 189–97.

Gervers, Michael, et al. 1990. 'The DEEDS Database of Medieval Charters: Design and Coding for RDBMS Oracle 5.' *History and Computing* 2: pp. 1–11.

Györffy, György. 1987. *Az Árpád-kori Magyarország történeti földrajza* [Historical topography of Hungary in the Árpád Age]. Vol. 2. Budapest: Akadémiai Kiadó.

Hunyadi, Zsolt. 1998. 'A székesfehérvári johannita konvent hiteleshelyi tevékenysége az Árpád-korban' [The Székesfehérvár Convent of the Order of St. John of Jerusalem in Hungary as a place of authentication in the Árpád Age], in *Capitulum I. Tanulmányok a középkori magyar egyház történetéből*, ed. L. Koszta, pp. 35–67. Szeged: Szegedi Középkorász Műhely.

———. 1999. 'The Knights of St. John and Hungarian Private Legal Literacy up to the Mid-Fourteenth Century', in . . . *The Man of Many Devices, Who Wandered Full Many Ways . . . Festschrift in Honor of János M. Bak*, ed. Marcell Sebők and Balázs Nagy, pp. 507–19. Budapest: Central European University Press.

Koszta, László. 1998. 'A pozsegai káptalan hiteleshelyi tevékenysége 1353-ig' [The activities of the Pozsega Chapter as a place of authentication up to 1353]. *Századok* 132: pp. 3–46.

———. 1998. *A pécsi székeskáptalan hiteleshelyi tevékenysége (1214–1353)* [The Pécs Cathedral Chapter as a place of authentication (1214–1353)]. Pécs: Pécs Története Alapítvány.

Kóta, Péter. 1987. 'A vasvári káptalan korai oklevelei' [The early charters of the Vasvár Chapter]. *Levéltári Szemle* 37: pp. 17–29.

Kumorovitz, Bernát L. 1928. 'A leleszi konvent oklevéladó működése' [Charter issuance of the Lelesz Convent]. *Turul* 42: pp. 1–39.

Kurcz, Ágnes. 1961. 'Az antikvitás hatásának nyomai XIII. századi oklevelekben' [Traces of the influence of Antiquity in thirteenth-century charters]. *Antik Tanulmányok* 8.

———. 1962. 'Arenga und narratio in der ungarischer Urkunden des XIII. Jahrhunderts'. *MIÖG* 70: pp. 323–54.

Mezey, László. 1967. 'A pécsi egyetemalapítás előzményei (A deákság és a hiteleshely kezdeteihez)' [The precedents of the foundation of the university in Pécs]', in *Jubileumi Tanulmányok*, ed. Andor Csizmadia, pp. 53–84. Pécs: JPTE.

———. 1972. 'Anfänge der Privaturkunde in Ungarn und der glaubwürdigen Orte.' *Archiv für Diplomatik* 18: pp. 290–302.

———. 1974. 'A hiteleshely a közhitelűség fejlődésében és III. Béla szerepe' [Places of authentication in the development of public authenticity and the role of Béla III], in *Középkori kútfőink kritikus kérdései*, ed. János Horváth and György Székely. Budapest: Akadémiai Kiadó, pp. 315–32.

Miklósy, Zoltán. 1940–41. 'Hiteles hely és iskola a középkorban' [Places of authentication and schools in the Middle Ages]. *Levéltári Közlemények* 18–19: pp. 170–78.

Parlagi, Márton. 1999. *A bácsi káptalan hiteleshelyi tevékenysége az Árpád-korban* [The Bács Cathedral Chapter as a place of authentication in the Árpád Age]. Szeged. (MA thesis, manuscript).

Reiszig, Ede. 1928. *A jeruzsálemi Szent János lovagrend Magyarországon* [The Order of the Knights of St. John of Jerusalem in Hungary]. Vol. 2. Budapest: Nemesi Évkönyv.

Solymosi, László. 1984. 'Észrevételek a Ciszterci Rend magyarországi repertóriumáról' [Notes on the Repertoire of the Cistercian Order in Hungary]. *Levéltári Közlemények* 55: pp. 242–43.

———. 1996. 'A székesfehérvári káptalan hiteleshelyi működésének főbb sajátosságai az Árpád-korban' [The major characteristics of the activities of the Székesfehérvár chapter as a place of authentication]', in *A székesfehérvári Boldogasszony bazilika történeti jelentősége*, ed. Gábor Farkas, pp. 180–201. Székesfehérvár.

Szakály, Ferenc. 1968. 'A szekszárdi konvent hiteleshelyi és oklevéladó működése 1526-ig' [The activities of the convent of Szekszárd as a place of authentication up to 1526]. *Tanulmányok Tolna megye történetéből* 1: pp. 9–60.

Szentpétery, Imre. 1930. *Magyar oklevéltan* [Hungarian diplomatic]. Budapest: Magyar Történeti Társulat.

Trostovszky, Gabriella. 1989. 'Az esztergomi káptalan XIII–XIV. századi oklevelei az országos levéltár diplomatikai levéltárában' [The 13th- and 14th-century charters of the Esztergom chapter in the National Archives of Hungary]. *Levéltári Közlemények* 60: pp. 57–81.

Appendix

The Structure of the Charters Issued by the Székesfehérvár Convent of the Knights of St. John

	LITTERAE PRIVILEGIALES	LITTERAE PATENTES	LITTERAE CLAUSAE
I. PROTOCOLLUM	intitulatio inscriptio salutatio	intitulatio	intitulatio (relatio – addressee) (relatio – salutatio)
II. CONTEXTUS	arenga promulgatio narratio dispositio clausulae sanctio corroboratio	promulgatio (narratio) dispositio clausulae sanctio	promulgatio (narratio) dispositio clausulae sanctio
III. ESCHATO-COLLUM	datatio (datum or actum) series dignitatum	datatio (datum or actum)	datatio (datum or actum)

THE PROBLEMS OF DATING THE QUEENS' CHARTERS OF THE ÁRPÁDIAN AGE (ELEVENTH–THIRTEENTH CENTURY)

Attila Zsoldos

The issuing of charters by Hungarian queens goes back to the beginning of official documents written in Latin in Hungary. Proof of this can be found in the fifteenth-century register of the lost estates of the monastery in Bakonybél, in which the donations of Queen Gisella, wife of King Stephen (1000–1038) are listed.[1] Although the register does not mention the charter explicitly, the fact that the text uses first-person singular verbs and pronouns – *me . . . contulli . . . dedi* – suggests that its writer knew and worked with Queen Gisella's charter, the tone of which was presumably fairly subjective. The probability of this is strengthened by the *evangeliarium* given by Queen Gisella to the monastery of Bakonybél, which included the charters of the monastery and which the monastery still owned in 1508.[2] It seems that Gisella's example was not followed by later queens: the first charter whose original copy survived is from 1224, issued by Queen Jolanta, the second wife of King Andrew II (1205–35).[3] The issuing of charters, however, did not become regular until the middle of the thirteenth century. It is not surprising, then, that the queens' charters only make up a small minority of the charters of the Árpádian Age: the total number of charters that remain from this period is about 10,000:[4] the 200 queens' charters we know of therefore constitute only two per cent of the whole.

Most of the queens' charters have a correct date. A minority give not only the year, but the day and month of issue, too.[5] Half of the charters we know only have the year of issue,[6] while in other cases they show the day but not the

From *Dating Undated Medieval Charters*. Ed. Michael Gervers. Copyright (by the Editor and Contributors 2000). Published by the Boydell Press (in association with Collegium Budapest), PO Box 9, Woodbridge, Suffolk, IP12 3DF, Great Britain. ISBN 0 85115 792 0.

1. National Archives of Hungary, Collected Photocopies of Medieval Charters (=DF) 287 859, published in *Diplomata Hungariae antiquissima I (ab anno 1000 usque ad annum 1131)*. Edendo operi praefuit Georgius Györffy, Budapestini 1992 (=*DHA*), 120.
2. Dezső Csánki, 'Magyarországi bencések egy bibliogaphiai becsű inventariuma 1508-ból' [A Book-Inventory of the Benedictines in Hungary from 1508], *Magyar Könyvszemle* 6 (1881): p. 294.
3. National Archives of Hungary, Collection of Medieval Charters (=DL) 24 383, published in *Codex diplomaticus Hungariae ecclesiasticus ac civilis*, 11 vols., stud. et op. Georgii Fejér, Budae 1829–44 (=*CD*), vol. III/1, p. 469.
4. György Györffy, *Az Árpád-kori Magyarország történeti földrajza* [The Historical Geography of Hungary in the Árpádian Age], 4 vols., Budapest, 1963–98, vol. I, p. 10.
5. For example, 1264: DF 248 144, published in *Monumenta ecclesiae Strigoniensis*, 3 vols., ed. Ferdinandus Knauz and Ludovicus Dedek, Strigonii, 1874–1924 (=*MES*), vol. I, p. 517; 1271: DF 282 130, published in *Urkundenbuch des Burgenlandes und der angrenzenden Gebiete der Komitate Wieselburg, Ödenburg und Eisenburg*, 4 vols., bearb. von Hans Wagner, Irmtraut Lindeck-Pozza, Graz–Köln–Wien, 1955–85 (=*UB*), vol. III, p. 276; 1282: DL 76 161, published in *CD* VI/2. 406.
6. For example, 1265: DF 248 643, published in *MES*, vol. I, p. 530; 1280: DF 243 678, published in *Árpádkori új okmánytár. Codex diplomaticus Arpadianus continuatus*, 12 vols., ed. Gusztáv Wenzel, Pest–Budapest, 1860–74 (=*ÁÚO*), vol. IV, p. 223.; 1284: DL 75 822.

year.[7] Finally, about one-tenth of the queens' charters have no date at all, but most of these are known only because they are mentioned in other charters.[8] Only one example of actual text remains.[9]

This short summary may suggest that dating problems are few and far between in respect of the queens' charters of the Árpádian Age. The situation is not so simple in reality, because the need for the precise date of issue obviously comes up both in the case of the charters which give only the year, and those which give only the day without the year. The traditional method used by Hungarian historians to solve these problems is content analysis.[10] I would like to demonstrate this by some examples.

It is a great help of course if the charter was transcribed later in the same year as another which has a full date. This was the case when King Ladislas IV (1272–90) transcribed on 30 May 1280 a charter which his mother, Queen Elisabeth, had issued in the same year: it is clear that the queen issued her charter before that date.[11] In other cases, what we know about the events or people mentioned in a charter helps us determine the date. One 1289 charter of Isabelle, the wife of Ladislas IV – who is often referred to as Queen Elisabeth in our sources – was definitely issued in the second half of that year, because the case it describes was dealt with after the assembly at Föveny (*post congregacionem regni Hungarie prehabitam circa Fuen*),[12] and this assembly was held around the feast of St John the Baptist (*generalis congregacio tocius regni nostri in Fuen anno Domini millesimo ducentesimo octogesimo nono, circa festum Beati Johannis baptiste celebrata*) – as is shown for example in another charter by the same Isabelle.[13] Yet another charter by Isabelle from 1290 must have been written

---

7. For example, DL 82 761, published in *Budapest történetének okleveles emlékei. Monumenta diplomatica civitatis Budapest*, vol. I (1148–1301), ed. Albert Gárdonyi, Budapest, 1936 (=*BTOE*), p. 71; DL 1159, published in *Hazai okmánytár. Codex diplomaticus patrius Hungaricus*, 8 vols., ed. Imre Nagy, Iván Paur, Károly Ráth, and Dezső Véghely, Győr–Budapest, 1865–91 (=*HO*), vol. VI, p. 307; DL 37 560, published in *HO*, vol. VII, p. 185.
8. For example, *MES*, vol. I, p. 560; *ÁÚO*, vol. IV, p. 258; *ÁÚO*, vol. XII, p. 312.; *ÁÚO*, vol. IX, p. 308.; *MES*, vol. II, p. 309.; *HO*, vol. IV, p. 124.
9. DF 207 088, published in *A pannonhalmi Szent Benedek-rend története* [The History of the Benedictine Monastery of Pannonhalma], 12 vols., ed. László Erdélyi and Pongrác Sörös, Budapest, 1902–16 (=*PRT*), vol. II, p. 326.
10. János Karácsonyi, *A hamis, hibáskeltű és keltezetlen oklevelek jegyzéke 1400-ig* [Forgeries and Undated Charters up to 1400], Budapest, 1902 (new edition: Szeged, 1988); Ubul Kállay, 'Új adatok keltezetlen oklevelek időpontjának meghatározásához' [New Data for Dating Undated Charters], *Századok* 47 (1913): pp. 110–31; *Az Árpád-házi királyok okleveleinek kritikai jegyzéke. Regesta regum stirpis Arpadianae critico-diplomatica*, 2 vols., ed. Imre Szentpétery and Iván Borsa, Budapest, 1923–87 (= *RA*) passim; Attila Zsoldos, 'Téténytől a Hód-tóig. Az 1279 és 1282 közötti évek politikatörténetének vázlata' [From Tétény to the Battle of Hód. A Study of Hungarian Political History between 1279 and 1282], *Történelmi Szemle* 39 (1997): pp. 69–73; *Erdélyi okmánytár. Codex diplomaticus Transsylvaniae*, vol. I (1023–1300), ed. Zsigmond Jakó, Budapest, 1997, passim.
11. 1280: DL 985, published *ÁÚO*, vol. XII, p. 301.
12. 1289: DF 200 713.
13. 1290: DF 200 719, published in *CD*, vol. VII/2, p. 127, cf. also Gyula Pauler, *A magyar nemzet története az Árpádházi királyok alatt* [The History of the Hungarian Nation under the Rule of the Árpádian Kings], 2 vols., Budapest, 1899 (reprint: 1984), vol. II, p. 406; Erzsébet S. Kiss, *A királyi generális kongregáció kialakulásának történetéhez* [The Genesis of the Royal Assemblies], Acta Universitatis Szegediensis de Attila József nominatae. *Acta Historica* 39 [Szeged] (1971): pp. 46–50.

before 10 July because it mentions her husband,[14] the king, as living – and he was killed on 10 July 1290.[15]

The charters of queens which describe measures of temporary validity – as well as those of kings – sometimes give the day, but not the year of issue. Nevertheless, the year of issue can usually be deduced. There is a summary, produced in 1390, of a charter issued by Queen Elisabeth, wife of King Stephen V (1270–72), according to which the original charter was written on 7 December (*in vigilia conceptionis Beate Virginis*).[16] It is possible to determine the missing year of the charter because of two facts: on the one hand, it speaks about Stephen V as living, and he died on 6 August 1272; on the other hand, the charter makes mention of the king's battle against the Czechs near the River Rábca (*in expedicione regni contra regem Bohemie iuxta aquam Rabcha*). Since the battle was fought in 1271,[17] and the king was dead by 7 December 1272, the charter was undoubtedly written on 7 December 1271. Another charter by Queen Elisabeth was issued "*tertio die post festum Passce*" without mention of the year.[18] The charter, however, tells of an event which was reported by the chapter of Pécs on 6 November 1282,[19] so we may well be justified in thinking that its date is 31 March 1282.

Sometimes we can date a charter only approximately. A charter by Queen Fenenna, the first wife of King Andrew III (1290–1301), in which she donated an estate near Pápa to Martin, the deputy chief justice of the royal court (*viceiudici curie domini regis*), was issued "*feria tertia proxima post octavas Pasce*". The charter is known only from György Fejér's edition, who gave 1292 as the date of issue.[20] This date cannot be accepted, because Martin became deputy chief justice of the royal court only in 1293.[21] Since Queen Fenenna died after 8 September 1295,[22] the possible dates of issue are 7 April 1293, 27 April 1294, or 12 April 1295. Evidence supporting the last date is given by the fact that in 1295 Queen Fenenna granted another estate near Pápa to the same Martin.[23]

It is not impossible to date the only queen's charter without proper dating which has survived intact. This was issued by Queen Mary, the wife of Béla IV, and in it she ordered the *comes* of the Great Island (*comiti de magna insula*) to report on the boundaries of the Újhely estate which had previously been given to the monastery of Pannonhalma, so that neither the abbot nor any noblemen living next to it would infringe upon the others' rights (*ita iura nobilium circumiacentium*

---

14. DF 200 719, published in *CD*, vol. VII/2, p. 127.
15. Chronici Hungarici compositio saeculi XIV, in *Scriptores rerum Hungaricarum tempore ducum regumque stirpis Arpadianae gestarum*, 2 vols. Edendo operi praefuit Emericus Szentpétery Budapestini 1937–38, vol. I, pp. 473–74.
16. DL 5777.
17. Pauler, vol. II, pp. 286–90.
18. DL 38 667.
19. *ÁÚO*, vol. XII, p. 372.
20. *CD*, vol. VI/1, p. 241.
21. Marcell, Martin's predecessor, held office on 31 March 1293 (see DL 90 763), and on 15 April 1293 it is Martin who issued a charter as deputy chief justice of the royal court (see *CD*, vol. VI/1, p. 260).
22. Cf. DL 40 288, published in *HO*, vol. VII, p. 242.
23. See previous note.

ex parte abbatis quicquam non derogetur et iidem nobiles ipsi abbati in suo iure nequeant iniurari).[24] Since Béla IV in 1264 – after 20 December[25] – passed judgement in a lawsuit between the monastery of Pannonhalma and the noblemen whose estates were next to the monastery's estate in Újhely,[26] it seems more than probable that the queen's charter was written in connection with this trial sometime in 1264.

There are some charters by queens which are dated, but clearly incorrectly. One of Queen Fenenna's charters was written *"anno Domini Mo CCo nonagesimo"*,[27] which would be acceptable if it did not mention a campaign of King Andrew III in Austria which – as is well-known – took place in 1291.[28] The same charter names a certain B., bishop of Veszprém, as the queen's chancellor. This name can be completed as Benedictus who followed Andrew, bishop of Eger, in the office in the autumn of 1291. The first mention of his name as the queen's chancellor is from 9 October,[29] so the date of issue can be given as after 9 October 1291. We may suppose that the word *"primo"* (after *"nonagesimo"*) was simply left out from the date by mistake.

The incorrect date of another charter calls attention to more serious problems. A charter by Queen Agnes, the second wife of Andrew III, was issued *"anno Domini Mmo CCo nonagesimo quinto, Kalendis Maii"*.[30] The date is obviously wrong, because Queen Fenenna – the first wife of King Andrew III – was alive on 1 May 1295. The fact that one summary transcription of the charter gives 1296 as its date,[31] when Queen Fenenna was already dead, does not solve the problem, because Agnes was not yet married to Andrew III; the marriage followed a year after the 1296 engagement, in 1297.[32] Agnes cannot possibly have issued a charter as Queen of Hungary before the marriage and her coronation as queen.

The greatest difficulty concerning this charter is not the dating problem, however. It mentions Theodore, the deputy chancellor of the king, as the provost of Székesfehérvár. In contrast, Theodore is last mentioned in a valid royal charter on 24 April as the provost of Székesfehérvár;[33] he is the elected bishop of Győr on 28 April,[34] and after that he is mentioned as the provost of Székesfehérvár only in forgeries.[35] Theodore's ecclesiastical dignity as given by the charter of Queen

---

24. *PRT*, vol. II, p. 326.
25. The abbot had to take an oath *"in octavis beate Lucie virginis"*, which refers to the approximate date.
26. DF 207 087, published in *PRT*, vol. II, p. 328.
27. DL 49 680, published in *ÁÚO*, vol. X, p. 36.
28. Mór Wertner, 'Az 1291. évi magyar–osztrák hadjárat' [The War between Austria and Hungary in 1291], *Hadtörténelmi Közlemények* 17 (1916): pp. 349–86.
29. *ÁÚO*, vol. XII, p. 510.
30. DL 70 724, published in *ÁÚO*, vol. X, p. 180.
31. DL 90 825.
32. Mór Wertner, *Az Árpádok családi története* [The Family History of the Árpáds], Nagybecskerek, 1892, pp. 576–77.
33. *RA*, no. 4013.
34. *RA*, no. 4018.
35. *RA*, nos. 4028, 4069, 4125, 4126.

Agnes is then incorrect – no matter whether the date is 1 May 1295 or 1296 – therefore, this charter must be a forgery.

Fortunately, there are some facts which help to determine the reason for, and approximate date of, the forgery. The supposed charter from Queen Agnes relates that the queen allows George, Peter, and Stephen, sons of Menna, nurse of King Ladislas IV, to keep the villages of Felnémeti, Középnémeti, and Alnémeti. These villages, according to the charter, were donated by Béla IV and his wife to the nurse, and the kings and queens who followed them confirmed the donation. Unluckily, these charters were burnt in the Dominican church of Patak when the Mongols invaded Hungary in 1285, during the so-called 'second Mongol invasion'.

The village of Felnémeti in the charter (today Milhost', Slovakia) was originally given to Michael, son of Stephen, and his wife, the nurse (*nutrix*) of Ladislas IV, by Queen Isabelle, wife of King Ladislas IV in 1278.[36] She also donated Középnémeti (today Tornyosnémeti, Hungary) in the same year to a certain George, who lived in Buda.[37] The anonymous nurse in Queen Isabelle's charter can be identified as Menna in the supposed charter by Queen Agnes, and George of Buda was one of her sons.[38] The circumstances in which Alnémeti (today Hidasnémeti, Hungary) was granted are not known, but the same family surely owned it in 1299.[39]

A charter from 1319 gives us some help in the problem of the forgery. It says that George, son of Nicholas, who was one of Menna's sons, had previously – between 1314 and 1319 – sued his cousins, Simon, Michael, and Stephen, sons of Stephen, whose mother was the same Menna, the nurse in the case of the villages Felnémeti, Köznémeti, and Alnémeti. The lawsuit ended with a compromise, which is described in the 1319 charter mentioned earlier. The parties divided Felnémeti and Alnémeti, and in the case of Középnémeti they agreed that if it was granted to George, the son of the nurse, then the other George, son of Nicholas (his nephew) had no claim to it; if, on the other hand, Középnémeti was given to nurse Menna or to anybody else, he had the same right to it as his cousins, sons of Stephen (*quod si continencia privilegii magistri Georgii filii nutricis habuerit, quod villa Kuzepnempty acquisicio fuerit eiusdem, extunc Georgius filius Nicolai prenotatus nullum ius haberet vel habere posset in eadem. Si vero dicta villa Kuzepnempty acquisicio domine nutricis, aut alicuius alterius extiterit, extunc Georgius filius Nicolai sicut unus ex filiis Stephani porcionem obtineret de eadem*).[40] This disposition makes sense only if Menna had two husbands (not at the same time, of course!). One of them was Michael, son of Stephen, whose name turns up in the 1278 charter mentioned earlier.[41] His sons were George, who lived

---

36. DF 266 088 and DL 75 382.
37. DF 266 087; see also DL 90 825 and DF 266 082.
38. Cf. 1319: DF 266 081.
39. DL 70 599, published in *ÁÚO*, vol. X, p. 351.
40. 1319: DF 266 081.
41. DL 75 382.

in Buda and who got Középnémeti, and Stephen, whose sons were sued by their cousin, George son of Nicholas.[42] This George (son of Nicholas) must have been the grandson of Menna's other husband, the name of whom is not known, because only then can we explain the following situation: his father is said to be the nurse's son, yet he still could not get part of the estate which was donated to George of Buda, his uncle.

Középnémeti was indeed donated to Menna's son, George – as is proven by the 1278 charter – so the other George, son of Nicholas, did not receive part of the estate after 1319. However, he could not accept this fact and started a new lawsuit against Simon, Stephen, and Michael, sons of Stephen, in 1325. He did not succeed this time either. It is more important for us that the supposed charter of Queen Agnes was not used in this new suit.[43] The forgery first appeared in 1346 when it was transcribed by the chapter of Eger at the request of Margaret, widow of Philip Druget, palatine (*legitimis et congruis postulacionibus eiusdem nobilis domine relicte Phylippi palatini et iusticie annuentes*).[44] Margaret was a granddaughter of one of the daughters of the nurse (see Family Tree of Menna the Nurse), and that same year (1346) in a lawsuit she had to exhibit the charter which proved that Középnémeti was granted to her great-grandmother, the nurse (*ipsa possessio Kuzepnimity fuisset acquisititia domine nutricis, que fuisset ava domine palatinisse*). However, Margaret did not possess such a charter – she could not have done so – so it is not surprising that she asked for a prorogation to show the document in question. After this, she exhibited the charter from Queen Agnes concerning the donation of the three Némethis (*quasdam litteras privilegiales domine Agnetis quondam regine Hungarie, que super collacione possessionum Kuzepnimity, Olnemity et Vegnemity quibusdam nobilibus facta emanatas*),[45] that is, the forgery. It is then certain that she had the forgery made.

42. 1319: DF 266 081 and 1324: DL 75 391.
43. 1325: DF 266 082; see also *Anjou-kori oklevéltár. Documenta res Hungaricas tempore regum Andegavensium illustrantia* [=*AOklt*], vol. IX, ed. Lajos Géczi, Budapest–Szeged, 1997, nos. 23–24.
44. DL 70 724.
45. 1347: DL 3796; cf. *ÁÚO*, vol. XII, pp. 648–50.

Bibliography

Codex diplomaticus Hungariae ecclesiasticus ac civilis. 11 vols. Stud. et op. Georgii Fejér. Budae, 1829–44.

Csánki, Dezső. 1888. 'Magyarországi bencések egy bibliogaphiai becsű inventariuma 1508-ból' [A Book-Inventory of the Benedictines in Hungary from 1508]. *Magyar Könyvszemle* 6: pp. 289–99.

Diplomata Hungariae antiquissima I. (ab anno 1000 usque ad annum 1131). Edendo operi praefuit Georgius Györffy. Budapest, 1992.

Erdélyi, László, and Pongrác Sörös, eds. 1902–16. *A pannonhalmi Szent Benedek-rend története* [The History of the Benedictine Monastery of Pannonhalma]. 12 vols. Budapest.

Gárdonyi, Albert, ed. 1936. *Budapest történetének okleveles emlékei. Monumenta diplomatica civitatis Budapest.* Vol. I: 1148–1301. Budapest.

Géczi, Lajos, ed. 1997. *Anjou-kori oklevéltár. Documenta res Hungaricas tempore regum Andegavensium illustrantia.* Vol. IX. Budapest–Szeged.

Györffy, György. 1963–98. *Az Árpád-kori Magyarország történeti földrajza* [The Historical Geography of Hungary in the Árpádian Age]. 4 vols. Budapest.

Jakó, Zsigmond, ed. 1997. *Erdélyi okmánytár. Codex diplomaticus Transsylvaniae.* Vol. I: 1023–1300. Budapest.

Kállay, Ubul. 1913. 'Új adatok keltezetlen oklevelek időpontjának meghatározásához' [New Data for Dating Undated Charters]. *Századok* 47: pp. 110–31.

Karácsonyi, János. 1902. *A hamis, hibáskeltű és keltezetlen oklevelek jegyzéke 1400-ig* [Forgeries and Undated Charters up to 1400]. Budapest. (New edition: Szeged, 1988.)

Kiss, Erzsébet S. 1971. *A királyi generális kongregáció kialakulásának történetéhez* [The Genesis of the Royal Assemblies]. Acta Universitatis Szegediensis de Attila József nominatae. *Acta Historica* 39 [Szeged].

Knauz, Ferdinandus, and Ludovicus Dedek. 1874–1924. *Monumenta ecclesiae Strigoniensis.* 3 vols. Strigonii.

Nagy, Imre, and Gyula Nagy, eds. 1878–1920. *Anjoukori okmánytár. Codex diplomaticus Andegavensis.* 7 vols. Budapest.

Nagy, Imre, Iván Paur, Károly Ráth, and Dezső Véghely. 1865–91. *Hazai okmánytár. Codex diplomaticus patrius Hungaricus.* 8 vols. Győr–Budapest.

Oklevéltár a gróf Csáky család történetéhez [Charters related to the history of the Csáky family]. 1919. Budapest.

Pauler, Gyula. 1899. *A magyar nemzet története az Árpádházi királyok alatt* [The History of the Hungarian Nation under the Rule of the Árpádian Kings]. 2 vols. Budapest. (Reprint: 1984.)

Pesty, Frigyes, and Tivadar Ortvay. 1896. *Oklevelek Temesvármegye és Temesvárváros történetéhez* [Charters Related to the History of County Temes]. Pozsony [now Bratislava].

Scriptores rerum Hungaricarum tempore ducum regumque stirpis Arpadianae gestarum. 2 vols. Edendo operi praefuit Emericus Szentpétery. Budapest, 1937–38.

Szentpétery, Imre, and Iván Borsa, eds. 1923–87. *Az Árpád-házi királyok okleveleinek kritikai jegyzéke. Regesta regum stirpis Arpadianae critico-diplomatica.* 2 vols. Budapest.

Wagner, Hans, and Irmtraut Lindeck-Pozza, eds. 1955–85. *Urkundenbuch des Burgenlandes und der angrenzenden Gebiete der Komitate Wieselburg, Ödenburg und Eisenburg.* 4 vols. Graz–Köln–Wien.

Wenzel, Gusztáv, ed. 1860–74. *Árpádkori új okmánytár. Codex diplomaticus Arpadianus continuatus.* 12 vols. Pest–Budapest.

Wertner, Mór. 1892. *Az Árpádok családi története* [The Family History of the Árpáds]. Nagybecskerek.

———. 1916. 'Az 1291. évi magyar–osztrák hadjárat' [The War between Austria and Hungary in 1291]. *Hadtörténelmi Közlemények* 17: pp. 349–86.

Zsoldos, Attila. 1997. 'Téténytől a Hód-tóig. Az 1279 és 1282 közötti évek politikatörténetének vázlata' [From Tétény to the Battle of Hód. A Study of Hungarian Political History between 1279 and 1282]. *Történelmi Szemle* 39: pp. 69–98.

The Family Tree of Menna the Nurse

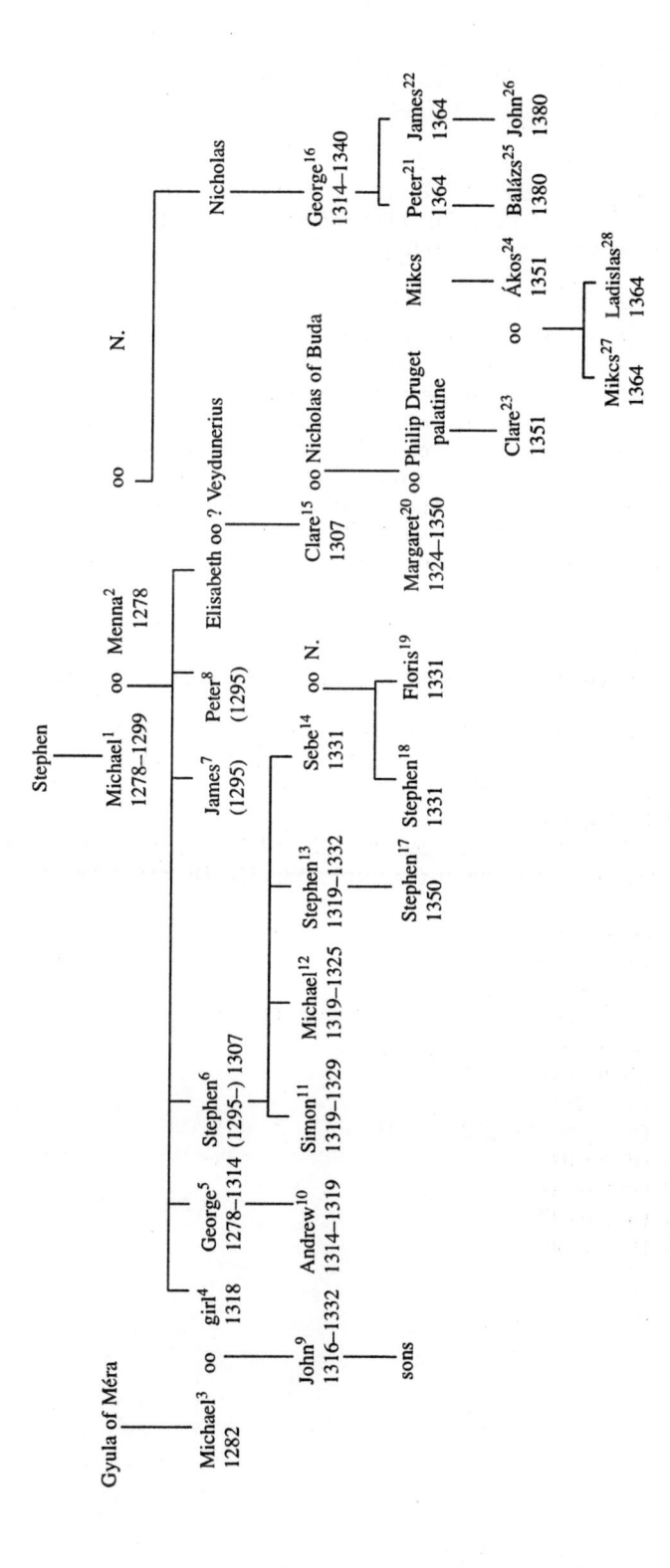

```
Stephen
   |
   ├── Michael¹ oo Menna²    Elisabeth oo ? Veydunerius        Nicholas
   |   1278–1299   1278                                           |
   |                                                              oo N.
   |                                                              |
   ├── James⁷ (1295)                                              ├── George¹⁶
   |                                                              |   1314–1340
   ├── Peter⁸ (1295) oo N.                                        |     |
   |                  |                                           |     ├── Peter²¹  James²²
   |                  ├── Sebe¹⁴ 1331                             |     |   1364    1364
   |                  ├── Stephen¹⁸ 1331                          |     |
   |                  |     └── Stephen¹⁷ 1350                    |     └── Balázs²⁵  John²⁶
   |                  └── Floris¹⁹ 1331                           |         1380     1380
   |                                                              |
   ├── Clare¹⁵ oo Nicholas of Buda                                └── Mikcs
   |   1307                                                              |
   |     └── Margaret²⁰ oo Philip Druget                                 ├── Clare²³
   |         1324–1350     palatine                                      |   1351
   |                                                                     └── Ákos²⁴ oo Mikcs²⁷  Ladislas²⁸
   |                                                                         1351     1364      1364
   |
Gyula of Méra
   |
   ├── Michael³ oo (wife)
   |   1282
   |     |
   |     ├── John⁹ 1316–1332
   |     ├── girl⁴ 1318
   |     ├── sons
   |
   ├── George⁵ 1278–1314 (1295–) 1307
   |     |
   |     ├── Andrew¹⁰ 1314–1319
   |     ├── Simon¹¹ 1319–1329
   |     ├── Michael¹² 1319–1325
   |     └── Stephen¹³ 1319–1332
   |
   └── Stephen⁶
```

For notes to Family Tree, see overleaf.

1. 1278: DF 266 088; 1299: ÁÚO, vol. X, p. 351, ÁÚO, vol. XII, p. 649.
2. 1278: DF 266 088; 1295: ÁÚO, vol. X, p. 180 (the forgery).
3. 1282: RA, vol. II/2–3, p. 290.
4. 1318: Györffy, vol. I, pp. 122–23.
5. 1278: DF 266 087; 1289: BTOE, vol. I, p. 248; 1295: ÁÚO, vol. X, p. 180 (the forgery); 1299: ÁÚO, vol. IX, p. 351; 1307: DF 266 085; 1314: DF 266 084.
6. 1295: ÁÚO, vol. X, p. 180 (the forgery); 1299: ÁÚO, vol. X, p. 351; 1307: DF 266 085.
7. 1295: ÁÚO, vol. X, p. 180 (the forgery).
8. 1295: ÁÚO, vol. X, p. 180 (the forgery).
9. 1316: Oklevéltár a gróf Csáky család történetéhez [Charters related to the history of the Csáky family], Budapest 1919 (= Csáky), vol. I, p. 75; 1317: Anjoukori okmánytár. *Codex diplomaticus Andegavensis*, vols. I–VII, ed. Nagy Imre, Nagy Gyula, Budapest 1878–1920, vol. I, p. 421; Csáky, vol. I, p. 76; 1318: Györffy, vol. I, pp. 122–23; 1320: *Oklevelek Temesvármegye és Temesvárváros történetéhez* [Charters related to the history of the county of Temes], ed. Pesty Frigyes, Ortvay Tivadar, Pozsony, 1896. Vol. I, p. 20; 1322: CD, vol. VIII/5, p. 122; 1324: DL 70 152, DF 266 087; 1325: CD, vol. VIII/5, p. 153; 1327: DL 86 986; 1332: DL 40 628.
10. 1314: DF 266 084; 1319. DF 266 081.
11. 1319: DF 266 081; 1324: DF 266 082, DF 266 087; 1325: DF 266 082 (cf. AOklt, vol. IX, no. 24); 1329: DL 2540.
12. 1319: DF 266 081; 1324: DF 266 082, DF 266 087; 1325: DF 266 082 (cf. AOklt, vol. IX, no. 24)
13. 1319: DF 266 081; 1324: DF 266 082, DF 266 087; 1325: DF 266 082 (cf. AOklt, vol. IX, no. 24); 1329: DL 2540; 1331: DL 70 615, DL 75 831; 1332: DL 40 628.
14. 1331: DL 70 615.
15. 1307: DF 266 085.
16. 1314: DF 266 084; 1319: DF 266 081; 1324: DF 266 082; 1325: DF 266 082 (vö. AOklt, vol. IX, no. 24); DL 70 610, CD VIII/5. 153; 1331: DL 70 615, DL 75 831; 1340: DF 266 084.
17. 1350: DF 266 087.
18. 1331: DL 70 615.
19. 1331: DL 70 615.
20. 1324: DF 266 087; 1340: DF 266 085; 1350: DF 266 087; 1351: DL 42 781.
21. 1364: DF 266 087.
22. 1364: DF 266 087.
23. 1351: DL 42 781.
24. 1351: DL 42 781; 1352: DL 42 781.
25. 1380: DF 266 088.
26. 1380: DF 266 088.
27. 1364: DF 266 087.
28. 1364: DF 266 087.

PART IV
DATING BY THE ASSOCIATION OF NAMES

SOCIAL GROUPS AS RECOGNITION PATTERNS: A MEANS OF DATING MEDIEVAL CHARTERS

Maria Hillebrandt

This paper is intended to describe an automatic procedure developed at the University of Münster for the analysis of prosopographical data, that is, names and groups of names, in charters from the early and high Middle Ages. Problems specific to questions of diplomacy or of the tradition of the charters and their critique were not taken into account while the procedure was being developed.[1] It was then also used to check and solve otherwise insurmountable problems in the chronology of charters, as a complement to the traditional diplomatic methods.[2]

The charters used in developing this procedure were those from the abbey of Cluny. They contain a huge number of personal names, virtually unmanageable with traditional means. The computer seemed from the start the ideal instrument to tackle the problems posed by hundreds of thousands of names, both for mathematical and statistical studies, the possible identification of names and groups of names, and improved dating of charters.

A description of the material used – that is, the charters of the abbey of Cluny – shall be followed here by a rough sketch of the automatic procedure developed to analyse names and groups of names in them.[3] It will be rounded off with a few remarks about the possibilities and limits of this procedure.

From *Dating Undated Medieval Charters*. Ed. Michael Gervers. Copyright (by the Editor and Contributors 2000). Published by the Boydell Press (in association with Collegium Budapest), PO Box 9, Woodbridge, Suffolk, IP12 3DF, Great Britain. ISBN 0 85115 792 0.

I would like to record a special debt of gratitude to Heiner M. Becker, who translated this text and whose influence on my ideas and formulations will be evident throughout. Thanks are also due to Michael Gervers for his invitation to this workshop and many useful talks and suggestions.

1. The work on the charters of Cluny was one of the projects on the history of Cluny and its houses undertaken at the Sonderforschungsbereich 7 at the University of Münster under Professor Joachim Wollasch. First results based on an earlier version of this automatic procedure were presented in 1982: Maria Hillebrandt, 'The Cluniac Charters. Remarks on a Quantitative Approach for Prosopographical Studies', *Medieval Prosopography* 3, no. 1 (1982): pp. 3–25, and no. 2 (1982): p. 103. On the prosopograhical research done in Münster, see Franz Neiske, 'Die Erforschung von Personen und Gemeinschaften des Mittelalters mit Hilfe der elektronischen Datenverarbeitung', in *L'histoire médiévale et les ordinateurs. Medieval History and Computers. Rapports d'une Table ronde internationale*, ed. Karl Ferdinand Werner, München, 1981, pp. 77–109.

2. I am preparing a comprehensive study on the chronology of the Cluniac charters; it will also consider in detail the diplomatic, prosopographical, and historical aspects, so that what is said here can be limited to a basic presentation of the automatic procedure.

3. Friedrich-Wilhelm Westerhoff, 'Gruppensuche: Ein Verfahren zur Identifizierung von Personen und Personengruppen in mittelalterlichen Namenquellen', in *Dokumentationsband zum EDV-Kolloquium 1985*, Schriftenreihe des Rechenzentrums der Westfälischen Wilhelms-Universität Münster LIX, Münster, 1985, pp. 67–77; Friedrich-Wilhelm Westerhoff, *Gruppensuche. Ein Verfahren zur Identifizierung von Personengruppen in mittelalterlichen Namen-Quellen. Beschreibung des Verfahrens und der Programme*, Schriftenreihe des Rechenzentrums der Universität Münster LXI, Münster, 1988. Here I can only sketch the general outlines of this procedure; for a detailed description of the program see Westerhoff, *Gruppensuche*.

1. The Charters of Cluny and Their Tradition

Thanks to a number of fortunate circumstances, the possessions and property of the abbey of Cluny (founded in 910) grew rapidly from the middle of the tenth century onwards. In South Burgundy, within a perimeter of roughly 70 kilometres around Cluny, the abbey soon became by far the largest landholder. The charters written between 910 and 1120, of which some 4,000 survive, bear witness to this development.[4]

These charters were recorded in the tenth and eleventh centuries, partly as originals and partly as copies, in the cartularies. Because of the considerable losses due mainly to the French Revolution, we have today only about 350 original charters left from the first two centuries of the abbey of Cluny. They can be complemented by a considerable number of copies made in the second half of the eighteenth century from original documents in the archives of the abbey. Another important complement is the cartularies produced mainly around the end of the eleventh century. They include some 3,100 documents and count among the most important cartularies of Western Europe. Compared with those documents still extant as originals or modern copies of originals, close to 55 per cent of the 4,000 charters mentioned survive only in these cartularies.[5]

The only overall criterion with which to arrange the documents in these cartularies is that of the abbot and his abbacy; although it seems that inside these cartularies for each abbot there are further criteria to group some documents, for example, regional or legal. These do not concern the chronology of the legal acts documented.

In most European monasteries one would still be able to place these documents in relatively short time-spans, if the name of an abbot is given in a document (provided this abbot and the time of his abbacy has been established). In Cluny, however, things are much more complicated, as over a period of some 150 years – between 950 and 1100 – there were only three abbots, each of whom held office for about fifty years.

2. Chronological Particularities in the Charters

The development of the writing of charters in Cluny resembles that of other French monasteries of the High Middle Ages. Towards the end of the tenth century and until about 1100 begins a process in the course of which the formulaic

---

4. Auguste Bernard and Alexandre Bruel, eds, *Recueil des chartes de l'abbaye de Cluny*, Collection de documents inédits sur l'histoire de France. Première série: Histoire politique, 6 vols, Paris, 1876–1903. The literature on Cluny and its history has grown immensely over the last few decades, but there is still no history of the *seigneurie* of the abbey. See also Georges Duby's classic study *La société aux XIe et XIIe siècles dans la région mâconnaise*, Bibliothèque générale de l'École Pratique des Hautes Études, VIe section, 1953, 2nd ed., Paris, 1971.

5. Maria Hillebrandt, 'Les cartulaires de l'abbaye de Cluny', *Mémoires de la Société pour l'Histoire du Droit et des Institutions des anciens pays bourguignons, comtois et romands* 50 (1993): pp. 7–18, with further references to literature and sources.

nature of the charter gets more and more lost. The exactitude of chronological details in dating formulae decreases progressively, until first the dating is reduced to the name of a ruler, and finally, after about 1050, they disappear completely.[6]

The problem of the dating of the charters was solved only very inadequately, when, at the end of the nineteenth century, the Cluniac charters were published in six volumes by Auguste Bernard and Alexandre Bruel. Although they arranged the documents chronologically, they used rather rough indicators for the placing of items whose dating formulae were either insufficient or lacking. These were, for example, the rule of a king or the time when an abbot held office – criteria which allowed only a very approximate positioning in relatively long spans – or they deduced a dating from the position given to the document by the copyists in the cartulary of an abbot. This, however, is rarely really useful, as – apart from the length of the abbacies – we encounter here the additional problem of documents being placed in the wrong order and at the wrong place in the cartularies. In the cartulary of Cluny's first abbot, Berno (910–927), for example, one finds a total of 156 charters of which 21 include the name of the abbot; only these were actually negotiated during his abbacy. All other documents were produced at a later stage, some even a century later.[7] These particularities were not noticed by the editors of the charters.

3. Means towards a Solution

The means to develop a quantifying method to solve these problems are to be found in the charters themselves. For although in the course of the eleventh century the dating formulae disappeared progressively, the writers of the charters continued to include the names of the witnesses, and this even when copying the documents into the cartularies, so that a lot of donors, witnesses, and monks are named repeatedly. Thanks to this, we find, up to about 1100, some 60,000 names in the charters. This massive body of names opens up a number of possibilities for the use of quantitative methods.

One of the prerequisites is that the names belong to persons from a comparable social context: they lived in relative proximity to the monastery and appear more than once in the charters, sometimes with different functions (author, tenant, neighbour, or witness of the document). As a first step in a quantitative analysis one should therefore try to identify persons in dated and in undated charters, which furnishes particular chronological relationships and sequences inside the

---

6. Olivier Guyotjeannin, '"*Penuria scriptorium*": le mythe de l'anarchie documentaire dans la France du nord (Xe–première moitié du XIe siècle)', in *Pratiques de l'écrit documentaire au XIe siècle*, ed. Olivier Guyotjeannin, Laurent Morelle, and Michel Parisse, pp. 11–44, Bibliothèque de l'École des Chartes 155, 1997; Dominique Barthélemy, 'Une crise de l'écrit. Observations sur les actes de Saint-Aubin d'Angers (XIe siècle)', in Guyotjeannin, Morelle, and Parisse, *Pratiques*, pp. 95–118.

7. On these particularities of the diplomatic sources from Cluny see my forthcoming study, referred to in note 2. See also Maurice Chaume, 'En marge de l'histoire de Cluny', *Revue Mabillon* 29 (1939): pp. 41–61, esp. p. 44f.

body of the charters.[8] The particularities of the charters, their tradition, and the edition mentioned above make it necessary to keep the frame for this comparison as large as possible, that is, to include the names from as many documents as possible from rather long periods.

When developing methods of how to study and structure the materials with this great number of personal names, we were able to draw upon the Münster research into so-called commemorative sources such as confraternity books or necrologies. These contain thousands of names, but generally only Christian (first) names.[9]

The first essential step, especially for an automatic comparison of names, is the unification of varying forms of names through a name index. As in the last-mentioned sources from the early and high Middle Ages, the charters of Cluny also show extreme variation in the ways in which names are written. These variations are due to the different local origins of the scribes or to the important time differences between the writing of the original documents and the copying. By a preliminary step called 'lemmatisation' the various forms of spelling are grouped according to philological criteria under a single entry or 'lemma' with the help of a complex dictionary of name variants, suffixes, and inflexes.[10]

Apart from the varying spellings of names, there are further difficulties in identifying persons in the Cluniac charters from the tenth and eleventh centuries:[11] for example, the additional information usually connected to the name of a person – such as surnames, titles, social status, or parental relationships – is either absent or has been added unsystematically or often wrongly. Therefore, the only more or less reliable information which the charters provide to identify a person is the context of names within which a name appears. This is, therefore, the most important criterion with which to analyse even those names which cannot be linked to an identifiable person.

To better identify a person, the program tries first to determine names as part of particular groups of names and to look for similar name groups in the database of the charters. Helpful in the process of identification is the fact that all persons named in a charter are linked in and by performing a legal act, and thereby provide a specific name context. In this way, additional information common to all

---

8. Maurice Chaume showed that this methodological approach is rewarding in the case of the Cluniac charters by giving extensive prosopograhical details for his corrections in the dating of the charters: 'Observations sur la chronologie des chartes de Cluny', *Revue Mabillon* 29 (1939): pp. 41–61, 81–89, 133–42; 31 (1941): pp. 14–19, 42–45, 69–82; 32 (1942): pp. 15–20, 133–36; 38 (1948): pp. 1–6; 39 (1949): pp. 41–43.

9. Dieter Geuenich, 'Die Lemmatisierung und philologische Bearbeitung des Personennamenmaterials', in *Die Klostergemeinschaft von Fulda im früheren Mittelalter*, ed. Karl Schmid, vol. 1, Münstersche Mittelalter-Schriften VIII/1, München, 1978, pp. 37–84; Dieter Geuenich, 'Methoden und Probleme der computerunterstützten Namenforschung', in *Namenforschung. Ein internationales Handbuch zur Onomastik*, ed. Ernst Eichler, Gerold Hilty, Heinrich Löffler, Hugo Steger, and Ladislav Zgusta, vol. 1, Berlin–New York, 1995, pp. 335–39.

10. Examples for lemmatised names can be found in the chart appended to this contribution.

11. It is generally characteristic for sources from this period that personal names lack distinctive features; see Dieter Geuenich, 'Personennamen und Personen- und Sozialgeschichte des Mittelalters', in *Namenforschung. Ein internationales Handbuch zur Onomastik*, ed. Ernst Eichler, Gerold Hilty, Heinrich Löffler, Hugo Steger, and Ladislav Zgusta, vol. 2, Berlin–New York, 1996, pp. 1719–722.

names in a charter – such as the name of the place in which property is being transferred – can be used in the process. As a person appears often in several charters, identification is usually possible in varying but comparable name groups and their contexts. At the same time, these patterns of groups can serve to constitute a kind of network, ideally linking dated, insufficiently dated, and undated documents.

4. Computerisation and Evaluation

These name groups are what the computer program searches for, and what it compares and evaluates. It is meant to determine in a list of elements – or, by way of comparison, in two or more lists – recurrent patterns, patterns which need not be preconfigured or programmed beforehand.

In our case, the 60,000 names of the more or less 4,000 Cluniac documents are treated as elements in an ordered list, which is divided into roughly 4,000 sub-lists. These sub-lists can be reorganised into strata which in our example represent documents from a particular chronological period. Every element is associated with its value, which here is the lemma, that is, the standardised form of the name. The fact that a name appears many times means that many elements have the same value. If elements from two sub-lists which are compared have the same value, they are regarded as corresponding. The task is therefore to find, if possible, all corresponding groups in two lists. The limitation of the context of a name group to a sub-list or charter mentioned above makes sense because the charters present independent units; but it is also sensible not to further narrow down the context as the names in two charters or sub-lists can follow different orders, and some names may have been left out or have been added in the second charter.

The program in any case establishes not just one, but usually many parallels with a given group, which in turn becomes the point of departure for a new search for further parallels and towards new, as yet unidentified but corresponding elements in different contexts, and so forth, so that this continuous process branches out progressively. In this way, it is possible to recognise even groups of names composed of changing elements or whose order follows varying principles; they can be considered and evaluated in all sorts of combinations.

Because of the huge number of these groups, the varying structures, and, consequently, the breadth of the possible interpretations, preliminary automatic selection and filtering are necessary at the next level. The problem is, of course, to formalise and render automatic the selection of the perspective in which one can make use of the parallels found. The basis for the evaluation is the degree of probability that this correlation is not purely accidental, but concerns a group which really existed. Several different parameters have therefore been integrated into the program, such as:

- The number of parallels (correlations) found in a group.
- The number of the individual names included.
- The similarity of the spelling of names.
- The compactness of a group of names: if a person is mentioned more than

once in a group, this does not alter the value, so that the group keeps the same extension as one in which this name has not been mentioned repeatedly.

The larger the number of parallels found in a group and the rarer some of the names included are, the more the spellings of names resemble each other or are identical, the more compact a group appears to be (that is, the less often the names belonging to a 'group' are interrupted by other names), the greater is the probability that the groups found and linked to each other concern the same people.

In addition to these essentially external – that is, formal – criteria, which cannot be influenced by the historian, one has to consider also internal criteria (that is, the contents); their weight can be determined by the user, for instance:

- The function a person had in the legal act concerned; if some functions, such as that of the scribe, are of lesser importance for the specific evaluation, their weight can be reduced; but it is also possible to accord greater weight to some concordances in witness lists.
- Similarly with placenames in different charters, such as those referring to locations where laymen held property. If corresponding groups are found in connection with the same placenames, they can be weighed more heavily, and so forth.

Taking into account these considerations, different weights can be given to specific criteria. The material and its evaluation can be individually adapted and controlled. This offers for a given database the opportunity, first to find millions of matching groups, and then to select by means of the program a number of different sequences of charters in which groups and their context are evaluated according to different patterns.

5. Possibilities and Limits of Automatic Evaluation

The program was written in PL/1 (Programming Language One) and was run on a mainframe with the MVS system. Even for a big mainframe at the university's main computer centre, the runtime of a job was tremendous. The output of the first step of the program, the recognition of groups of identical names, filled a large magnetic-tape. The charters selected for the time up to 1100 contain approximately 9,600 different names which could be attributed to about 3,200 different lemmas. The largest sub-list contains 175 elements. A run executed with a coefficient 15 for the size of the group resulted in more than three million parallels, constituting some 740,000 groups. It is obvious that only a limited number of these could be printed to be treated by the historian: those in which the evaluation of the parallels had a relatively high evaluation result. What then remains to be done for the historian is the long, one might even say infinite, study of the printed lists.

To illustrate this, one example of the results of the automatic comparison is given here: it brought together charters which in the edition are more than 3,000 numbers apart, and where the number of parallels found is relatively high. The appended chart shows, in a somewhat simplified form, the kind of synopsis produced by the program: for the so-called starting list, the names from charter no. 124, the program found parallels in four other charters, the so-called sub-lists, nos. 131, 948, 2018, and 3283. The sub-list from charter no. 948 received the highest coefficient in the automatic evaluation (=22). The reason is that (i) with the exception of abbot Maiolus, all names have parallels in charter no. 124, and (ii) the context of both groups is nearly identical; this concerns as much the external criteria – the size of the group and the order of the names – as the internal criterion of the function of the name in relation to the legal act treated in the charter.

When working with these lists, one has first to check and countercheck, by means of traditional historical prosopographical methods, all the way from the name to the historical person suggested by the program. Here the criteria already used in the automatic procedure have to be refined and at the same time extended. These criteria differentiate in the first place two social groups: laymen and monks.

For the first group, kinship, property, or social status can be relevant. For the chronology of the charters information such as the sequence of generations in one and the same kin group can be of particular importance and has to be solved, or the different career steps of individual persons have to be traced.

We can refer here again to the charters shown in the appended chart, and the groups of names one can see there: in charter no. 2018 Gauzerannus/Jocerannus, Ebrardus and Humbertus are described as sons of Alindrada. In a further charter (no. 2181) which contains also a list of names corresponding to our starting list from charter no. 124, but which for reasons of space has not been included here, another son of Alindrada is mentioned, Eldebertus. These details on Alindrada's family can now be added in those instances where the charters contain no information on parental relationships (charters nos. 124, 131, 948, and 3283: Eurardus/Ebrardus, Eldebertus).

As none of the five charters used here has a date, one needs to find other clues to place them chronologically. In this instance, a result can be approached by combining three different steps:

A first rough chronological orientation is possible thanks to the mention of abbots Maiolus and Odilo in charters nos. 948 and 1028; their combined abbacies lasted from about 950 to 1049. In the same period one can also place charters nos. 124, 131, and 3283, which were 'dated' by the editors Bernard and Bruel according to their place in the cartularies: charters nos. 124 and 131 in the cartulary of the first abbot, Berno (910–927); charter no. 3283 in the cartulary of abbot Hugh, whose abbacy in Cluny lasted from 1049 to 1109.

In a second step, all information in the charters regarding the family of Alindrada is analysed more closely; in this case the designation of a donation for the salvation of a family member (no. 2018: for Humbertus; no. 2181: for Eldebertus), or their presence in the group of witnesses can provide further biographical indications regarding some individuals.

The third step cannot be gathered from what is shown in the chart, but can be deduced from material provided by the program. It is achieved by studying the sub-lists which the program has delivered for charters with names, which have no parallels in the starting list from charter no. 124, but instead in charters nos. 131 and 2018 (italicised in the chart). In our case, this refers to charters with a precise date (no. 1724: 986/987; no. 1917: 992).[12]

Summing up all these observations we can say that the persons named in these five charters were active towards the end of the tenth century, at the time of the transition from the abbacy of Maiolus to that of abbot Odilo.

The second social group of major importance in the Cluniac charters is, of course, that of the monks. For a period of some eighty years we have a relatively large number of charters with six, ten, twenty, or even more names of monks in witness lists. To establish here a chronological order, the context of the names, and the order in which they appear is of particular importance – a prerequisite if one wants to arrive at a more precise chronological determination of the charters.[13]

At this stage of the work, two advantages of the automated search procedure for groups are particularly striking. First, by concentrating on the comparison of names when searching for parallels, all the complementary information is left aside which – as it is often unreliable – usually renders a prosopographical analysis so difficult (I mean references to titles, social status, or parental relationship). These details are instead carried along as mere supplementary information which – by means of an automatic procedure – can be added in the following prosopographical analysis as to a puzzle in order to build up a differentiated picture. By making it possible to interpret better the succession of generations or different career steps of individuals mentioned in this way one also obtains a better grasp of the material for the more precise chronological determination of charters.

The second advantage is the flexibility with which the criteria for the automatic evaluation of the groups of names found can be determined. This makes possible the successive treatment and evaluation of the material from various points of view. For example, can the results of an evaluation which accorded the highest importance to identical placenames be compared with those which give precedence to the legal function a person performs in a charter?[14]

The limits of the procedure are to be found first of all in the material itself. For example, one cannot apply it to the Cluniac charters from the twelfth or thirteenth century. The reason is that around the end of the eleventh century the monastery's territorial expansion ended; for the following period there is therefore a much

---

12. In addition to the chronological analysis one may have to use also other criteria, for example, questions of the tradition of the documents; in our case, the manuscripts have been used apart from the edition.

13. Examples for the study of lists of monks by means of this automatic procedure are: Franz Neiske, 'Der Konvent des Klosters Cluny zur Zeit des Abtes Maiolus. Die Namen der Mönche in Urkunden und Necrologien', in *Vinculum societatis. Joachim Wollasch zum 60. Geburtstag*, ed. Franz Neiske, Dietrich Poeck, and Mechthild Sandmann, Sigmaringendorf, 1991, pp. 118–56; Maria Hillebrandt, 'Les moines de Cluny en Provence (v. 950–v. 1050)', in *Saint Mayeul et son temps. Actes du congrès international, Valensole, 12–14 Mai 1994*, Chroniques de Haute-Provence 330–331, Digne-es-Bains, 1997, pp. 99–115.

14. Unfortunately, as a consequence of the difficulties mentioned below, not all of the possibilities of the program could be exploited.

smaller number of donations, sales, or disputed transactions. This means, of course, that persons became much less frequently active and the number of names is greatly reduced. Consequently, there is no longer enough material for the statistical procedure described here.[15]

Further limits may be found in the way documents from the tenth and eleventh centuries were originally structured. The criterion of the sequence of names, for example, has to be used with care, because the copyists have written the lists of witnesses in straight lines, possibly destroying the original charter order of the names in columns.[16] Another problem is that especially the number of monks mentioned in the cartularies decreases continuously from the middle of the eleventh century onwards, so that in the end it becomes impossible to place this social group clearly in its context.[17] In these cases it is more useful for a chronological analysis to use traditional methods by looking for individuals such as priors.[18]

But as a result of this procedure, the dating of an astoundingly large number of charters could be revised, refined, or corrected, sometimes establishing differences of up to a century. Due to lack of funding, however, and the substantial technical changes which occurred over the same period, the project in this very comprehensive and refined form had to be abandoned.

The programming had to be extremely sophisticated, and with every new release of the PL/1 Optimising Compiler the problems encountered getting the program running again proved at times extremely difficult. It was therefore decided to abandon it and it has not been transferred to more recent platforms. However, the algorithm has been used in later applications which can be run on PCs, although in a much more modest version than the original program.

---

15. Duby, *La société*, pp. 8–10, with an account of the development of diplomatic sources in southern Burgundy.

16. For the establishment of a chronology of charters on the basis of witness lists, see, for example, Wendy Davies, ed., *The Llandaff Charters*, Aberystwyth, 1979. A peculiarity can be observed in the copies of charters in the cartulary of Montier-en-Der: the scribe who copied the major part of the cartulary around 1127, arranged the names of the witnesses in columns, even when in the original they were written in lines; see Laurent Morelle, 'Des moines face à leur chartrier: étude sur le premier cartulaire de Montier-en-Der (vers 1127)', forthcoming. I am very grateful to Laurent Morelle for sending me a copy of his article before its publication.

17. This changes for a short period at the beginning of the twelfth century when the group of monks belonging to the entourage of abbots Hugh and Ponce are mentioned more frequently: Maria Hillebrandt, 'Albertus Teutonicus. Copiste de chartes et de livres à Cluny', *Études d'histoire du droit médiéval en souvenir de Josette Metman. Mémoires de la Société pour l'Histoire du Droit et des Institutions des anciens pays bourguignons, comtois et romands* 155 (1988): pp. 215–32.

18. Michael Gervers gives a good survey of the different traditional methods of dating medieval charters as well as a convincing critique in 'The Dating of Medieval English Private Charters of the Twelfth and Thirteenth Centuries', in *A Distinct Voice. Medieval Studies in Honor of Leonard E. Boyle*, ed. Jacqueline Brown and William P. Stoneman, Notre Dame, 1997, pp. 455–80, esp. pp. 455–59.

Bibliography

Barthélemy, Dominique. 1997. 'Une crise de l'écrit? Observations sur les actes de Saint-Aubin d'Angers (XIe siècle)', in *Pratiques de l'écrit documentaire au XIe siècle*, ed. Olivier Guyotjeannin, Laurent Morelle, and Michel Parisse, pp. 95–118. *Bibliothèque de l'École des Chartes* 155.

Bernard, Auguste, and Alexandre Bruel, eds. 1876–1903. *Recueil des chartes de l'abbaye de Cluny (Collection de documents inédits sur l'histoire de France. Première série: Histoire politique)*. 6 vols. Paris.

Chaume, Maurice. 1939. 'En marge de l'histoire de Cluny'. *Revue Mabillon* 29: pp. 41–61.

Davies, Wendy, ed. 1979. *The Llandaff Charters*. Aberystwyth.

Duby, Georges. 1971 (1953). *La société aux XIe et XIIe siècles dans la région mâconnaise*. Bibliothèque générale de l'École Pratique des Hautes Études, VIe section. 2nd ed. Paris.

Gervers, Michael. 1997. 'The Dating of Medieval English Private Charters of the Twelfth and Thirteenth Centuries', in *A Distinct Voice. Medieval Studies in Honor of Leonard E. Boyle*, ed. Jacqueline Brown and William P. Stoneman, pp. 455–80. Indiana: Notre Dame.

Geuenich, Dieter. 1978. 'Die Lemmatisierung und philologische Bearbeitung des Personennamenmaterials', in *Die Klostergemeinschaft von Fulda im früheren Mittelalter*, ed. Karl Schmid, vol. I, pp. 37–84. Münstersche Mittelalter-Schriften VIII/1. München.

——. 1995. 'Methoden und Probleme der computerunterstützten Namenforschung', in *Namenforschung. Ein internationales Handbuch zur Onomastik*, ed. Ernst Eichler, Gerold Hilty, Heinrich Löffler, Hugo Steger, and Ladislav Zgusta, vol. I, pp. 335–39. Berlin–New York.

——. 1996. 'Personennamen und Personen- und Sozialgeschichte des Mittelalters', in *Namenforschung. Ein internationales Handbuch zur Onomastik*, ed. Ernst Eichler, Gerold Hilty, Heinrich Löffler, Hugo Steger, and Ladislav Zgusta, vol. II, 1719–1722. Berlin–New York.

Guyotjeannin, Olivier. 1997. '"*Penuria scriptorum*": le mythe de l'anarchie documentaire dans la France du nord (Xe – première moitié du XIe siècle)', in *Pratiques de l'écrit documentaire au XIe siècle*, ed. Olivier Guyotjeannin, Laurent Morelle, and Michel Parisse, pp. 11–44. *Bibliothèque de l'École des Chartes* 155.

Hillebrandt, Maria. 1982. 'The Cluniac Charters. Remarks on a Quantitative Approach for Prosopographical Studies'. *Medieval Prosopography* 3, no. 1: pp. 3–25; 3, no. 2: p. 103.

——. 1988. 'Albertus Teutonicus. Copiste de chartes et de livres à Cluny'. *Études d'histoire du droit médiéval en souvenir de Josette Metman. Mémoires de la Société pour l'Histoire du Droit et des Institutions des anciens pays bourguignons, comtois et romands* 155: pp. 215–32.

——. 1993. 'Les cartulaires de l'abbaye de Cluny'. *Mémoires de la Société pour l'Histoire du Droit et des Institutions des anciens pays bourguignons, comtois et romands* 50: pp. 7–18.

——. 1997. 'Les moines de Cluny en Provence (v. 950–v. 1050)', in *Saint Mayeul et son temps. Actes du congrès international, Valensole, 12–14 Mai 1994*, pp. 99–115. Chroniques de Haute-Provence 330–331. Digne-es-Bains.

Neiske, Franz. 1981. 'Die Erforschung von Personen und Gemeinschaften des Mittelalters mit Hilfe der elektronischen Datenverarbeitung', in *L'histoire médiévale et les ordinateurs. Medieval History and Computers. Rapports d'une Table ronde internationale*, ed. Karl Ferdinand Werner, pp. 77–109. München.

———. 1991. 'Der Konvent des Klosters Cluny zur Zeit des Abtes Maiolus. Die Namen der Mönche in Urkunden und Necrologien', in *Vinculum societatis, Joachim Wollasch zum 60. Geburtstag*, ed. Franz Neiske, Dietrich Poeck, and Mechthild Sandmann, pp. 118–56. Sigmaringendorf.

Westerhoff, Friedrich-Wilhelm. 1985. 'Gruppensuche: Ein Verfahren zur Identifizierung von Personen und Personengruppen in mittelalterlichen Namenquellen', in *Dokumentationsband zum EDV-Kolloquium 1985*, pp. 67–77. Schriftenreihe des Rechenzentrums der Westfälischen Wilhelms-Universität Münster LIX. Münster

———. 1988. *Gruppensuche. Ein Verfahren zur Identifizierung von Personengruppen in mittelalterlichen Namen-Quellen. Beschreibung des Verfahrens und der Programme*. Schriftenreihe des Rechenzentrums der Universität Münster LXI. Münster.

Appendix

The names from charter no. 124 and their parallels in charters 131, 948, 2018, and 3283
(*Recueil des chartes de l'abbaye de Cluny*, ed. Auguste Bernard and Alexandre Bruel, vols 1–4, Paris, 1876–88).

In the first line, the number of the charters is complemented by its date and its evaluation rating. The names are standardised: reduced to their *rectus*, they are preceded by a number indicating their position in their charters and followed by the lemma in small capitals. The first column gives the number of parallels to each name; the numbers in columns 3, 5, 7, and 9 refer to the position of the respective names in the first charter (BB 124; col. 2). The names are followed by supplementary information from the charters: ABB for *abbas*, LEV for *levita*, FRN for *francus*; V means that there is a family relationship; the final letter after each name designates the function of the person in the charter (A = donator; Z = witness; E = receiver; S = scribe). Names which have no parallels are italicised.

1	2	0124 (910–927)	3	4	0131 (910–927)	14	5	6	0948 (954–994)	22	7	8	2018 (993–1048)	09	9	10	3283 (1049–1109 ?)	13
8	1	Alindrada (ALIANRAD F)	A	1	Rannulfus (RAGINWULF)	A	1, 3	1	Alindrada (ALIANRAD F)	A	1, 3	1	Alindrada (ALIANRAD F)	A	1, 3	1	Alindrada (ALIANRAD F)	A
6	2	Rannulfus (RAGINWULF)	X	2	Maynardus (MAGINHARD)	X		2	Maiolus ABB (MAG-L)	E		2	Gauzerannus (GAUTHRABAN)	V	A	1, 32	Alindrada (ALIANRAD F)	F
8	3	Alindrada (ALIANRAD F)	F	3	Arleyus	X	1, 3	3	Alindrada (ALIANRAD F)	F	8	3	Ebrardus V (EBURHARD)	A	8	3	Ebrardus V (EBURHARD)	A
1	4	Ildinus (HILDI-N)	Z	4	Alindrada (ALIANRAD F)	X	4	4	Ildinus (HILDI-N)	Z		4	Umbertus (HUNBERHT)	V X	9	4	Eldebertus (HILDIBERHT)	Z
1	5	Rannaldus (RAGINWALD)	Z	5	Rannulfus (RAGINWULF)	X	6	5	Noe (NOAH)	Z		5	Odilo ABB (AUD-L)	X	2, 11	5	Ramnulfus (RAGINWULF)	X
1	6	Noe (NOAH)	Z	6	Alindrada (ALIANRAD F)	X	5	6	Rannaldus (RAGINWALD)	Z		6	Martinus FRN (MARTINUS)	X	10	6	Durannus (DURANDUS)	Z
2	7	Uuandalmunt (WANDILMUND F)	Z	7	Rannulfus (RAGINWULF)	F	7	7	Uuandalmunt (WANDILMUND F)	Z		7	Adaltrudis (ATHALTHRUTH F)	X	7	7	Uuandalmundis (WANDILMUND F)	Z
5	8	Eurardus (EBURHARD)	Z	8	Eurardus (EBURHARD)	Z	8	8	Eurardus (EBURHARD)	Z	1, 3	8	Alindrada (ALIANRAD F)	V	A	8	Rotbertus LEV (HROTHBERHT)	S
3	9	Eldebertus (HILDIBERHT)	Z	9	Eldebertus (HILDIBERHT)	Z	9	9	Eldebertus (HILDIBERHT)	Z		9	Ioceramnus (GAUTHRABAN)	V	A			
4	10	Durantus (DURANDUS)	Z	10	Bernardus (BERINHARD)	Z	10	10	Durantus (DURANDUS)	Z	8	10	Ebrardus (EBURHARD)	V	A			
6	11	Rannulfus (RAGINWULF)	Z	11	Odilo (AUD-L)	Z	2, 11	11	Rannulfus (RAGINWULF)	Z		11	Odilo (AUD-L F)	Z				
				12	Bernoardus (BERINHARD)	Z						12	Letprannus (LEUDBRAND)	Z				
				13	Durantus (DURUNDUS)	Z					10	13	Durannus (DURANDUS)	Z				
				14	Rodbertus LEV (HROTHBERHT)	S						14	Martinus (MARTINUS)	Z				
												15	Christianus (CHRISTIANUS)	Z				
												16	Berardus (BERINHARD)	Z				
												17	Letaldus (LEUDWALD)	X				
											2, 11	18	Ramnulfus (RAGINWULF)	X				

BEYOND DEEDS: A ROLE FOR PERSONAL NAMES?

Trevor Chalmers

There is an automaton by the English artist and inventor Tim Hunkin which consists of two Greek philosophers' heads, respectively labelled 'Inspiration' and 'Frustration'. You put in a coin, the installation rumbles ominously for a few moments, then there is a loud bang, and 'Inspiration' is illuminated from within by a light-bulb. 'Frustration', on the other hand, emits a disconsolate puff of smoke.

There is an unfortunate tendency for the end users of computer applications to assume that the systems they employ are, or ought to be, infallible and omniscient, delivering inspiration--or at least illumination – at the bang of a button. Such users are often highly offended when frustration results and, all too often, identify as so-called 'bugs' weaknesses in the underlying logic of the processing or in the data – weaknesses which in many cases are wholly inevitable. Yet in practice nobody using the very impressive user interface which Rodolfo Fiallos demonstrated at this conference would for a moment underestimate its scope for trial and error, and for exercise of the historian's judgement; nor imagine that the DEEDS database is like some sort of microwave oven into which a document is placed, and from which it eventually emerges as 'done', that is, dated with final and oracular certainty.

On the contrary, DEEDS is a tool, a subtle and powerful test to which an undated document can be subjected, with the understanding that an inconclusive outcome is always possible and in many cases unavoidable. On that basis, as the DEEDS team themselves stress, parallel tests are desirable, to refine the methodology and cross-check its results, again always on the understanding that the outcome may be uncertain.

The present paper is a brief response to a remark by Professor Michael Gervers to the effect that he is looking for ideas to further develop and refine the DEEDS methodology. Admittedly, the idea considered here is hardly a new one – rather an old one reheated, perhaps: the use of personal names in the dating process, one which might be set up in parallel to the word-pattern matching performed in the DEEDS database. Maria Hillebrandt covers much of this territory from the historian's standpoint, in much scholarly detail, in her paper in the present volume (Chapter 12).[1] The present paper offers some sidelights, hopefully complementary, from the perspective of an archivist-turned-programmer.

Professor Gervers has pointed out the shortcomings of witness lists as evidence for dating, in terms of their inaccuracy, truncation, or suppression – in cartulary

---

From *Dating Undated Medieval Charters*. Ed. Michael Gervers. Copyright (by the Editor and Contributors 2000). Published by the Boydell Press (in association with Collegium Budapest), PO Box 9, Woodbridge, Suffolk, IP12 3DF, Great Britain. ISBN 0 85115 792 0.

1. Maria Hillebrandt, 'Social Groups as Recognition Patterns: A Means of Dating Medieval Charters', Chapter 12 of the present volume.

copies at least – as well as of the often wildly misleading effect of dating with reference to a name which recurs in an unvarying form from generation to generation.[2] Moreover, medieval names, with their associated problems of identification, do not lend themselves to word-pattern matching, and their presence in the DEEDS database would seriously interfere with the operation of the analysis routines. In consequence, names are altogether filtered out of the working data.[3]

Yet I understand from Rodolfo Fiallos that the system includes an impressive audit-trail, which allows all editorial steps to be retraced, if necessary. It should in theory be possible to recover the name-elements mechanically if it should be desired to subject them to further processing. And where names exist it seems a shame not to use them, even if only in a corroborative or otherwise supplementary technique.

The really major problem with personal names, of course, is that of identification. The archive community has eagerly borrowed from the library world the concept and use of the name authority file; and certainly this is – or should be – a major step towards achieving a uniformity of identification nationally, and even internationally, in cases where identifications are possible. Name authority systems used in the library world have the drawback for archival use that they are based on the principle that all authors may be considered to be identifiable, however tenuously, by virtue of having published something. Records, on the other hand, throw up a preponderance of individuals whose only claim to modern attention is that they flitted momentarily into the headlights of some administrative juggernaut, and are otherwise unidentified and, frankly, unidentifiable. This is true of modern records, and vastly more so in the case of medieval ones. Ideally, identification of personal names needs to be no more than an optional element in the preparation of detailed electronic finding-aids, in which the identifiable and unidentifiable must appear side by side. Devising a computer index that does justice to name-lists in archival material of this sort can call for a fair bit of cunning and complexity.

However, for purposes of computer-assisted dating, there is perhaps a case for ignoring the question of identification altogether and, rather than tracing individuals, taking any names, in association with any other names occurring in some common context, not only in witness lists, but also as parties to a transaction, or in any other formal or informal association evident within a document. Logically, at least, the matching of two or more names occurring in an undated document with similar combinations of names in a sufficient number of dated documents ought to help in assigning a date, or at least to refine or act as a second check on a date arrived at by other means. After all, as Maria Hillebrandt illustrates, names occurring in record sources – legal documents above all – tend to be there not through mere random quirk, but in consequence of a social or institutional connection, or an

---

2. Michael Gervers, 'The Dating of Medieval English Private Charters of the Twelfth and Thirteenth Centuries', in *A Distinct Voice: Medieval Studies in Honor of Leonard Boyle, OP*, ed. Jacqueline Brown and William P. Stoneman, Indiana: Notre Dame, 1997, p. 457.

3. Gervers, 'The Dating', p. 478.

administrative process; and there is a fair probability that the association of names will recur from one document to another.

Even where within any given area exactly the same names recur from generation to generation, if looked at in bulk, concentrating on name forms alone one might hope for just a slight variation of detail. The indication of a spouse, an epithet, an office, or some other specific feature can give an individual characteristic to a name, and so help to associate the list in which it occurs with cognate lists of the same area and period.

I propose to give a brief illustration of name-group matching, on a scale smaller and far less sophisticated than that of the methodologies employed by Maria Hillebrandt. It is crude in the extreme, but has the virtue of simplicity: anyone with not-too-advanced database skills, or access to average IT support, could build such a set of procedures for their own research uses.

The data-set I have used relates to what, from the point of view of the Conference, is the 'wrong end' of the Middle Ages, consisting as it does of a body of fifteenth- and early sixteenth-century Scottish royal charter witnesses. They are derived from the Register of the Great Seal of Scotland, which in this period is more than anything else a central record of landholding, Scotland being then still in a pre – *Quia Emptores* state of galloping subinfeudation.[4]

Although almost by definition the witnesses are known individuals, they vary considerably in number, identity, and order within the list. They provide a reasonable body of material for establishing how well the computer can 'pin the tail on the donkey', as it were, in running names from unregistered charters against the names in the Register entries.

The Register contains about 3,000 entries for the half-century between 1463 and 1513; about 2,500 of those entries have witness lists given in full, or as cross-references to other charters. In cases where the originals of registered charters can be checked against the Register entries, those cross-references can be demonstrated to be accurate in most instances, at least until 1508, at which date this point of office detail becomes decidedly casual, even slapdash.[5]

These data allow the matching of name-groups to be demonstrated quite clearly. Normally, such matching would be done on the basis of known individuals with a specific set of titles, or official designations, or both; however, in order more closely to simulate the matching of names pure and simple, irrespective of

---

4. *Registrum Magni Sigilli Regum Scotorum: The Register of the Great Seal of Scotland II, 1424–1513*, ed. James Balfour Paul, Edinburgh, 1882.

5. The Register, although it contained engrossments of documents emanating from the royal Chancery, was maintained not by the Chancery staff but by the lord clerk register and his depute, the clerk of council. In about 1507, John Murray of Blackbarony, an ambitious layman, succeeded to the latter post, which had hitherto been largely, although not exclusively, the preserve of clerics, and which, partly in consequence of a number of changes in the organisation of the king's council, had grown in prominence from a predominantly scribal function into a minor but essential office of state. It is probable that relative accuracy in the witness lists, preserved hitherto by the diligence of proceduralists, was abandoned as one of the consequences of a new incumbent challenging received nostrums, in this case that the detailed composition of witness lists was especially meaningful in the conveyancing practice of the period.

identification, the test queries ignored the individuals' titles and offices. A search would therefore pick up any occurrence of each individual throughout his career. In a Microsoft Access database, basic date information was entered from the charters, also the associated witness lists, amounting to about 23,000 attestations by about 140 individuals occurring in various guises.[6] A record for each individual was created in this process.

The procedure used for the group matching of names is illustrated in *Figure 1* (see Appendix, p. 184). For each test, a search set consisting of a list of witnesses taken from an unregistered charter is entered in a temporary table as a list of numeric pointers to the individuals occurring as witnesses. Here, the basis of the search is the record representing the identifiable person who underlies the name, matching being performed on the 'person ID', that is, the machine-generated numeric identifier of the individual.

A query is then run to match each 'person ID' in the temporary table with equivalent ID numbers occurring in the table of attestations. In turn, each matched number links through to the table of register entries in order to derive the year of the matching entry. This query returns a crude list of the matching entries, illustrated in *Figure 2* (see Appendix, p. 185). The list gives for each entry the year, and the number of witnesses that match an individual in the search set.

Another query further summarised these results, and presented them as a list of years, giving, for each year, the total number of register entries with matches on two names, three names, four names, and so on. Each number of names appears as a separate column in the query output.

Figure 3 (see Appendix, p. 186) shows the results of such a trial query using an unregistered charter internally dated 1470.[7] The persons used as search criteria are shown on the left, the pattern of matches on the right. Among the register entries for 1470 itself there were three matches for eight of the names, and eight matches for seven of the names; moreover, in that year the results form a visible peak. There were no matches at all on more than eight names: the witness list of the unregistered charter is absolutely characteristic of the period, but the amount of movement within the group represented in the lists is sufficient to prevent a point-to-point match. Other trials had similar results, although not always so clean and consoling.

Another example is illustrated in *Figure 4* (see Appendix, pp. 187). This time, entry of witnesses from an unregistered charter of 1486 produced a visible peak with a single eight-name match three years too early; but there is a comfortingly solid block of fifteen seven-name matches in the two subsequent years, and a total of 31 seven-name matches in the actual year of the unregistered charter.

Of course, such results are hardly surprising in a data-set that is small, relatively formulaic, and, on the whole, homogeneous, especially since the matching

---

6. 'Inspeximus of grant under the great seal, 5 July 1470', in William Fraser, *The Red Book of Grandtully*, vol. 1, Edinburgh, 1868, no. 17.

7. 'Confirmation under the great seal, 6 October 1486', National Archives of Scotland, Leven and Melville Papers, GD 25/38.

was in this case done on the basis of identified individuals. So, in order to approximate more to the matching of unidentified names, the queries were modified and re-run with the matching performed on the name-elements alone. The individuals were thus deprived not only of their dignities, but also of their identities. This had the effect of levelling the pitch a bit, as about a dozen names are duplicated among the charter witnesses, some as many as four or five times.

The results of running the revised queries in relation to the two earlier examples are presented in *Figures 5* and *6* (see Appendix, pp. 188–89). They show that the peaking effect is – as one might expect – less distinct; but the rough pattern which emerges suggests that crude group-matching on name-forms alone, even using such a crude computer procedure as outlined above, might at least help to provide checks on other dating techniques. A full-scale mechanism for comparing groups of names would require special consideration of some rather more tricky technical issues.

It is desirable to permit equivalence of name-forms in order to allow for uncertainties of reading, or to permit the recording of aliases and allow their incorporation in the search pattern. In this way, name A in the search set might be allowed to match name X or name Y in the substantive data; alternatively, name A or name B in the search set might match name Y. Such equivalence, which ideally is desirable on both sides of the query equation, would require a rather more complex data structure and a rather more ambitious algorithm than the simple queries outlined above.

It is probably desirable to provide a facility for structurally linking names in a list in order to cater for interrelationships. As with built-in equivalence, such a facility would require further complexity in the data structure; and the algorithm to match sets of records daisy-chained in this way would pass well beyond the reach of raw Standard Query Language, and require hefty and devious programmatic intervention.

It is probably essential to impose an artificial distinction between multiple occurrences of the same name-form within a list of names in order to ensure that the count of query hits is accurate. Left to its own dumb devices, the computer will cheerfully deceive itself; for however many times a name-form occurs discretely in the search-set, the machine will be satisfied if it finds a single match in the substantive data, and report as though a match had been made in each case, whereas in fact the substantive data might contain only the single instance, matched repeatedly with unerring simple-mindedness. A perfectly adequate remedy may be to impose an arbitrary identifier on each repeated occurrence – for example, flagging each one as 'A', 'B', 'C', and so on.

A weighting might usefully be given to the relative order in which matched names appear in a list. Whether any such discernible order relates to local precedence or to the use in drafting of a common exemplar, the information might help to narrow down otherwise unhelpful results.

A method of restricting a search to documents emanating from a specific area, desirable when looking at word-patterns alone, will be essential in narrowing queries down to a sensible domain. Broad-brush geographical units – for example,

English counties – may be adequate, but in order to make adequate provision for provenance and content, it needs to be possible to associate any document with one or more such units. Also, in order to avoid arbitrary exclusion of documents from an adjacent or otherwise related region, it would be a good idea to provide a mechanism for weighting matches by proximity. A table of proximity weightings, possibly based on nothing more sophisticated than raw distances between the closest points of each of the places used, might greatly help to refine the search results.

In conclusion, it might be worth a little cautious experimentation with the use of names, in bulk and perhaps without too much sophistication, as a secondary dating technique in relation to the word-pattern matching of the DEEDS process. Reverting to the little extravagance with which I began this paper, perhaps such a supplementary technique might at least tilt the balance further away from frustration, in the direction of inspiration.

Bibliography

Fraser, William. 1868. *The Red Book of Grandtully*. Vol. 2. Edinburgh.

Gervers, Michael. 1997. 'The Dating of Medieval English Private Charters of the Twelfth and Thirteenth Centuries', in *A Distinct Voice: Medieval Studies in Honor of Leonard Boyle, OP*, ed. Jacqueline Brown and William P Stoneman, pp. 455–80. Indiana: Notre Dame.

Hillebrandt, Maria. 1999. 'Social Groups as Recognition Patterns: A Means in Dating Medieval Charters', in *Dating Undated Medieval Charters*, ed. Michael Gervers, The Boydell Press, pp. 163–76.

Paul, James Balfour, ed. 1882. *Registrum Magni Sigilli Regum Scotorum: the Register of the Great Seal of Scotland*. Vol. 2, 1424–1513. Edinburgh.

APPENDIX

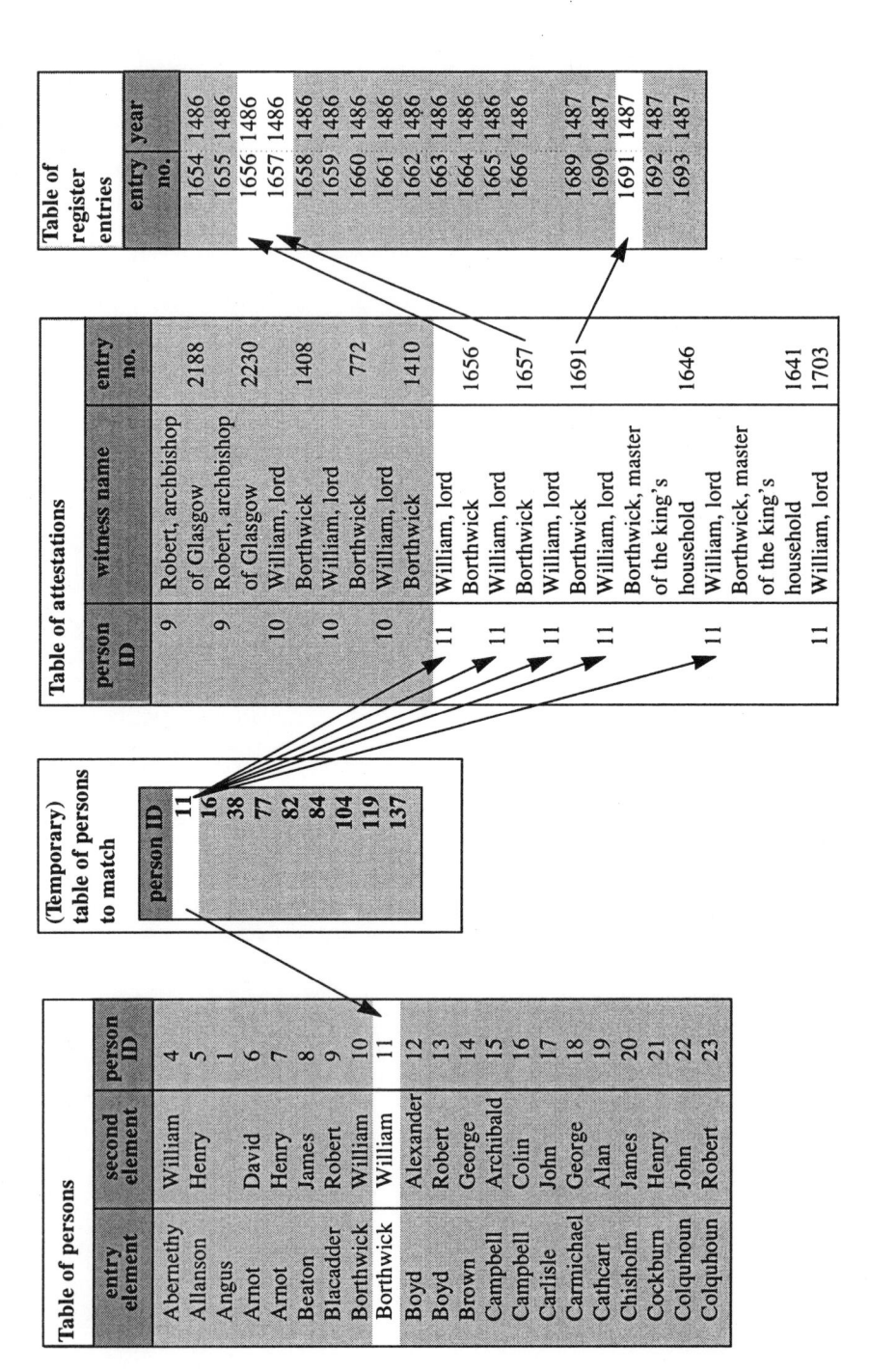

Table of persons		
entry element	second element	person ID
Abernethy	William	4
Allanson	Henry	5
Angus		1
Arnot	David	6
Arnot	Henry	7
Beaton	James	8
Blacadder	Robert	9
Borthwick	William	10
Borthwick	William	11
Boyd	Alexander	12
Boyd	Robert	13
Brown	George	14
Campbell	Archibald	15
Campbell	Colin	16
Carlisle	John	17
Carmichael	George	18
Cathcart	Alan	19
Chisholm	James	20
Cockburn	Henry	21
Colquhoun	John	22
Colquhoun	Robert	23

(Temporary) table of persons to match

person ID
11
16
38
77
82
84
104
119
137

Table of attestations		
person ID	witness name	entry no.
9	Robert, archbishop of Glasgow	2188
9	Robert, archbishop of Glasgow	2230
10	William, lord Borthwick	1408
10	William, lord Borthwick	772
10	William, lord Borthwick	1410
11	William, lord Borthwick	1656
11	William, lord Borthwick	1657
11	William, lord Borthwick	1691
11	William, lord Borthwick, master of the king's household	1646
11	William, lord Borthwick, master of the king's household	1641
11	William, lord Borthwick	1703

Table of register entries	
entry no.	year
1654	1486
1655	1486
1656	1486
1657	1486
1658	1486
1659	1486
1660	1486
1661	1486
1662	1486
1663	1486
1664	1486
1665	1486
1666	1486
1689	1487
1690	1487
1691	1487
1692	1487
1693	1487

Figure 1 *Schematic representation of a query for matching individuals in witness lists*

Beyond DEEDS: A Role for Personal Names? 185

year	entry no.	no. of matches
1485	1626	7
1485	1627	7
1485	1628	7
1485	1629	6
1485	1630	7
1486	1631	6
1486	1632	6
1486	1633	7
1486	1634	7
1486	1635	7
1486	1636	7
1486	1637	7
1486	1638	7
1486	1639	3
1486	1640	7
1486	1641	7
1486	1642	7
1486	1643	7
1486	1644	7
1486	1646	7
1486	1647	4
1486	1648	7
1486	1649	7
1486	1650	4

Figure 2 *Results of initial query to match individuals in witness lists*

Dating Undated Medieval Charters

Names to match
Colin Campbell
John Colquhoun
David Guthrie
William Knollis
Thomas Spens
Andrew Stewart
James Stewart
John Stewart
William Tulloch
Archibald Whitelaw

Year	\multicolumn{7}{c}{No. of docs per no. of matches}						
	2	3	4	5	6	7	8
1463	12	1					
1464	14	8	10				
1465		8	15	3	1		
1466	1	18	14				
1467		21	6	5			
1468		10	21				
1469		4	4	1	1	1	
1470			1	1	2	8	3
1471	1	2	8	11	3		
1472		3	6	6	25		
1473		2	13	24	2		
1474		3	6	20			
1475			13	2	1		
1476	12	16	1	16			
1477		12	16	24	1		
1478		3	7	41	3		
1479		3	11	8			
1480			14	1	1		
1481	2	30					
1482	10	11	1				
1483	8						
1484	31						
1485	20						
1486	33	1					
1487	24						
1488	16	36					
1489		78					
1490		76					
1491	3	63					
1492	10	28					
1504	1						

Figure 3 *Distribution by year of matches on named individuals. Example 1: witnesses to an unregistered charter of 1470 compared with witnesses listed in the Register of the Great Seal of Scotland*

Beyond DEEDS: A Role for Personal Names? 187

Names to match
James Livingstone
William Elphinstone
David Livingstone
Archibald Whitelaw
Alexander Scot
Colin Campbell
David Lindsay
Andrew Stewart
William Borthwick

Year	\multicolumn{7}{c}{No. of docs per no. of matches}
	2	3	4	5	6	7	8
1463	12	1					
1464	17	16					
1465	10	9					
1466	33						
1467	32						
1468	29	1					
1469	9	1					
1470	10	4					
1471	1	24					
1472	4	34					
1473	1	40					
1474		28					
1475		15	1				
1476	27	18					
1477	10	43					
1478	3	51					
1479	5	14	3				
1480		5	1				
1481	3	28	1				
1482	4	13	7				
1483		1	15	2	4	7	1
1484				4	12	15	
1485					5	15	
1486		1	2		2	31	
1487					19	9	
1488	36	1	4	1	10	10	
1489	45	33					
1490		25	51				
1491	2	64					
1492	9	30					
1493	56						
1504	1						

Figure 4 *Distribution by year of matches on named individuals. Example 2: witnesses to an unregistered charter of 1486 compared with witnesses listed in the Register of the Great Seal of Scotland*

Results of search on names alone:

Year	\multicolumn{7}{c}{No. of docs per no. of matches}
	2	3	4	5	6	7	8
1463	2	12		1			
1464	4	13	7	8	9	1	
1465			8	10	6	3	
1466		1	18	5	9		
1467			21	6	5		
1468		9	2	19	1		
1469		4	3	1	1	2	
1470			1		2	9	3
1471		4	7	11	2	1	
1472		3	5	8	21	3	
1473		3	6	27	6		
1474		3	6	20			
1475			13	2	1		
1476	12	12	5	16			
1477		12	16	24	1		
1478		3	7	41	2	1	
1479		3	9	9	1		
1480		14	1	1			
1481	1	30	1				
1482		11	11				
1483	13	7	1				
1484		30	1				
1485		17	3				
1486	2	34					
1487	4	24					
1488	9	50					
1489		78					
1490		76					
1491	3	53					
1492	15	28					
1493	40						
1504	1						

Results of search on identified individuals:

Year	\multicolumn{7}{c}{No. of docs per no. of matches}
	2	3	4	5	6	7	8
1463	12	1					
1464	14	8	10				
1465		8	15	3	1		
1466	1	18	14				
1467		21	6	5			
1468		10	21				
1469		4	4	1	1	1	
1470			1	1	2	8	3
1471	1	2	8	11	3		
1472		3	6	6	25		
1473		2	13	24	2		
1474		3	6	20			
1475			13	2	1		
1476	12	16	1	16			
1477		12	16	24	1		
1478		3	7	41	3		
1479		3	11	8			
1480		14	1	1			
1481	2	30					
1482	10	11	1				
1483	8						
1484	31						
1485	20						
1486	33	1					
1487	24						
1488	16	36					
1489		78					
1490		76					
1491	3	63					
1492	10	28					
1504	1						

Figure 5 *Comparative results, based on the search-set of example 1, of queries for matches on names alone (left-hand table) and on identified individuals (right-hand table)*

Beyond DEEDS: A Role for Personal Names?   189

Results of search on names alone:

Year	\multicolumn{8}{c}{No. of docs per no. of matches}
	2	3	4	5	6	7	8	9
1463	2	11	2					
1464	9	15	18					
1465	8	9	10					
1466		33						
1467		23	9					
1468	12	18	1					
1469	7	3						
1470	1	10	4					
1471		2	23					
1472	2	11	27					
1473		5	36					
1474	1		28					
1475			15	1				
1476		27	18					
1477		10	43					
1478		3	49	2				
1479		7	12	3				
1480			15	1				
1481		3	28	1				
1482		5	15	4				
1483			3	15		9	2	1
1484					4	11	16	
1485						5	15	
1486			1	2		2	31	
1487						19	9	
1488	36		1	5	1	11	8	
1489	45	33						
1490		25	51					
1491	2	64						
1492	4	35						
1493	18	39						
1496	6							
1504	1							
1508	1							
1509	6							
1510	12							
1511	10							
1512	36							
1513	1							

Results of search on identified individuals:

Year	\multicolumn{7}{c}{No. of docs per no. of matches}
	2	3	4	5	6	7	8
1463	12	1					
1464	17	16					
1465	10	9					
1466	33						
1467	32						
1468	29	1					
1469	9	1					
1470	10	4					
1471	1	24					
1472	4	34					
1473	1	40					
1474		28					
1475		15	1				
1476	27	18					
1477	10	43					
1478	3	51					
1479	5	14	3				
1480		15	1				
1481	3	28	1				
1482	4	13	7				
1483		1	15	2	4	7	1
1484				4	12	15	
1485					5	15	
1486		1	2		2	31	
1487					19	9	
1488	36	1	4	1	10	10	
1489	45	33					
1490		25	51				
1491	2	64					
1492	9	30					
1493	56						
1504	1						

Figure 6 *Comparative results, based on the search-set of example 2, of queries for matches on names alone (left-hand table) and on identified individuals (right-hand table)*

PART V
PALAEOGRAPHY AND SIGILLOGRAPHY

ON THE MARGINS OF BOOK AND CHARTER PALAEOGRAPHY. THE DATING OF SOME HUNGARIAN MANUSCRIPTS FROM THE ELEVENTH TO THE THIRTEENTH CENTURY

László Veszprémy

István Hajnal, perhaps the most prominent Hungarian palaeographer of this century, was acutely aware, even in the years between the wars, that new perspectives – and, naturally enough, new tasks – were being offered to the discipline of palaeography by the growing number of charter- and book-script facsimile collections spreading throughout Europe with the improvement of printing techniques. As a scholar of great erudition, he took it for granted that Hungarian scripts should be compared to Western and Central European analogies.[1] That was the procedure he adopted for his *Palaeography*, published in 1921, and the same principle guided him towards the end of his life in his synthesising monograph on the medieval universities and script development, especially in its appendix of charter copies, finished by his talented Hungarian disciple László Mezey.[2] Hajnal's attention was in all likelihood directed towards charter writing because the large number of deeds and the advancement of chancellery techniques and practice, which anticipated mass production, better suited the requirements of his sociological, social–historical approach, and his research methods.[3]

Of course, as far as methodological problems are concerned, there are quite different, solely technical reasons which explain why the study of codex scripts was given less attention. Codices survive in very small numbers from the first three centuries of Hungarian history, and even their Hungarian provenance is impossible to verify due to the lack of scribal or ownership ('possessor') inscriptions. Research increasingly came to focus on individual manuscripts: it was proved, for example, that the *Admont Bible* (Vienna, ÖNB, Ms. Ser. nov. 2701–2702) had not been copied in Hungary, but was brought into the country at a later date.[4] Even manuscripts which exhibit written evidence of local Hungarian usage – such as the *Song of Songs Commentary* and the *Schoolbook of Esztergom* (Esztergom, Archiepiscopal Library Ms. III, 184) – raised doubts concerning whether they had been copied in Hungary. It was even suggested by some scholars that the only

---

From *Dating Undated Medieval Charters*. Ed. Michael Gervers. Copyright (by the Editor and Contributors 2000). Published by the Boydell Press (in association with Collegium Budapest), PO Box 9, Woodbridge, Suffolk, IP12 3DF, Great Britain. ISBN 0 85115 792 0.

1. István Hajnal, *Vergleichende Schriftproben zur Entwicklung und Verbreitung der Schrift im 12–13. Jahrhundert*, Budapest–Leipzig–Milan, 1943.
2. István Hajnal, *Írástörténet az írásbeliség felújulása korából* (Palaeography from the period of the intellectual revival), Budapest, 1921; and *L'enseignement de l'écriture aux universités médiévales*, Budapest, 1959.
3. For an appreciation of Hajnal, see M. T. Clanchy, *From Memory to Written Record in England 1066–1307*, London, 2nd ed., 1993, p. 98; and Bernhard Bischoff, *Latin Palaeography. Antiquity and the Middle Ages*, Cambridge, 1993, p. 98.
4. *Kódexek a középkori Magyarországon* (Codices in medieval Hungary), Budapest, 1985, no. 20.

manuscript of the Hungarian Anonymous Chronicler's *Gesta Hungarorum* (Budapest, OSzK, Ms. Cod. Lat. 403) was a non-Hungarian copy.[5] The Budapest codex exhibition in 1985–86, which presented a remarkable number of known and unknown codices from the Hungarian medieval period, either in the original or in photographic form, was of epochal significance for the history of this discipline. I am inclined to agree with the assumption of the editors of the exhibition catalogue that the liturgical, legal, and scientific manuscripts with Hungarian references were probably copied in Hungary if there is no evidence to the contrary: a manuscript or fragment mistakenly included in this group will not falsify the picture; the less so, as there is no reason to assume the existence of a local scribal tradition or script region (*Schriftprovinz*) for the initial centuries, and it can rightly be hypothesised that Central Europe, including a part of southern Germany and Bohemia–Moravia, displays common features. This assumption still awaits verification, but István Hajnal's valuable observations about the similarities between Western and Central European charter writings should be borne in mind.

With further reference to the abovementioned exhibition of codices, one may emphasise the importance of the twelfth century within the Árpád Age (1000–1301). Compared to the eleventh century, the number of documents multiplied and, no less significantly, the script type preserving the characteristics of the late Caroline script tradition began to tend towards the Gothic script by the end, with more and more features of this script cropping up in the documents. When I was studying the scripts of the *Pray codex* (Budapest, OSzK, Ms. MNy 1) in 1983 I unfortunately took it to be a lone Hungarian document, palaeographically backward compared to West European developments, and a proof of a relatively conservative Central European writing practice.[6] During my later researches, I have found analogies with the charter and book scripts of south Germany. The present paper is concerned with the exposition of these common regional traits.

What characterises Hungarian twelfth-century manuscripts in general is the survival of late Caroline book writing and a relatively late appearance of mature Gothic script. Anticipating my conclusion, it is perhaps not mistaken to assume that the reason for this might be sought in the direct and indirect effects of the so-called slanting oval style (*schrägovaler Stil*) widespread in south Germany, Bavaria, and Austria. Although in these areas this style was by no means used exclusively, it did preserve a type of writing bearing late Caroline characteristics. In my view, this type of writing, which was used for a considerable number of Hungarian codices, can be traced to this region. This backwardness as compared to Western European, especially French, practice, where the ascendancy of Gothic script was faster and more spectacular, was part of Central European regional practice and not a specifically Hungarian development. Needless to say, that does not mean that scribal characteristics remained unchanged from the eleventh to the thirteenth century, but it does indicate that the slanting oval type left enough room for the spreading of Gothic features in the *ductus* and *tractatio* of writings. This

---

5. *Kódexek*, nos. 25 and 26.
6. *Kódexek*, no. 23.

fact, in turn, raises the question, particularly within the framework of Hajnal's sociological approach, as to whether the social and cultural development of this region was reflected in the comparatively conservative script, or whether it was typical of monastic ecclesiastic writing practice. In Hungary, the principal writing style was obviously based upon monastic writing practice.

Acceleration of writing speed did not necessarily require a radical break with the script type, at least until the early thirteenth century. Of course, the above-mentioned writing practice also suited the genre of the surviving manuscripts (sacramentaries, liturgical manuals, legendaries, representative legal collections, and so on). It is not by chance that the '*dictamen*' character of writing began to predominate, with some elements of the letters tending towards cursivity, and more frequent abbreviations when it came to school tracts, the copying of council decrees for practical purposes, and so on.

The *Pray codex*, a sacramentary, can be dated precisely, by the work of its third scribe, to between 1192 and 1195. The *Micrologus* section of this sacramentary, copied by a different scribe, can probably be dated to the same period. The scripts of this manuscript offer an insight into the writing practice of a smaller Benedictine *scriptorium*, and it cannot be ascribed to chance that two scribes – of the sacramentary and of the *Micrologus* – worked in succession without any trace of Gothic influence. The characters are not exactly slanting oval, but suggest the indirect influence of that form. In the script-pattern collection of Karin Schneider one can find several examples which show that late twelfth-century writings only resemble the slanting oval type in their *ductus* and in the lack of Gothic features; otherwise the character 'o' is neither slanting (leaning to the right) nor oval.[7] Very few documents offer themselves as illustrations of the slanting oval type proper because the scripts of a more crowded *ductus*, but already at a right angle, were partly developed from this script. As far as we know, the first Hungarian document of this script type is the *Esztergom/Gran benedictionale* (Zagreb, Chapter Library, MR 89) from the late eleventh century, preserved today in Zagreb (I. plate 1).[8]

In general, it is very hard to place undated manuscripts in the eleventh and twelfth centuries, without some features of content to guide us. Yet, with the expansion of Hungarian comparative material, it would perhaps not be premature to outline the relative chronology of the codices. I, too, have faced the difficulty of dating separately each new-found Latin manuscript or fragment, because of the

---

7. Karin Schneider, *Gotische Schriften in deutscher Sprache vom späten 12 Jahrhundert bis um 1300*, Wiesbaden, 1987.

8. Károly Kniewald, 'Az esztergomi Benedictionale' (The Benedictionale of Esztergom), *Magyar Könyvszemle* 51 (1941): pp. 213–31. This was analysed most recently by József Török, who suggested that, as one of the earliest surviving copies of the Magdeburg-Braunschweig family, the *Benedictionale* reached Hungary from Germany, and was copied in the territory of the Esztergom archbishopric: see József Török, 'Az esztergomi Benedictionale' (The Benedictionale of Esztergom), in *Strigonium Antiquum*, vol. 2, Budapest, 1993, pp. 69–72. For a general overview of the earliest Hungarian liturgical manuscripts, see László Veszprémy, 'Eleventh- and Thirteenth-Century Liturgical Manuscripts (mostly from Zagreb) as Historical Sources', *Povijesni Prilozi* 17 (1998): pp. 261–68.

small number of available Hungarian parallel scripts. Let me mention by way of illustration the problems of dating a fragment from this period. At first, during the preparation of our representative catalogue of fragments of Hungarian codices, the script of this *sermonarium* fragment of Augustine and Caesarius Arelatensis was believed to date from the late eleventh century.[9] The famous German palaeographer Bernhard Bischoff modified this date to the latter half of the twelfth century and I followed this in my publication in the *Magyar Könyvszemle* [Review of Hungarian Book History], while the pre-publication reader of the volume found it typical of the first half of the twelfth century.[10]

Let me make a few brief remarks about the slanting oval style (*schrägovaler Stil*). The latest discussion of the question can be found in the catalogue of the codex exhibition 'Kalligraphie in Bayern' in Munich in 1981, written by the late Bernhard Bischoff.[11] This practice can be traced back to the writings of a tighter *ductus* used around the turn of the tenth and eleventh centuries. The name derives from the slight initial right-leaning of the letter 'o' and the curves of some other letters as well. The script may possibly have evolved in the first decades of the eleventh century, possibly in Regensburg. An outstanding representative of this style was Otloh, a monk at St Emmeram who was born *c*.1010 and died *c*.1070. He copied more than twenty liturgical books and spent several years away from his monastery also engaged in copying; in this way, he contributed much to the spread of this script type (see I. plate 2). This popular and widely used script, prevalent until around 1200, naturally also varied, as one would expect given its large geographical spread.

With regard to our earliest codices, very careful dating is needed. This is borne out by the case of the so-called *Szelepchényi evangelistarium* from Nitra (Slovakia, Hung. Nyitra, Chapter Library), whose date was estimated to be some time from the early eleventh to the mid-twelfth centuries. Since the Hungarian saints are missing from it, its copying cannot be dated long after 1083.[12] Analogies of its script type can be found, for example, among dated French manuscripts of the mid-eleventh century (Cluny, prior to 1049, Manuscrits, vol. 3, III. plate XVIII; 1058, St Maur-des-Fosses, vol. 2, plate X; 1059, Echternach vol. 3, plate XXII); the script of the *Evangeliarum* in Zagreb (Zagreb, Chapter Library MR, 153), admittedly of French origin, is also similar.[13] The three oldest

9. *Fragmenta Latina codicum in Bibliotheca seminarii cleri Hungariae centralis*, ed. László Mezey, vol. I/2, no. 2, pp. 20–21, Budapest and Wiesbaden, 1989.
10. László Veszprémy, 'Egy 12. századi sermonarium-töredék' (A sermonary fragment from the twelfth century), *Magyar Könyvszemle* 102 (1986): pp. 53–60.
11. Bernhard Bischoff, *Kalligraphie in Bayern. Achtes bis zwölftes Jahrhundert*, Wiesbaden, 1981, pp. 34–36; *Palaeography*, pp. 120–22; Karin Schneider, *Gotische Schriften*, pp. 9–24.
12. A facsimile edition published by Július Sopko and Július Valach, *Codex Nitriensis*, Matica Slovenská, 1987; László Veszprémy, 'A Nyitrai Evangelistarium' (The Evangelistary of Nitra), *Ars Hungarica* 21 (1993): pp. 5–10.
13. C. Samaran and R. Marichal, *Catalogue des manuscrits en écriture latine portant des indications de date, de lieu, ou de copiste*, vol. 1, Paris, 1959. For its French origin, see Tünde Wehli, 'A zágrábi püspökség Szt. László-kori kódexei' (Codices of the Zagreb bishopric from St Ladislas' age), in *Szent László és Somogyvár. Tanulmányok a 900 éves somogyvári bencés apátság emlékezetére* (St Ladislas and Somogyvár. In memory of the foundation of the Benedictine monastery at Somogyvár), Kaposvár, 1992a, pp. 83–97.

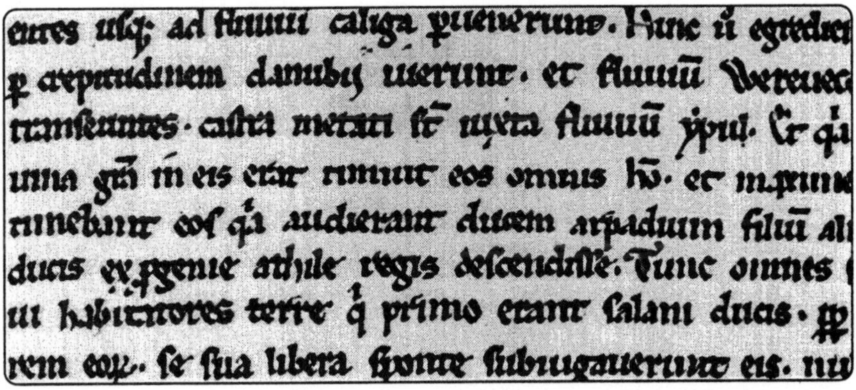

Plate I, 1

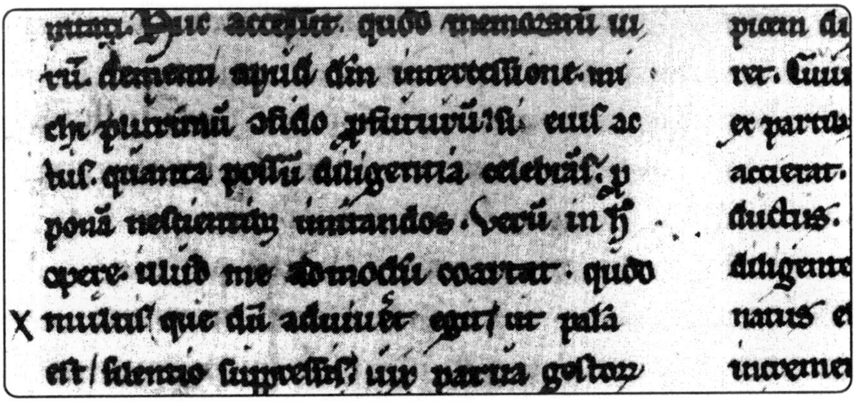

Plate I, 2

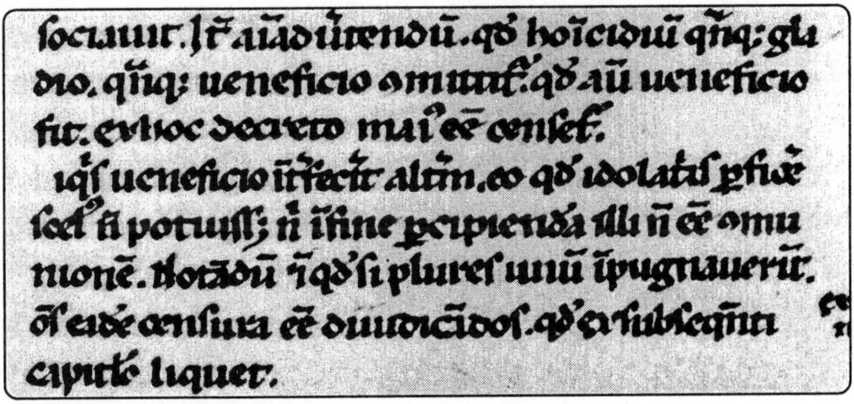

Plate I, 3: Unterkircher, *Die datierte Handschriften*, vol. 1, no. 24.

Hungarian liturgical manuscripts preserved in Zagreb are customarily related to the foundation of the bishopric, hence their copying is dated to around 1090. This, however, is not incontestable, since the tradition of the foundation by the Hungarian King Ladislas – later canonised – could also have been attached to these manuscripts during the decades after the foundation, to which they owe their survival. One of them, the *Esztergom benedictionale*, is undoubtedly written in an eleventh-century – especially its latter half or end – script. It is less elegant than the Otloh copies, but it is rightly regarded as the first Hungarian document of the south German writing tradition.[14]

The script of a Sacramentary fragment attributed to the monastery of Hronsk Beòadik (Hung. Garamszentbenedek) was written far earlier: in the first half of the eleventh century, on the evidence of foreign analogies (Bischoff, *Kalligraphie*, plates 20–22).[15] Some of our earliest liturgical manuscripts may be compared with the charters. The scripts of the *St Margaret sacramentarium* (previously known as the *Hahót codex*, Zagreb, Chapter Library, MR 126) and the *Győr Agenda* (Zagreb, Chapter Library, MR 165) are not so far removed from that of the deeds of the Hungarian King Coloman [Kálmán] (1109: DL 11), the charter of *Fulco hospes* dated 1146 (DF 206 815), and a number of non-Hungarian charters.[16] Therefore, the copying of these codices should possibly be dated to the turn of the eleventh and twelfth centuries, or to the first decades of the twelfth.

Fortunately for us, the date of the *Codex Albensis*, which very likely originated in Alba Iulia, Transylvania (Hung. Gyulafehérvár, today in Graz, Universitätsbibliothek, Ms. 211), and which earlier research had already attributed to the first decades of the twelfth century, can be verified on the basis of the conspicuous similarity between its script and that of the charter of Felician, Archbishop of Esztergom (DF 251 974) dated 1134.[17]

Charters influenced by the slanting oval style appear from the mid-twelfth century. These charters can be taken as adumbrating the writing type known from the *Pray codex*, a fact which also shows how charter writing tried to adapt the book script to its purposes. One of its finest documents is a charter by the Hungarian

---

14. Bischoff, *Kalligraphie*, plate 25; Franz Unterkircher, *Die datierten Handschriften der Österreichischen Nationalbibliothek bis zum Jahre 1400*, Vienna, 1969, vol. 1, plates 23–24

15. A picture of this fragment was printed in *Könyv és könyvtár a magyar társadalom életében* (Book and library in Hungarian society), ed. Máté Kovács, vol. 1, Budapest, 1969, no. 1.

16. László Veszprémy, 'Legkorábbi hazai sacramentariumaink' (The first sacramentaries in Hungary), in *Tanulmányok a középkori magyarországi könyvkultúráról* (Papers on medieval book culture in Hungary), ed. László Szelestei, Budapest, 1989, pp. 121–35; Károly Kniewald, 'Hartwick győri püspök Agenda pontificalisa' (The *Agenda pontificalis* of Hartwick, Bishop of Győr), *Magyar Könyvszemle* 61 (1941): pp. 1–21. For the Hungarian charters, we used the medieval charter collection of the Hungarian National Archive (*DL*), and its photographic collection (*DF*); for the non-Hungarian charters, Walter Koch, *Die Schrift der Reichskanzlei im 12. Jahrhundert (1125–1190). Untersuchungen zur Diplomatik der Kaiserurkunde*, Vienna, 1979, plate 1; and J. Stiennon, *L'écriture diplomatique dans le diocèse de Liège du XIe siècle au milieu du XIIIe siècle*, Paris, 1960, p. 215, plate 24.

17. *Kódexek*, p. 21. A facsimile edition was published by Zoltán Falvy and László Mezey, *Codex Albensis. Ein Antiphonar aus dem 12. Jahrhundert*, Budapest and Graz, 1963. See also László Dobszay and Gábor Prószéky, *Corpus Antiphonalium Officii Ecclesiarum Centralis Europae*, vol. 1, Budapest, 1988.

King Géza II, preserved in Pannonhalma and possibly copied there (DF 206 816). A precedent for a looser *ductus* is King Béla II's deed, also of Pannonhalma, dated 1137 (DF 206 810). Later documents from Pannonhalma include Géza II's deed of 1151 (DF 206 817), Lady Margit's of 1152 (DF 206 818), King Stephan III's of 1171 (208 422), and John, Abbot of Pannonhalma's, dated 29 March 1201 (DF 206 831). These examples should not prompt the conclusion that this style, or the script evolved from it, was characteristic only of Pannonhalma. It is more likely that one of the country's largest *scriptoria* also used this script, as reflected in the charters copied there. Modern researchers may be especially grateful for the survival of the 1201 charter, since it proves that this script practice was still alive at a time when charters had long been copied in a more rapid, charter-specific, more cursive *ductus*. From the 1180s, efforts to separate book and charter writing appear to have become increasingly pronounced, with the ascendancy of Gothic characteristics in charter writing.[18]

A fine document of the mature slanting oval style survives from the mid-twelfth century. Although the Hungarian copying of the *Ezekiel commentary* of Nuremberg (Germanisches Nationalmuseum, Cod. Lat. 22 922) is not yet verified, its use in Hungary is certain, as its provenance was the library of the Dominicans in Košice (Hung. Kassa). Foreign examples suggest that the writing of the manuscripts of the *Ezekiel* type should be dated to the middle or third quarter of the century. The best known example of a similar but somewhat earlier script is the *Admont Bible*, said to have been copied in Salzburg in the 1130s (Vienna, ÖNB, Ms. Ser. nov. 2701-02) as well as the *Augustine manuscript* in the Chapter library of Prague (Ms. A 21,1) from the 1130s–1140s, and a codex from St Florian from 1134 (Unterkircher, *Die datierte Handschriften*, plate 27). The *Sermonarium* fragment mentioned above also seems to belong here.[19]

Another Nuremberg manuscript from Košice (Germanisches Nationalmuseum, Cod. Lat. 23 375), that of Isidore of Seville's *Etymologiarum libri*, also dates from the middle or third quarter of the twelfth century. Its use in Hungary is supported, apart from its Košice provenance, by a marginal note referring to a certain Briccius, Bishop of Vác, who lived in the early thirteenth century.[20] The style of its writing is somewhat related to *dictamen* script, but its *tractatio* preserves traces of a careful book hand, nowhere near the level of the Esztergom school book. The calligraphy of the Council decrees of the *Pray codex*, also dated to the mid-twelfth century, is also relevant here. Apparently, the choice of script was also influenced by the manual, practical school-book character of Isidore's work. Among charters, King Béla II's (1137, DF 206 810) and Lady Színes's (1146, DF 206 814), both of Pannonhalma, may be mentioned here. The writing of the *prima manus* of the

---

18. For the Pannonhalma charters see László Veszprémy, 'Pannonhalmi oklevelek a 13–14. században' (Charters from Pannonhalma in the thirteenth and fourteenth centuries), in *Mons Sacer 996–1996*, vol. 1, ed. Kornél Szovák and Imre Takács, Pannonhalma, 1996, pp. 471–80.

19. Július Sopko, 'Najstaršie košické rukopisné knyhi', *Kniha* (1975), p. 82; *Kataloge des Germanischen Nationalmuseums Nürnberg*, vol. 2, part 2, ed. Hardo Hilg, Wiesbaden, 1986, pp. 21–23. I used a microfilm deposited in the National Széchényi Library, Budapest.

20. See note 19.

Song of Songs Commentary of Esztergom (Archiepiscopal Library, Ms. III. 184) appears to prove what we have said about the writing type of the Isidore manuscript. The smaller script of looser *tractatio* suited the non-representative didactic copies better.[21]

After the abovementioned commentary comes the *Esztergom schoolbook*, preceding the supplementary Hungarian historical note, which closes the manuscript. The treatise on rhetoric and grammar displays the typical traits of the *dictamen* genre in both its *tractatio* and the number of abbreviations. The looseness of its *tractatio* and *ductus*, tending to cursivity, is not a singular phenomenon: King Béla II's charters of 1137 and 1138 provide illuminating evidence (Pannonhalma: DF 206 811; Esztergom: DF 286 216). These charters are also the first documents of the transformation of book writing, and its opening towards cursiveness. Mention of Pannonhalma should also serve to warn us that individual *scriptoria* – and even individual scribes – used the different types of writing where appropriate.

Let us briefly touch on the problem of the list of the burial places of Hungarian kings copied after the *Esztergom schoolbook*, which was until recently – rather exaggeratedly – called the *Esztergom chronicle*. The authenticity of its insertion in an undoubtedly strange script has raised serious doubts for a long time. Interestingly, scholars have overlooked the calligraphy of an Esztergom deed of King Emeric dated 1198 (DF 248 310) whose palaeographic features coincide largely with the disputed script. It is presumed that there was a period in the course of the adoption of Gothic charter writing when, in the hands of some scribes, the *tractatio* of the writing all but collapsed and a seemingly casual, rather uncouth script emerged. It is illuminating in this connection to look at another charter of King Emeric written between 1198 and 1202 (DL 38).[22]

From the second half of the twelfth and the beginning of the thirteenth century, there are several manuscripts which display some signs of the conservative writing style under consideration. The first group of these includes those which do not show signs of the extremely tight *ductus* of the end of the century and no powerful Gothic tendency is apparent in their *tractatio*. In my opinion, this group includes the *Cerbanus translation* of the texts of Maximus Confessor and Joannes Damascenus from Rein (Rein, Zisterzienserstift, Ms. 65).[23] In contrast to its most recent dating, I would tend to place it closer to the death of Abbot David also mentioned in the preface (1150), that is, in the third quarter of the century.

I take the view that the St Stephen legends in the *Ernst codex* (Budapest, OSzK, Cod. Lat. 431) are far later, dating the manuscript, copied by several hands, to the end of the century (Schneider, *Gotische Schriften*, plates 4, 13).[24] The Hungarian

---

21. *Kódexek*, no. 24.
22. *Kódexek*, no. 25. For an up-to-date survey on the problems concerning this manuscript, see István Mészáros, 'Egy Árpád-kori iskoláskönyv Esztergomban' (A schoolbook from the Árpád age in Esztergom), in *Strigonium antiquum*, vol. 2, pp. 73–79.
23. *Kódexek*, no. 14. See also Iván Boronkai, 'Die Maximos-Übersetzung des Cerbanus', *Acta Antiqua Academiae Scientiarum Hungaricae* 24 (1976): pp. 307–33; István Kapitánffy, 'Cerbanus és Maximus fordítása' (Cerbanus and his Maximus translation), in *Mons Sacer*, vol. 1, pp. 357–68.
24. *Kódexek*, no. 16. A facsimile edition with an introduction was published by Elemér Varjú, *Legendae Sancti regis Stephani*, Budapest, 1928.

scholar Elemér Varjú has clearly demonstrated the differences between the writings by different hands, attempting to attribute them to a generation gap between younger and older scribes. It is, however, more probable that the Gothic script moulded the writing of different scribes to different degrees. The fourth hand which copied the Hungarian legends appears to be the most conservative, the rest of the scribes producing a more markedly Gothic script.

The *Legendary of Rein* (Rein, Zisterzienserstift, Ms. 69) and the manuscript of the *Hartvick legend* (Budapest, OSzk, Cod. Lat. 17) are dated to the years around the turn of the century.[25] The latter is also in several hands. These manuscripts lead into the early thirteenth century when this type of script already bears the mark of regular Gothic book writing, preserving much of the *ductus* of the older writing practice. The process by which the south German scripts turned Gothic is well known from Karin Schneider's important handbook. Scripts similar to that of the manuscripts of Rein and Budapest can be encountered in documents from the last quarter of the twelfth century (Schneider, *Gotische Schriften*, plates 28, 29). A second *Augustine fragment* in our Catalogue of Latin Manuscript Fragments in Hungary can be dated to the end of the twelfth century, illustrating the potential of the slanting oval style to develop into Gothic.[26] The *Lectionarium* of Hronsk Beòadik (Garamszentbenedek*)* is presumably also from the end of that century, displaying characteristic features of a writing type called Rhine quadrate by Schneider, and also used elsewhere in German territories (Schneider, *Gotische Schriften*, plate 28).[27]

The gradual adoption of Gothic characteristics could have taken place in a number of ways. Of these, two can be illustrated from the first half of the thirteenth century. One is the *Zagreb missal* (earlier known as the *Güssing Missal*, Güssing, Klosterbibl. Ms. I, 43). A fine analogy can be found with the large-size characters of the missal in Schneider's collection (plate 57, first quarter of the century). As for small-size characters, examples can be found in Hungarian charters of the 1220s (for example, the charter of Nicholas, Provost of Esztergom, dated 1225, DL 118). The genre of the document also influenced the choice of writing type.[28]

The other possible course can be exemplified by the much-disputed manuscript of the Anonymous chronicler's *Gesta Hungarorum* (II. plate 1). In my view, the dating and palaeographic evaluation of the manuscript have inspired so much uncertainty precisely because Hungarian palaeography has failed to reckon with the survival of the south German style in the Gothic script, and also because the publication of palaeographic aids has developed significantly only in recent

---

25. *Kódexek*, nos. 18, 17
26. *Fragmenta Latina*, vol. I/2, no. 5, plate 4.
27. For the problems of provenance see Kinga Körmendy, *A Knauz-hagyaték kódextöredékei és az esztergomi egyház középkori könyvtárának sorsa* (Codex fragments of the Knauz-collection and the fate of the medieval ecclesiastical library at Esztergom), Budapest, 1979, pp. 73–75.
28. *Kódexek*, no. 30. See also László Dobszay, 'Árpád-kori kottás misekönyvünk provenienciája' (The provenance of a missal with notations from the Árpád age), *Zenetudományi dolgozatok* (1984): pp. 7–12.

decades.[29] Research was misled by a hypothesised French antecedent, derived from the generalisation of French influence demonstrable in charter writing. The dating of the codex of the Anonymous chronicler to the middle of the century is supported by German examples (Schneider, *Gotische Schriften*, plates 52, 60, 85, and so on [II. plates 2–3]), as well as by some Hungarian charters written between 1220 and 1250; for example, a charter of the Székesfehérvár Convent of the Knights of St. John of Jerusalem dated 1256 (DL 83128), although the *ductus* and *tractatio* are not perfectly identical with those of Anonymous.

In his university textbook *The History of the Latin Script*, published in 1962, László Mezey, almost the only follower of the paleographical school initiated by Hajnal in Hungary, attempted to describe the eleventh-century codices and to attribute them to various territorial writing styles. He rightly listed the *Hronsk Beòadik sacramentary* fragment and the *Esztergom benedictionale* as proof of the influence of the south German Latin script tradition. Clearly differentiated from these was the writing of the *Szelepchényi evangelistarium*, connected more closely with northern French writing patterns, such as the *Evangeliarium* of non-Hungarian provenance preserved today in Zagreb.[30]

I have attempted to trace the tendencies mentioned by Hajnal and Mezey in the Hungarian Latin manuscripts and fragments known to us today. In the eleventh and twelfth centuries, a period from which only a few historical sources have survived, the use of book and charter palaeography has become much more important in helping us to reconstruct the cultural background and the borrowings of Hungarian book culture from Western and Central Europe.

---

29. *Kódexek*, no. 30. See also László Veszprémy, 'Anonymus Gestájának kézirata' (The manuscript of the Anonymous Notary's Gesta), *Magyar Könyvszemle* 108 (1991): pp. 44–52. Tünde Wehli, 'Anonymus Gesta Hungarorumjának helye a magyarországi könyvfestészet körében' (The place of the Anonymous Notary's *Gesta Hungarorum* in Hungarian book illumination), *Magyar Könyvszemle* 108 (1992b): pp. 52–55. Another striking parallel with the script of the Hungarian *Gesta* can be found in a Zagreb *Pontificale*, from the first part of the thirteenth century – see Dragutin Kniewald, *Zagrebaèki liturgijski kodeksi XI–XV., stoljeæa*, Zagreb, 1940, pp. 16–17.

30. László Mezey, *A latin írás története*, Budapest, 1962.

SEC'DUM IOHANNEM:·

nno ab incarnatione dñi ñri ihu xp̄i mill· xc· iii· inditio
ne ii· dedicata ē hec capella iiii· id· Iulii a nemone sc̄e iuua
uensis ecl̄e archiep̄o· in honore sc̄e & induē trinitatis· & sc̄issim
crucis· & sc̄e marie matris dñi· & sc̄i nycolai cōfessoris dñi.
Continent aū in altari reliquie recondite. De spongia dñi n
de fimbriis uestimenti ei· De ligno sc̄e crucis· De sudario dñi

Plate II, 1

in domo dñi ordinent psone· p quas dia
bolus pcul pellatur: & clerus d̄o ñro mul
tiplicetur. Archidiaconus
Quantum ad humanū spectat exameñ·
natura· scientia· & moribs dignus habe
tur: & pbr cooperatores effici in his d̄o

Plate II, 2

gione urbis parisiorū incolle qui antea mōs
mercurii quo inibi idolū ipsius principalit
colebat agallis· nunc ū mons martyrū uoca
tur sc̄oq̄ dñi gr̄a· qui ibide triumphale mar
tyriū pperarunt· celebrata ē ·vii· id octob
anno ab incarnatione dñi ñri ihu xpi non
gesimo sexto· a passione aut sexagesimo· iiii

Plate II, 3

Bibliography

Bischoff, Bernhard. 1981. *Kalligraphie in Bayern. Achtes bis zwölftes Jahrhundert.* Wiesbaden: Harrassowitz.

———. 1993. *Latin Palaeography. Antiquity and the Middle Ages.* Cambridge: Cambridge University Press.

Boronkai, Iván. 1976. 'Die Maximos-Übersetzung des Cerbanus'. *Acta Antiqua Academiae Scientiarum Hungaricae* 24: pp. 307–33.

Clanchy, M. T. 1979. *From Memory to Written Record in England 1066–1307.* London: Edward Arnold.

Codex Albensis. Ein Antiphonar aus dem 12. Jahrhundert. 1963. Edited by Zoltán Falvy and László Mezey. Budapest: Akadémiai and Graz: Akademische Druck.

Codex Nitriensis. 1987. Edited by Július Sopko and Július Valach. Matica Slovenská.

Dobszay, László. 1984. 'Árpád-kori kottás misekönyvünk provenienciája' (The provenance of a missal with notations from the Árpád age).' *Zenetudományi dolgozatok*: pp. 7–12.

Dobszay, László, and Gábor Prószéky. 1988. *Corpus Antiphonalium Officii Ecclesiarum Centralis Europae.* Vol. I. Budapest: Zenetudományi Kiadó.

Fragmenta Latina codicum in Bibliotheca seminarii cleri Hungariae centralis. 1989. Edited by László Mezey. Vol. I/2. Budapest: Akadémiai and Wiesbaden: Harrassowitz.

Hajnal, István. 1959. *L'enseignement de l'écriture aux universités médiévales.* Budapest: Akadémiai Kiadó.

———. 1921. *Írástörténet az írásbeliség felújulása korából* (Palaeography of the period of the intellectual revival). Budapest: Budavári Tudományos Társaság.

———. 1943. *Vergleichende Schriftproben zur Entwicklung und Verbreitung der Schrift im 12–13. Jahrhundert.* Budapest–Leipzig–Milan: Danubia.

Kapitánffy, István. 1996. 'Cerbanus és Maximus fordítása', in *Mons Sacer 996–1996*, ed. Kornél Szovák and Imre Takács, pp. 357–68. Vol. I. Pannonhalma: Pannonhalmi Főapátság.

Kataloge des Germanischen Nationalmuseums Nürnberg. 1986. Edited by Hardo Hilg. Vol. II, part 2. Wiesbaden: Harrassowitz.

Kniewald, Károly. 1941a. 'Az esztergomi Benedictionale' (The benedictional of Esztergom). *Magyar Könyvszemle* 151: pp. 213–31.

———. 1941b. 'Hartwick győri püspök Agenda pontificalisa' (The Agenda pontificalis of Hartwick, bishop of Győr). *Magyar Könyvszemle* 61: pp. 1–21.

Kniewald, Dragutin. 1940. *Zagrebaèki liturgijski kodeksi XI–XV.* Zagreb: Stoljeæa.

Koch, Walter. 1979. *Die Schrift der Reichskanzlei im 12. Jahrhundert (1125–1190). Untersuchungen zur Diplomatik der Kaiserurkunde.* Vienna: Akademie.

Kódexek a középkori Magyarországon (Codices in medieval Hungary). 1985. Budapest: Országos Széchényi Könyvtár.

Kovács, Máté, ed. 1969. *Könyv és könyvtár a magyar társadalom életében* (The book and the library in the life of Hungarian Society). Vol. I. Budapest: Gondolat.

Körmendy, Kinga. 1979. *A Knauz-hagyaték kódextöredékei és az esztergomi egyház középkori könyvtárának sorsa* (Codex fragments of the Knauz-collection and the fate of the medieval ecclesiastical library at Esztergom). Budapest: Magyar Tudományos Akadémia.

Mészáros, István. 'Egy Árpád-kori iskoláskönyv Esztergomban', in *Strigonium antiquum*, pp. 73–79. Vol. II.

Mezey, László. 1962. *A latin írás története* (History of the Latin script). Budapest: Tankönyvkiadó.

Samaran, Charles, and Robert Marichal. 1959–. *Catalogue des manuscrits en écriture latine portant des indications de date, de lieu, ou de copiste.* Vol. I. Paris.

Schneider, Karin. 1987. *Gotische Schriften in deutscher Sprache vom späten 12 Jahrhundert bis um 1300.* Wiesbaden: Harrassowitz.

Sopko, Július. 1975. 'Najstaršie košické rukopisné knyhi.' *Kniha*: pp. 80–85.

Stiennon, Jacques. 1960. *L'écriture diplomatique dans le diocèse de Liège du XIe siècle au milieu du XIIIe siècle.* Paris.

Török, József. 1993. 'Az esztergomi Benedictionale' (The benedictional of Esztergom), in *Strigonium Antiquum*, pp. 69–72. Vol. II. Budapest: Márton Áron.

Unterkircher, Franz. 1969. *Die datierten Handschriften der Österreichischen Nationalbibliothek bis zum Jahre 1400.* Vol. I. Vienna: Akademie.

Varjú, Elemér. 1928. *Legendae Sancti regis Stephani.* Budapest: Singer and Wolfner.

Veszprémy, László. 1986. 'Egy 12. századi sermonarium-töredék' (A sermonary fragment from the 12th century). *Magyar Könyvszemle* 102: pp. 53–60.

——. 1989. 'Legkorábbi hazai sacramentariumaink' (The first sacramentaries in Hungary), in *Tanulmányok a középkori magyarországi könyvkultúráról* (Papers on medieval book culture in Hungary), ed. László Szelestei, pp. 121–35. Budapest: Országos Széchényi Könyvtár.

——. 1991. 'Anonymus Gestájának kézirata' (The manuscript of the Anonymous Notary's *Gesta*). *Magyar Könyvszemle* 108: pp. 44–51.

——. 1993. 'A Nyitrai Evangelistarium' (The Evangelistary of Nitra). *Ars Hungarica* 21: pp. 5–10.

——. 1996. 'Pannonhalmi oklevelek a 13–14. Században' (Charters from Pannonhalma in the 13th and 14th centuries), in *Mons Sacer 996–1996*, ed. Kornél Szovák and Imre Takács, pp. 471–80. Vol. I. Pannonhalma: Pannonhalmi Főapátság.

——. 1998. '11th- and 13th-Century Liturgical Manuscripts (mostly from Zagreb) as Historical Sources.' *Povijesni Priloziu* 17: pp. 261–68.

Wehli, Tünde. 1992a. 'A zágrábi püspökség Szt. László-kori kódexei' (Codices of the Zagreb bishopric from St Ladislas' age), in *Szent László és Somogyvár. Tanulmányok a 900 éves somogyvári bencés apátság emlékezetére* (St Ladislas and Somogyvár. Studies in memory of the foundation of the Benedictine monastery at Somogyvár), pp. 83–97. Kaposvár: Somogy Megyei Múzeumok Igazgatósága.

——. 1992b. 'Anonymus Gesta Hungarorumjának helye a magyarországi könyvfestészet körében' (The place of the Anonymous Notary's *Gesta Hungarorum* in Hungarian book illumination). *Magyar Könyvszemle* 108: pp. 52–55.

SEALS AND THE DATING OF DOCUMENTS

P. D. A. Harvey

In Britain, relatively little use has been made of the historical evidence offered by medieval seals. To be sure, seals used in royal administration have been extensively investigated in both England and Scotland,[1] and seals have been used as part of the evidence for clerical arrangements in some aristocratic families,[2] but there has been no study of monastic or urban seals from this viewpoint, or of what they could tell us about bishops' chanceries. Certainly, little attention has been paid to the non-heraldic personal seals that make up some four-fifths of surviving medieval seals. Yet potentially all these seals have much to tell us. They survive in large numbers – 300,000 seal impressions from before 1500 is a conservative estimate – and one would suppose that the style, the chronology, and the geographical distribution of their design and use could throw new light, not only on medieval law and administrative history, but also on cultural, social, and economic history.

Catalogues of existing British medieval seal impressions are weighted heavily towards the seals of the upper levels of society: of royalty, bishops, and monasteries, the equestrian and heraldic seals of nobles and knights. In continuing the work on the systematic and comprehensive catalogue of the seals in the Public Record Office in London, begun by the late Mr R. H. Ellis,[3] it became apparent that a database offered enormous advantages over the traditional printed catalogue which arranges seals either in the order of the archive, document by document, or else by the name of the owner. To use the evidence offered by the non-heraldic personal seals one needed to be able to assess them quantitatively, and to order them by a variety of different criteria: not just by owner's name, but by user's name (not necessarily the same by any means), by date, by geographical area, by their legends, and by their designs. All this a computer can achieve effortlessly; and a relational database for cataloguing the seals at the Public Record Office was designed by Dr Trevor Chalmers and extensively tested by entering nearly 4,000 seal impressions from the Ancient Deeds of the Duchy of Lancaster and of the Auditors of Land Revenue.[4] Alongside the development of the database was the compilation of editorial rules governing its use: standardised wording for describing,

From *Dating Undated Medieval Charters*. Ed. Michael Gervers. Copyright (by the Editor and Contributors 2000). Published by the Boydell Press (in association with Collegium Budapest), PO Box 9, Woodbridge, Suffolk, IP12 3DF, Great Britain. ISBN 0 85115 792 0.

1. For example, H. C. Maxwell-Lyte, *Historical Notes on the Use of the Great Seal of England*, London, 1926; R. K. Hannay, 'The Early History of the Scottish Signet', in *The Society of Writers to His Majesty's Signet*, Edinburgh, 1936, pp. 3–51.
2. Notably by T. A. Heslop, 'The Seals of the Twelfth-Century Earls of Chester', *Journal of the Chester Archaeological Society* 71 (1991): pp. 179–97.
3. R. H. Ellis, *Catalogue of Seals in the Public Record Office*, 3 vols, London, 1978–86.
4. P. D. A. Harvey, 'Computer Catalogue of Seals in the Public Record Office, London', *Janus*, 1996, part 2: pp. 29–36. The classes of Public Records entered are DL 25, 26 and LR 14, 15.

especially, the design so that a search would accurately bring together all relevant seals – which it would not do if the same design was, for example, sometimes called 'lion walking to left', sometimes 'lion walking facing left', sometimes 'lion facing left, walking'.

Following interest shown in the project outside the Public Record Office, in 1998 the database was adapted to accept references from other repositories as well, and this facility was tested by entering about a hundred seals from the Additional Charters in the British Library. Now a consortium has been formed, consisting at present of four public repositories and one private archive – the British Library, the National Archives of Scotland, the National Library of Wales, the Public Record Office, and the archives of the Dean and Chapter of Canterbury – to initiate the use of the database for a union catalogue of seals in British repositories. Planning is under way for a first stage of perhaps one person/year's work in each repository, entering in all some 20,000 seals in the database. An essential component of the project is to incorporate in the database a digital image of every seal impression that is entered, and this adaptation, with the entry of images of the seals already catalogued, is already in progress. Since every impression from a single seal-die is linked to a single description – the seal is not described separately for each impression – there has to be a way of telling whether a seal impression in one repository was or was not made by the same die as an impression of similar appearance in another. The impressions themselves cannot be placed side by side, and a digitised image is the only practicable solution – besides of course offering many other advantages. When I succeeded R. H. Ellis as the Public Record Office's cataloguer of seals he wrote to me, quoting G. C. Bascapé: "Ma nessuna descrizione sarà mai efficace come l'immagine" [no description will ever be as effective as a picture].[5] "Every editor of a seal catalogue", Ellis added, "should bear these words inscribed on his heart."

All this is more relevant to the dating of medieval charters than may appear at first sight. In the first place, any work based on the evidence of seals is bound to rely heavily on the accurate dating of undated charters. The twelfth and thirteenth centuries saw crucial developments in the use and design of seals, developments that we shall fully understand – so making it possible to apply the evidence of the seals in a wider context – only if we can establish a satisfactory chronology. The projected union catalogue of British seals, as well as everyone concerned in it, has the strongest possible interest in the development of any technique which offers the possibility of dating undated charters easily and precisely.

There is also the possibility that the seal may occasionally – no more – help us in dating the charter. This appeared in a short preliminary exercise in using the database to investigate the development of particular types of seal. Although it does not yet contain enough material to establish a reliable chronology for any type, it is notable that one late-medieval design, a single initial with crown above and a branch on one or both sides, first appears in the database on documents of

---

5. G. C. Bascapé, *Sigillografia*, 2 vols, Milan, 1969–78, vol. I, p. 111.

the late 1360s and early 1370s, rapidly becoming very common. It also appears on two seals attached to documents where the dates are incomplete or lost: one of them on documents which can be dated between 1337 and 1361, the other on a document that can be dated only to the reign of Edward III, 1327–77.[6] Even from our present limited knowledge we can say that the seal suggests in each case a date late in the range. As we learn more of the chronology of particular seal designs we shall find ever more cases where the seal can offer at least contributory evidence to the date of the document it authenticates. The most it can do, however, is to point to the earliest possible date, the *terminus a quo*, the date when a particular design first appears; even personal seals bearing the owner's name might be in use long after that first owner's death, while corporate seals might continue in use almost indefinitely – the city of Exeter was still using its twelfth-century seal at the beginning of the twentieth.[7]

But beyond this, the cataloguing of seals and the dating of charters are potentially still more closely linked. The automated seal catalogue was developed at the Public Record Office, where the major collections of early deeds have been fully catalogued but without an account of their seals – the descriptions do no more than say how many seals are attached to the document. The situation is similar at the British Library and in some other large repositories: catalogues of medieval deeds have largely ignored the seals. But the more time and thought go into the development of databases for cataloguing seals, the more archivists – in Britain and elsewhere – are questioning the policy of cataloguing the seal separately from the document it authenticates. Doubts arise on both theoretical and practical grounds. The seal is an integral part of the document, not a distinct entity, and to catalogue it separately from the text of the document is to infringe one of the accepted premises of archival description: that the piece, the individual document, is the smallest unit that can be described. But there are pragmatic reasons too for cataloguing the seal as a part of the document. Any catalogue of seals is bound to draw much information from the text of the document. The British automated catalogue includes the document's date, explicit or implicit, the names of the parties who used – or may have used – the surviving seals, the places they came from, the places the document relates to, and the place where it was sealed, whether there is a sealing clause, and whether the seal explicitly supports or replaces the seal of someone else. All this comes from the text of the document, and by the time it is all entered in the database – placenames identified in their counties, surnames in standardised modern form, as well as in the form of the document – the cataloguer has advanced a long way towards cataloguing the document's text, as well as its seal: relatively little further work would be needed to produce a complete description of the document, seal and text. Simple efficiency demands a single bite at the cherry, not two.

A likely way forward is a system of linkage between the catalogue of seals and the online catalogue of documents – this is, after all, the kind of flexibility that is

6. Public Record Office, DL 25/1202, 1210, 1212; DL 25/1057.
7. H. Lloyd Parry, *The Exeter Civic Seals*, Exeter, 1909.

one of the great virtues of computer catalogues. This lies in the future, but probably not the far-distant future. It is in this context that – again not too far ahead – the computer system for entering the text and analysing it as a means of dating may well come to be part of the package.

Bibliography

Bascapé, G. C. 1969–78. *Sigillografia*. 2 vols. Milan.
Ellis, R. H. 1978–86. *Catalogue of Seals in the Public Record Office*. 3 vols. London.
Hannay, R. K. 1936. 'The Early History of the Scottish Signet', in *The Society of Writers to His Majesty's Signet*. Edinburgh.
Harvey, P. D. A. 1996. 'Computer Catalogue of Seals in the Public Record Office, London.' *Janus*, part 2. Paris.
Heslop, T. A. 1991. 'The Seals of the Twelfth-Century Earls of Chester'. *Journal of the Chester Archaeological Society* 71. Chester.
Lloyd-Parry, H. 1909. *The Exeter Civic Seals*. Exeter.
Maxwell-Lyte, H. C. 1926. *Historical Notes on the Use of the Great Seal of England*. London.

PART VI
COMPARATIVE METHODOLOGIES

DENDROCHRONOLOGY AND HISTORY

András Grynaeus

At first sight, it may appear that there are no similarities between the dating of written sources on the basis of word patterns and dendrochronological dating on the margins of archaeology and biology. Closer acquaintance with the former has caused me to revise my rash view, however. Although the two methods are quite different, a number of parallels may be observed which could be useful for scholars working in both disciplines.

Dendrochronological Dating

In the temperate zone – and in all regions where there are seasons which follow one another – one can clearly discern the yearly growth produced by the cambium (the outer, growing part of the structure which is only a few cell-rows thick)[1] of the trees, namely the year-ring or tree-ring.[2]

If we count the tree-rings we can estimate the age of the tree when it was felled. It must be emphasised that this is only the age of the tree, not an absolute age which may be linked to a particular year. There are trees which produce large tree-rings (for example, the poplar) and others which produce narrow ones (for example, the oak).[3]

The thickness of tree-rings varies and does not repeat periodically, depending as it does not only on species, site, and density of population, but also on external influences – moisture, temperature, parasites, and so on – which change from year to year. These are complemented by extraterrestrial components, above all the activity of sunspots, to which different species have very different sensitivities: for example, while the growth of the fir (Abies alba Mill.) is fundamentally influenced by this factor,[4] the oak reacts hardly at all. As a result of all these factors, the changing of the thickness of the tree-rings is not periodical. Of a given series of at least 30 tree-rings we can declare with certainty that it will never be found again in the life of the given tree species, that is, it can be regarded as a historical feature. This, the so-called *historical principle*, is one of the cardinal principles of dendrochronology.

Variation in the thickness of tree-rings will be similar in two or more contemporaneous trees of the same species and growing close together, since in this case

---

From *Dating Undated Medieval Charters*. Ed. Michael Gervers. Copyright (by the Editor and Contributors 2000). Published by the Boydell Press (in association with Collegium Budapest), PO Box 9, Woodbridge, Suffolk, IP12 3DF, Great Britain. ISBN 0 85115 792 0.

1. Babos, *Faanyagismeret*, p. 12.
2. Babos, *Faanyagismeret*, p. 7.
3. Babos, *Faanyagismeret*, p. 8.
4. Grynaeus, *Dendrokronológia*, p. 357.

the environmental influences will be approximately the same. Conversely, if variations in tree-ring thickness show numerous similarities in the case of two trees the ages of which are unknown, we would be justified in attributing the same age to them. This, the so-called *synchronic principle*, is the second cardinal principle of dendrochronology.

If we have an old and a recent piece of wood – for example, a piece of recently fallen tree and another from the beam of an old house – there may be a part of the tree-ring series in each case which overlaps the other, that is, the old tree was still alive when the young began to grow somewhere in the same area. On the basis of the common part the two series may be brought together and the absolutely dated series extended. This is the third cardinal principle, the so-called *overlapping principle*.[5] Using this *overlapping* method we can produce a series or chronology which is specific for a given species in a given territory and goes back far into the past (*Figure 1*).

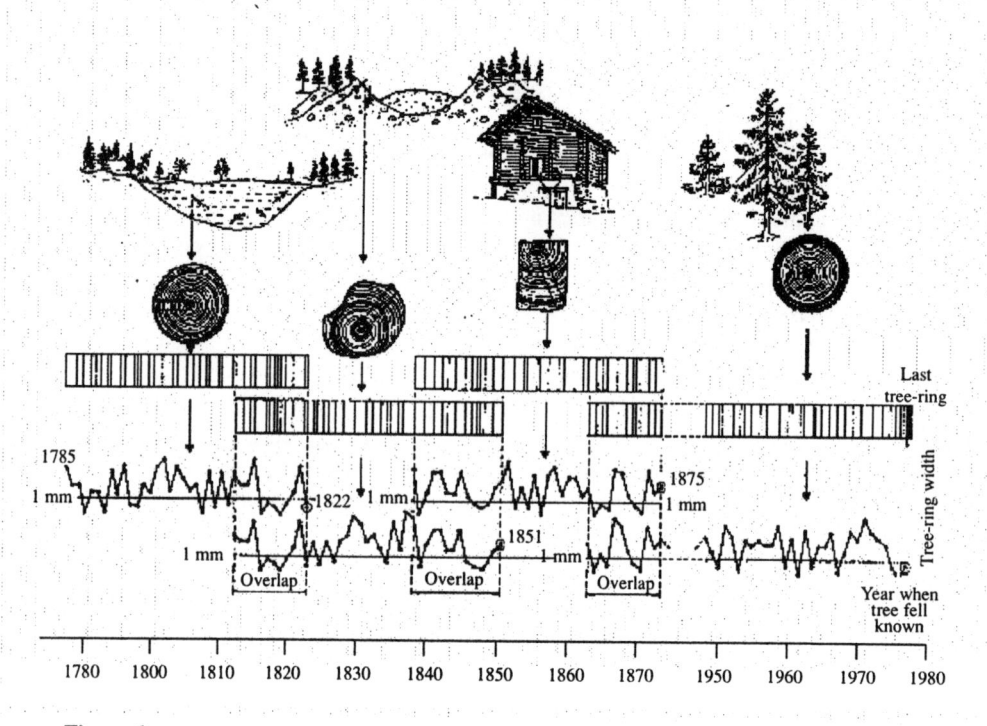

Figure 1
Source: Schweingruber, *Der Jahrring*, p. 85.

5. Grynaeus, *Dendrokronológia*, p. 358.

In the case of a sample of unknown age we 'only' have to find that part of our chronology which corresponds to its tree-ring thickness series. If we can connect each year of the sample to those of the basic chronology, it will be datable.

The main advantages of dendrochronological dating compared to other scientific methods (for example, C14) are its cost-effectiveness and the fact that even seasonal features can be identified, since in most cases the tissues produced at the beginning of the vegetation period (spring timber) can easily be differentiated from those produced at the end (autumn timber). It is for these reasons that the method came to be applied in archaeological research soon after its discovery; indeed, the dating possibilities of this method have always been at the forefront of European research.

The main limitation of this approach to dating should by now have become clear: for useful results we require samples of the same species and a territorial chronology (the size of territories differs considerably: in southern Germany the diameter of the circle is 1,000 km, while in northern Germany it is only 100 km).

The work begins with the sample collection, followed by the measuring of tree-ring thicknesses and computer processing of the data. Finally, we come to the evaluation and comparison, the main element of which is the *dating*: the bark not only protects the body of the tree and the augmenting cells below the bark (cambium), but it also plays a decisive role in the transportation of water to the crown of the tree. The sapwood is the outer, living part of the body of the tree: by its means the nutriments dissolved in water synthesised in the crown are brought to each cell of the tree, while in the autumn starch is stored in it. The heartwood or duramen is the dead, central wood of the tree; its inactive cells do not participate in the life processes of the tree.

This distinction is important for dating purposes since the thickness of the sapwood is constant for a given species in a given territory: the cambium produces a new tree-ring each year, while the innermost tree-ring of the sapwood becomes part of the heartwood. In this way, the sapwood always has the same number of tree-rings, while the diameter of the tree grows from year to year.

If we know the thickness of the sapwood, we can date the falling time or earliest possible falling time of the tree relatively precisely, even if the bark is missing (*Figure 2*).

After this brief excursus, let us investigate the parallels between dendrochronological dating and the dating of manuscripts by means of word patterns.

All researchers must have an adequate database, for which there are two principal criteria of adequacy. First, the database should be specific to a territory, that is, I cannot use the database of German trees in the investigation of Hungarian samples – similarly, the expressions used in charters change from territory to territory. (Another important parallel is that the territories in question do not always correspond to medieval states, as a result of which we have to discover the limits of validity of the given word pattern or tree-ring database.) Secondly, dendrochronology is species-specific, that is, data concerning the oak cannot be compared with those of the poplar. The situation of charter researchers is somewhat better in this respect since most medieval charters were written in Latin, while the

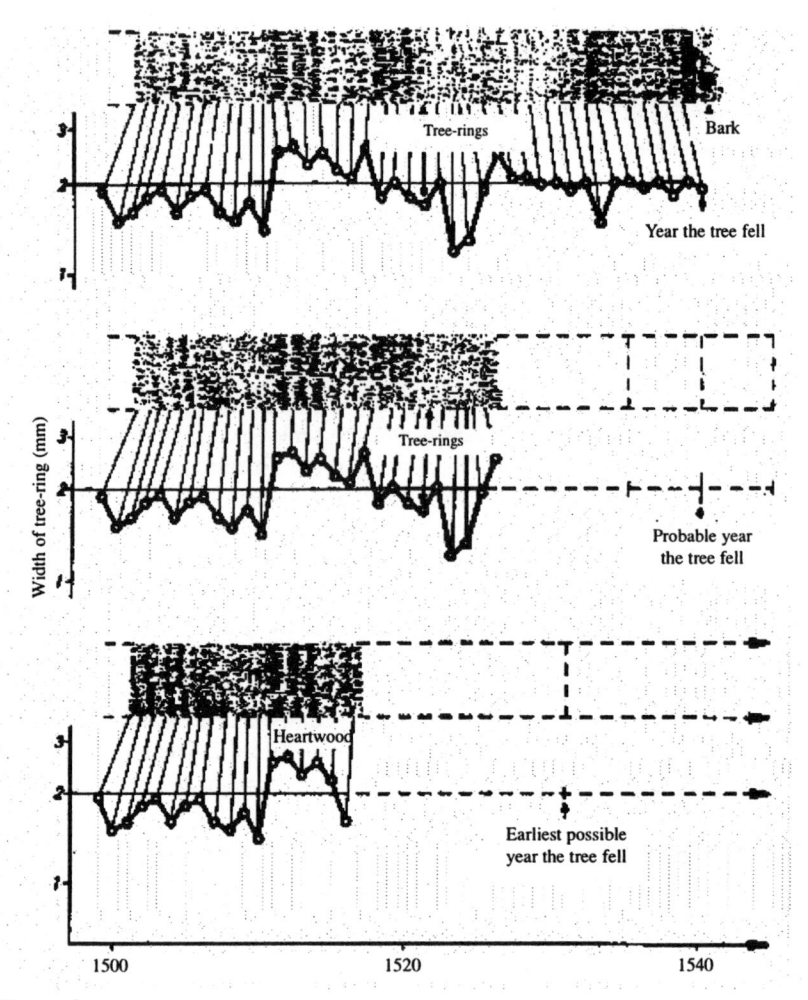

Figure 2
Source: Eckstein and Bedal, 'Dendrochronologie', p. 228.

number of tree species is quite large. At the same time, in medieval Hungary only oak was used as a building material – why, we do not know – which considerably simplifies the work of Hungarian dendrochronologists.

It is extremely important that the investigated sample or tree-ring series be of substantial size, which means a data series of at least 30 elements. The size depends on the species: in the case of the pine, a piece of barrelwood 5–10 cm long may be sufficient, but we often need a span-long piece of medieval oak. The age of the sample is also important: a similar piece of Roman oak may contain as many as 100 tree-rings.

While 30 tree-rings constitute the minimum quantity required, we usually need at least 45–50 tree-rings for precise dating. On the other hand, if we are

Dendrochronology and History 217

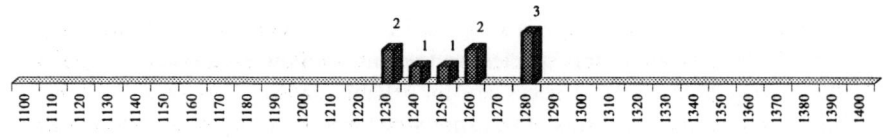

Contra omnes homines et feminas warantizabimus

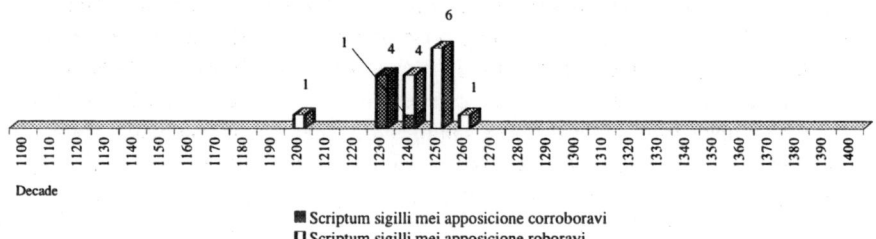

■ Scriptum sigilli mei apposicione corroboravi
□ Scriptum sigilli mei apposicione roboravi

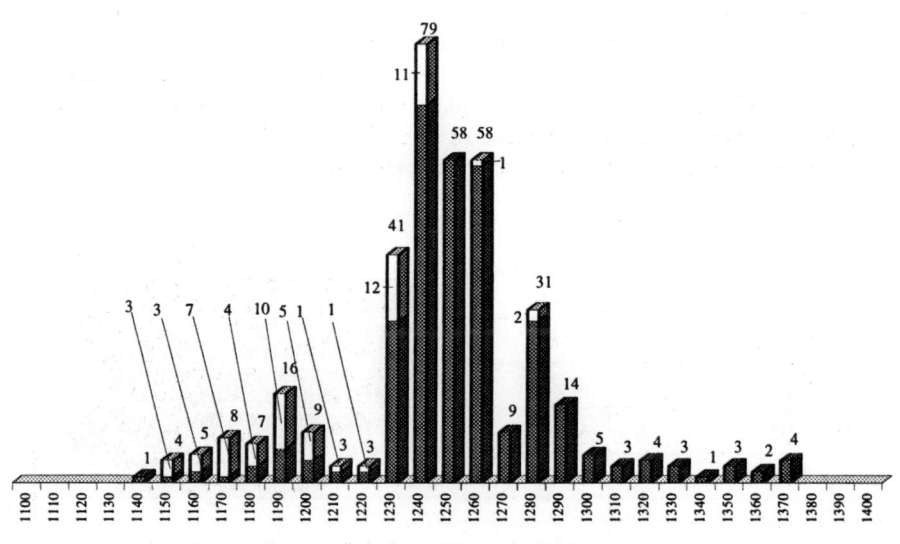

■ Beate Marie   □ Sancte Marie

Figure 3
Source: Gervers, 'Dating', pp. 472–73 (data derived from Hospitaller cartulary: British Library, Cotton ms. Nero E vi).

investigating a redwood (Sequoia sp.), a 0.5 m sample containing 250 tree-rings will hardly be enough: in this species the tree-rings follow each other so regularly that a very long series is necessary for reliable dating. This phenomenon is described numerically in terms of an expression taken from statistics, used to indicate the sensitivity of a data series.

Data series specificity is common to both research fields (*Figure 3*). Something similar may be observed in charter dating, too: as can be seen in *Figure 3*, the length of the 'data series' is also specific: some consist of only one expression, while others contain 5–6 words.

There are years in which a climatic event took place which was sufficient in scope to influence fundamentally the growth of all trees. This can be recognised in each and every sample in the form of a characteristically broad or narrow tree-ring. The identification of such a year can help to date even quite small samples. It must be emphasised, however, that samples are datable even without a significant number of tree-rings if the data series is long enough: this is echoed in charter dating by those charters which, although not containing any specific expression, are nevertheless datable on the basis of their features taken as a whole.

Dendrochronology cannot always give an exact result, only a relative chronology, that is, the place of the investigated sample within the site. This is illustrated by a Roman settlement in the case of which we dated wells of wooden structure. For a long time we could give only their relative chronology (*Figure 4*). We knew how many years there were between the construction of individual wells, but we could not attribute particular dates. Luckily, other sources – for example, a coin and a ceramic fragment – helped us to place the wells in the time series. Finally, the moment came when we were able to date one of the data series exactly, and so all the investigated wells in the settlement (*Figure 5*).

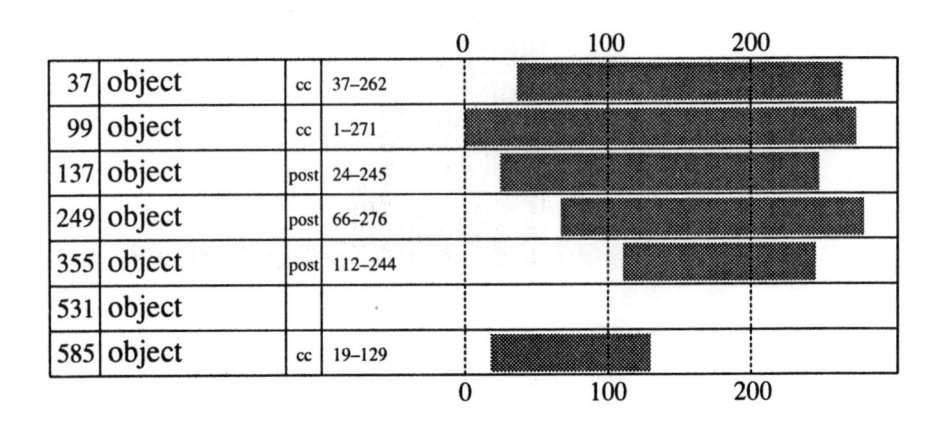

37	object	cc	37–262
99	object	cc	1–271
137	object	post	24–245
249	object	post	66–276
355	object	post	112–244
531	object		
585	object	cc	19–129

Period I: post X + 130
Period II: from X + 260 to X + 280
Period III: before X + 30 or after X + 246

Figure 4 *Meenfoecsanak-Szeles Objects*

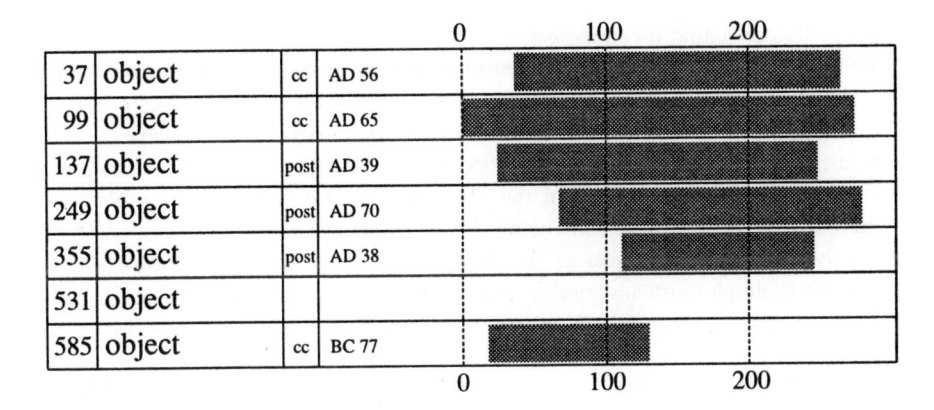

Dendrochronology and History

37	object	cc	AD 56	▰▰▰▰▰
99	object	cc	AD 65	▰▰▰▰▰
137	object	post	AD 39	▰▰▰▰
249	object	post	AD 70	▰▰▰▰
355	object	post	AD 38	▰▰
531	object			
585	object	cc	BC 77	▰▰

Period I: post BC 77
Period II: AD 56–70
Period III: before BC 134, or after AD 40

Figure 5 *Meenfoecsanak-Szeles Objects*

When comparing data series, I try to define two values with the help of computer analysis and a calculus of probabilities. I plot the data and compare the graphs to determine the extent to which they correspond. I then scan the identity of the values (I do this by means of the so-called *t*-test), and whether the degree of discrepancy is constant. Some trees can weather adverse circumstances in much the same shape as other trees in rather better circumstances. In this case, the two data series will be largely similar, but while in one tree yearly growth can be measured in tenths of a millimetre, in the other the same figure will be measured in several millimetres (*Figure 6*).

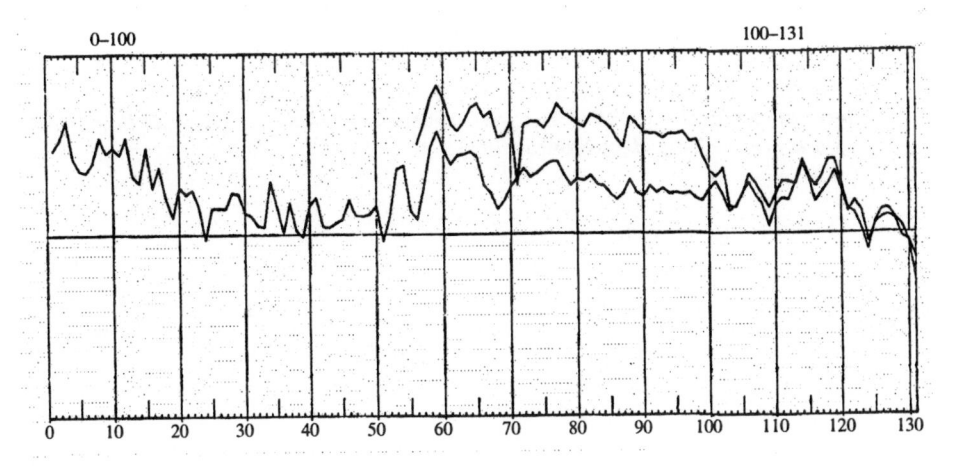

Figure 6

In charter dating it can happen that a number of significant word patterns can be found in the same source: this does not always make life easier for the historian. The situation is similar in the case of trees: although we are sometimes able to recognise the traces of a number of characteristic periods in the thickness of the tree-rings, their number and importance do not constitute an independent source: the individual characteristics of the given sample are decisive. If we have one sample from a young tree and another from an ancient tree of the same period, the number and meaningfulness of the characteristics will be different, since a weak sapling is much more susceptible to the effects of a dry month than a giant oak whose roots stretch hundreds of metres. We therefore need to know something about the history of the investigated wood samples (compare the criticism of sources in charter dating).

By way of conclusion, although the primary purpose of dendrochronology is the dating of a given building or object, we can of course obtain other interesting information as well. For example, in the course of a large-scale rescue excavation in Northern Hungary pieces of a barrel came to light in one of the wells. It turned out that the barrel had been made somewhere in the Baltic region, and that herrings were probably imported in them. Similarly, the dating of charters is only one of the aims of investigation: the persons who used the investigated word patterns are also important, since through them we can learn something new about unknown or barely known aspects of medieval life.

Bibliography

Babos, Károly. 1994. *Faanyagismeret és fafaj-meghatározás restaurátoroknak*. Magyar Nemzeti Múzeum.
Eckstein, Dieter, and Konrad Bedal. 1973–74. 'Dendrochronologie und Gefügeforschung.' *Ethnologica Europea* 7, no. 2: pp. 223–45
Gervers, M. 1997. 'The Dating of Medieval English Private Charters of the Twelfth and Thirteenth Centuries', in *A Distinct Voice: Medieval Studies in Honor of Leonard E. Boyle, O.P.*, ed. J. Brown and W. P. Stoneman, pp. 455–504. Notre Dame.
Grynaeus, András. 1998. 'Dendrokronológia', in *A régésztechnikus kézikönyve*, vol. I, ed. Ilona Gábor, pp. 357–66. Panniculus Ser. B. No. 3. Szombathely, Hungary.
Schweingruber, Fritz Hans. 1983. *Der Jahrring. Standort, Methodik, Zeit und Klima in der Dendrochronologie*. Bern–Stuttgart 1983.

DATING PROBLEMS AND METHODS IN THE MIDDLE AGES OF EARTH HISTORY

József Pálfy

Introduction

It is not only humans and their societies which have a history worth studying: the Earth, our 4.6 billion-year-old planet, also has an exciting and tumultuous past. Much like historians who are concerned with past events, geologists and palaeontologists are keen to unravel the history of the Earth and life on Earth. Their timescale is vastly different, however: the 'deep-time' of geological history involves millions, or even billions of years. Nevertheless, time and chronology are of paramount importance to historians and geologists alike. Continents drift apart and collide, ocean basins form and vanish, volcanoes erupt and wane, sea levels rise and fall, mountain ranges build up and erode, new species evolve and become extinct, wholly new forms of life emerge and die out in the course of millions of years. We need to date these events if we are to reconstruct and understand the geological and biological evolution that led to our very existence and to the physical world which surrounds us.

In the context of the present volume I attempt to address some of the fundamental issues of geological dating and present them in a manner accessible to the non-specialist. History and geology may be far apart as scholarly disciplines; however, each may learn lessons from the other's methodologies, as there are clear parallels in the subjects and aims of our studies. Comprehensive coverage cannot be the goal of a short paper; instead, I focus on selected issues and provide the interested reader with references to a few key articles and monographs as sources of in-depth information. My treatment is guided by the search for common ground, where similarities may exist between dating problems and methods in human history and geological history. Particular emphasis is placed on possible parallels with the charter dating method developed by Michael Gervers,[1] which is based on transient word patterns.

Rocks, Fossils, and Stratigraphy

The primary sources of information for the geologist and palaeontologist are the rock record and the fossil record contained within it. The Latin saying *Ex libro*

From *Dating Undated Medieval Charters*. Ed. Michael Gervers. Copyright (by the Editor and Contributors 2000). Published by the Boydell Press (in association with Collegium Budapest), PO Box 9, Woodbridge, Suffolk, IP12 3DF, Great Britain. ISBN 0 85115 792 0.

This research was supported by Hungarian Scientific Research Fund (OTKA) grants F23451 and T29965.

1. M. Gervers, 'The Dating of Medieval English Private Charters of the Twelfth and Thirteenth Centuries', in *A Distinct Voice*, ed. J. Brown and W. P. Stoneman, University of Notre Dame Press, 1997, pp. 455–504.

lapidum historia mundi concisely catches the essence of our science. To read the book whose pages are layers of rocks, one must first be able to establish temporal relationships. The law of superposition, originally formulated by Steno in the seventeenth century, states that in a normal succession of layers of rock, the lower one was deposited before the higher one, and so the lower one is also older. On this simple rule rests most of our interpretation of geological history. The law of superposition can be used in a single outcrop, or correlations can be made within a region where the types of rocks do not change. Lithostratigraphy deals with such ordering and correlation of formations of rocks. Because the properties of rocks are determined primarily by their depositional environment rather than by the time of deposition, the use of rock units as markers of time can be seriously compromised or misleading. However, sedimentary rocks commonly contain fossils which can be arranged in a temporal sequence based on observation of their occurrence in individual outcrops. Near the end of the eighteenth century, William Smith was the first to recognise that particular kinds of fossils can be used to correlate the rocks which contain them, and the fossils keep their sequence irrespective of changes in the enclosing rocks. This observation, originally made by the pragmatic engineer while digging canals in the English countryside, was placed on a firm footing with the proposal of Darwin's evolutionary theory. Biological evolution is the underlying principle which explains why the fossil record provides us with a versatile tool with which to infer geological time. There is a constant and unidirectional change of organisms through time, which makes possible the use of fossils for correlation, an endeavour termed biostratigraphy. There is an obvious parallel here with the dating of undated charters, where one also needs to turn to observation of word patterns, seals, and so on – anything which consistently changes through time.

Simultaneously with the development of evolutionary theory, significant advances in biostratigraphy were made by the mid-nineteenth century. A hierarchical subdivision of geological time was established, principally on the basis of fossils. At least at higher levels, it has remained remarkably stable since then. Thus the Middle Ages of geological history is properly called the Mesozoic Era, which consists of, from oldest to youngest, the Triassic, Jurassic, and Cretaceous periods. Each period in turn contains epochs, which are subdivided into ages. Thus the Lias is the first epoch of the Jurassic, and itself consists of the Hettangian, Sinemurian, Pliensbachian, and Toarcian ages. The ages are further subdivided into chrons. These time-units are abstracted from their corresponding time-rock units, that is, they are defined as the time represented by the deposition or formation of their corresponding rock units. Thus, a chron is based on a zone, which is defined by the assemblages of its characteristic fossil species. By the 1860s, a zonal scheme for the Jurassic of north-western Europe had essentially been established by the German palaeontologists Quenstedt and Oppel. Ongoing work has led to refinements, thus zones are further divided into subzones, which in turn contain faunal horizons, the smallest possible biostratigraphic units.[2]

2. J. H. Callomon, 'Time from Fossils: S. S. Buckman and Jurassic High-Resolution Geochronology', *Geological Society of London Memoir* 16 (1995): pp. 127–50.

In an attempt to stabilise chronology – that is, the system of our contiguous time-units – a locality is selected by an international committee of experts for each age, which thereafter serves as a global stratotype section and point. A physical marker in an actual rock outcrop, the so-called Golden Spike, will mark there a unique point as the lower boundary of a stage – that is, the time-rock or chronostratigraphic unit – and the corresponding time-plane in geological history, which is taken as the beginning of the equivalent time-unit. Only the lower boundary of a unit will be designated; the upper boundary is automatically defined by the lower boundary of the next youngest unit.[3]

Before turning to questions of methodology in biochronology, we shall briefly consider some important characteristics of the rock and fossil record which may hinder the interpretation of observations. A fundamental property of the rock record is that it commonly records episodic sedimentation.[4] A sequence of rocks that appears to result from temporally continuous sedimentation is only so beyond a certain, often coarse level of time resolution. Typical sedimentation rates and the episodic nature of deposition sets limits to the minimum time intervals we can distinguish. Clearly, there are sediments that record annual events – for example, phytoplankton blooms in lakes or in the sea – yet the majority of sedimentary rocks can be regarded as recorders of short events of deposition and longer intervening gaps. Under most circumstances, geological time cannot be resolved to less than tens of thousands of years; sometimes the resolution is significantly coarser.

The fossil record is also inadequate and biased to some extent, so that caution is needed not to read it literally. Preservation is the single most important constraint as only organisms with a durable skeleton leave a reliable fossil record. Only a minute fraction of the individuals which once existed will ever be found and several factors control the spatial and temporal distribution of fossils.[5] Chance plays a role in both the preservation and the discovery of each fossil specimen. Rocks formed during the time when a species existed may not contain the fossils of that species if the organism did not live there – because the environment was not suitable, or the area was outside the geographic range of the species – or its remains did not get preserved there (due to the activity of scavengers or chemical processes of lithification called diagenesis). Collection failure can cause observed ranges – that is, the interval between the first and last appearance of a species – to be shorter than the true life-span of the species.[6]

3. The sometimes confusing but necessary dichotomy of time vs. time-rock units – in other words, chronology vs. chronostratigraphy, and their relationship to biostratigraphy – is concisely elucidated by J. H. Callomon, 'Biostratigraphy, chronostratigraphy and all that – again!' in *Proceedings of the International Symposium on Jurassic Stratigraphy, Erlangen*, ed. O. Michelsen and A. Zeiss, Geological Survey of Denmark, 1984, vol. 3, pp. 611–24.
4. For an extremely readable account, see D. V. Ager, *The Nature of the Stratigraphic Record*, London: Macmillan, 1973.
5. S. K. Donovan and C. R. C. Paul, *The Adequacy of the Fossil Record*, New York: John Wiley, 1998.
6. For a concise summary of this and related problems pertinent to biostratigraphy, see Chapter 5 in A. B. Smith, *Systematics and the Fossil Record: Documenting Evolutionary Patterns*, Oxford: Blackwell, 1994.

Fossils are not the only means of stratigraphy. In fact, any signal which changes globally through time and is preserved in the rock record can be used to infer the ages of rocks. Presently popular methods include sequence stratigraphy (based on global sea-level changes), magnetostratigraphy (based on polarity switches of the Earth's magnetic field), and strontium isotope stratigraphy (based on a fluctuating 87Sr/86Sr isotope ratio in ancient seawater). These methods, although increasingly important and widely used, are not discussed here as they have little in common with the study of human medieval history.

Biochronological Methods: Telling the Time from Fossils

Biochronology uses the vertical or stratigraphic distribution of fossils in actual outcrops to infer the age of the enclosing rocks.[7] The distinction between biostratigraphy and biochronology is a subtle one which is nevertheless important. Biostratigraphy is concerned with the correlation of rocks based on their fossil content. Equivalence in time is not explicitly implied. On the other hand, biochronology seeks to establish precise time correlation based on fossils. To be successful, patterns and properties of temporal and geographic distribution of fossils have to be carefully assessed. Fossil groups that are useful for biochronology should have the following attributes: rapid evolutionary tempo, wide geographic distribution, independence of depositional environment, and easy recognition of its species through distinctive morphologies. Some of the biochronologically important marine fossil groups of the Mesozoic are the ammonoids (extinct molluscs), conodonts (microscopic tooth-like structures of animals of uncertain affinity which became extinct in the Triassic), radiolarians (single-celled siliceous microfossils), and foraminifera (single-celled calcareous microfossils).

Vagaries of the fossil record – that is, the role of chance in preservation and recovery – and complexities of the original distribution of the organism in space and time make biochronology a less than straightforward exercise. Traditional biochronology is most commonly based on assemblage zones, whereby a time-unit is represented by its characteristic suite of taxa (a taxon is any of the hierarchical entities of systematic palaeontology, for example, a species, genus, family, and so on). More restricted is the use of range zones, which are defined by the first and last appearances of a single taxon. When comparing distant localities, correlation is often rendered problematic due to geographic differences. Of special concern is the case when a taxon's true range varies from one area to another, thus introducing a potential for incorrect temporal correlation. In traditional biochronology, expert judgements are relied upon to carefully screen out such cases.

As the number of taxa and the complexities of distribution patterns increase, the need arises for the application of quantitative methods to solve the correlation

---

7. A somewhat dated, but comprehensive source of information on this subject is E. G. Kauffman and J. E. Hazel, eds, *Concepts and Methods in Biostratigraphy*, Stroudsburg, Pennsylvania: Dowden, Hutchinson, and Ross, 1977.

problems. The 1980s saw significant developments in the field of quantitative biostratigraphy and major advances were reported in several books.[8] Quantitative biostratigraphy is a misnomer, unfortunately entrenched in the literature, for mathematical methods of biochronology.[9] Several methods are now available, which differ in their philosophy, mathematical approach, and usefulness, depending on the available raw data.[10] Variants of multivariate analytical techniques that have been applied to biochronological problems have generally met with limited success. Archaeological seriation is one of these methods which may be most familiar to scholars of history.[11] Seriation, however, does not perform well in solving more complex problems commonly encountered in geological correlation.[12] In-depth treatments of various other multivariate methods can be found in the volumes referred to above. Here we narrow the choice to those techniques which have gained more widespread use and may merit consideration for non-geological applications. The general aim of these methods is to achieve time correlation by means of producing range charts of taxa. The range chart displays the first and last appearances of each taxon in stratigraphic, that is, temporal order. One widely used technique, the graphic correlation, relies on graphic logs which record first and last appearances in measured stratigraphic sections. This method exploits the spatial aspect of stratigraphic information as recorded in actual rock outcrops, thus it is not directly comparable to historical data sources and is not discussed here further. Two other methods can be broadly called probabilistic stratigraphy and relational stratigraphy, so revealing the basic difference in their approach. Probabilistic methods seek the most likely sequence of events, that is, first and last appearances. Discrepancies between the sequence recorded in different sections are resolved in a way that a sequence with the highest probability is derived. The resulting ranges can be considered as average ranges. The best developed variant, the ranking and scaling method (RASC),[13] is automated and it produces statistically significant results when large datasets are available.

The most widely used relational or deterministic method is the unitary association (UA) method developed by Guex.[14] In many ways, it can be regarded as a

8. J. M. Cubitt and R. A. Reyment, eds, *Quantitative Stratigraphic Correlation*, Chichester: John Wiley and Sons, 1982; F. M. Gradstein, F. P. Agterberg, J. C. Brower, and W. S. Schwarzacher, eds, *Quantitative Stratigraphy*, Dordrecht: Reidel Publishing, 1985; F. P. Agterberg, ed., *Automated Stratigraphic Correlations*, Amsterdam: Elsevier, 1990.

9. L. E. Edwards, 'Quantitative Biostratigraphy', in N. L. Gilinsky and P. W. Signor, eds, *Analytical Paleobiology*, Knoxville, Tennessee: University of Tennessee, 1991, vol. 4 of *Short Courses in Paleontology*, pp. 39–58.

10. L. E. Edwards, 'Quantitative Biostratigraphy: The Method Should Suit the Data', in Cubitt and Reyment, *Quantitative Stratigraphic Correlation*, pp. 45–60.

11. D. G. Kendall, 'Seriation from Abundance Matrices', in *Mathematics in the Archaeological and Historical Sciences*, ed. F. R. Hodson, D. G. Kendall, and P. Tautu, Edinburgh: Edinburgh University Press, 1971, pp. 215–52; B. M. Wilkinson, 'Techniques of Data Analysis-Seriation Theory', *Archaeo-Physika* 5 (1974): pp. 1–142; J. C. Brower, 'Archaeological Seriation of an Original Data Matrix', in Gradstein et al., *Quantitative Stratigraphy*, pp. 95–108.

12. See p. 180 in J. Guex, *Biochronological Correlations*, Berlin: Springer-Verlag, 1991.

13. Gradstein et al., *Quantitative Stratigraphy*.

14. Guex, *Biochronological Correlations*.

rigorous formulation of the assemblage-zone concept of traditional biochronology. The basic information here is the co-occurrence of taxa in samples from different stratigraphic levels, rather than the first and last appearances in the studied sections. The ranges obtained by the method are maximum ranges, which are especially effective in solving correlation problems arising from temporal shifts in the geographic range of taxa. The method produces a set of so-called 'unitary associations', which are minimal sets of co-occurring taxa. Individual UAs have biochronological value only if they can be recognised over wide geographic areas. If this is not the case, several UAs need to be combined and only such composite units will be meaningful for time correlation between different areas. Here we need not be concerned with the details of the method, which is described in full detail by Guex.[15] Suffice to say that it relies on a branch of mathematics called graph theory. The graph is built of points – termed vertices of the graph – corresponding to each observed taxon. If two taxa are found together in a sample, their vertices are connected by a line (called an edge of the graph). If one taxon is found to occur consistently above the other, it is displayed by an arrow – called an arc of the graph – pointing to the younger taxon. Unobserved relationships can be determined by completing the graph without violating established superpositions and co-occurrences, in effect inferring the virtual coexistence of coeval taxa which have not been found together in nature. Unitary associations are determined from this completed biostratigraphic graph, as minimal sets of coexisting taxa connected by edges. *Figure 1* presents a simple example of three stratigraphic sections from which six taxa were collected. A computer algorithm for the unitary association method has been implemented and the BioGraph program enables a user-friendly automated application of the method on an IBM-compatible personal computer.[16]

Geochronology: Determining Numeric Ages from Isotopes

Establishing the temporal succession of rock units and assigning them to intervals of geologic time – that is, eras, periods, epochs, and so on – can be achieved using fossils. This is often called relative dating, but determining the numeric age of rock units requires different methods. The area of geochronological dating is not of immediate relevance for historians; we only briefly discuss it here to emphasise that not only relative time is important in geology, but absolute time, too. Whereas a framework of calendar years can be directly read from certain documents in medieval history, in Mesozoic geology it can only be achieved through tedious analysis. Much as radiocarbon dating is used in archaeology, various other radioactive isotopes are employed as geochronometers for dating rocks which are tens or hundreds of millions of years old. Currently, the two most precise and accurate methods are U-Pb and 40Ar/39Ar geochronology, which are based on the radioactive decay of uranium isotopes into lead, and potassium into argon, respec-

---

15. Guex, *Biochronological Correlations*.
16. Chapter 6 in Guex, *Biochronological Correlations*.

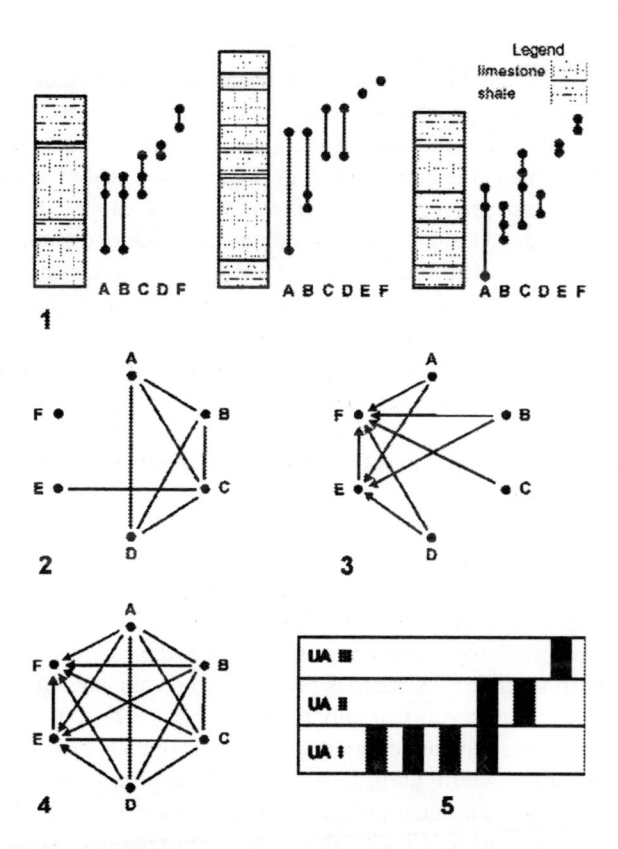

Figure 1 Steps of constructing biochronologic subdivisions from field data using the Unitary Association method. 1 - Simplified stratigraphic columns from three localities, showing rock types and occurrences of fossil taxa A through F; 2 - Graph representing co-occurrences of taxa using vertices and edges; 3 - Graph representing superposition of taxa using vertices and arcs; 4 - Combined biostratigraphic graph; 5 - Unitary Associations deduced from 4 (simplified from Edwards 1991).

tively. For Mesozoic rocks, today's technology permits error margins which are typically smaller than 1 per cent (for example, less than ±1 million years for a rock formed 200 million years ago). In essence, the age of the rock is calculated by measuring the ratio of radioactive parent and radiogenic daughter isotopes, since the rate of decay is known and remains constant through time.[17] Minerals suitable for radiometric dating primarily occur in igneous – volcanic or plutonic – rocks. The aim of dating these minerals is the determination of the crystallisation age of the rock. Most sedimentary rocks cannot be directly dated by isotopic methods.

17. For details of geochronology, see G. Faure, *Principles of Isotope Geology*, 2nd ed., New York: John Wiley and Sons, 1986.

The ages of volcanic ash layers interbedded with fossiliferous sediments allow the calibration of the geological time scale. Radiometric ages can thus be integrated with fossil-based biochronological ages. Utilising a reliable time-scale, numeric ages expressed in millions of years can be translated into chronostratigraphic ages using the named divisions of geological time, and vice versa.[18] This is essential for reconstructing geological events whose ages were determined by different methods. The duration of biochronological and chronostratigraphic units can also be deduced from a time scale. For example, the Jurassic Period lasted from 200 to 145 million years ago. The average duration of stages is 5 million years, whereas a typical ammonoid zone represents approximately 1 million years. Finer subdivisions, subzones, and horizons may push the limit of biochronological resolution near to 100,000 years.

A Case Study of Traditional and Quantitative Methods in Toarcian (Early Jurassic) Biochronology

An example may be used to illustrate the general points made above. Let us consider a section of marine shales and minor sandstones exposed along the banks of the Yakoun River in the Queen Charlotte Islands, western Canada. This locality contains the best preserved ammonoid fauna from the Toarcian stage of the Jurassic of North America.[19] Numerous beds have yielded many ammonoid taxa, whose level of occurrence was carefully recorded (*Figure 2*). Our goal is to correlate these beds to the standard chronological scale, which is based on the zones established in north-western Europe. A traditional approach was followed by Jakobs. Realising the significant differences in the faunal composition of North America and Europe, she subdivided the section into regional, North American zones by delineating assemblages of taxa that are consistently found together. Analysing the occurrences of common taxa with Europe, also using indirect correlation through other areas, such as South America, she suggested correlations between the North American and European zonal schemes. Apparently anomalous ranges – that is, cases when the sequence of first or last appearances of taxa was different in North America from that in Europe – were noted but filtered out.

An alternative approach utilised the unitary association method after compiling a dataset based on 16 of the best known ammonoid-bearing middle Toarcian stratigraphic sections of the world.[20] From the occurrences of more than one hundred taxa, a framework of 40 UAs was constructed. As discussed earlier, a typological

---

18. The most widely used time-scale is W. B. Harland, R. L. Armstrong, A. V. Cox, L. E. Craig, A. G. Smith, and D. G. Smith, *A Geologic Time Scale 1989*, Cambridge: Cambridge University Press, 1990.

19. G. K. Jakobs, P. L. Smith, and H. W. Tipper, 'An Ammonite Zonation for the Toarcian (Lower Jurassic) of the North American Cordillera', *Canadian Journal of Earth Sciences* 31 (1994): pp. 919–42.

20. J. Pálfy, R. R. Parrish, and P. L. Smith, 'A U–Pb age from the Toarcian (Lower Jurassic) and its use for time scale calibration through error analysis of biochronologic dating', *Earth and Planetary Science Letters* 146 (1997): pp. 659–75.

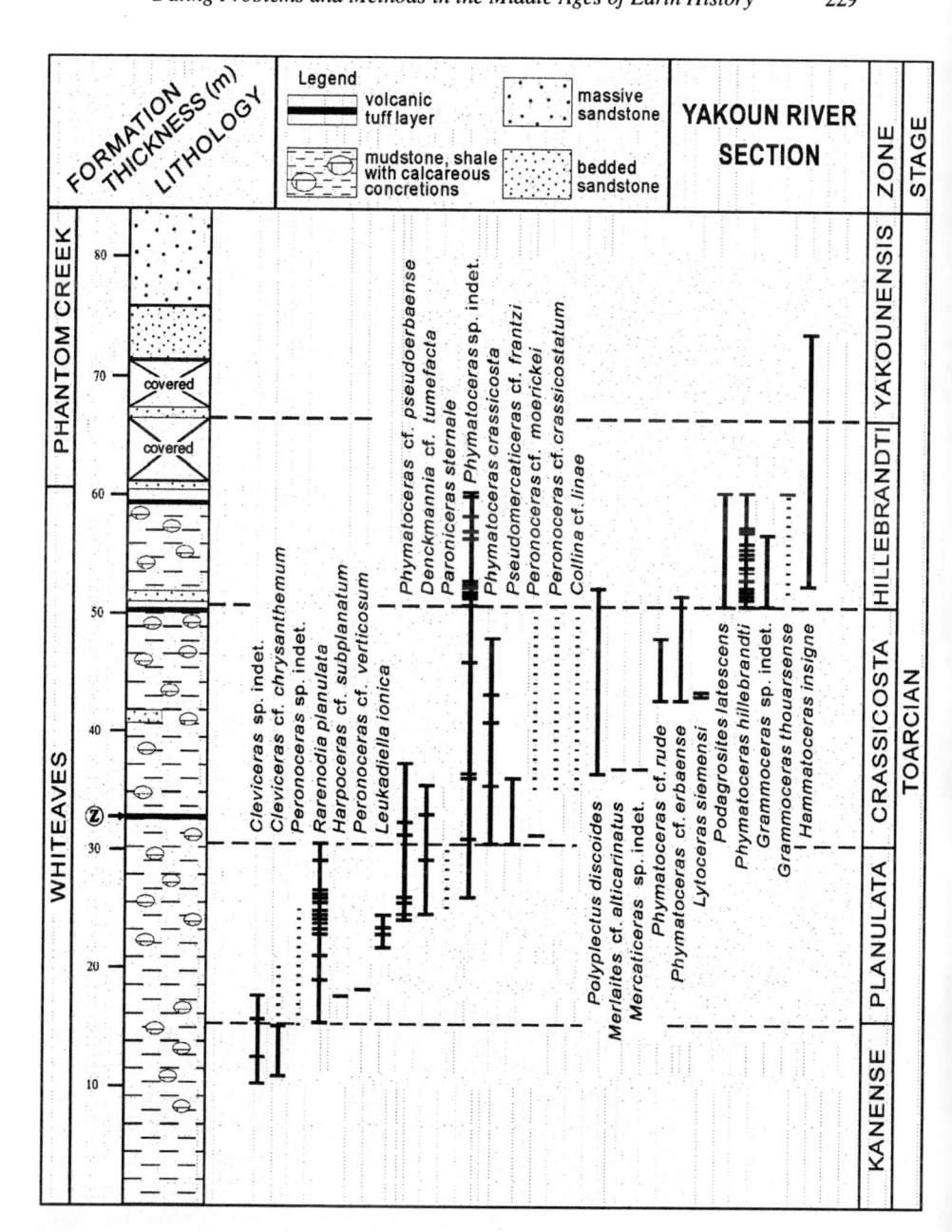

Dating Problems and Methods in the Middle Ages of Earth History   229

Figure 2 Litho- and biostratigraphy of the Toarcian of the Yakoun River section (after Jakobs 1994 and Pálfy 1997). "Z" denotes the volcanic tuff dated radiometrically by the U–Pb method as 181.4±1.2 m. y. old. Ammonite ranges (vertical lines) with collection levels (horizontal bars) are shown for the Planulata, Crassicosta, and Hillebrandti zones only. The assemblage zones were defined by traditional biochronology in Jakobs 1994. Dotted lines denote imprecisely located collections.

definition of chronological units is pursued to ensure uniform and stable use of these units in stratigraphy. No type section has been designated for the Toarcian, but the generally accepted region where a reference section can be located is around Thouars in France, from where the stage takes its name. It was possible to express the traditional ammonoid zones and their constituent subzones recognised in a section in the type region in France in terms of the minimum required sets of UAs,[21] as well as their maximum permissible sets (*Figure 3*). Any ammonoid assemblage from a Toarcian sample can be assigned to one or several contiguous UAs, which in turn can now be correlated to the standard zonation, giving both the most likely age and the maximum permissible range of ages.

An additional significance of the Yakoun River locality is that a precise U-Pb radiometric date was obtained from the section. A volcanic ash layer near the base of the Crassicosta Zone yielded an age of 181.4±1.2 million years, which is used as an important tie-point for the calibration of the numeric time scale. One of the outputs of the UA method when executed using the BioGraph software is a correlation table which provides a UA or a range of UAs for each collection level in a given section. Thus an age expressed as UA 22–25 could be assigned to the dated volcanic layer, which in turn best correlates with the Variabilis Subzone of the Variabilis Zone in the reference section in France. However, using the maximum permissible correlation from *Figure 3*, the age of the volcanic layer could be as old as the underlying Semipolitum Subzone of the Bifrons Zone or as young as the overlying Illustris Subzone of the Variabilis Zone. Thus a plus-or-minus-one-subzone uncertainty in ammonoid-based intercontinental biochronological correlation is demonstrated.

Discussion

A more than superficial resemblance can be noted between a number of dating problems and methods of Mesozoic Earth history and medieval history. Fossils, remains of organisms which have evolved through time, are used to date the rocks from which they were recovered. In a method analogous to this in many regards, undated charters can be dated on the basis of their word patterns which record the evolution of language. The geographic and temporal distribution of organisms may be controlled by a complex history of migration, which introduces potential errors in time-correlation based on fossils. Quantitative analysis which seeks to establish maximum ranges of taxa is the most efficient way of dealing with this problem. Because the evolution of language may also show regional differences, similar problems may be encountered in language-based methods of document dating. Hypothetically, the unitary association method appears to offer the most immediate comparison with, hence an application potential for, charter dating using word patterns. If taxa are substituted with word patterns, and the 'stratigraphic' order of samples is deduced from documents with known dates, a

---

21. J. Gabilly, 'Le Toarcien a Thouars et dans le centre-ouest de la France', *Les Stratotypes français*, Centre Nationale de la Recherche Scientifique, Paris, 1976, vol. 3.

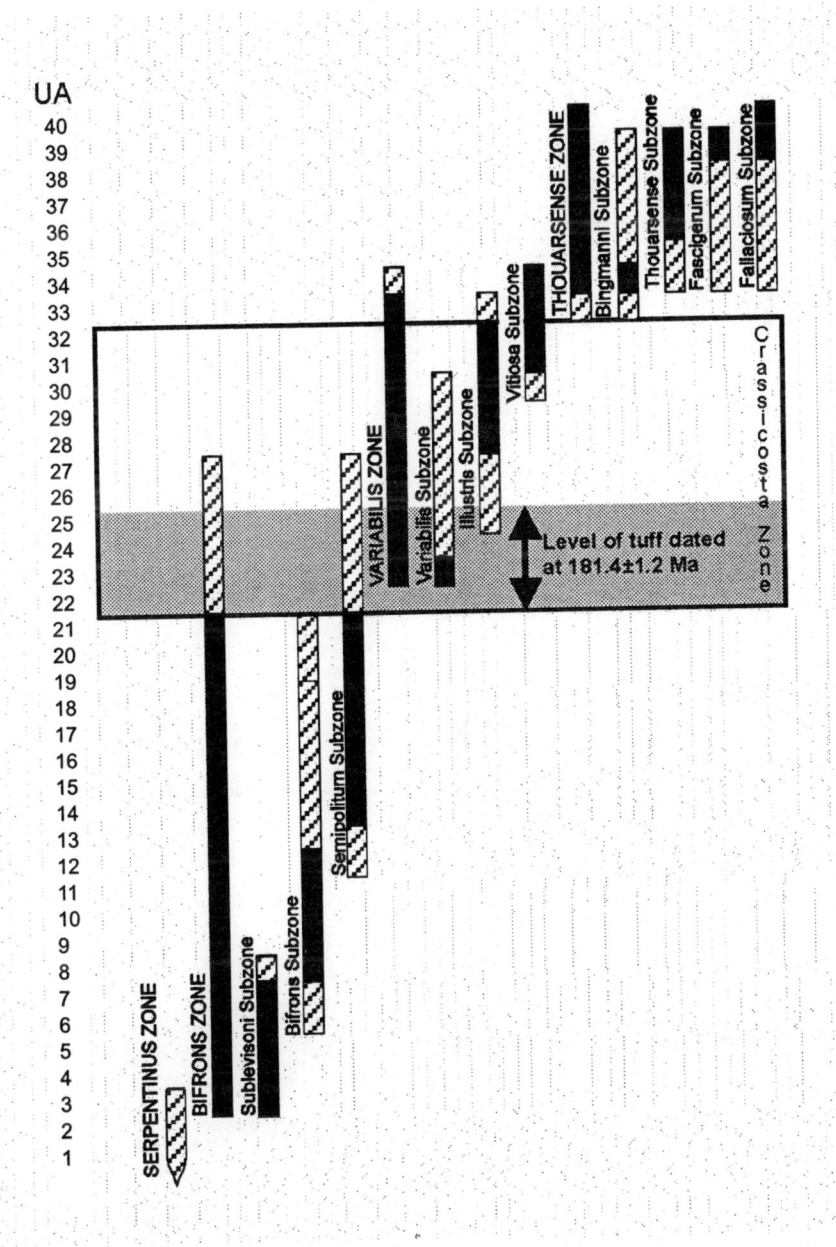

Figure 3 Traditional zones correlated with the 40 Unitary Associations recognized in middle Toarcian ammonoid faunas analyzed using the BioGraph program. Minimal (solid bars) and maximal (hatched bars) groupings of UAs corresponding to the northwest European standard zones and subzones are shown. The box denotes correlation of the North American Crassicosta Zone and the isotopically dated level (gray shaded) within it.

chronologically calibrated framework of Unitary Associations of word patterns could be established. Occurrence of assemblages of word patterns could then be compared against the reference range chart in much the same way as in fossil dating.

Bibliography

Ager, D. V. 1973. *The Nature of the Stratigraphic Record*. London: Macmillan.
Agterberg, F. P. ed. 1990. *Automated Stratigraphic Correlations*. Amsterdam: Elsevier.
Brower, J. C. 1985. 'Archaeological seriation of an original data matrix', in *Quantitative Stratigraphy*, ed. F. M. Gradstein, F. P. Agterberg, J. C. Brower, and W. S. Schwarzacher, pp. 95–108. Dordrecht: Reidel Publishing.
Callomon, J. H. 1984. 'Biostratigraphy, chronostratigraphy and all that – again!', in *Proceedings of the International Symposium on Jurassic Stratigraphy, Erlangen*, ed. O. Michelsen and A. Zeiss, pp. 611–24. Geological Survey of Denmark, vol. 3.
———. 1995. 'Time from fossils: S. S. Buckman and Jurassic high-resolution geochronology'. *Geological Society of London Memoir* 16: pp. 127–50.
Cubitt, J. M., and R. A. Reyment, eds. 1982. *Quantitative Stratigraphic Correlation*. Chichester: John Wiley and Sons.
Donovan, S. K., and C. R. C. Paul. 1998. *The Adequacy of the Fossil Record*. New York: John Wiley.
Edwards, L. E. 1982. 'Quantitative biostratigraphy: The method should suit the data', in *Quantitative Stratigraphic Correlation*, ed. J. M. Cubitt and R. A. Reyment, pp. 45–60. Chichester: John Wiley and Sons.
———. 1991. 'Quantitative biostratigraphy', in *Analytical Paleobiology*, ed. N. L. Gilinsky and P. W. Signor, vol. 4 of *Short Courses in Paleontology*, pp. 39–58. University of Tennessee, Knoxville, Tennessee.
Faure, G. *Principles of Isotope Geology*. 1986. 2nd ed. New York: John Wiley and Sons.
Gabilly, J. 1976. 'Le Toarcien a Thouars et dans le centre-ouest de la France', in *Les Stratotypes français*. Vol. 3. Paris: Centre Nationale de la Recherche Scientifique.
Gervers, M. 1997. 'The Dating of Medieval English Private Charters of the Twelfth and Thirteenth Centuries', in *A Distinct Voice. Medieval Studies in Honor of Leonard Boyle, OP*, ed. J. Brown and W. P. Stoneman, pp. 455–504. Indiana: Notre Dame.
Gradstein, F. M., F. P. Agterberg, J. C. Brower, and W. S. Schwarzacher, eds. 1985. *Quantitative Stratigraphy*. Dordrecht: Reidel Publishing.
Guex, J. 1991. *Biochronological Correlations*. Berlin: Springer-Verlag.
Harland, W. B., R. L. Armstrong, A. V. Cox, L. E. Craig, A. G. Smith, and D. G. Smith. 1990. *A Geologic Time Scale 1989*. Cambridge: Cambridge University Press.
Jakobs, G. K., P. L. Smith, and H. W. Tipper. 1994. 'An ammonite zonation for the Toarcian (Lower Jurassic) of the North American Cordillera'. *Canadian Journal of Earth Sciences* 31: pp. 919–42.
Kauffman, E. G., and J. E. Hazel, eds. 1977. *Concepts and Methods in Biostratigraphy*. Stroudsburg, Pennsylvania: Dowden, Hutchinson and Ross.
Kendall, D. G. 1971. 'Seriation from abundance matrices', in *Mathematics in the Archaeological and Historical Sciences*, ed. F. R. Hodson, D. G. Kendall, and P. Tautu, pp. 215–52. Edinburgh: Edinburgh University Press.
Pálfy, J., R. R. Parrish, and P. L. Smith. 1997. 'A U–Pb age from the Toarcian (Lower Jurassic) and its use for time scale calibration through error analysis of biochronologic dating'. *Earth and Planetary Science Letters* 145: pp. 659–75.
Smith, A. B. 1994. *Systematics and the Fossil Record: Documenting Evolutionary Patterns*. Oxford: Blackwell.
Wilkinson, B. M. 1974. 'Techniques of data analysis-seriation theory'. *Archaeo-Physika* 5: pp. 1–142.

THE MEDIEVAL CHARTER COLLECTIONS IN THE NATIONAL ARCHIVES OF HUNGARY

Iván Borsa

The National Archives of Hungary have two medieval collections. One constitutes documents (charters, public records, registers, letters, and so on) taken from the different record groups/fonds kept in the National Archives; the other is a collection of photographic enlargements of microfilms made of documents kept in other archives.

In Hungary, the end of the Middle Ages is considered to be the date of the Battle of Mohács – 29 August 1526 – and all archival documents or texts which originated in the Middle Ages are generally known as charters (*oklevél*).

After the defeat of the 1848–49 Revolution and Freedom Fight, and the demise of Austrian absolutism, a new political system came into being, with the result that the documents of the now defunct central administrative bodies – Cancellaria regia, Camera Hungariae aulica, Consilium locumtenentiale – were transferred to the Archivum regni (National Archives). By far the majority of the documents which were collected by the Camera Hungariae aulica came from church and family archives. Most of these were documents relating to defunct church communities, dissolved religious orders, and extinct families.

In 1876, the new director of the National Archives decided that all its charters, letters, registers, censuses, and so on – even later copies – originating before 1526 should be put together in a single collection. These documents were given a reference number, beginning with '1'. Since a document can contain a number of texts – *mandatum* and *relatio* are already two texts, while *protocollum* and *chartularium* sometimes amount to several hundred – it was necessary to create a chronological catalogue card for each text in a particular document.

These catalogue cards were put into chronological order in such a way that the number or numbers of a charter text issued on a given day or in a given year could be found. On the catalogue card it was necessary to indicate not only the date of the document and its reference number in the new collection, but also who issued the charter, in what form the document existed (original, transcription of the whole text, transcription of the contents, copy, *protocollum*, *formularium*), and what reference number it had had before it came into the collection. In the case of original documents it was necessary to note the mode of sealing of the document (pendent, beneath the text or on the back, closing), and in the case of a number of seals, how many.

The history of the National Archives' other medieval collection goes back to 1935. Many difficulties were caused for historical research, especially to

From *Dating Undated Medieval Charters*. Ed. Michael Gervers. Copyright (by the Editor and Contributors 2000). Published by the Boydell Press (in association with Collegium Budapest), PO Box 9, Woodbridge, Suffolk, IP12 3DF, Great Britain. ISBN 0 85115 792 0.

researchers of Hungarian medieval history, by the division of the territory of what had been medieval Hungary into four countries at Trianon in 1920, which meant in practical terms that the archives which subsequently came into being were no longer easily accessible to Hungarian scholars. The National Archives decided in 1935 to seek permission to have the medieval documents kept in the – now foreign – archives put onto microfilm, from which enlargements would be prepared. On this basis up until 1945 several thousand enlargements were made. After the Second World War at first only documents kept in the archives of Hungarian church communities, counties, and towns were put onto microfilm; then, when it became possible, and on an exchange basis – each party putting something onto microfilm for the other – microfilms of several tens of thousands of documents from neighbouring countries were gathered in the microfilm collection of the National Archives. Anyone who has read a number of documents on a microfilm reader can understand why something had to be done to improve the situation. With the special assistance of the Hungarian Academy of Sciences and the Ministry of Culture, between 1974 and 1982 the second medieval collection was established from the photographs made from the microfilms then available. (Photographs made from a single document were put into one envelope, the chronological catalogue cards were prepared, and these were given a reference number within the photograph collection, starting from 200001, although the catalogue cards remained separate.) Microfilms prepared from medieval documents after that time and hopefully in the future are photographically enlarged and put into the medieval photograph collection.

In 1982, the National Archives began to pursue the suggestion, rejected in 1970, that the five items of information found on the catalogue cards of the first collection – reference number, date, issuer, form in which the document has survived, and the reference number of the original (in the case of photographs, the original archive reference number) – should be put into machine-readable form so that they could be searched not only on the basis of chronology, but also on the basis of the other data – and permutations thereof – on the catalogue cards.

The reference numbers of the items in the first collection today exceed 108,000, those of the photograph collection 292,000, while the reference numbers of medieval texts are approaching 320,000. This is immediately clear because each text of a given document has its own entry in the database.

It was foreseeable at the time of the decision to render the catalogue cards into machine-readable form that it would be necessary to solve the problem of the 12,000 catalogue cards lacking a date. Prior to this, however, it was necessary to examine the document texts in order to see whether it would be possible, using traditional methods, new source publications, monographs, and so on, to establish the year of the document. If this was not possible, it would be necessary to find a *terminus ante quem* and a *terminus post quem*.

After the completion of the work, '9999' was entered into the record's 'Date' field in the case of documents without a year date. The two dates between which the document's date of issue may be searched is found in the 'Notes' field. There are 9,865 of these undated records.

The question may arise: How complete are these collections? The answer is: They are not complete. We are not unaware of the fact that in Hungarian archives there are still documents transcribed after 1526 which have not been examined: I estimate that the two collections represent approximately 90 per cent of all the relevant documents currently in existence. Presumably, there are still medieval documents to be put onto microfilm in all seven neighbouring countries. (It is to be noted that the Österreichisches Staatsarchiv, the Archivio Segreto Vaticano, and many other European archives also contain numerous medieval documents, photographs of which could be included in the medieval document collections of the Hungarian National Archives.)

Vivant sequentes